THE RENAISSANCE IN EUROPE: A CULTURAL ENQUIRY

Courts, Patrons and Poets

EDITED BY DAVID MATEER

D1307867

Yale University Press, New Haven & London in association with The Open University

This publication forms part of an Open University course: AA305, *The Renaissance in Europe: A Cultural Enquiry.* Details of this and other Open University courses can be obtained from the Course Reservations Centre, PO Box 724, The Open University, Milton Keynes MK7 6ZS, United Kingdom: tel. +44 (0)1908 653231, e-mail ces-gen@open.ac.uk

Alternatively, you may visit the Open University website at http://www.open.ac.uk where you can learn more about the wide range of courses and packs offered at all levels by the Open University.

For availability of this or other course components, contact Open University Worldwide Ltd, The Berrill Building, Walton Hall, Milton Keynes MK7 6AA, United Kingdom: tel. +44 (0)1908 858785; fax +44 (0)1908 858787; e-mail ouwenq@open.ac.uk; website http://www.ouw.co.uk

First published 2000 by Yale University Press in association with The Open University

Yale University Press
23 Pond Street
London
NW3 2PN

The Open University
Walton Hall
Milton Keynes
MK7 6AA

Edited, designed and typeset by The Open University

Printed and bound in the United Kingdom by Alden Press Ltd, Osney Mead, Oxford OX2 0EF

Cover and colour printing by Spine Offset Ltd, Rainham, Essex

British Library cataloguing in publication data
A catalogue record for this book is available from the British Library

Library of Congress cataloging in publication data
Card number 99-68043

ISBN 0 300 08219 3 (C)
ISBN 0 300 08225 8 (P)

8179B/aa305b2i1.1

1.1

THE RENAISSANCE IN EUROPE: A CULTURAL ENQUIRY

Courts, Patrons and Poets

Contents

Preface

This is the second of three books in the series *The Renaissance in Europe: A Cultural Enquiry* which form the main texts of an Open University third-level course of the same name. This interdisciplinary course has been designed for students who are new to cultural history and the Renaissance as well as for those who have already undertaken some study in these areas. The purpose of this series is to introduce the idea of the Renaissance both as it developed during the fifteenth and sixteenth centuries and as it has since been interpreted. Through a wide-ranging series of case studies, we hope to provide a broad overview of current scholarship in the field of Renaissance studies. The subject is not tackled chronologically, although the earlier phases of the Renaissance tend to be considered in the first two volumes and the later in the third. Each book engages with different themes and aspects of the Renaissance and is self-sufficient and accessible to the general reader. This second book, *Courts, Patrons and Poets*, examines the cultural impact of humanist ideas at a variety of courts in Renaissance Italy, and then traces their reception and modification in other parts of Europe.

As part of the course, this book includes important teaching exercises which in most cases are followed by some discussion of the points raised. At the beginning of each chapter the expected outcomes for the reader are listed in the form of objectives. A bibliography has been prepared for each chapter and where applicable this is followed by a source list for texts from the set Reader and Anthology (see below) and for musical extracts. At the end of the book is a glossary. Entries in the glossary are emboldened in the text, usually the first time they appear. The convention for dating adopted throughout the series is to use CE (Common Era) and BCE (Before Common Era) in preference to the more traditional AD and BC.

For each volume in the series there are set texts to which the reader will need access in order to engage fully with the material. Throughout the series references to the two volumes of source material are to the 'Reader' and the 'Anthology' followed by an extract number; no page references to the Reader and Anthology are given. References to other set texts are in the standard author/date system. For this book the set texts are:

P. Elmer, N. Webb and R. Wood (eds) (2000) *The Renaissance in Europe: An Anthology*, New Haven and London, Yale University Press.

K. Whitlock (ed.) (2000) *The Renaissance in Europe: A Reader*, New Haven and London, Yale University Press.

Jacob Burckhardt (1990) *The Civilization of the Renaissance in Italy* , trans. S.G.C. Middlemore, introduction by Peter Burke, Harmondsworth, Penguin.

Alison Cole (1995) *Art of the Italian Renaissance Courts: Virtue and Magnificence*, London, Weidenfeld & Nicolson.

J.L. Halio (ed.) (1993) W. Shakespeare: *The Merchant of Venice*, The Oxford Shakespeare, Oxford, Oxford University Press.

D. Norbrook (1993) *The Penguin Book of Renaissance Verse: 1509–1659*, ed. H.R. Woudhuysen, Harmondsworth, Penguin.

The three books in the series are:

The Impact of Humanism, edited by Lucille Kekewich

Courts, Patrons and Poets, edited by David Mateer

Challenges to Authority, edited by Peter Elmer

The course editors were Julie Bennett, Christine Considine and Rachel Crease, picture research was carried out by Tony Coulson and the course secretary was Sam Horne. Roberta Wood was the course manager, Ruth Drage was the course designer, Ray Munns was the course artist and Robert Gibson was the compositor.

Introduction

BY DAVID MATEER

Courts, Patrons and Poets is a multi-disciplinary enquiry into the cultural activity of fifteenth- and sixteenth-century Europe. Its title does not do justice to the wide range of activities examined between its covers: painting, manuscript illumination, sculpture and the striking of portrait medals, music, architecture, poetry and drama. For obvious reasons, none of these areas has been subjected to exhaustive treatment. Such is the richness and diversity of 'Renaissance culture', and such the variety of its geographical, political and social contexts, that some attempt had to be made to balance the delicate equation between depth of treatment on the one hand and breadth of coverage on the other. The scope of this book, therefore, has been deliberately limited in the hope that the salient features of a key moment in the history of western civilization, in both its national and international aspects, will appear in sharper focus.

To a large extent the critical perspective adopted in this book differs from the traditional art-historical approach, which tends to see the Renaissance as a system of socially disembodied ideas and to study its art and artists in isolation from the wider world. A major theme running through the early chapters is the extent to which art both shaped and reflected the values of the society for which it was created. To gain a deeper understanding of this process, one must examine not just artists but also the interaction and collaboration between those who produced, paid for, exploited and appreciated the artefact. From Peter Elmer's general discussion of the hierarchical structures of a typical Renaissance court, it should quickly become apparent that every aspect of court life was designed as a manifestation of its 'prince' and an embodiment of his, or her, values. The architecture and decoration of the palace, and the court ceremonies and festivities that took place there, all combined to enhance the ruler's reputation as well as give pleasure. As a patron of the arts, he or she would naturally pay close attention to the development of any commissioned work and expect to participate in the creative process as an active collaborator. This notion that an artefact was the result of a 'partnership' may at first seem outrageous, for it subverts one of our cherished beliefs about Renaissance cultural production, namely, that artists worked in an atmosphere of creative and intellectual freedom, producing masterpieces that were received passively by enlightened patrons. Such a view is demonstrably a romantic myth. The fifteenth-century sculptor and architect Filarete (Antonio Averlino) affords an insight into the contemporary reality when he describes the relationship between patron, architect and building as that of a father, mother and child. We can deduce much from this provocatively gendered simile. In a hierarchically structured and patriarchal society such as that of Renaissance Italy it was clearly the patron not the artist who was perceived, until late in the period, as the dominating figure in artistic creation. Mary Hollingsworth sums up this view in forceful terms:

> Fifteenth-century patrons were not passive connoisseurs: they were active consumers. It was the patron, and not the artist, who was seen by his contemporaries as the creator of his project and this gave him the strongest possible motive for controlling its final appearance. Above all, the traditional art historical approach disguises the function of art in the fifteenth century and the central role it played in the construction of images for wealthy, powerful and ambitious patrons in Renaissance Italy.
>
> (*Patronage in Renaissance Italy: From 1400 to the Early Sixteenth Century*, London, John Murray, 1994, pp.1–2)

The ruler therefore both created, and was created by, the commissioned work of art.

Although most of us think first of the visual arts when we hear the word 'Renaissance', in the period itself it was literature and letters (the so-called 'liberal' arts) that were taken more seriously by patrons. Painting, sculpture and architecture were regarded as 'mechanical' arts, along with agriculture, weaving and navigation. Especially at the beginning of the period, the social status of a painter or musician was little different from that of a carpenter, weaver or stonemason. However, there is evidence that by the end of the fifteenth century this situation was changing. In the late 1490s, for instance, Duke Ercole I of Ferrara received a letter from his secretary advising him to engage the composer Heinrich Isaac in preference to Josquin Desprez, the most distinguished musician of his age. According to the letter, Isaac: 'is able to get on with his colleagues better and composes new pieces more quickly. It is true that Josquin composes better, but he does it when it suits him and not when one wishes him to' (quoted in Gustave Reese, *Music in the Renaissance*, W.W. Norton, New York, 1959, p.229). Josquin was not the only creative artist to acquire a reputation with employers for being 'difficult'; his younger contemporary Michelangelo showed a similar lack of deference to popes, cardinals and government officials, whom he treated as equals rather than as his masters. Little wonder, then, that later generations

Contents

Preface

This is the second of three books in the series *The Renaissance in Europe: A Cultural Enquiry* which form the main texts of an Open University third-level course of the same name. This interdisciplinary course has been designed for students who are new to cultural history and the Renaissance as well as for those who have already undertaken some study in these areas. The purpose of this series is to introduce the idea of the Renaissance both as it developed during the fifteenth and sixteenth centuries and as it has since been interpreted. Through a wide-ranging series of case studies, we hope to provide a broad overview of current scholarship in the field of Renaissance studies. The subject is not tackled chronologically, although the earlier phases of the Renaissance tend to be considered in the first two volumes and the later in the third. Each book engages with different themes and aspects of the Renaissance and is self-sufficient and accessible to the general reader. This second book, *Courts, Patrons and Poets*, examines the cultural impact of humanist ideas at a variety of courts in Renaissance Italy, and then traces their reception and modification in other parts of Europe.

As part of the course, this book includes important teaching exercises which in most cases are followed by some discussion of the points raised. At the beginning of each chapter the expected outcomes for the reader are listed in the form of objectives. A bibliography has been prepared for each chapter and where applicable this is followed by a source list for texts from the set Reader and Anthology (see below) and for musical extracts. At the end of the book is a glossary. Entries in the glossary are emboldened in the text, usually the first time they appear. The convention for dating adopted throughout the series is to use CE (Common Era) and BCE (Before Common Era) in preference to the more traditional AD and BC.

For each volume in the series there are set texts to which the reader will need access in order to engage fully with the material. Throughout the series references to the two volumes of source material are to the 'Reader' and the 'Anthology' followed by an extract number; no page references to the Reader and Anthology are given. References to other set texts are in the standard author/date system. For this book the set texts are:

P. Elmer, N. Webb and R. Wood (eds) (2000) *The Renaissance in Europe: An Anthology*, New Haven and London, Yale University Press.

K. Whitlock (ed.) (2000) *The Renaissance in Europe: A Reader*, New Haven and London, Yale University Press.

Jacob Burckhardt (1990) *The Civilization of the Renaissance in Italy*, trans. S.G.C. Middlemore, introduction by Peter Burke, Harmondsworth, Penguin.

Alison Cole (1995) *Art of the Italian Renaissance Courts: Virtue and Magnificence*, London, Weidenfeld & Nicolson.

J.L. Halio (ed.) (1993) W. Shakespeare: *The Merchant of Venice*, The Oxford Shakespeare, Oxford, Oxford University Press.

D. Norbrook (1993) *The Penguin Book of Renaissance Verse: 1509–1659*, ed. H.R. Woudhuysen, Harmondsworth, Penguin.

The three books in the series are:

The Impact of Humanism, edited by Lucille Kekewich

Courts, Patrons and Poets, edited by David Mateer

Challenges to Authority, edited by Peter Elmer

The course editors were Julie Bennett, Christine Considine and Rachel Crease, picture research was carried out by Tony Coulson and the course secretary was Sam Horne. Roberta Wood was the course manager, Ruth Drage was the course designer, Ray Munns was the course artist and Robert Gibson was the compositor.

Introduction

BY DAVID MATEER

Courts, Patrons and Poets is a multi-disciplinary enquiry into the
cultural activity of fifteenth- and sixteenth-century Europe. Its title
does not do justice to the wide range of activities examined between
its covers: painting, manuscript illumination, sculpture and the
striking of portrait medals, music, architecture, poetry and drama.
For obvious reasons, none of these areas has been subjected to
exhaustive treatment. Such is the richness and diversity of
'Renaissance culture', and such the variety of its geographical,
political and social contexts, that some attempt had to be made to
balance the delicate equation between depth of treatment on the one
hand and breadth of coverage on the other. The scope of this book,
therefore, has been deliberately limited in the hope that the salient
features of a key moment in the history of western civilization, in both
its national and international aspects, will appear in sharper focus.

To a large extent the critical perspective adopted in this book differs
from the traditional art-historical approach, which tends to see the
Renaissance as a system of socially disembodied ideas and to study its
art and artists in isolation from the wider world. A major theme
running through the early chapters is the extent to which art both
shaped and reflected the values of the society for which it was
created. To gain a deeper understanding of this process, one must
examine not just artists but also the interaction and collaboration
between those who produced, paid for, exploited and appreciated the
artefact. From Peter Elmer's general discussion of the hierarchical
structures of a typical Renaissance court, it should quickly become
apparent that every aspect of court life was designed as a
manifestation of its 'prince' and an embodiment of his, or her, values.
The architecture and decoration of the palace, and the court
ceremonies and festivities that took place there, all combined to
enhance the ruler's reputation as well as give pleasure. As a patron of
the arts, he or she would naturally pay close attention to the
development of any commissioned work and expect to participate in
the creative process as an active collaborator. This notion that an
artefact was the result of a 'partnership' may at first seem outrageous,
for it subverts one of our cherished beliefs about Renaissance cultural
production, namely, that artists worked in an atmosphere of creative
and intellectual freedom, producing masterpieces that were received

passively by enlightened patrons. Such a view is demonstrably a romantic myth. The fifteenth-century sculptor and architect Filarete (Antonio Averlino) affords an insight into the contemporary reality when he describes the relationship between patron, architect and building as that of a father, mother and child. We can deduce much from this provocatively gendered simile. In a hierarchically structured and patriarchal society such as that of Renaissance Italy it was clearly the patron not the artist who was perceived, until late in the period, as the dominating figure in artistic creation. Mary Hollingsworth sums up this view in forceful terms:

> Fifteenth-century patrons were not passive connoisseurs: they were active consumers. It was the patron, and not the artist, who was seen by his contemporaries as the creator of his project and this gave him the strongest possible motive for controlling its final appearance. Above all, the traditional art historical approach disguises the function of art in the fifteenth century and the central role it played in the construction of images for wealthy, powerful and ambitious patrons in Renaissance Italy.
>
> (*Patronage in Renaissance Italy: From 1400 to the Early Sixteenth Century*, London, John Murray, 1994, pp.1–2)

The ruler therefore both created, and was created by, the commissioned work of art.

Although most of us think first of the visual arts when we hear the word 'Renaissance', in the period itself it was literature and letters (the so-called 'liberal' arts) that were taken more seriously by patrons. Painting, sculpture and architecture were regarded as 'mechanical' arts, along with agriculture, weaving and navigation. Especially at the beginning of the period, the social status of a painter or musician was little different from that of a carpenter, weaver or stonemason. However, there is evidence that by the end of the fifteenth century this situation was changing. In the late 1490s, for instance, Duke Ercole I of Ferrara received a letter from his secretary advising him to engage the composer Heinrich Isaac in preference to Josquin Desprez, the most distinguished musician of his age. According to the letter, Isaac: 'is able to get on with his colleagues better and composes new pieces more quickly. It is true that Josquin composes better, but he does it when it suits him and not when one wishes him to' (quoted in Gustave Reese, *Music in the Renaissance*, W.W. Norton, New York, 1959, p.229). Josquin was not the only creative artist to acquire a reputation with employers for being 'difficult'; his younger contemporary Michelangelo showed a similar lack of deference to popes, cardinals and government officials, whom he treated as equals rather than as his masters. Little wonder, then, that later generations drew striking parallels between the work of these two figures. Their 'attitude' may be taken as symptomatic of the growing prestige of the artistic professions at this time. You will be able to detect earlier signs of this increased esteem and artistic self-awareness in the course of reading Chapters 1–3.

Perhaps the most distinctive aspect of the Renaissance was its attempt to revive Graeco-Roman antiquity across a wide range of cultural fields and media. From being the concern of a small group of fourteenth-century Florentines, this enthusiasm for classical forms was, by 1600, shared by a large section of the European upper and middle classes. The Renaissance was therefore an international movement; but this is not to say that it was a homogeneous one. England, Hungary, Spain and Poland all participated in the Renaissance, but their renaissances were not mere mechanical copies of a model produced in Italy. Elsewhere in Europe the revival of letters and the generation of new currents in artistic expression had many sources independent of the Italian well-spring, and those Renaissance ideas that *were* imported were adapted to local circumstances. It is not so much a case of the imitation of Italian models as of their reconstruction, and the development of hybrid forms from a process of appropriation and creative misinterpretation. In Chapters 4 and 5 Ceri Sullivan and Richard Brown describe this process of cultural translation and filtering in the context of the British literary Renaissance, while at the same time giving due weight to the strong indigenous forces at work there.

CHAPTER ONE

Court culture in the Renaissance

BY PETER ELMER[1]

Objectives

The objectives of this chapter are that you should:

- understand the role of the court as a site of cultural production, particularly in the field of the visual arts;
- assess the role of patronage in court culture;
- examine, through selective case studies, the degree of stylistic consistency in Renaissance court culture;
- assess the diffusion of court culture in Italy and Europe in the late fifteenth and early sixteenth centuries.

Introduction: definitions and debates

In this and the following two chapters, we look at a particular institutional context, the court, as a site for the creation and development of Renaissance culture. In examining the historical role of the court in Renaissance Europe, scholars have frequently cited Baldassare Castiglione's celebrated work, *Il libro del cortegiano* (*The Book of the Courtier*) (published 1528), as their starting point. Written during the period of the 'destruction of Italy' by the forces of the French and Spanish armies in the early sixteenth century, it depicts a golden age of courtly accomplishment in which the arts and learning were reborn. For Castiglione, the court of Guidobaldo da Montefeltro (d.1508) and his wife Elizabetta Gonzaga (d.1526) (Figure 1.1, overleaf) at Urbino represented the peak of cultural refinement – a sentiment echoed by Jacob Burckhardt (1990, pp.46–7). But as much as we are tempted to embrace Castiglione's vision of a courtly golden age in the late fifteenth century, we need to be aware that his image of Urbino was coloured by a deep-seated nostalgia for the past. Castiglione himself was sufficiently honest to acknowledge as much when he warned his readers not to give too much credit to those who wax lyrical about earlier courts. In attempting to reconstruct the

---

[1] This chapter was originally planned by Nick Webb.

cultural life of the Renaissance court we must therefore make allowance for the rhetoric of eulogy, while at the same time acknowledging the real contribution this distinctive institution made to the cultural development of Europe in our period.

Figure 1.1 Raphael (attributed), *Elizabetta Gonzaga*, 1504–5, oil on panel, 58 x 36 cm. Uffizi Gallery, Florence. Photo: Scala

In order to appreciate fully the role played by the Renaissance court in the promotion of the visual arts, we need first to wrestle with the problem of definition. One near-contemporary description defines the court as 'a company of well-bred men in the service of a distinguished superior' (Cesare Ripa, in Bertelli, 1986, p.8). Burckhardt reaffirmed the corporate nature of the court when he described it, like the state, as 'a work of art and organization' (p.46). It therefore existed as an artificial creation of the ruler designed to uphold and enhance the authority of its creator. Implicit in this analysis is the idea that the Renaissance court represented an important stage on the road from medieval barbarism to modern (i.e. post-Enlightenment) civility. The conscious appropriation of the arts and learning to promote civility and good government marks out the court as a special site of innovatory practice in the Renaissance (Elias, 1980). This account of the evolution of the court is not universally accepted today. Just as some scholars have balked at Burckhardt's anachronistic reading of the origins of the individual in Renaissance society, so others have emphasized continuity between the medieval and the Renaissance court (e.g. Bertelli, 1986, pp.35–6; Anglo, 1990). In addition, few historians of the Renaissance court today subscribe to the view, first popularized by Elias, that the prime function of the court was to serve as an instrument to 'domesticate' the nobility and so consolidate the growing political authority of the 'absolutist' prince. Increasingly, the court is seen as 'ambivalent' in terms of its political significance. Though some Renaissance rulers did undoubtedly encourage an aristocratic presence at court, neither this nor the affirmation of **seigneurial** authority that accompanied it necessarily guaranteed dynastic and political stability. Furthermore, proximity to the centre of political gravity in the Renaissance state reinforced the nobility's own claims to power as they bathed in the reflected political glory of their sovereign prince (Asch, 1991, pp.1–4).

None of this is to deny, however, that the Renaissance court was influenced and shaped by new social, political, religious and cultural developments. For example, there is little doubt that during the fifteenth century, particularly in Italy, important changes in the nature and personnel of government were effective in reshaping the appearance of many courts. Political conditions in Italy dictated a growing need for professional and educated bureaucrats who might intercede on behalf of their lord in diplomatic missions. A **humanist** education was increasingly considered an essential accomplishment for those courtier-administrators who aspired to high office in the employ of the state (see Book 1, Chapter 3).

As these functions grew, so did the need for the court to establish firmer roots. In the Middle Ages, and even to some extent in the Renaissance, the court possessed no single fixed abode. It was to be found wherever the lord happened to be. But with the growth of large staffs of trained administrators, secretaries and a host of other minor and semi-public officials, it became increasingly necessary for courts to establish a more permanent base. The Italian word for a court, *corte*, reflects this sense of permanence and place, suggesting as it does an enclosed and defined space (Cole, 1995, p.8). A unique feature of the Renaissance court was therefore its specific location in a complex of buildings which housed, among others, the ruler and his family, attended by a large number of men and women who carried out a great variety of functions.

We can, however, go beyond this rather broad simplification. Two other characteristics of the Renaissance court, both with their origins in earlier times, help us to define its essential features: the hierarchical and closed nature of its structure. The court was conceived of as a microcosm, both of the state and of the natural world, and as such it was felt to reflect the God-given hierarchical principles which contemporaries saw as integral to the smooth operation of the human and natural world. This was manifest, for example, in the physical layout of the court and the variable access and proximity which individual courtiers, diplomats and guests might possess to the ruler and his family. It also reflected the notion of the special sanctity of the person of the lord, whose charismatic authority and presence required the observation of strict rituals and codes of behaviour. For some, these developments mark a definitive break with the medieval court. Whereas the ritual celebrations (marriages, coronations, funerals) of the Renaissance court continued to function, as before, as public celebrations of the bond between prince and subject, now there was a growing emphasis on the more private world of the court as 'a platform for the cult of majesty' (Asch, 1991, p.10).

The world of the Renaissance court was then both hierarchical and elitist. It constituted a world within a world, a sacred space whose well-policed boundaries accentuated its separation from the world outside. These boundaries were both visible and invisible. Frequently, the court was located in, but apart from, its host city, and entry into the inner sanctum was restricted to all but a select few. But even if one was granted access to the court, its rule-bound nature meant that only those in the know, the *cognoscenti*, were able to avail themselves of its prized facilities. Every Italian court, following the lead of the French and Burgundian courts in the fifteenth century, had its set of rules or orders (*ordini*) which governed every aspect of life at court. Dress codes, or sumptuary laws, governed the physical appearance of courtiers, while strict rules of etiquette established correct behaviour for activities as diverse as banqueting and entertainment. Such concern for social decorum also informed the protocols surrounding the reception and entertainment of foreign dignitaries and ambassadors. Limits were even set on the distance a princely host might expect to travel to greet a guest, according to their social and political status (high-ranking VIPs might expect an escort from the borders of the state to the court itself).

The preoccupation of Renaissance society with rules and codes of conduct was most evident at court and must have reinforced the elitist and closed nature of court society. In artistic terms, this was accentuated by the contemporary vogue for emblems and sophisticated iconography, the revival of pagan culture and classical mythology providing the knowing courtier with a private and exclusive language through which to express refined notions of courtly taste.

Exercise

Read Alison Cole's introduction to the Renaissance court in her *Art of the Italian Renaissance Courts* (pp.7–14) and answer the questions below.

1 To what extent does Cole offer a different picture of the court from the one depicted above?

2 How many different 'types' of Italian court does she identify?

Discussion

1 Though Cole mentions most of the points raised in our initial discussion, she also injects an element of paradox into her understanding of the way in which Italian Renaissance courts functioned. Thus, she refers to the closed nature of the court (particularly its physical location) while at the same time arguing for a degree of accessibility which undermined its exclusiveness. The ruler was both accessible and inaccessible to subjects and visiting dignitaries. Similarly, the court was both fixed and mobile (pp.8–9). Above all, though membership of the court was uncertain (courtiers rarely possessed security of income or preferment), the court itself retained 'a remarkably consistent character', as roles and rituals were predetermined (p.9).

2 Cole suggests a great variety of courts in Italy. There were those established by the *condottieri*, seigneurs, urban patricians and ecclesiastical princes (popes, bishops and cardinals). In many cases, there was room for overlap. Some noblemen combined incomes from land with incomes drawn from warring. The pope was both a spiritual and a secular lord – he controlled large parts of central Italy (the papal states). ❖

Clearly, one of the key features of the Italian Renaissance court was its sheer diversity. It could take many forms, dependent on a wide range of factors, including size, wealth and origin (Cole, p.13). A court might also contain a number of smaller and separate households, usually reserved for the wife or sons of the ruler. These courts acted as a focus of political intrigue, and they also frequently engaged in competition with each other, particularly in the context of cultural exchange and production. Any attempt therefore to reduce the court to a single, simple definition is almost certainly doomed to failure. We can, however, isolate a number of features which, in combination, provide the skeleton of a definition. First and foremost, the court consisted of a physical space in which the ruler lived, worked and played. Here, the prince 'made laws, received ambassadors, dispatched letters, gave commands, decided cases, made appointments, took his meals, entertained, and proceeded through the streets' (Martines, 1979, p.221). Secondly, the court was circumscribed by those men and women who were given privileged access to this sacred space. These included not just the prince himself and his immediate family and entourage, but also a wide variety of personnel, ranging from visiting ambassadors, secretaries and noblemen to a host of minor functionaries. But in addition to place and personnel, a third element of the Renaissance court which increasingly set it apart from its medieval predecessor was the sense of spectacle or 'event' which dominated everyday life (Asch, 1991, p.9). The careful stage management of courtly existence in this period has frequently led scholars to perceive life at the Renaissance court as a form of theatre in which the ruler and the rest of the *dramatis personae* acted their respective roles according to a well-worn script. Burckhardt would no doubt have approved of such definitions of the court, for they dovetail neatly with his own notion of the 'state as a work of art'.

As an institution of critical significance in the social, political and cultural history of early modern Europe, the Renaissance court is the subject of a growing literature. Our interest, however, will focus on the role played by courts (particularly those of Italy) in the propagation of the visual arts, with particular emphasis on the relationship between courtly patronage and the promotion of Renaissance aesthetic values and ideas. We shall also seek to compare these developments across a range of court types in order to investigate links between cultural and political forms. The case studies of Milan, Mantua, Urbino and Buda are intended to provide a wide cross-section of court types (seigneurial, princely and monarchical). In Chapter 3, the case of a republican city-state, Florence, is addressed in order to determine the extent to which court culture might permeate an urban and mercantile environment which was otherwise hostile to the political trappings of courtly life. In exploring and comparing these examples, the aim is to show how the Renaissance court provides important evidence for a number of questions which have preoccupied historians since the time of Burckhardt. The medieval origins of the institution of the court, for example, raise the issue of continuity. Burckhardt (see Book 1, Chapter 1) assumed that the Renaissance marked a comprehensive break with the past, the innovative and secular spirit of the Italian people standing in marked contrast to the traditionalism and religious superstition of their European forbears. Increasingly, however, scholars have rejected this view, many citing the example of the Renaissance court as an institution which incorporated both old and new features in its propagation of social, political and cultural values (see, for example, Anglo, 1990).

Two further features of the court raise important issues for the student of the Renaissance. First, the question of reception. Because Burckhardt assumed that the Renaissance was above all the product of Italian genius, he had little to say about the process of transmission, whereby classical culture was adopted by Renaissance Italians and then exported to the rest of Europe. We now know that this was not a simple process of passive reception and acceptance of classical culture which spread across western Europe in neat concentric circles from its epicentre in Italy. Renaissance Europeans were selective and discriminatory in their evaluation and appropriation of the heritage of the classical past. Certain art forms and styles were preferred above others, the choice often reflecting the broad political climate in which this process of reception took place. In addition, the continuing vitality of certain aspects of medieval culture (e.g. chivalric literature, **Gothic** architecture and art, religious piety) encouraged interesting forms of cultural hybridization which often mask any clear break between 'medieval' and 'Renaissance'. The well-documented role of the court as one of the chief sites of cultural patronage and artistic display in the Renaissance thus provides an invaluable opportunity to study the related processes of dissemination and reception at first hand, as well as providing a wealth of comparative material.

Our second area of concern relates to this comparative dimension in recent studies of the court. One of the more common explanations for the uneven spread and selection of types of Renaissance culture in Europe has focused on the politics of *renovatio*. Far too often, however, this has resulted in an over-simplistic tendency to reduce art and culture to the status of mere ideology, a propagandistic tool, which, in the words of one critic, 'reinforces the assumption that the aesthetic and the political occupy different realms' (Starn, 1990, p.12). Citing Burckhardt as a corrective force in this respect, Starn believes that we should avoid the temptation to distinguish Renaissance art, ideology and politics in this way and view them instead as part of a seamless whole. If one accepts the logic of this argument, we need no longer see 'image' and 'reality' as separate and distinct elements in the analytical armoury of the historian. In Renaissance society, image *was* reality. At court, images of the prince such as those found in paintings and medals conveyed a range of meanings which were shared by both the subject of the image and the onlooker (the courtier). Under the circumstances, the prince was as much a product of the courtly conventions which informed the creation of such art forms as their original creator. Both were expected to perform their allotted role in the drama of court life. In the case of the former, this demanded the careful cultivation of image as a vital adjunct of conventional forms of political life. With respect to the latter, it required due reverence, bordering on adoration, for the semi-divine status of the prince, either in person or in representation. None of this is to deny the political significance of courtly patronage of the arts, nor does it diminish the importance of the court as an object of historical investigation. On the contrary, as Burckhardt himself intuitively recognized, the court provided powerful evidence to sustain one of his most cherished assumptions – namely, that the Renaissance in Italy witnessed the emergence of the 'state as a work of art' (Starn, 1990).

Patronage and the Renaissance court

The system of patronage which linked one individual (a superior) to another (an inferior) in a reciprocal bond of allegiance and support derived from the medieval world of feudal social relations. In the context of Renaissance art and culture, the patron–client relationship lay at the heart of cultural production. Though it permeated all aspects of society, such a system was most prominent in the courts of Renaissance Europe where scholars, artists and writers vied for commissions from wealthy and independent patrons. The court, of course, was not the only site of patronage for the arts and learning, but during the course of the fifteenth and sixteenth centuries it provided a rich and often stimulating environment for a range of media which rapidly outshone other centres of cultural production such as the universities and monasteries.

Patronage of the visual arts, in the broadest sense, was not limited to the demands and tastes of the individual. In some Italian city-states, for example, communal bodies such as lay confraternities and public boards of work might exert as much influence in commissioning works of art as private individuals. But it was at court that the taste of an individual patron was most likely to receive satisfaction. Patrons might commission works of art for a wide variety of reasons. Some undoubtedly were inspired to do so out of concern for the aesthetic pleasure that it gave, or the principle of what we might refer to today as 'art for art's sake'. Others (and, one is inclined to believe, the majority) were more likely to be inspired to commission works of art because of the glory or kudos they reflected on the patron. Pious noblemen and wealthy businessmen often sought to raise their standing in the here and now, while at the same time securing future glory in the world to come, through the purchase of religious art, much of which was displayed publicly in the churches and chapels of their respective communities.

The political potential of artistic patronage was not lost on the rich and powerful, and gained an added stimulus in the Renaissance through the revival of Aristotelian notions of *magnificentia* and **decorum**. These concepts were rooted in the idea that one with authority demonstrates the right to rule through magnanimous actions and gestures. Typically, these might include conspicuous expenditure on building projects or works of art, which exemplified the ruler's magnanimity or 'greatness of soul'. Artistic patronage of this kind therefore reflected the personal virtue of the patron as well as projecting a powerful image of the political authority he wielded (Cole, pp.21–4). In the last book of *The Courtier* Castiglione drew attention to the permanent enhancement of a princely reputation that might be achieved through the patronage of architecture. In contrast to the more ephemeral forms of splendour and magnificence which were the natural pursuits of the prince (hunting and banqueting, for example), public building, according to Castiglione, promised both honour in this life and a form of immortality in the next (Castiglione in Bull, 1976, pp.310–11, 315).

Castiglione's source was probably the Roman orator Cicero, who, in his *De officiis* (*On Duties*), recommended that public works of this kind reflected more credit on the patron than other forms of ostentation. This work by Cicero was also the chief humanist source for the Renaissance understanding of the notion of decorum. He argued that decorum was a vital aspect of the **cardinal virtue** of Temperance which allowed the virtuous man to know his rightful place in society, to exercise self-control and to behave in a natural and dignified manner (*De officiis* 1.27.93–8). In terms of Renaissance artistic patronage, this might be construed to mean that pornography in art was permissible if displayed in private (see, for example, the decorations of Giulio Romano in the Palazzo Te in Mantua, discussed below) and that the elements of an architectural scheme should be harmonious and consistent with the principles of the **Vitruvian canon**. In all cases, a concern for context was paramount. Not surprisingly, a sensitivity to the concept of decorum was a necessary attribute of any aspiring courtier, writer or artist who wished to secure patronage. In similar fashion, the possession of *sprezzatura* (the seemingly effortless facility of the artist or courtier to demonstrate their abilities) became a hallmark of the successful Renaissance artist and connoisseur. Increasingly, a humanist education, which included study of the ethical treatises of Aristotle and Cicero and the works of classical rhetoricians like Quintilian, groomed patrons and clients for their respective courtly roles. It also equipped the former with a suitable 'language' for art appreciation.

That the court was a sympathetic environment for artistic activity is shown by the frequency with which art was discussed there. The polite conversation about the relative merits of Raphael as a painter and Michelangelo as a sculptor recorded in the first book of *The Courtier* is similar to what we know of real or imagined conversations that were said to have taken place at the courts of Mantua, Milan and Buda in the fifteenth century. These accounts suggest that visual art was appreciated at court for its own sake and purely in terms of its aesthetic appeal. Drawing was increasingly regarded as an appropriate pastime for courtiers (Aristotle, *Politics* 8.3; Castiglione in Bull, 1976, pp.96–101). There is also evidence to suggest that the architectural patron was expected to play an active role in the planning and construction of new buildings, rather than simply to pay for the work. In the influential architectural treatise of Filarete (discussed further in Chapter 2), Ludovico Gonzaga, marquis of Mantua, is depicted holding a discussion with the duke of Milan about the range of artistic styles available to the discerning patron. He concludes by opting for the 'antique' or ***all'antica*** style, rather than the outmoded Gothic, on the recommendation of a courtier 'very learned in such things' (Spencer, 1965, vol. 1, pp. 174–5). The courtier in question was none other than Leon Battista Alberti (1404–72), who worked for Ludovico in Mantua and whose influential humanist treatise on painting, *De pictura* (*On Painting*), was dedicated in its Latin version to Ludovico's father. Moreover, interest in the *all'antica* style of building was not confined to the realms of theoretical discourse. Between 1471 and 1476, the same Ludovico paid for the construction of the *rotonda* of the church of S. Annunziata in Florence in the new *all'antica* style. Similar examples of courtly patronage of architectural innovation can be found at Urbino and Mantua, as well as royal Buda, providing ample evidence of the particular appeal that building exerted for learned patrons of the day.

Court culture and the Renaissance: themes and issues

One of the key issues we will address in this chapter is the extent to which Renaissance visual arts flourished in the environment of the court, and the reasons for their appropriation by rich and wealthy court patrons. A number of factors may affect our judgement of these important issues:

- the extent to which humanism fostered and informed such art;
- the process whereby classical culture was transmitted to Italy and the rest of Europe;

- what we mean by 'the visual arts' in the context of the court;
- the relationship between patron and client within the context of artistic production at court.

Central to the following discussion is the role of humanism in the promotion and development of the arts at court. Book 1 in this series looked at how the development of humanism was closely linked to seigneurial support for a variety of cultural endeavours. Patrons of the new humanist learning might, for example, sponsor the production and publication of a philosophical treatise, or provide a permanent pension or position at court or university for a humanist or philosopher. During the second half of the fifteenth century, a series of epic poems was produced by humanists in imitation of the Roman poet Virgil in which the deeds of contemporary seigneurial families were eulogized. Such poems were in many respects the verbal equivalents of the classicizing architecture. Indeed, the architect and art theorist Alberti, in his treatise on painting, specifically recommended that artists should work closely with poets in order to extend their knowledge of the classical world:

> For their own enjoyment, artists should associate with poets and orators, who have many embellishments in common with painters and who have a broad knowledge of many things. These could be very useful in beautifully composing the *istoria,* whose greatest merit consists in the *invenzione*. A beautiful invention has such force ... that even without painting, it is pleasing in itself alone.
>
> (Spencer, 1966, p.90)

Alberti's reference to the humanist predilection for allusive imagery or iconography highlights one of the main areas of constructive collaboration between artists and poets. Humanists frequently provided inscriptions for paintings, as well as devising *invenzione,* or programmes of decoration, in which images were matched with suitable inscriptions. Humanism certainly assisted in promoting the visual arts and music, and ultimately laid the foundation for a new literary genre, art criticism, which helped to provide an accessible vocabulary for art appreciation and connoisseurship (Baxandall, 1988; Hope and McGrath, 1996). In time, academies of the visual arts were founded by wealthy patrons, thus emulating the literary academies of poets and humanist scholars which were more common in the period.

The diffusion of Renaissance culture raises a number of questions about the way in which new artistic ideas circulated in Europe at this time. It is not possible here to do justice to the vast number of courts in northern and southern Europe (for example, those of the kings of

Spain, France, England, the duchy of Burgundy, the German lands of the emperor) which were all influenced and shaped to some extent by Italian visual culture. We may, however, make some general points.

Exercise

Read the extract from Earl Rosenthal's article 'The diffusion of the Italian Renaissance style in western European art' (Reader, no.13) and briefly summarize his main points.

Discussion

Rosenthal's chief point is to contrast the fate of Renaissance painting with that of antique architecture and sculpture. Whereas all three art forms were equally prized in Italy from an early stage, the rest of Europe was far more receptive to the new style of architecture and sculpture. Rosenthal attributes such discrimination to the greater role played by princely and seigneurial patrons in northern Europe, who valued artistic developments in these spheres (especially palace building and funerary monuments) more highly on account of their symbolic, rather than their aesthetic, value. He also stresses the role played by humanist-educated diplomats and court officials, as well as dynastic networks, in preparing the way for the reception of these particular art forms.

A further point of contrast is suggested by the fact that the chief patrons of art were equally divided among the clergy, upper middle classes and seigneurs. The subject matter of painting was overwhelmingly religious, not secular, and the relative shortage of princely patrons for such art further restricted its appeal and spread. Finally, in northern Europe it was more common to commission tapestries to adorn the walls of palatial chambers (they were also warmer), as opposed to the Italian preference for frescoes. ❖

The artefacts, objects and texts which provide evidence for material culture in the Renaissance invite further comment. We should not, for example, limit our understanding of visual culture to the common categories of the present-day 'fine arts', namely painting, sculpture and architecture. For one thing, the distinction which exists today between the so-called 'fine' and 'applied' arts is not appropriate to our period. Manuscripts, medallions, tapestries, clothing, jewels and personal ornaments, pottery, banners, theatrical contraptions, fortifications and urban design were all the province of the 'artist'. We should also proceed with caution in analysing the surviving literary evidence as a guide to our understanding of the visual culture of the Renaissance. A rhetorical description of a work of art written by a humanist scholar is unlikely to accord with the criteria established in the contract document between the artist and patron for the same object. (This and related issues are discussed in the extract from Baxandall's *Painting and Experience in Fifteenth-century Italy* (Reader, no. 10).) Such a source is unlikely to reflect the kinds of aesthetic judgement we might bring to bear today on a work of art. Approaching the material culture of the Renaissance, we need to go back to first principles and, to some extent, employ the methodology of the cultural anthropologist. In so doing, we need to reconsider the relationship between individual artefacts and the wider culture from which they acquire their 'meaning'. Only when we know the collective norms of a community or society can we make educated inferences as to the range of meanings which a given object might possess at a particular time and place. But such meanings often remain tantalizingly elusive. In the case of the court festival, the quintessential art form of the Renaissance, we are reminded of just how little we know of the place and importance of the arts at court. The ephemeral nature of these performances, and the fact that our knowledge of them is restricted to written accounts, provides a major challenge to historical analysis. At the same time, the manner in which the individual arts (painting, drama, music, architecture) often acted as little more than a backdrop for the main event (a tournament, feast or celebration) reminds us yet again of the alien nature of cultural priorities in the Renaissance (Anglo, 1990, pp.80–97).

It has been argued that Italian court patronage of the visual arts did not 'shape and direct demand as it did in the more traditional feudal-type monarchies' of northern Europe (Goldthwaite, 1993, p.175; see also Martines, 1979). One consequence of this approach is the greater freedom Italian court patronage appeared to bestow on the artist. This is underlined by the observation that artists working in Italian courts tended to be more innovative and original, unconstrained as they were by the conservative guild system which operated in the communal states (e.g. Venice and Florence) (Warnke, 1993, esp. pp.243–59). The greater appreciation of artists' skill or genius at court also provided a valuable opportunity for them to ascend the social ladder. It was not unknown for some to achieve noble status. The itinerant sculptor Giovanni Dalmata, for example, received a castle from Matthias Corvinus, the grateful king of Hungary. As ever, humanist scholars might support such ennoblement of the artist by reference to classical precedent. Pliny the Elder's *Natural History*, for example, one of the main literary sources for antique art, eulogized the relationship between Alexander the Great and the Greek painter Apelles (Pliny, *Naturalis historia* 35.36.77–8).[2] In order to underline his claim for an aestheticization of politics in the Renaissance,

---

[2] In 1526 the Mantuan court artist Giulio Romano was referred to as a second Apelles, his patron Marquis Federico Gonzaga assuming the role of a second Alexander (Verheyen, 1977, p.44).

Burckhardt too refers to the 'elective affinity' between court rulers and those who were paid to broadcast their fame through works of art. The 'state as a work of art' was thus the outcome of a collaborative approach on the part of the ruler and artist. Court patrons also seem to have paid better than their communal counterparts. Working for a court, however, could, on occasion, prove dangerous. In 1500, Giacomo Andrea da Ferrara, who had been employed alongside Leonardo da Vinci as an engineer at the Sforza court in Milan, was summarily executed by the French for wearing the livery of his patron (Warnke, 1993, p.253).

Italian court culture: style and sensibility

The word 'style' can have several different meanings. Most frequently when applied to art it refers to those formal elements commonly adopted and employed by a group of practitioners. In the broadest sense of the term, an artistic style is said to represent an art movement or a collective and distinctive phase in artistic development. Defined in this way, most Renaissance art is said to possess the stylistic attributes of classical art and naturalistic representation. We need to be careful, however, not to create too broad a definition. Meyer Schapiro (1994), for example, has shown how stylistic labels are an artificial construct which frequently masks the fact that it is always possible to locate degrees of difference in the work of individual artists or craftworkers.[3] We also use the phrase in respect of the 'lifestyles' of individuals or societies. Courtiers in our period were conspicuous in their search for 'stylishness' in their dress, speech and formal behaviour. These, like artistic styles, are liable to change and adaptation over time. In the case of the Renaissance, it is usual to describe various phases of artistic development culminating in **mannerism**, a product of the high or late Renaissance (roughly coinciding with the middle decades of the sixteenth century), which was characterized by the tendency of its practitioners to subvert the 'rules' of the orthodox style through virtuoso displays of technical skill. For specialist art historians, the question of continuity in Renaissance art is a tortuous one. For our purposes, it is sufficient to acknowledge the problem while at the same time recognizing that throughout the fifteenth and sixteenth centuries Renaissance art, regardless of the specific context in which it flourished, was based largely on naturalism and classical ideals of perspective and proportion.

[3] These issues are discussed more fully in the extract from Schapiro (1994) given in the Reader (no. 12).

Stylistic distinctions therefore need to be treated with caution and used as working definitions rather than as universally acknowledged categories. This is particularly evident when one is faced with the division between Gothic and *all'antica* art works. Any attempt to draw a clear-cut boundary between the two styles is undermined in practice by the existence of numerous examples of co-existence and hybridity. The Medici Palace in Florence, for example, contains frescoes in the private chapel which were influenced by the **International Gothic** style, while the main courtyard has arcades of *all'antica* composite columns. Both of these were created at the same time. Painters like Botticelli (whom you will encounter in Chapter 3) drew on the conventions of both styles. In the same way, public festivals and civic displays with roots in the medieval past easily assimilated the Renaissance passion for motifs and emblems derived from classical mythology and history (Anglo, 1990). Florence, widely celebrated as the home of the Renaissance, incorporated the medieval pageantry of the joust and the tournament into its civic festivities (Figure 1.2). In the process, it allowed the republican commune to demonstrate its familiarity with the new cultural fashions, as well as providing a safety valve for leading families to express their rivalries through artistic displays rather than civil conflict (Trexler, 1980, pp.240–70).

The chivalric origins of such militaristic performances lay of course in the feudal societies of medieval Europe. During the fifteenth century, chivalric fashion continued to exert a strong influence upon the princes of north-western Europe, nowhere more so than at the court of Charles the Bold, duke of Burgundy (1433–77), a figure whom Burckhardt saw as thoroughly antipathetic to the spirit of Renaissance Italy (pp.27–8). There are grounds, however, for viewing Charles and his court in a different light. Not only was he personally attracted to a range of artistic styles in the development of his court, but Burgundy itself often exported many of its cultural products to the seigneurial

Figure 1.2 Workshop of Apollonio di Giovanni, *A Tournament in Piazza Santa Croce*, c.1460–5, cassone panel, egg tempera on panel, 45 x 153 cm. New Haven, Conn., Yale University Art Gallery. University Purchase from James Jackson Jarves

courts of Italy (Paravicini, 1991, p.94). Widely regarded as the epitome of chivalric culture in his age, Charles was none the less a great admirer of Italian cultural products. Contact with Italy and the new Italian court culture was undoubtedly facilitated by the fact that the duke regularly recruited soldiers from Italy and employed Italian secretaries and officers in his household (Walsh, 1976, pp.146–97). The French chronicler Philippe de Commynes wrote of Charles's repudiation of medieval chivalric romances in favour of classical literature, citing his wish to imitate the heroism of ancient princes as the main reason for his incessant pursuit of warfare. During the siege of Neuss in 1475, Charles, who insisted that his knights maintain courteous behaviour in camp, retired each evening to read the histories of Livy or stories which recounted the deeds of Alexander the Great. Classical heroes were particularly popular at court and were readily appropriated in the apocryphal histories of royal dynasties in order to strengthen claims of lineage and legitimacy. Hercules, for example, was regularly cited in Burgundian history as one of the early ancestors of Charles the Bold. The centrepiece of the festivities to honour the marriage of Charles to Margaret of York was an extensive **masque** celebrating the twelve labours of Hercules, held at Bruges in 1468 (Anglo, 1990, pp.81–2, 88–9).

Exercise

Plate 1 depicts a scene from one of the eleven tapestries on the theme of the Trojan War that were made for the magistrates of Bruges and subsequently given to Charles the Bold. To which style, International Gothic or *all'antica*, is it indebted?

Discussion

Apart from its subject matter, which is clearly inspired by the vogue for classical learning and literature, the tapestry is largely a product of the International Gothic style. The cluttered narrative scene is composed in two planes – background and foreground – with little sense of depth or perspective. The sense of space is crudely established through the use of overlapping forms and the recession of lances and tents. Titles help us to identify individuals among the Greeks, Trojans and Amazons, but there is no attempt to depict the personal features of the cast of characters. All are stereotypes dressed in contemporary costume; Pyrrhus (the figure on the right) dons medieval armour and not a classical breastplate. Finally, the richness of colour and texture testify to the tapestry's debt to an older style of art work which is at odds with the Renaissance vogue for naturalism, perspective and the use of classical dress and motifs. ❖

It would be a mistake, however, to conclude that Charles's support for the International Gothic style in art was a manifestation of cultural backwardness. Popular throughout the courts of northern Europe, tapestries of this nature were equally sought after by leading Italian princes who collected and hung them on the walls of their Renaissance palaces. Tapestries depicting the Trojan Wars were owned by, among others, Ludovico Sforza of Milan and Federico da Montefeltro of Urbino. In the case of Ludovico, they were hung publicly to mark the entrance of the Emperor Maximilian's delegation into the city in 1493, while those of Federico decorated a large room in which plays were performed. Reference to tapestries of tournaments and hunting scenes which once belonged to the duke of Burgundy can also be found in an inventory of Medici property dating from 1492 (Spallanzani and Bertelà, 1992, pp.8, 37). (This inventory is discussed in Chapter 3.)

If tapestry production was an art form that was most closely associated with the late medieval International Gothic, this did not of itself preclude its potential role as a vehicle for Renaissance-style art work. This is apparent in the designs created by Bramantino (*c.*1465–1530) for a series of tapestries on the subject of the months of the year in 1509 (see January in Plate 2). Made at Vigevano in northern Italy, they were the work of a local weaver, Benedetto da Milano.

Exercise

Compare Bramantino's work, shown in Plate 2, which depicts the god Janus, with Plate 1, discussed above. Why is Bramantino's work deserving of the stylistic label 'Renaissance'?

Discussion

Whereas Bramantino's general subject matter is not of itself classical (interest in astrology and zodiacal signs was as much a part of intellectual and everyday life in the Middle Ages as it was in the Renaissance), the treatment of the subject demonstrates a thorough grounding in the principles of the new art. Throughout, there is concern for perspectival space. The composition is balanced and clear (note in particular how Bramantino uses empty spaces to accentuate the realistic nature of the scene), and individuals are accurately defined and dressed in classical garb. The classical buildings and inscription further highlight the cultivated learning of its designer, the former reminiscent of the depictions of ideal cities which were a popular feature of Renaissance art (see, for example, Cole, Plate 53). Finally, one is struck by the far more subtle approach to colour in this composition. Instead of gold and silver thread, plain colours are picked out in wool and silk. ❖

Stylistically, then, Bramantino's work is readily identifiable as Renaissance. In terms of content, it also demonstrates a knowledge and passion for classical culture. The figure in the centre depicts Janus, the double-faced Roman god, holding the key to the start of the Roman year. He stands on a classical plinth on which is inscribed a Latin description of the agricultural activities associated with the first month of the year. The figures in the roundels are the Sun (top left) and Aquarius (top right). The arms of the patron, Giangiacomo Trivulzio, are set in the roundel directly above Janus, while shields and coats of arms of other members of the family decorate the border. Despite its classical appeal, the work also owes much to contemporary religious preoccupations. The figures on the right represent idleness, and those on the left, dressed in Moorish costume (probably the three Magi), celebrate the feast of Epiphany (6 January).

These examples demonstrate the two-way nature of cultural exchange in fifteenth- and sixteenth-century Europe. The process of cultural diffusion in the Renaissance was not confined to the simple export of (superior) Italian classical culture to the rest of (inferior) Europe. This is readily apparent in the esteem with which the two Flemish painters Jan van Eyck and Rogier van der Weyden were held in the humanistic courts of Italy. Altarpieces and secular paintings by northern artists were commissioned by Florentine merchants and Italian princes. One such, a *Nativity*, painted by Hugo van der Goes for Tommaso Portinari, one of the directors of the Medici bank in Bruges, was installed in the family chapel in S. Egidio in Florence in 1483 (Plate 3). Its subsequent influence on Italian masters like Ghirlandaio and Botticelli is unmistakable and provides one example among many of the general admiration for Netherlandish painting in Italy at this time. Indeed, such was the interest of cultivated patrons and artists in Italy in the art of the northern schools that one historian has been tempted to suggest that it was 'Netherlandish painting, not Italian, that held centre stage for much of the fifteenth century' (Christiansen, 1998, p.39).

Other examples from the fifteenth century provide ample evidence of the growing taste for northern art at the Italian courts. In 1449, Ciriaco of Ancona (the intrepid traveller and collector of inscriptions, encountered in Book 1, Chapter 3), on visiting the art collection of the Este court at Ferrara, remarked that the work which most impressed him was a **triptych** by Rogier van der Weyden who, after Van Eyck, he considered 'the outstanding painter of our time'. It was admiration of this sort that led Francesco Maria Sforza, duke of Milan, to send a local painter to Brussels in 1460 to study with van der Weyden. It also ignited a desire in many leading Italian patrons to secure at first hand the services of northern masters. Thus, on the authority of the bookseller-biographer Vespasiano da Bisticci, we hear that Federico da Montefeltro, one of the most cultivated patrons in fifteenth-century Italy:

> was much interested in painting, and because he could not find in Italy painters in oil to suit his taste he sent to Flanders and brought thence a master who did at Urbino many very stately pictures, especially [for] Federigo's study.

(Christiansen, 1998, p.41)

It is evident that one of the features of Netherlandish art which appealed to patrons like Federico was the innovative use of oil paint. The advantage of working exclusively in oil was that it produced much subtler colour schemes which enhanced the illusionistic aspect of painting. Leonardo da Vinci's use of techniques such as *sfumato* (smoked finish) and *chiaroscuro* (the combination of light and dark tonal registers) derived ultimately from this northern style of painting. In addition, the use of oil in paint – a cheap and relatively accessible medium – redirected the attention of patrons towards the artist's inventiveness and away from the earlier infatuation with rich and expensive materials (Spencer, 1965, vol. 1, pp.310–11).

The emergence of a distinct Italian Renaissance style in art was ultimately indebted to the humanist revival of learning in the fifteenth century. In time, the dominance of a classically informed style of art would lead Italian artists to reconsider and downgrade the achievement of their northern colleagues. Viewed through a lens 'fully polished with the pumice of classical learning', Netherlandish art was made to 'appear deficient to an informed public' and in the process was itself transformed and Italianized (Christiansen, 1998, p.40). The critical apparatus was provided then by the vogue for classical literature and learning. The steady growth of new translations and editions of authors such as Vitruvius, Pliny the Elder, Livy and Ovid, allied to the invention of printing, familiarized a growing audience with the mythological, historical and architectural details of *all'antica* art. During the course of the fifteenth century the trade in antiquities flourished in centres such as Rome, Florence and Venice. Gift-giving, another characteristic feature of courtly life and the patron–client system, helped to create a shared sense of aesthetic taste and artistic sensibility in Italy. Small sculptures and bronze figurines – often modelled on recently excavated examples from the classical past – were widely collected and exhibited. Classical literature also provided precedents for new approaches to interior decoration. By the 1440s the ancient custom of adorning houses, villas, courtyards, gardens and studies with images and paintings of ancestors was cited by the Florentine humanist Poggio Bracciolini as evidence to support the contemporary fad for the public display of antique sculpture (Gilbert, 1980, p.169). The use of harmonious proportion and the depiction of accurate physiognomy in the Renaissance portrait bust combined the humanist interest in ideal types with the desire to recreate an accurate portrayal of a particular person (for an example of such a bust, see Cole, Plate 23). Writers of the period produced classically inspired poetic eulogies with similar intent.

In the absence of actual Roman paintings, the 'spirit' of ancient art was invoked through literary and mathematical treatises on proportion and perspective, as well as through the contemporary revival of interest in anatomy (discussed in more detail in Book 3, Chapter 5). The master of this approach was of course Leonardo da Vinci (1452–1519), whose work in these fields is treated more fully in the next chapter. It was Leonardo who developed the initial investigations of pioneers such as the Florentine Brunelleschi into the nature of linear perspective. He was the first to establish, for example, that because of optical distortions in the field of vision caused by the central bias of the eye (the fact that most people look with two eyes rather than one, causing objects to blur at the periphery of sight), a perspectival grid ought to be created to offset this effect.[4] This research was begun during his stay in Milan, where he illustrated the geometrical treatise of the celebrated mathematician Luca Pacioli (c.1445–1517) (Figure 1.3). Pacioli was supported in his mathematical humanism by the patronage of Guidobaldo da Montefeltro, whose father, Federico, was a keen student and patron of the mathematical arts. Among those artists whom Federico cultivated were others, like Leonardo, with a special interest in the revival of mathematics. Most celebrated of these was Piero della Francesca, who dedicated his *De prospettiva pingendi* (*On the Perspective of Painting*) (1435) to his learned patron.

During the course of the fifteenth century a distinctive Renaissance style of art did evolve in Italy, characterized by a growing concern among artists for clear and balanced spatial construction, varied composition, and formal and expressive naturalism. Its roots lay in the classical revival, but it was also influenced – as our brief discussion of Netherlandish art suggests – by the creative potential of the northern Gothic style, as well as by direct observation of man and nature. The role of the artist therefore was not restricted to mere copying or imitation of classical prototypes. It was rather guided by a spirit of experimentation which led artists both to equal and to

[4] For Leonardo's views on this subject, see the extracts from his notebooks in the Anthology (no. 31).

Figure 1.3 Jacopo de' Barbari, *Luca Pacioli*, c.1495, oil on canvas, 99 x 120 cm. Capodimonte Gallery, Naples. Photo: Scala

surpass the achievement of their classical predecessors. Whatever the case, by the end of the fifteenth century there is evidence to suggest that the *all'antica* style was fully domesticated in Italy. This is evident, for example, in the fresco cycle by Ghirlandaio in the church of S. Maria Novella, Florence, which depicts a contemporary interior (Figure 1.4, overleaf). The *putti* playing along the frieze are comparable to examples found on the singing galleries in Florence Cathedral, and the classical candelabra ornamentation on the panelling recalls the abstract designs found in the Domus Aurea, the 'Golden House' of the Emperor Nero, recently discovered in the 1480s. The scenic realism of the fresco suggests that this is an actual contemporary interior. As such, it serves as a useful indicator of just how far the Renaissance had infiltrated everyday life in the upper echelons of Italian society. And though it would be foolish to overstate the extent to which individual artists, patrons and workshops were committed to the ideals of the new aesthetic, the examples of men like Federico da Montefeltro in Italy and Matthias Corvinus in Hungary suggest that some wealthy patrons did aim to effect a deliberate and conscious policy of cultural renewal based on the classical revival.

Figure 1.4 Domenico Ghirlandaio, *Birth of the Virgin*, 1485, fresco, approx. life size. Tornabuoni Chapel, S. Maria Novella, Florence. Photo: Alinari

Book illumination: advertising culture?

One source for a better understanding of the aesthetic tastes of the Renaissance patron is the illuminated book. This embodied many of the values of the Renaissance and was avidly collected for a variety of reasons. Above all, in an age when the advent of printing (from about the mid fifteenth century) increased the luxury value of individually produced and illustrated books, ownership of such items represented an important symbol of wealth, power and status. Books were of course made to be read or listened to, both for education and for entertainment. But this was not their sole function. They were frequently collected for their physical attractiveness or were given as gifts either by grateful clients or by fellow princely collectors. Many were read only by a select few. Books in Greek, for example, commonly fell into this category as only a small number of humanist scholars and even fewer patrons were able to read this little-known language.

Exercise

One of the most celebrated book collectors of the fifteenth century was Federico da Montefeltro, the lord of Urbino. Read the extract from the 'Life of Federigo da Montefeltro' by the Florentine bookseller Vespasiano da Bisticci (Anthology, no. 32). What features of Federico's library and book collecting strike you as particularly noteworthy?

Discussion

One of the most curious aspects (to the modern reader) of Federico's book collecting is that according to Vespasiano this wealthy patron refused to have printed books in his library (although it is now known that he did in fact possess some printed books). One gains the impression that from Federico's perspective, possession of such items would have constituted a demeaning act. Illuminated books of the kind collected by Federico were a luxury consumer item and attested to the owner's elevated status as one who was not only sufficiently wealthy to purchase them but also sufficiently learned to appreciate their educational and aesthetic value. Whether or not Federico actually read and studied the tomes in his library is, however, another question. Book collecting, then as now, did not necessarily imply scholarship. In addition, two other features of Federico's library are worthy of comment: first, its size and the diversity of its contents (it had cost 30,000 ducats[5]); and secondly, the fact that Federico's book collection at Urbino was a working library to which visiting scholars and other luminaries were allowed access. Though by no means a public library in the modern sense of the word, it was none the less a valuable collection which suggested the erudition and magnanimity of its owner. ❖

The production of illuminated books such as those collected by Federico at Urbino was undoubtedly boosted by the growing demand for such luxury items among the learned patrons of Europe. Personal libraries of the kind described by Vespasiano were increasingly common at the courts of fifteenth-century Italy. By the end of the century the libraries of the Medici in Florence and the Sforza in Milan each contained about a thousand volumes. By comparison, a self-respecting humanist may have been fortunate to own as many as 50 books, few of which would have been decorated. Nor was book collecting on this scale confined to the Italian courts. One of the largest collections in Europe was to be found in Hungary at the court of King Matthias Corvinus. This may have contained over two and a half thousand tomes (roughly as large as that of the Vatican library in Rome). The impetus for the royal collection seems to have stemmed from the influence of Italian humanists attracted to Matthias's court in the mid fifteenth century. From the 1460s onwards many volumes were commissioned from Italian workshops, and so great was the demand that within a short time a school of illumination was set up in Buda, the royal capital, to supply the native market (Csapodi and Csapodi-Gárdonyi, 1969). In this instance, there can be little doubt that Matthias's promotion of bookish culture represented a conscious

---

[5] At a rough estimate, one ducat would have possessed the purchasing power of about £64 today.

attempt on the part of the king to copy and even emulate the sophisticated artistic and intellectual tastes of the north Italian courts.

Illuminated books were produced at a number of different centres, each of which was characterized by its own particular style and specialism. Padua, for example, initiated a vogue for antiquarianism, while at Ferrara illuminators imitated the work of jewellers and goldsmiths. The portable nature of books, however, guaranteed a degree of cross-fertilization and imitation, with motifs originating in one centre readily transferred and incorporated into styles found elsewhere (Alexander, 1995). Book illumination could also take several forms. It might simply be used to illustrate the subject matter of the text. Alternatively, it might help to amplify the physical layout of the text or allow the inclusion of independent images, whether decorative, **representational** or **emblematic**. Manuscripts also varied considerably in size, from those that could be held in the palm of the hand to the large liturgical books positioned on lecterns around which singers might gather. Whatever the case, the basic unit of artistic composition was either the single or double page. Size clearly determined to some extent the parameters of this particular art form. It did not, however, prevent ingenious practitioners from producing complex and detailed images – often whole scenes – in very limited spaces such as the **historiated** initials which graced the pages of many such works. As for the extent of such decoration, few manuscripts were illustrated throughout. Most artistic work was confined to specific locations: the frontispiece; decorated initials on the first page of text; smaller initials introducing new sections or chapters in the body of the work; the end of chapters; or a **colophon**.

Some of the features discussed here are apparent in the illuminated manuscript Bible produced for Matthias Corvinus (see Plates 4 and 5). This lavishly illustrated three-volume edition was the work of two Florentine workshops, but was unfinished at the time of the king's death. In 1498 it was valued at 1,400 ducats. The text illustrated here is the first verse of the first Psalm: '*Beatus vir*' (Blessed is the man). The illuminations provide a good example of how word and image can work together to extend the range of meanings attaching to a particular text. The principal images on the left-hand (verso) page, or frontispiece (Plate 4), depict scenes from the life of David. From left to right, we see young David searching for stones, old David praying to God, young David smiting Goliath and the Philistines in flight, with Jerusalem in the background. Above the text on the right-hand (recto) page (Plate 5), David's Israelite supporters (on the left) engage in battle with armies representing the rebel forces of Absalom (the city behind, Hebron, where David was crowned, is clearly modelled on Florence as is evident in the inclusion of the Loggia dei Signoria (later known as the Loggia dei Lanzi)). Beneath this scene, and inserted within the text, David, wearing armour, is seated on a throne, playing the lyre. The allusion here is to his role as the person traditionally regarded as the composer of the Psalms.

It would be a mistake, however, to construe these images as a straightforward commentary on the biblical life of the psalmist, David. Throughout, it is the intention of the authors of this work, the Giovanni brothers, to associate the royal patron, Matthias Corvinus, with the figure of David. This is made explicit in a number of ways. Most significant is the inclusion of the French king, Charles VIII (1470–98) (he is the crowned figure with hooked nose wearing the fleur-de-lys), in the image depicting David at prayer. Following his triumphant invasion of the Italian peninsula in 1494, Charles had called for a crusade against the Turks. This was a cause close to Matthias's heart. During the 1480s the Turks were once again amassing on the borders of Hungary, and Matthias was eager to counter the threat. An alliance with Charles was not therefore out of the question. The artists' equation of the Philistines, and their champion Goliath, with the hated Turks seems natural in the circumstances (Plate 4). A further strand of analysis has associated the military engagement between David and the rebellious Absalom (Plate 5) with Matthias's own struggle to assert his supremacy in Hungary over rival claimants to the throne (Garzelli, 1985, vol. 2, pp.303–7). An active reading of these images within the context of contemporary events and concerns thus allows the historian to uncover many layers of meaning which might otherwise be lost.

Exercise

Identify the chief stylistic features of Plates 4 and 5. How might our knowledge of Renaissance stylistic conventions add to a contemporaneous 'political' reading of this text?

Discussion

The illustration contains a mixture of styles. Traces of the International Gothic are evident in the use of rich and expensive colours such as purple and bright red. But the chief inspiration for the design is clearly the revival of the antique. The text, for example, is written in the new 'Roman' book script (although in gold on a purple background). The architectural-style frame of the border is reminiscent of a Renaissance doorway or window, and the four corners of the left-hand sheet (Plate 4) contain fictive reliefs of subjects taken from classical mythology and history. Elsewhere, the abstract candelabra decoration on the vertical sides of the same frontispiece recalls that found in the newly discovered Domus Aurea of Nero (see above, p.21), while some borders contain military trophies and the paraphernalia of war. Other classical touches include the figure of David selecting pebbles, closely modelled on a typical pose of classical sculpture (that of the legendary Narcissus who fell in love with his own reflection), and the antique roundels depicting coats of arms and classical figures. The dominant style is Renaissance, though the landscape setting, with the suggestion of aerial perspective and changing shades of light, is reminiscent of northern European painting.

The contemporary resonance of the scene – particularly its relation to Matthias's current predicaments (Turkish threat, dynastic instability) – is accentuated by the way in which the biblical text and associated images are dressed up in the visual language of the classical past. David's status as king, military leader and musician/poet is reaffirmed by the introduction into the design of various elements of antique art, architecture and sculpture (including jewellery and cameos) which add an imperial flavour to the proceedings. Further evidence for a contemporary reading is provided by the use of Renaissance-style clothing (Goliath as a Turk, soldiers in fifteenth-century battle dress). All that is missing is the Corvinian coat of arms – a timely reminder perhaps that because of the death of the intended patron such images could be easily redesigned to suit the needs of a wide range of potential clients. ❖

Italian court culture

This section explores the cultural life of three Italian courts: those of the Sforza, Montefeltro and Gonzaga. All three share similar political and cultural traits. Their ruling dynasties, for example, were acutely aware of the political advantages to be gained through the promotion and patronage of the arts. But there are also subtle differences of emphasis which reflect, in part at least, the varying extent to which the classical revival in art and letters penetrated the aristocratic sensibilities of Renaissance Italians.

The Sforza court

Patronage and politics

The last two independent Sforza dukes of Milan, Galeazzo Maria (1466–76) and his brother Ludovico (regent 1479–94; duke 1494–1500), acquired European-wide reputations for their support of the arts and the magnificence of their courts.[6] In the process, they were clearly assisted by the size and wealth of their territories and estates.

[6] Giangaleazzo, the son of Galeazzo Maria, who held the title of duke from 1476 to 1494, was largely subservient to his uncle, Ludovico, who acted as regent in these years. In 1494, after his nephew's death, Ludovico became duke of Milan.

Stretching from the Alps in the north to the Apennines in the south, and including the fertile provinces of the plain of Lombardy, the duchy of Milan was one of the richest states in Europe in the fifteenth century. Despite outward appearances, however, Sforza rule in Milan was beset by problems, two of which, insolvency and dynastic insecurity, were to play an important role in determining the nature of cultural patronage and production at the Milanese court.

From the outset, the Sforza dukes were perpetually in debt. In 1482, for example, total annual expenditure in the duchy exceeded income by approximately 300,000 ducats. One does not have to look far for the source of insolvency. In the same year, almost three quarters of the duke's income was spent on warfare and the cost of maintaining a standing army.[7] A further 80,000 ducats were set aside for maintaining the court and household, while 140,000 ducats were lavished on the refurbishment of Giangaleazzo's private chamber. The duke's horses, hawks and hounds cost another 16,000 ducats. In addition, a whole army of officers, administrators and clients required payment. The duke's astrologer, for example, was paid about 290 ducats per annum.

The fact that so much money was spent on defence reflected in part the insecurity of the Sforza, whose title to the imperial fiefdom of Milan was not officially confirmed until the investiture of Ludovico (involving the formal acknowledgement by his overlord, the emperor, of his right to rule as duke) in 1494. Francesco Sforza (1450–66), the founder of the dynasty, had assumed power following the fall of the heirless Visconti and a short-lived popular republic. The Sforza claim to legitimacy was pursued through traditional channels such as marriage and diplomacy (most notably with France and the empire), but throughout the period of their rule in Milan the undercurrent of dynastic instability remained a consistent factor which affected both their style of government and their patronage of the arts. With the possible exception of Galeazzo Maria, the promotion and pursuit of cultural and artistic *magnificentia* preoccupied the Sforza dukes of Milan and helped to offset continuing uncertainty surrounding their claim to the duchy.

Financial constraints at court meant that artists and architects had to compete for the relatively small and insecure stipends which they received from their Sforza masters. Not infrequently, they sought commissions and patronage elsewhere. Under Ludovico Sforza, the celebrated architect and painter Donato Bramante of Urbino (*c.*1444–1514) received an annual salary of just 62 ducats for services

---

[7] In addition to paying their own troops, the Sforza made regular payments to *condottieri*. Galeazzo Maria Sforza, for example, paid a retainer of 36,000 ducats to Ludovico Gonzaga of Mantua.

to the duke. Bramante continually complained to his friend and patron, the courtier Gaspare Visconti, that remuneration from the Sforza court was unreliable, so much so that on one occasion he claimed he was unable to buy a pair of shoes. Bramante only survived because he could rely on alternative sources of patronage such as that offered by his friend Visconti, a fact which highlights the multi-layered levels of patronal support which existed in any large court. Visconti was himself a member of the former ruling family of Milan, a ducal counsellor and a favourite of the duchess, Beatrice d'Este, the wife of Ludovico. A keen humanist, Visconti first began to employ Bramante from about 1487, probably as a private tutor. As a wealthy courtier-patron, he was able to provide additional work and supplementary income for artists otherwise employed by the duke. He was also, most importantly, able to commission work comparable in style, content and quality to that produced at the ducal court. The wall paintings for his new palace in Milan, for example, are on an equal footing with those commissioned by the duke for his household. They also reflect the deep-seated humanist aspirations and interests of the patron, as, for example, in the half-length portraits of the two Greek philosophers, Heraclitus and Democritus, which Bramante painted on the walls of Visconti's palace (Figure 1.5).

Figure 1.5 Bramante, *Heraclitus and Democritus*, *c*.1490, fresco from the 'Casa Panigarola', 102 x 127 cm. (The depiction of these two philosophers in this way – Heraclitus crying and Democritus laughing – was a common iconographic conceit in the period.) Pinacoteca di Brera, Milan. Photo: Alinari

The *all'antica* style and subject matter stand direct comparison with the fresco of the mythological figure *Argus* which Bramante and a pupil painted for the treasury of the Sforza at the Castello Sforzesco (Cole, Plate 71).

If shortage of funds often forced artists to seek elsewhere for patronage within the entourage of the Sforza court, political expediency none the less demanded an important role for the arts in Milan. Humanists, scholars, artists and architects were actively involved in the creation of artefacts which celebrated the achievements of their newly ennobled patrons. The legitimation of the Sforza was achieved in two seemingly contradictory ways: first, by reinforcing the sense of continuity between the Sforza and their Visconti predecessors; and secondly, by affirming their independence from that same tradition. In cultural terms, the first objective was achieved by various means. Visconti symbols, for example, frequently appear on buildings, coins, medals and in illuminated manuscripts commissioned by the Sforza. Continuity is also evident in the Sforza patronage of artists who had previously been employed at the Visconti court. In 1492 Ludovico even went so far as to commission a monumental tomb for his illustrious predecessor Giangaleazzo Visconti, in the Certosa, Pavia (Norris, 1990, p.20; Cole, pp.104–5 and Plate 77). As important as it was for the Sforza to demonstrate the legitimacy of their descent from the noble Visconti,[8] it was also imperative that they were able to portray themselves as rulers of Milan in their own right. Again, patronage of learning and the arts provided a powerful medium for the assertion of such claims. Francesco Sforza, for example, employed the humanist scholar Francesco Filelfo (1398–1481) to construct a family history which, based on Homer's *Iliad*, glorified the military prowess of the new duke (Hollingsworth, 1994, p.167).[9] Thirty years later, Ludovico attempted to bestow the appearance of longevity and legitimacy on his family by commissioning from Leonardo a monumental equestrian statue of his father Francesco, the first duke (discussed further in Chapter 2). A similar motive almost certainly lay behind Ludovico's attempt to move the sacred seat of the dynasty from the Certosa in Pavia to the Sforza church of S. Maria delle Grazie in Milan (discussed in more detail below, p.34).

---

[8] Francesco Sforza married the illegitimate daughter (Bianca Maria) of Duke Francesco Maria Visconti – another aid to his claim to the title.

[9] The family history, a lengthy Latin epic poem entitled *Sphortias* (*Sforziade*), was continued by Ludovico, who employed writers, translators and printers to produce multiple copies of this work which extolled the virtuous rule of his father, the first duke (Norris, 1990, p.20; Cole, Plate 68).

Defining the Sforza court

The Sforza court was a complex entity which contained scores of officials, dignitaries, servants and others, all of whom were ranked according to an elaborate hierarchy (see Figure 1.6). The focal point of the court, and the figure who helped most to define its purpose and function, was the duke. Rank within the court was largely determined by access and proximity to his physical presence. The feudal pecking order, in which the duke's immediate family and other noble courtiers occupied the living space closest to him, was largely a by-product of the Middle Ages. During the course of the fifteenth century, first under the Visconti and then under the Sforza, the social and political significance of these arrangements was further enhanced by the growing tendency to visualize the person of the duke as semi-divine and sacrosanct:

> The ducal court became an earthly paradise, occupying a special place in the earthly universe. Those who participated in it were presumably blessed with wonders denied to those outside the sacred precincts. According to the logic of the image, the prince's greatness transcended all earthly particularism and united all his subjects and other inferiors on a higher plane, imbued with sacral power. In the later medieval period, secular rulers were absorbing and appropriating the quality of sacrality that had once been a monopoly of the church. The very language of Roman law in the Milanese dominion supported such pretensions, for it spoke of the duke as 'the image of the Divine presence'.
>
> (Lubkin, 1994, p.71)

Precedence and the observation of due deference were an obsession of courtiers and rulers alike. Distinction of place at court carried real meaning in terms of offices, rewards and pensions. It was also central to an individual's self-image, which informed the aristocratic virtue of magnanimity and was reflected in the way in which courtiers and noblemen received and entertained eminent visitors from neighbouring courts. Rules had to be established to ensure the maintenance of propriety and to avoid embarrassing blunders. The Sforza archives contain a number of guest lists which incorporate this kind of thinking. In 1468, for instance, the ducal chancellery drew up a memorandum listing those lords and ambassadors who should be received by the duke and, most importantly, the order for their reception. First came the ambassadors of the pope, the imperial electors and worthy princes (including the marquis of Mantua). Other ambassadorial guests were to be evaluated according to the richness of their gifts (30 ducats and more was noteworthy), the number of people in their entourage, and even the number of horses they brought with them (Maspes, 1890). Critical to social decorum

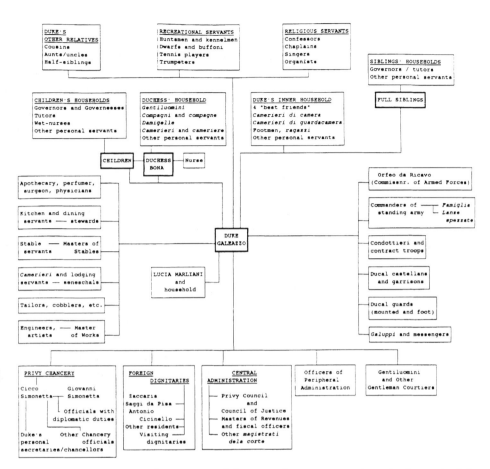

Figure 1.6
Diagram of court-related persons and offices in the court of Galeazzo Maria Sforza. Reproduced from Lubkin, 1994, p.250, Figure 5

was an appropriate sense of dress and ornamentation. Ambassadorial reports of the period frequently describe in detail the costumes and jewellery worn on such occasions. In 1489 the Florentine ambassador to Milan wrote to Lorenzo de' Medici to relate the good impression his son's brocaded tunic had made on the Milanese court when he attended the wedding of Giangaleazzo Sforza. The bride on this occasion, Isabella of Aragon, the daughter of the king of Naples, was escorted all the way from Genoa to Milan (Magnani, 1910).

Though many of the officers and servants of the duke's household were also servants of the state whose location in the physical space of the court was fixed by virtue of their appointment, others frequently travelled with the duke as he visited the various homes and palaces scattered throughout the duchy. The unfixed nature of the court is a useful reminder of the fact that the court was largely defined by the personal presence of the duke. Among his various residences were the ducal palace at the Castello Sforzesco di Porta Giovia in Milan, the Palazzo Arengo near Milan Cathedral and the castle at Pavia, as well as villas and hunting lodges elsewhere in the duchy, such as that at Vigevano which was converted into a ducal complex by Ludovico

Sforza. The court, then, was both the physical space surrounding the duke and the personnel who served, advised and entertained him. Flexibly defined before the mid 1450s, its boundaries became more fixed in the second half of the fifteenth century when rules of conduct and orders of protocol were devised by advisers to the duke. The strict etiquette and elaborate ceremonies and rituals which dominated the life of the Sforza court testify to this process and may owe much to similar developments in the courts of the kings of France and dukes of Burgundy (Lubkin, 1994, pp.95, 126–47).

The court as an institution therefore guaranteed restricted access to the duke at the same time as it brought together the upper echelons of Lombard society. Some among the urban elite – the richer merchants, magistrates, nobility and civic office-holders – served as salaried courtiers on the duke's privy and judicial councils and acted as agents of government in the duchy. The duke also counted many senior clerics among his retinue of trusted servants. Of the 40 vacant ecclesiastical offices in the duchy between 1450 and 1500, 35 were filled by ducal appointments, 5 of whom were members of the duke's own family. Cardinal Ascanio Sforza (1455–1505), Ludovico's brother, served as an orator and diplomat in addition to performing his ecclesiastical functions. Among other services to the state of Milan, he negotiated the marriage of Bianca Maria Sforza to the Emperor Maximilian (1493–1519) in 1493, an act of enormous importance for her uncle, Ludovico, who as a result secured in the following year the official recognition of the emperor to his claim to the duchy.

The cardinal's significance as a patron of art, music, architecture and letters is noteworthy in its own right. As archbishop of Pavia he had been responsible for organizing the plans for the reconstruction of the new transept for the cathedral, a project which involved both Leonardo and Bramante. He was also an extremely wealthy man and used his fortune (based in Rome) to sponsor the work of a number of humanist scholars, musicians and artisans from his native Lombardy (his patronage of music is discussed in more detail in Chapter 2). Among those to whom he gave commissions was Bramante, who was responsible for designing the classical-style cloisters in the old monastery of S. Ambrogio in Milan (Ambrose was the patron saint of the city). It was then perhaps fitting that his humanist-inspired tomb in the church of S. Maria del Popolo in Rome was located in one of the churches renovated by his former client, Bramante (Figure 1.7). Sforza's position within the ecclesiastical hierarchy, combined with his family connections, made him a powerful figure in terms of artistic patronage. His ability to treat parish churches in Milan as part of his personal domain also provided the family with a further platform to demonstrate their authority in the duchy.

Figure 1.7 Andrea Sansovino, tomb of Cardinal Ascanio Sforza, 1508. S. Maria del Popolo, Rome. Photo: Alinari-Anderson

Religious commissions

Occasionally, artistic projects involving the city of Milan were debated in council. One such case was the expression of concern over progress on the spire of the fourteenth-century Gothic cathedral which had been preoccupying the dynasty since the days of Francesco Sforza (1450–66). Leonardo's proposal is discussed in Chapter 2. Religious life in the city was centred on the public services in Milan's churches which brought together the urban population and the court. It also found expression in the many lay organizations, confraternities and charities which existed in the city and which helped to fund and administer, among other things, Filarete's Ospedale Maggiore (see Chapter 2, pp.106–12). During the second half of the fifteenth century, however, most large-scale religious projects were financed by the dukes, who were able to use such commissions for their own dynastic ends as well as demonstrating, ostensibly at least, their Christian piety. For example, the sumptuous display of interior decoration and sculpture at the Certosa in Pavia was intended in part to reinforce dynastic continuity between the Sforza and their illustrious predecessors, the Visconti (Cole, pp.104–9).

Another important ecclesiastical site of Sforza patronage was the church of S. Maria delle Grazie in Milan, which Ludovico 'appropriated' partly as a prospective mausoleum for himself and his wife. The church had been founded in the 1460s through a charitable donation by a local noble family. Thirty years later it became the focus of Sforza attention and was transformed for their private use. In 1493 the old choir was pulled down and a new transept, choir and sacristy constructed in its place. The work of rebuilding has been attributed to Bramante, largely on the grounds of its similarity to a signed engraving by the architect of an imaginary church interior, dated 1481 (Figures 1.8 and 1.9), and because of the debt of the design to complex geometrical and numerological reasoning. Whatever the case, the circular decorations in the apse suggest that the architect was well read in the literature of mathematics and proportion and may have been influenced by the writings of the mathematician Luca Pacioli. At the same time as the rebuilding, Ludovico paid for frescoes to adorn the walls of the refectory, including Leonardo's *Last Supper*. He also gave the church a sumptuous set of new vestments and altar cloths (Cole, Plate 70). Following the sudden death of his wife Beatrice d'Este in 1497, Ludovico was moved to make a substantial new donation to the church, including the funding of commemorative masses and new building works. It seems highly likely that he had already made the decision to have himself buried in the church, alongside his wife and other prominent courtiers. In 1564, long after the fall of the Sforza, the effigies of Ludovico and his wife were moved from S. Maria delle Grazie to the Certosa in Pavia, where they now stand (Cole, p.110 and Plates 81 and 82; Giordano, 1995).

In commissioning Leonardo to paint the *Last Supper*, Ludovico was undoubtedly influenced by earlier work produced by the artist in the city of Milan, including a highly original altarpiece, the *Madonna of the Rocks* (Plate 6). Begun shortly after Leonardo's arrival in the city, this was commissioned in 1483 by the lay confraternity of the Immaculate Conception for the church of S. Francesco Grande. The original

Figure 1.8 Bramante, *The Prevedari Print*, 1481, engraving. Raccolta Stampe Achille Bertarelli, Castello Sforzesco, Milan. Photo: Saporetti

Figure 1.9 View of the crossing, S. Maria delle Grazie, 1495–9, Milan. Photo: Scala

contract stipulated that the painting of 'Our Lady with Her son made in oil in all perfection' should form the centrepiece of a much larger wooden structure. The final version, however, which was not completed until 1508, was not entirely faithful to the commissioning document. In addition to the Madonna and Child accompanied by angels, Leonardo included the figure of an infant John the Baptist receiving the blessing of Christ.[10] The innovative qualities of the work lay in the naturalistic landscape (rocks, mist, water and plants, all observed carefully from nature), the concern for realistic lighting and life-like figures, and the absence of any indication of the divine, such as a halo. All indicate a profound break with convention. The emotional atmosphere created by the figure group is only tangentially related to the subject matter of the composition and is probably indicative of Leonardo's concern to demonstrate his stylistic virtuosity.

We do not know what the original patrons thought of Leonardo's execution of their commission, but the duke was sufficiently impressed to commission a similar altarpiece from a local, unknown artist which imitated many of the features of Leonardo's *Madonna of the Rocks*. The *Pala Sforzesca* (see Cole, Plate 87 and p.115) is a curious combination of styles and conventions. The influence of Leonardo is evident in the *sfumato* effect. The artist may also have sought to imitate a number of features of the earlier work, including the figure of Christ in the process of blessing, the down-turned gaze of the Madonna and the accurate depiction of drapery. The *Pala*, or altarpiece, takes the form of a *sacra conversazione*, or 'holy conversation', in which a group of saints (Ambrose, Gregory, Augustine and Jerome) surround the enthroned Madonna and Child.[11] The space in which they appear is articulated through the perspective of the surrounding architectural detail, here supported by piers of a classical design.

The church of S. Ambrogio was situated close to the garden of the Castello Sforzesco di Porta Giovia and so provided a valuable

[10] The scene may derive from an apocryphal story which relates how St John the Baptist, under the tutelage of the archangel Uriel, met the infant Christ during the Holy Family's flight into Egypt. One explanation for the inclusion of John the Baptist is that he is intended to represent St Francis, who was described by his official biographer, Bonaventure, as a second John the Baptist. The confraternity's chapel was located in a Franciscan church and the Franciscans were the great defenders of the dogma of the Immaculate Conception (Paoletti and Radke, 1997, pp.316–17).

[11] The small church of S. Ambrogio, outside the city walls of Milan, where the completed altarpiece was displayed, was dedicated to these four saints, who were also leading patristic theologians.

opportunity for the duke to demonstrate allegiance to his local parish through the donation of such a gift. It was also customary for altarpieces commissioned by individual patrons to include representations of the donor and his family. This was not simply a reflection of the donor's piety. In most cases it provided a valuable opportunity for the patron to convey political and dynastic messages. In this particular instance, some confusion exists as to who exactly is depicted in the scene. According to Cole (p.115), who dates the picture to 1496–7, the ducal family includes images of Ludovico's two legitimate sons, Massimiliano (b. 1493) and Francesco (b. 1495). It is possible, however, that the children may be representations of Ludovico's other children, including an illegitimate son born to his mistress, Cecilia Gallerani (see Chapter 2, p.135 and Plate 12), in 1491. Uncertainty over the succession (as mentioned above, Ludovico was only confirmed as duke in 1494) may therefore be reflected in the final work. Whatever the case, there can be little doubt that the depiction of St Ambrose, the patron saint of Milan, resting his hand on the shoulder of the duke was intended to bestow a sense of legitimacy on Ludovico's rule. The overwhelming impression one has in looking at this picture is of a this-worldly approach to the subject matter of the altarpiece. The fashionable apparel of the duke's family, juxtaposed with the rich vestments of the saints, suggests that the former are somehow on a par with, and sanctified by, the presence of the latter. Like the grand design of the Certosa and the architectural splendours of the church of S. Maria delle Grazie, Ludovico demonstrates in this commission the potential importance of religious art as a medium to register his dynastic claims to the duchy of Milan.

Portraiture and self-representation

Political aims were well served by portraiture. The portrait was a particularly useful accoutrement to the tortuous process of marriage negotiation since it could be used to demonstrate not only the beauty of prospective marriage partners but also their wealth and authority. A good example of this process in action is suggested by the various attempts of Ludovico to marry off his niece, Bianca Maria Sforza, to one of the royal houses of Europe. As a prelude to marriage negotiations, her portrait was circulated to the courts of France, Austria and Hungary before she was betrothed to János, the illegitimate son but nominated heir of Matthias Corvinus of Hungary. Further portraits and gifts were exchanged, with Ludovico's brother, Cardinal Ascanio Sforza, acting as go-between. When János failed to secure the throne following the death of his father in 1490, Ludovico successfully re-arranged the marriage of his niece to the Hapsburg Emperor Maximilian I. A portrait of Bianca Maria was now produced by the Milanese court portraitist Giovanni Ambrogio de Predis (he had also assisted Leonardo in painting the side panels to the *Madonna of the Rocks*), and elaborate festivities were held in Innsbruck in March 1494 to celebrate the wedding (see Figures 1.10 and 1.11). The marriage represented an astonishing success for Ludovico. (Such coups, however, did not come cheap. Ludovico had to pay a dowry of 300,000 ducats, plus a further 100,000 ducats for his investiture. Jewels and furnishings cost an additional 70,000 ducats.) The portrait was thus a vital medium of diplomatic and political life. It advertised the wealth and status of noble families and helped to legitimate and underwrite their often uncertain lineage and authority. Moreover, portraits were frequently inscribed with familial mottoes and personal devices or *imprese*. The use of such iconography in court portraiture was a commonplace of Renaissance art.

Figure 1.10 Giovanni Ambrogio de Predis, *Bianca Maria Sforza*, c.1493, oil on panel, 51 x 32.5 cm. Widener Collection. © 1999 Board of Trustees, National Gallery of Art, Washington DC

Figure 1.11 Giovanni Ambrogio de Predis, *Maximilian I Hapsburg*, portrait dated 1502 (i.e. not contemporaneous with the wedding), oil on panel. Gemäldegalerie des Kunsthistorisches Museum, Vienna

Portraits, whether of the living or the dead, were also a means of extending the ducal presence in both time and space. Zanetto Bugatto (d. 1476), a jobbing artist employed by both Francesco and Galeazzo Maria Sforza, painted portraits of the latter which he was allowed to sell to clients and courtiers who wished to ingratiate themselves with the duke. While little is known of his career (he does not appear to have caught the attention of humanists, and few pictures can definitely be attributed to him), he was none the less sent by the duke of Milan to study portraiture under Rogier van der Weyden in Bruges (1460–3). He was also commissioned by the duke to produce gold medals depicting his patron in 1473. A portrait of the duke attributed to Bugatto depicts his subject in a conventional profile position which may well be modelled on representations devised for coins or medals (Figure 1.12).

This type of image was also commonly used to decorate homes and to provide a visual representation of a genealogy or family tree. At Pavia and Milan, Bugatto was hired along with other artists to decorate rooms with the portraits of earlier rulers of Milan as well as the members of the current court. Similar wall paintings also included reference to the daily life of the duke, who was shown engaged in typical courtly pursuits such as hunting, receiving ambassadors, entertaining and feasting. Special payments were made for painting likenesses of people, horses and dogs. An early, but uncompleted, scheme for the Castello Sforzesco in Milan included two decorated rooms, hunting scenes in the Sala della Balla (room of dancing) and four court scenes in the adjacent room. In 1471 Galeazzo Maria Sforza and his wife Bona of Savoy paid a visit to their *condottiere*, Ludovico Gonzaga, at Mantua. While there, the duke saw Mantegna's highly innovative frescoes for the Camera Picta (literally 'painted room', but also known as the Camera degli Sposi, or 'room of the husband and wife') which formed the backdrop to

Figure 1.12 Zanetto Bugatto (attributed), *Galeazzo Maria Sforza, c.*1472?, oil on panel. Pinacoteca del Castello Sforzesco, Milan. Photo: Saporetti

Ludovico's audience chamber. Not only was his Mantuan neighbour inferior to him in rank and wealth, but the duke was conspicuous by his absence from the painted scenes of court life at Mantua which *did* include the two men (Emperor Frederick III and Christian I of Denmark) who most thwarted his own dynastic ambitions. He was, however, sufficiently impressed by what he saw to plan something similar for his own palaces (see Cole, pp.149–55). It was probably with this in mind that Bugatto was sent by the duke to Mantua to study at first hand the compositions of Mantegna. Fresco cycles of the kind designed by Mantegna at Mantua, and imitated by lesser artists at Milan and elsewhere, chronicled life at court, demonstrating in the process not just the joys of court life but also its perilous and fickle nature. Patronage and favouritism were by their very nature ephemeral and the wall paintings which adorned the rooms of the court must have acted as a constant reminder to onlookers of this fact of life. On the other hand, such designs might have served another function, for they also represented powerful *exempla*, or models of morality, which projected an image of court life as the ultimate goal of the civilized nobleman.

One of the most popular modes of self-advertisement in the Renaissance was the symbolism of heraldry. Of medieval origin, the heraldic device had evolved from the need of soldiers in battle to identify their enemies and comrades in arms. In time, the range of geometric designs on shields was extended to more elaborate devices such as helmets and crests. By the second half of the fourteenth century, mottoes were commonly added to coats of arms, which were used as statements of genealogical significance and evidence of long lineage and legitimacy. The question of legitimacy was one which preoccupied Ludovico Sforza following the death of his nephew, Giangaleazzo (it was widely rumoured that Ludovico had poisoned him), in 1494. Prior to this, his 'inferior' status is indicated in a *cassone* (chest) panel dating from some time before 1495 in which he carries the title of Dux Bari (duke of Bari) (Plate 7). The illustrations on the panel further demonstrate the contemporary obsession with *imprese*. The shields on the horses' coats, for example, portray the favourite devices of the three men destined to rule over Milan in its golden age: the buckets for Galeazzo Maria and his son, Giangaleazzo, and the brush for Ludovico. Ludovico was also nicknamed 'il Moro' (the Moor), probably on account of his swarthy appearance. His nickname is alluded to in the *cassone* panel by the inclusion of a black squire standing behind him.

The brush was only one of a number of *imprese* which Ludovico and his wife, Beatrice d'Este, employed in referring to themselves. Others include the image of a dove below a flaming sun, a bridle and a cloth for sifting flour. One might reasonably conclude from this brief foray into the place of heraldic symbolism in the Renaissance court that the fascination with such imagery represented little more than an elaborate means of self-aggrandizement. In large part, this was probably true. Construed, however, within the context in which it appeared – a building, event, person – the use of such a device also carried the connotation of personal ownership or property (Boulton, 1990). A further boost to the popularity of this particular art form was provided by the humanist appropriation and development of the genre. Humanists extended the use of personal devices from the visual to the literal. Classical proverbs, adages and pithy quotations were avidly collected as potential mottoes for new *imprese* and formed the basis of a new Renaissance parlour game of 'spot-the-source'. Nor was this game confined to seigneurial courts such as that of the Sforza in Milan. In 1490, the Medici poet and learned humanist Angelo Poliziano (1454–94) complained that he was bombarded with requests for witty verses, symbols and emblems which, by the nature of the 'game', could only be understood by the most intimate acquaintances of the subject of the device (Maier, 1971, vol. 1, p.26).

In this study of the Sforza court we have examined the way in which art and artistic patronage both reflected the transient prestige of the ruling house and actively helped to define the authority of the ruler and his court. The extent to which powerful seigneurial patrons such as the Sforza were themselves able or willing to engage with, and fully appreciate, the new humanist-based art forms of the Renaissance, however, remains questionable. They frequently delegated, for example, the process of commissioning portraits and interior decoration to high-ranking servants or knowledgeable courtiers. And in the case of Duke Galeazzo Maria there is little evidence, apart from his patronage of music, to suggest any preference for either classical art or literature. Galeazzo Maria treated artists as mere skilled artisans or decorators and never bothered to employ court painters as such. His taste was generally for the Gothic. He was equally remiss in his patronage of humanist letters, despite his excellent classical education. The celebrated Sforza library was regarded by him as little more than 'a collection of precious objects [rather than] a reservoir of knowledge and inspiration' (Lubkin, 1994, pp.108–10). Not all Italian princes or lords were so negligent in their cultivation of *all'antica* culture, as is evident from the following case study of Federico da Montefeltro.

The Montefeltro court

In contrast to the court of the Sforza at Milan, the celebrated court of Urbino was largely the creation of a single princely patron, Federico da Montefeltro, who ruled over the principality of Urbino from 1444 until his death in 1482. Lauded at the time as one of the most important cultural centres in Renaissance Italy, the court that Federico created at Urbino provides a wealth of material for a case study in the full-scale reception of classical culture in fifteenth-century Italy, as well as important evidence for the wider social and political significance that contemporaries attached to the revival of the antique.

The small and remote court of Urbino was financed, like so many other Italian courts, by the mercenary activities of its ruling house, the Montefeltro. Soldiering for the minor nobility in Italy was a way of life, and a profitable one, which frequently allowed mercenary princes or *condottieri* to devote large sums of money to the pursuit of **otium**, or leisure, in contrast to **negotium**, or the day-to-day demands of running a small state. In the case of the Montefeltro, it enabled the spectacularly successful Federico to build on a grand scale and invest huge sums in the new learning and arts. The source of Federico's wealth was the *condotta*, or contract through which he hired his military services to the highest bidder.[12] This provided the bulk of an annual income of approximately 50,000 ducats. During the period of his rule he was involved in only one major war. He received regular payments from Milan, was paid a retainer by the pope, and supplemented his income with one-off contracts such as that signed with Florence in order to secure the recapture of Volterra (Cole, p.68). Federico's wealth from this source was in fact so great that he was not obliged to tax his subjects, a wise option in view of the fate of his half-brother and predecessor, Oddantonio, who was murdered by his subjects, indignant at the oppressive levels of taxation levied by their lord. Military success and financial stability thus formed the bedrock of Federico's successful rule as lord of Urbino. Various honours soon followed. Not only was he awarded the Neapolitan Order of the Ermine and the English Order of the Garter, but in 1474 he was appointed to the rank of *gonfaloniere*, or commander of the papal armies and was rewarded with the title of duke. In typical fashion, the symbols of these successes feature prominently on the façade of the new palace at Urbino which he constructed in the 1470s with the profits of war.

During the middle decades of the fifteenth century, Federico was much preoccupied with a long-running feud with his neighbour and fellow *condottiere* Sigismondo Malatesta of Rimini (1417–68). The dispute between the two men is interesting not simply for the light it sheds on the nature of warfare and politics in Italy at this time, but also because of their shared cultural interests. Both men, for example, commissioned artistic work of a similar nature, infused with the spirit

---

[12] The *condotta* was divided into two parts: payment for a fixed period of service followed by a retainer fee (see Mallett, 1974, p.12).

of the new humanism, and both frequently 'shared' or employed the same artists, such as Piero della Francesca (Cole, p.69 and Plate 49). Some similarities in their artistic patronage may also be ascribed to their common profession of soldiering. For example, the similarity of their images on medals probably reflects the use of stereotypical gestures of military command in such artefacts, as well as the circulation in Italian courts of standard moulds (Figures 1.13 and 1.14). The international reputation of Federico as a chivalric and scholarly figure undoubtedly owes much to the support he received from the humanist Pope Pius II in his prolonged conflict with Sigismondo. Thanks in large part to Pius's autobiographical *Commentaries*, Federico was lauded as a benign, cultivated and prudent ruler, while Sigismondo was castigated as a hot-headed, pagan

Figure 1.13 Sperandio di Mantua, *Federico da Montefeltro*, medal, obverse and reverse, c.1482, bronze, diameter 89.5 mm. British Museum, London. Photo: © British Museum

Figure 1.14 Pisanello, *Sigismondo Pandolfo Malatesta*, medal, obverse and reverse, c.1445, lead, diameter 104 mm. Samuel H. Kress Collection. © 1999 Board of Trustees, National Gallery of Art, Washington DC

debauchee whom Pius publicly condemned to hell during his own lifetime. This image of Sigismondo was perpetuated by Burckhardt (p.39), though recent scholarship has tended to paint a more balanced picture of the ruler of Rimini as an urbane and learned man who, like Federico, dedicated himself to the cultivation of the arts and learning (Pernis and Adams, 1996; Woods-Marsden, 1989).

The centrepiece of Federico's patronage of the arts was the ducal palace at Urbino, built in successive stages between 1447 and the 1490s (Figures 1.15 and 1.16). According to Castiglione, writing in the early sixteenth century, it looked more like a city than a palace, and was adorned with all manner of priceless objects:

> such as silver vases, wall-hangings of the richest cloth of gold, silk and other similar material [and] countless antique statues of marble and bronze, with rare pictures, and with every kind of musical instrument.

(Bull, 1976, p.41)

The design of the palace owes much to earlier examples, most notably the restrained magnificence of Cosimo de' Medici's palace in Florence and the model hill-top city that Pope Pius II created at his birthplace, Corsignano, which he named Pienza in his own honour. The former undoubtedly influenced the design of the main courtyard

Figure 1.15 Print map of Urbino, 1689. Photo: by courtesy of Istituto di Storia dell'Arte, Urbino/Prof. Giuseppe Cucco

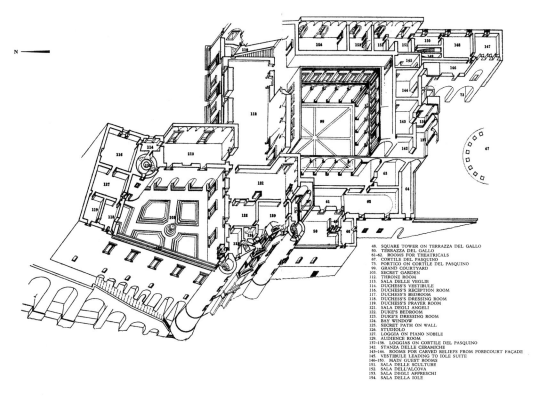

48. SQUARE TOWER ON TERRAZZA DEL GALLO
50. TERRAZZA DEL GALLO
61-62. ROOMS FOR THEATRICALS
67. CORTILE DEL PASQUINO
73. PORTICO ON CORTILE DEL PASQUINO
99. GRAND COURTYARD
103. SECRET GARDEN
112. THRONE ROOM
113. SALA DELLE VEGLIE
114. DUCHESS'S VESTIBULE
116. DUCHESS'S RECEPTION ROOM
117. DUCHESS'S BEDROOM
118. DUCHESS'S DRESSING ROOM
119. DUCHESS'S PRAYER ROOM
121. SALA DEGLI ANGELI
122. DUKE'S BEDROOM
123. DUKE'S DRESSING ROOM
124. BAY WINDOW
125. SECRET PATH ON WALL
126. STUDIOLO
127. LOGGIA ON PIANO NOBILE
129. AUDIENCE ROOM
137-138. LOGGIAS ON CORTILE DEL PASQUINO
142. STANZA DELLE CERAMICHE
143-144. ROOMS FOR CARVED RELIEFS FROM FORECOURT FAÇADE
145. VESTIBULE LEADING TO IOLE SUITE
146-150. MAIN GUEST ROOMS
151. SALA DELLE SCULTURE
152. SALA DELL'ALCOVA
153. SALA DEGLI AFFRESCHI
154. SALA DELLA IOLE

Figure 1.16 Axonometric projection of the ducal palace, Urbino, drawn by Renato Bruscaglia. Reproduced from Rotondi, 1969, Figure 54

(Cole, Plates 10 and 55), while the siting of the loggias between the twin turrets, or *torricini*, was intended to provide a spectacular view over the surrounding countryside in imitation of the position chosen by Pius for Pienza. A third possible influence was the main entrance to the Castel Nuovo in Naples (Cole, Plate 43), built for King Alfonso of Aragon, which featured a similar arrangement of loggias flanked by towers and inscribed with classical decoration.

The first stage of construction, begun in about 1447, envisaged the completion of a new town palace in what is now the Piazza Rinascimento. This building, which incorporated two older houses, was a long, rectangular block topped with crenellations, extending towards the palace of Federico's stepfather to the south and to the *castellare*, or former civic palace, to the north. Among the rooms situated in this wing of the palace, the most impressive is the Sala della Iole, so-called after the bas-reliefs on the fireplace depicting statues of the Greek hero Hercules and his mistress, Iole. Another room contains the painted figures of Roman heroes in contemporary armour, though most of the rooms in the palace, according to a contemporary description, were decorated with plain walls and tapestries.

The second stage in the development of the site seems to have begun shortly after Federico's marriage to his second wife, Battista Sforza, in

1459. In 1465 he hired Luciano Laurana (1420/5–79), a Dalmatian architect who had earlier worked in Mantua and Pesaro (the native city of Federico's new wife). Laurana's plan envisaged the development of the southern slope, where the private apartments overlook the valley from the **belvedere** set between two turrets, and the integration into the design of a number of Renaissance features, including the courtyard, grand staircase, hanging garden and *studiolo*:

> the whole project, a vast complex of articulated buildings to be fitted in with others of medieval date on a very different site, demanded careful and subtle balance of the new idiom with what was traditionally acceptable as monumental architecture in a town. The two facades offer an inspired contrast. That facing out to the country, with the chivalric, fairytale reference and vertical emphasis of the soaring *torricini*, seems to belong to a tall medieval fortress; the other, broad and horizontal, faces the town across a wide square and seems trustingly to welcome guest and citizen.

(Cardini, 1986, p.85)

Laurana's concern for form and function is apparent in all aspects of the palace's construction and is informed throughout by classical precedent. His debt to ancient authorities, for example, is apparent in his desire to combine elements from Vitruvian palace design with those features of rural villas mentioned in the *Letters* of Pliny the Younger (see the Anthology, no. 42). Likewise, the hanging garden situated between the old *castellare* and new *torricini* seems to derive from the Roman predilection for formal gardens set within an architectural setting. Laurana's desire to integrate the various parts of the complex into a harmonious whole is evident in the creation of the courtyard which acts as a link between the public and private functions of the palace. He also varied the size of the rooms in the palace in relation to their function. These range in scale from the small, intimate space occupied by Federico's private study, his *studiolo*, to the large reception rooms such as the Sala Grande (or throne room) (Figure 1.17). A further notable feature of the palace is its relationship to the city of which it formed an integral part. Unlike some city palaces (e.g. Mantua), that of the Montefeltro was planned to facilitate ease of access from the city. The openness of the design is accentuated by the situation of the L-shaped Piazza Duca Federico (also known as the Piazza Ducale), underneath the eastern walls of the palace, which was used as the site of public festivities and ceremonial occasions. Castiglione, for example, recounted watching a comedy performed here set against the backdrop of a triumphal arch and tapestries on the walls depicting the Trojan Wars, accompanied by an inscription which read: 'Wars outside, games at home: the great man has concern for both' (La Rocca, 1978, vol. 1, pp.343–8).

Figure 1.17 View of the Sala Grande (throne room), ducal palace, Urbino. Photo: Scala

After the death of Battista Sforza in 1472, Laurana left Urbino and was eventually replaced by the Sienese painter, sculptor, architect and engineer Francesco di Giorgio Martini (1439–1502) who worked intermittently at the palace until 1490. He was responsible for the completion of some of the principal structural features of the palace, such as the main courtyard and the hanging garden, as well as for the supervision of much of the interior decoration. One of the most eye-catching features of the latter was Martini's designs for the intarsia (wood-inlay) panelling in the doorframes and *studiolo* of the duke. The work was carried out by Florentine craftsmen such as Baccio Pontelli, who sent plans of the palace to Lorenzo de' Medici. Martini was also responsible for a similar courtyard and intarsia-panelled *studiolo* at the Montefeltro palace of Gubbio to the south of Urbino.

At Urbino, Martini made further improvements and extensions to the existing plan. He developed, for example, the block known as the Cortile del Gallo (to the right of the main turrets) with a south-facing loggia, and planned the construction of a small round building to house Federico's mausoleum. This, however, was never built, though it did survive in the form of a wooden model which was exhibited in the ducal library until the sixteenth century. The original design may have reflected the keen interest of Renaissance artists and architects in pagan round temples which featured prominently in ideal cityscapes of the period (see, for example, the one that has survived at Urbino, shown in Cole, Plate 53). Martini, moreover, was not simply an architect. As befitted a man who made his living by designing and constructing military defences, he was also responsible at Urbino for a number of structural and technological innovations which vastly improved the practical, as well as the aesthetic, appearance of the palace. Among his many improvements were the ventilation and water systems. The former, through the construction of special flues, guaranteed smokeless rooms. The latter consisted of an intricate hydraulic system of pipes which allowed water from a cistern at the top of the tower beside the *castellare* to serve the fountain in the garden. He also made a major contribution to the construction of the service area, stable blocks and fortifications. In one of his architectural treatises he specifically mentions his *data*, or bastion, which, set immediately in front of the west turrets of the palace, also contained space for the stabling of over 300 horses. He transformed the western slope below the palace into a *mercatale*, or new market, and was responsible for numerous new religious buildings and private developments which enhanced the appearance of the city (Rotondi, 1969; Heydenreich, 1996, pp.74–81).

One reason why the ducal palace quickly came to be regarded by contemporaries as a textbook example of Renaissance architecture was because it appeared to follow to the letter the guidelines laid down by one of the foremost experts in this field, Leon Battista Alberti, in his *De re aedificatoria* (*On Architecture*) (Rykwert, et al., 1988).[13] The composite style of the **capitals** on the columns, for example, follow closely the Albertian definition for this type of structure, which he terms specifically 'Italic'. A precedent for this *all'antica* style of building existed in the design which Alberti had provided for the mausoleum church of Federico's great rival, Sigismondo Malatesta, at Rimini (Cole, Plate 17). Alberti is known to have visited Urbino in 1464, and at a later date Federico was sufficiently impressed to order a copy of his architectural treatise to be made from a manuscript in the ducal library at Ferrara. Fundamental to Alberti's architectural aesthetic was the idea, drawn from antiquity, that beauty was determined by a combination of the principles of *numerus* (perfect number), *finitio* (proportioned outline) and *collocatio* (harmonious positioning). Whether or not Alberti was influential in the actual design of the palace at Urbino, there can be little doubt that the building was constructed according to these criteria.

[13] This work by Alberti constituted the only humanist text on architecture actually to be printed in the fifteenth century. Composed about 1450, but not published until 1485, it was largely an exposition of the architectural theories of the Roman Vitruvius. It has been described as 'very much a book addressed to a classically trained audience, rather than a guide to architectural practice' (Hope and McGrath, 1996, p.169; and see Cole, pp.27–8).

Exercise

Read the extract from Vespasiano da Bisticci's life of Federico (Anthology, no. 32) and the extract from the translation of the contract issued to Laurana in 1468 (Anthology, no. 33) and answer the questions below.

1 What style of building did Federico have in mind when he issued the contract to Laurana?

2 What does the contract suggest about the duke's involvement in the building project?

3 How does this compare with what we know of Federico's intellectual accomplishments as detailed by Vespasiano?

Discussion

1 According to the document confirming Laurana as the architect, Federico wished to commission the construction of a building which would be beautiful, worthy and appropriately indicative of the status of the patron and his ancestors.

2 Although the contract certainly testifies to Federico's undoubted enthusiasm for, and understanding of, the classical principles of architecture (the preface to the agreement records that architects who design according to 'arithmetic and geometry' were most appreciated by both ancients and moderns), it none the less acknowledges a degree of independence for the architect. The licence makes clear that once Federico has approved Laurana's design, the architect is free to sub-contract his staff of stonemasons and woodcarvers (note that Laurana's title of 'architect' distinguishes him from the overseer of building work, the *capomaestro*).

3 Vespasiano's account strongly confirms the image of Federico as a man well versed in the art of architecture and its related and subsidiary disciplines. He records, for example, that Federico had studied mathematics and took an active interest in the related fields of music, sculpture and painting, and he notes Federico's desire to create a style which is 'grand, with due measure and proportion'. ❖

Not surprisingly, Federico's preferred self-image is consciously inscribed on the palace, and not just in the formal, classical design of the complex, but also in the iconographical and symbolic references which decorate both the interior and the exterior of the building. Federico's sensitivity to his growing authority and status is evident, for example, in the prominent use of the initials FC and FD (or sometimes FE.DUX) to indicate his various titles (*Federicus Comes* or Count Federico, and *Federicus Dux* or Duke Federico) which often appear alongside the

Montefeltro coat of arms. His personal symbol, the eagle, is a recurring motif, as is an exploding mine, an appropriate *imprese* for a mercenary warlord. Moreover, the orderly and harmonious appearance of the palace echoes the duke's own preoccupation with the orderly and disciplined nature of his court. Shortly after Federico's death in 1482, a set of detailed instructions was drawn up for his servants which itemized each of their respective functions, down to the number of torches to be lit and when. Significantly, Federico seems to have passed on his own love of the new style of architecture to his courtiers, who frequently imitated the stylistic innovations seen at the ducal palace in their own townhouses, castles and rural retreats. Ludovico Odasi, for instance, a humanist counsellor at the court of Urbino and sometime tutor to Federico's son, had the motto 'Always through Federico' inscribed on the ceiling of the portico of his palace which was fronted with **Doric-Ionic** composite columns reminiscent of those found in the ducal palace (Figures 1.18 and 1.19).

Understandably, many of the references to Federico in the palace allude to his role as a military man. This is apparent in the tall turrets fronting the entrance to the palace which owe more to an idealistic

Figure 1.18 Palazzo Bonaventura Odasi, entrance portico with inscription inset in beam. Photograph after the restoration of 1972. Photo: by permission of Soprintendenza Beni Ambientali e Architettonici delle Marche, Ancona

Figure 1.19 Baccio Pontelli, intarsia door leading from the Sala degli Angeli to the Sala del Trono, ducal palace, 1470s, Urbino. Photo: INDEX/Archivio Fotografico Soprintendenza BAS, Urbino

vision of a chivalric past than to the practical considerations of Renaissance warfare. A throw-back to French castle design in the age before gunpowder, they have little value as fortifications, but say much about the mind-set of Federico (see the modern defences constructed by Martini at the fort of Rocca S. Leo in the 1470s: Cole, Plate 60). Federico's military cast of mind is also reflected in the relief decorations along the backrest of the bench that lines the façade overlooking the Piazza Duca Federico, or Piazza Ducale; these are direct quotations from Martini's sketchbook and Roberto Valturio's *De re militari* (*On Military Matters*) which was first published in 1472 (Cole, p.82; and see Figures 1.20 and 1.21). The images on the panels range from depictions of Arab siege engines to machines for pumping water and classical armour. Further evidence of the militaristic nature of much of the iconography on display in the palace can be seen in the main courtyard; here a Latin frieze inscription praises Federico as *gonfaloniere* who, undefeated in battle and assisted by the virtues of Justice, Clemency, Liberality and Religion, 'built this house to his glory and that of his heirs' (Figure 1.22).

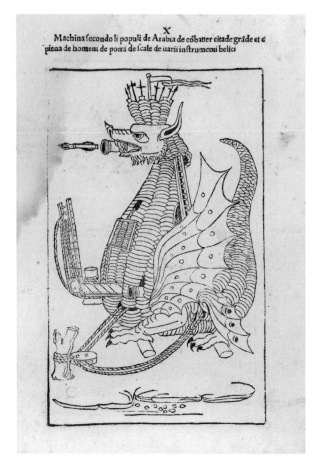

Figure 1.20 Dragon rocket launcher. From Roberto Valturio, *De re militari*, 1483, Verona, Boninus de Boninis. British Library I.B. 30748. Reproduced by permission of the British Library

Figure 1.21 Ambrogio Barrocci, panel relief showing the same dragon machine, 1470s, Istrian stone. Ducal palace, Urbino. Photo: INDEX/Archivio Fotografico Soprintendenza BAS, Urbino

Figure 1.22 Interior view of main courtyard, ducal palace, Urbino. (Top attics were added later in the history of the building.) Photo: INDEX/Archivio Fotografico Soprintendenza BAS, Urbino

Other representations of the Montefeltro focus on the role played at court and within the state by Federico's extraordinary second wife, Battista Sforza. Unusually for a woman, she had received a thoroughly humanist education in her native Pesaro and Milan. Consequently, she could read and write Latin and Greek, and, as Federico's consort, was able to perform various offices during his absences from Urbino (she also acted as his ambassador at Rome). She and her husband were keen supporters of the Monte di Pietà, the charity for unmarried women, which was run by the religious fraternity known as the *Corpus Domini* (Body of the Lord). The members of this lay association venerated the Host, or wafer-bread, the consumption of which forms the focus of the Catholic Mass. Following Battista's death, various humanist orations were commissioned to celebrate and honour her virtuous life, and several paintings included her posthumous portrait. One such can be found in an altarpiece commissioned by the *Corpus Domini* fraternity and sponsored in part by Federico, which consists of a central panel by the Flemish painter Justus of Ghent showing the enactment of Holy Communion at the Last Supper (Cole, Plate 66 (note that the plate here is reversed)). Beneath this was a **predella** sequence by Paolo Uccello, based on a religious play, depicting the story of the Profanation of the Host, in which the Jew accused of the crime is burned at the stake, together with his family. For the centrepiece and the predella sequence, see Plate 8. Something of a counterbalance to this tale is provided in the main panel where a Jewish convert, Isaac, ambassador to the shah of Persia, is included among the onlookers. The recently deceased Battista, with her new-born son, Guidobaldo, are shown in the doorway at the rear.

Battista Sforza also appears with her husband in a famous double portrait by Piero della Francesca which was commissioned shortly after the former's death (see Cole, Plate 62 and Figure 3.20 in Chapter 3). On the reverse side, Federico and Battista appear in two triumphal scenes (Cole, Plate 7). Here, the allegorical images are accompanied by Latin inscriptions which extol their respective virtues. Battista is praised for her female modesty, her honour reinforced by the manly exploits of her husband. Federico, on the other hand, receives plaudits for his moderate government and military supremacy: 'He rides illustrious in triumph – just as he wields the sceptre with moderation, so the eternal fame of his virtues commends him as equal to the greatest general.'

Exercise

What stylistic features of these two pictures are familiar from earlier descriptions in this chapter?

Discussion

Two features which stand out are: first, the presentation of the two portraits in profile – reminiscent of the format used by Bugatto in the striking of medallions and antique coins (see above, p.39); and secondly, the intricately crafted background landscape, a familiar element in the popular portraits of the northern artist Hans Memling of Bruges (*c*.1440–94). ❖

The allegorical triumph is suffused with humanist learning. This type of image was hugely popular in the Renaissance as a result of Petrarch's poems in his *Trionfi* (*Triumphs*) of 1372. These depict imaginary victory processions in which various abstract qualities – Love, Chastity, Death, Fame, Time and Divinity – appear, as in a dream, before the poet. Here, the four cardinal virtues (Justice, Prudence, Courage and Temperance), in the allegorical form of four women, accompany Federico and personify his virtues. Opposite him, Battista, shown reading a book (probably a holy book), is surrounded by the **theological virtues** (Faith, Hope and Charity), her chariot pulled by two unicorns, mythical beasts which symbolized chastity. The impression of a classical victory parade (see Cole, Plates 5, 31, 45 and 116) is further underscored by the painted inscription in Roman lettering beneath each of the chariots. Subjects like these, particularly Petrarch's *Trionfi*, were frequently found on household furniture, the panels of *cassoni*, in manuscripts and, in Urbino, on the intarsia doors of the Sala della Iole (Cole, Plate 57). Cole suggests that Federico 'chose the portable diptych format so that he could carry the portrait of his late wife with him when he journeyed from palace to palace'. This was a common practice in the Renaissance. Some devotional images were likewise transportable in much the same way as we today carry keepsake photographs of family and close friends (Cole, p.83).

Nowhere are Federico's humanist credentials more readily apparent than in his suite of private rooms which include his *studiolo* (or 'small study') (Figure 1.23). Refurbished in the 1470s, it contains vital clues to Federico's complex personality and devotion to learning and the arts, combining as it does a variety of stylistic and thematic subjects. At the lower level, the room is decorated with intricately carved intarsia panels which depict symbols of Federico's passion for music, books and the contemplative life. They also contain a series of *trompe-l'oeil*[14] designs which suggest open cabinets and other illusionary images, such as the stored armour – another indication that this room served as a retreat from Federico's active life as a soldier. In one panel, Federico himself appears dressed in a long gown, the epitome of the Christian knight, while other panels illustrate the theological virtues. The skilled craftsmanship was probably the work of Florentines, following designs by several artists, including Botticelli.

[14] Literally 'deceive-the-eye', and regarded by Pliny the Elder as a sign of artistic virtuosity.

Figure 1.23 Diagram showing the arrangement of the *studiolo* in the ducal palace, Urbino, drawn by Renato Bruscaglia. Reproduced from Rotondi, 1950

Beneath these panels were a range of Montefeltro symbols and devices (Cole, Plate 58), while above, on the upper storey of the walls, were a series of 28 paintings of *uomini famosi* (famous men), mostly the work of Flemish-based artists such as Justus of Ghent and the Spaniard Pedro Berruguete (Cole, Plate 59). The painted **coffered** ceiling is covered with further symbolic allusions to Federico, along with an inscription which gives his noble titles.

Scholars have long debated the meaning of this elaborate iconographical programme and the significance of the arrangement of the various motifs, both to each other and to the paintings above. The subject matter of some of the panels consists of puns on the general theme of peaceful recreation set within a flourishing landscape, and thus evoke the classical topos of the *locus amoenus*, or 'pleasant place'. Others perform a celebratory function and 'may be taken as a visual parallel to encomiastic biographies, with their enumerations of the ruler's qualities – moral, aesthetic, intellectual and political' (Cheles, 1986, p.55). A good example of this can be found in the image of the squirrel (see Plate 9 and Cole, Plate 58). The squirrel's habit of acquisitive industriousness (represented here by the full basket of fruit) made the animal 'a recognised image of the prudent ruler' (Paoletti and Radke, 1997, p.287). Taken as a whole, the *studiolo* can be seen not only as an expression of the personality of its cultured patron but also as a constitutive element in the creation of the persona of Federico. If study helped to shape *l'uomo universale*, as Federico undoubtedly believed, then an environment filled with the books and images of past men of letters, both Christian and pagan, was clearly an inspiration to men like the lord of Urbino. In conclusion, it has been argued that Federico's *studiolo* 'more than any single work of art from Urbino ... embodies the aesthetic, intellectual and moral achievements and aspirations of its outstanding patron' (Cheles, 1986, p.92). Here:

> Federico brought together a wide range of learning, both ancient and modern, Christian and pre-Christian, and also several contemporary artistic styles. To Federico our categorically opposed labels of 'ancient' and 'modern', 'Italian' and 'Flemish', 'Gothic' and 'Renaissance' would have seemed strangely and unnecessarily exclusive. Neither he nor the artists who worked for him were disturbed by the variety within his decorative scheme. If anything, rich diversity gave the scheme much of its particular power.
>
> (Paoletti and Radke, 1997, p.287)

While Federico was regarded as a role model in his own lifetime, and his court at Urbino a recognized centre of excellence in the promotion of cultural renewal, the fate of the dynasty he founded was less secure. Lacking Federico's financial and political acumen, his successors as dukes failed to preserve the independence of the duchy of Urbino, and during the course of the sixteenth century it once again resumed its role as a cultural and political backwater. The family's bad fortune, however, has proved a bonus for posterity. Today, the palace remains largely untouched by the refurbishments of subsequent generations and stands as one of the finest examples of the expression of the new-found confidence and cultural vitality so often associated with the Renaissance in Italy.

The Gonzaga court

Art and architecture in fifteenth-century Mantua

Our final example of an Italian Renaissance court is that of the Gonzaga at Mantua. In addition to providing a valuable opportunity for comparisons with our previous two courts, this study also seeks to demonstrate how Renaissance cultural fashions changed over time, reflecting as they did alterations in the personal and political fortunes of the ruling family. In the person of Isabella d'Este (1474–1539), the wife of Francesco Gonzaga, it also provides us with an interesting case study in female patronage of the arts.

Gonzaga rule in Mantua originated with the military take-over of the city by the family in 1328. Thereafter, successive generations extended their control over the city and surrounding countryside by selling their services as *condottieri* to neighbouring city-states, forever mindful to preserve a careful balance of power in this most disputed region of northern Italy. Despite its topographical limitations as a political power base (it was situated in a low-lying valley which was not only susceptible to flooding but was also difficult to defend), Mantua possessed a number of advantages which the Gonzaga scrupulously cultivated. Located as it was at the crossroads of important trade routes running from west to east (linking Milan and Venice) and from north to south (Germany and Rome), the city became an important commercial centre which also attracted visitors on account of its reputation as a popular pilgrimage site. The possession of a relic of the Precious Blood of Christ (reputedly brought to Mantua by Longinus, the soldier who had pierced Christ's side on the Cross) was to provide the Gonzaga, by association, with all manner of opportunity to consolidate their rule in the city. In addition to religious relics, the Gonzaga were also acutely aware of the potential political significance of the cultivation of arts and learning. Mantua was after all the birthplace of the celebrated Roman poet Virgil. The Gonzaga also benefited from an unusual degree of dynastic continuity, which may in part explain the unprecedented political stability the family enjoyed in the internal government of their principality (Woods-Marsden, 1990, p.27).

The court of the Gonzaga was focused on a group of buildings on the north-east side of the city which successive generations of the family developed in the fifteenth and sixteenth centuries. The oldest part of the palace complex included the Palazzo del Capitano and the Magna Domus (large house) which faced on to the Piazza Sordello. This square also contained the *duomo* (cathedral), the bishop's palace and the townhouses of several noble families, including that of the Castiglione family. Originally separate from the old core of the palace was the late fourteenth-century residence of the Gonzaga, the fortified Castello di S. Giorgio. During the course of the fifteenth century, however, it was incorporated into the main complex to create a ducal palace which extended over 34,000 square metres (Figure 1.24).

Under Gonzaga rule, this palace complex underwent large-scale rebuilding and refurbishment. During the 1480s, the Domus Nova (new house) was constructed and an arcaded courtyard was added to the Castello by the Florentine Luca Fancelli (*c*.1430–95), who had begun his career as a stonemason executing designs composed by Alberti. Between 1515 and 1524 a new set of ground-floor apartments for Isabella d'Este was designed by Lorenzo Leonbruno (*c*.1489–1537) who later served as court artist to the Gonzaga following the death of Mantegna. Finally, in the 1520s and 1530s a more extensive programme of modernization was undertaken for Federico II (marquis, 1519–30; duke, 1530–40), based on the designs of Giulio Romano (1492–1546), culminating in the refurbished Appartimento

Figure 1.24 General aerial view of ducal palace site, Mantua. Photo: INDEX/ Giovetti

di Troia (named after the series of wall paintings on the theme of the Trojan War) and the Cortile della Mostra (courtyard of the show) which was completed after the death of Giulio. During its heyday, the Gonzaga court was home to a large collection of valuable art works and antiques, many of which eventually found their way to England when they were sold by the impoverished Gonzaga to King Charles I in 1627 (Chambers and Martineau, 1981).

Like the Montefeltro, the Gonzaga were first and foremost military men whose control of Mantua was largely dependent on the income and titles they accrued as *condottieri*. Not surprisingly, therefore, they too were attracted to chivalric imagery which formed an important element of both their public and their private self-image. This can be seen, for example, in the fresco cycle commissioned by Ludovico Gonzaga in the late 1440s from the artist Pisanello (*c.*1395–1455) which depicts scenes from Arthurian legend. The choice of subject and its prominent position in the main reception hall of the Magna Domus were clearly intended as a compliment to the martial qualities of Ludovico, and may have possessed a special appeal in a city which, by virtue of its holy relic, could claim an affinity with the search for the Holy Grail (Cole, Plate 108). Despite the growing reputation of Mantua as a centre for humanist studies (as early as 1423 the humanist Vittorino da Feltre had established a school in the city which acquired an international renown), this preoccupation with chivalric literature continued into the second half of the fifteenth century. Isabella d'Este, for example, the wife of the Marquis Francesco (1484–1519), was a life-long devotee of chivalric romances.

Her fascination with the deeds of King Arthur and his chivalrous knights probably began in her native Ferrara where the mythical English king was enthusiastically, if somewhat improbably, lauded as an ancestor of the Este family. Isabella, however, as we shall see, was a knowledgeable patron of the arts and letters who was equally devoted to the new humanism. The combination of chivalry and humanism found an outlet in her support for the Ferrarese poet Matteo Maria Boiardo (*c.*1441–94) whose epic fantasy *Orlando innamorato* (1483–95) attempted to suffuse the medieval form of the chivalric romance with the humanist style of classical literature (Cole, p.119; Verheyen, 1971, pp.29, 43n.).

By the middle decades of the fifteenth century, however, there is evidence to suggest the beginnings of a shift in cultural taste in Mantua. The catalyst appears to have been provided by two artists, Leon Battista Alberti and Andrea Mantegna (1430/1–1506), both of whom shared a passion for classical ideals. Their patron, Ludovico Gonzaga, was equally well schooled in classical humanism (he had been educated at Vittorino's academy) and was therefore able to appreciate the significance of the stylistic innovations which both men brought to their respective areas of expertise. In the case of Alberti, whose treatise *De pictura* (*On Painting*) had been dedicated to Ludovico's father, the city and its patron were rewarded with the construction of one of the finest classical buildings in Renaissance Italy, the church of S. Andrea (Cole, Plates 109 and 110).

The initial stimulus for the planned renovation of the church was the visit of Pope Pius II to Mantua for the church congress that was held there in 1459. On this occasion the papal council recognized the relic of the Blood of Christ as authentic. Shortly afterwards, Ludovico Gonzaga began to plan the rebuilding of the church in such a way as to magnify the glory of this most holy of relics, one which not only brought fame and wealth to the city but also cast its princely protector in a supremely positive light. Initial plans were scrapped, however, when Alberti substituted a new architectural design for the original. In a letter addressed to Ludovico in October 1470 Alberti set out new guidelines for the proposed renovation:

> I have also heard in the last day or two that Your Lordship and your citizens have been discussing the building scheme here at Sant' Andrea. And that the principal intention was to have a great space where many people might go to behold the Blood of Christ. I saw Manetti's model. I liked it. But it did not seem the right thing to realise your intention. I thought it over and devised what I am sending you. This will be more practical, more immortal, more worthy and more gladdening. It will cost much less. This form of temple the

Ancients called Sacred Etruscan. If you like it I will do a correct version in proportion.

(Chambers, 1970, pp.113–14)

Exercise

Comment on the general tone of this letter. What does it suggest about the relationship between architect and potential patron?

Discussion

Perhaps the most notable feature of this letter is its relatively informal tone. Though the writer addresses Ludovico in suitably deferential terms ('Your Lordship'), there is a brevity and a familiarity which suggests that Alberti was on close speaking terms with the marquis. It also strongly suggests that the architect was addressing a well-informed and educated man who was capable of understanding the finer details of the plan without recourse to excessive flattery or description. ❖

Alberti's plan envisaged the creation of a monumental structure which would provide good visibility of the high altar and its sacred relic. This was to be achieved through the construction of a wide, single-aisled space covered with a coffered barrel vault, the largest of its kind since classical times (Cole, Plate 109). The external portico façade is largely indebted to the Roman triumphal arch, but the design itself does not simply attempt to replicate classical precedent. Rather, it marks a break with convention by adapting classical forms to contemporary usage. Hence the large central arch with its coffered barrel vault imitates the vault of the nave. This is flanked by smaller openings which also relate to the internal layout of the church, while the whole design of the façade is unified by a giant **order** of paired **Corinthian pilasters**. A triangular pediment provides a fitting finish to this mock Etruscan-style temple. The project was actually completed after Alberti's death in 1472 by Luca Fancelli, who, despite his more lowly origins as an engineer, none the less inherited the role of court architect from his illustrious and learned predecessor. Further evidence of Albertian design in the refurbishment of Mantua is in the Domus Nova (1480–4) which incorporates an alternate pattern of pilasters and windows across thirteen bays (Figure 1.25, overleaf). A number of possible sources have been suggested for this work, including the convent of S. Chiara at Urbino by Francesco di Giorgio Martini and the theoretical architectural treatise of Filarete (discussed in more detail in Chapter 2). Like the Franciscan convent at Urbino, the façade of the Domus Nova was arranged with a uniform frontage set between two wings. Originally it was intended to form part of a square block situated around a central courtyard, but the other wings were never in fact constructed (Heydenreich, 1996, pp.84–6).

Figure 1.25 View of the Domus Nova garden façade, Mantua. Photo: Scala

Just as Alberti's design for S. Andrea and other commissions in the city marked a turning point in Gonzaga patronage of new architecture, so the appointment of Mantegna as court painter in 1460 symbolized a break with the past in terms of painting. Mantegna's style of painting was in marked contrast to that of his predecessor Pisanello. Not only was it informed by a thorough-going appreciation of antique art (Mantegna's figures resemble those of classical sculpture), but it was also deeply indebted, particularly in terms of subject matter, to the revival of classical and humanist learning which Ludovico so admired. Like Alberti, then, Mantegna was no mere artisan. His presence at the Mantuan court (he served the Gonzaga for 46 years) represented a real coup for Ludovico. Henceforth the small court of Mantua was in the vanguard of artistic innovation, rather than merely imitating the styles of grander courts, a fact on which the Gonzaga were able to capitalize with respect to their political and dynastic aspirations.

Mantegna was not employed by the Gonzaga simply to paint. Again like Alberti, he performed a wider role as artistic adviser to the family, and encouraged them in their attempt to recreate at Mantua a model *all'antica* court. Among his many duties, for example, was the role of antique collector (Ludovico and his grandson's wife, Isabella d'Este, were assiduous collectors of ancient sculpture and classical remains). Nor was his work limited to commissions for the Gonzaga. He was frequently employed by prestigious foreign patrons to produce works of art, and was allowed to do so by his patron in part because of the political capital which might accrue as a result. In this way, Mantegna's work reached a wide audience and he too was able to indulge in a degree of self-promotion, a feature of artistic life which was accentuated by the trend in the late fifteenth century for artists of Mantegna's calibre to produce engraved copies of their work. Mantegna was not simply a court painter whose artistic imagination was restricted by the daily routine of court life. His fame today, none the less, rests primarily on the large-scale projects he undertook at Mantua that helped transform the appearance of the Gonzaga court into one of the most admired of the period. In addition to the painted murals for the Camera Picta (Cole, Plates 111–15 and pp.152–5) and the canvas series *The Triumphs of Caesar* (Cole, Plate 116 and pp.155–6), Mantegna produced a variety of smaller works, including gifts for foreign dignitaries, as well as devotional and religious pieces such as the altarpiece for Francesco Gonzaga, the *Madonna della Vittoria* (Cole, Plate 117). While this and the Camera Picta include portraiture, his contemporary fame seems to have lain in his imaginative reconstruction of historical and classical subjects. Isabella d'Este for one did not rate his skill as a portraitist (Elam, 1981).

Isabella d'Este

Mantegna's work at the court of Mantua overlapped with the period of the marriage of Isabella d'Este to Francesco Gonzaga in 1490. Isabella's influence on the court was considerable and ushered in a new phase in Mantuan artistic and cultural patronage. Her husband happily conceded that he knew more about horses than cameos, and his own patronage of the arts was largely confined to using it as a vehicle to extol the merits of his military exploits (Cole, pp.158–9 and Plate 117; Hollingsworth, 1994, p.220). Isabella, on the other hand, was deeply committed to the humanist revival of arts and letters, her passion for all things antique stemming from an early humanist education at her native court of Ferrara.

Exercise

Read pages 160–9 of Cole. What were the chief features of Isabella d'Este's patronage of the arts?

Discussion

Isabella d'Este wanted to use her commissions to enhance her reputation and self-image as a woman of taste. She purchased as much work as she could afford, though these were mostly smaller pieces. She could rarely afford to bring the best painters to Mantua, but she did request work from them as well as buying paintings at second hand. She was particularly unusual in her desire to collect works by select Italian artists, irrespective of their subject matter.

None the less, Isabella was often highly prescriptive about the content of proposed commissions, a situation which frequently led to conflict with her agents and prospective artists. She was also largely reliant on humanist advisers like da Ceresara and Bembo to provide the iconographic schemes for her many acquisitions.

Her self-image was clearly an important part of her role as patron, as is evident from her portrait commissions as well as her purchase and display of clothing and jewellery. Humanist scholarship was an important adjunct to self-publicity; Isabella associated herself with the virtue of Prudence. In contrast to male princely patrons, she does not seem to have been overly concerned with the propagation of political or dynastic imagery. Instead, she seems to have devoted her energies to cultivating her image as a learned and pious woman at court. ❖

Isabella's intellectual interests were wide-ranging and were fostered by humanist advisers whom she employed in a number of capacities. Paride da Ceresara (b. 1466), for example, a minor humanist at the court of Mantua, was instructed by Isabella to provide an allegorical *invenzione* for the artist Perugino's *Battle between Love and Chastity* (1505) (Plate 10), one of a series of similar compositions intended for her *studiolo* in Mantua (Chambers, 1970, pp.133–43). The complex iconography and subject matter of these works demanded a thorough grounding in classical literature. The extent to which the average courtier might be expected to decipher the message of such art is open to question. What is undisputed, however, is Isabella's own familiarity with this sphere of learning. Among the many humanist enterprises which she supported was that of the Venetian printer Aldus Manutius (*c.*1450–1515), who pioneered the idea of pocket editions of classical texts.

Another important aspect of Isabella's intellectual persona was her love and patronage of music. She herself was an accomplished singer and was able to play several musical instruments. The inventory of possessions to be found in her *studiolo* and *grotta* includes two books of French songs and a theoretical treatise on music by the Milanese teacher Franchino Gaffurio. Isabella's *grotta* in the S. Croce suite of the Corte Vecchia also includes intarsia panels depicting musical instruments and a view of Mantua, underneath which is inscribed the notation of a love song by the Flemish composer Johannes Ockeghem (Figure 1.26). Isabella's passion for music, and its symbolic significance within the context of court life, is similarly apparent in the decoration of her former *grotta* with her personal device comprising an alto clef, nine rests and a repeat sign (Figure 1.27). Music and musicians also provided access to other arts and their

Figure 1.26 Lorenzo Leonbruno, intarsia panelling showing view of city, *grotta* of Isabella d'Este. Corte Vecchia, S. Croce apartments, ducal palace, Mantua. Photo: INDEX/Giovetti

Figure 1.27 Panelling design showing musical rests, *grotta* of Isabella d'Este. Castello di S. Giorgio, ducal palace, Mantua. Photo: INDEX/Giovetti

practitioners. Isabella's instrument maker in Venice, for example, also acted as her agent with various painters (Fenlon, 1981).

Above all, Isabella was an insatiable collector who became a connoisseur of contemporary as well as ancient art. This was partially achieved through the activities of trusted intermediaries who were instructed to secure the services of painters, sculptors, goldsmiths and a host of other craftsmen. But it was also stimulated by Isabella's own travels, either to neighbouring courts or to places of particular significance for antiquarians, such as Rome. The 'eternal city', with its classical ruins and heritage, fascinated Isabella. During her visits to the city in 1514 and 1525, she purchased antiques and made notes on the latest interior design which she hoped to emulate in her own private suite of rooms at Mantua (Brown, 1997). She was also a tireless negotiator who often bullied into submission those with whom she was engaged in the purchase of precious works of art. Even faithful courtiers like Mantegna were not immune to her persuasions. After much haggling, Isabella secured a portrait bust of the Roman Empress Faustina from the aged painter as he lay on his death-bed.

In securing the services of artists like Giovanni Bellini (1435–1516), Giorgione (*c.*1478–1510), Leonardo da Vinci (1452–1519), Raphael (1483–1520) and Perugino (1446–1523), Isabella employed a variety of strategies ranging from the deferential to the dictatorial. Letters to agents in Venice, Florence and Rome demonstrate that she was not entirely even-handed in her treatment of potential employees (Chambers, 1970, pp.124–50; Hope, 1981, pp.308–11). Perugino, for example, received specific instructions as to what was to be included in the commission for the *Battle between Love and Chastity* (see above). Isabella's letter to the artist is exhaustive in its requirements, and although she was willing to leave some freedom for him to use his own initiative, the tone of her comments leaves little doubt as to who should play the chief role in defining the finished product. She concludes:

> I am sending you all these details in a small drawing, so that with both the written description and the drawing you will be able to consider my wishes in this matter. But if you think that perhaps there are too many figures in this for one picture, it is left to you to reduce them as you please, provided that you do not remove the principal basis, which consists of the four figures of Pallas, Diana, Venus and Cupid. If no inconvenience occurs I shall consider myself well satisfied; you are free to reduce them, but not to add anything else. Please be content with this arrangement.
>
> (Chambers, 1970, p.137)

We might contrast these instructions to those which were issued to the Venetian painter Giovanni Bellini, brother-in-law of Mantegna, who was simply asked to paint 'some ancient story or fable with a beautiful meaning' (Chambers, 1970, p.127). Delays in the completion of commissions also elicited a variety of responses from Isabella. On occasion, she could be terse and vitriolic. Yet with Leonardo she was positively deferential. Writing to the head of the Carmelite Order in Florence where the artist was engaged, she asked if Leonardo might be persuaded to produce a picture for her *studiolo*, or, failing that, 'a little picture of the Madonna, holy and sweet as is her natural manner'. There is no record of her reaction to the response, which politely pointed out that the artist was currently working for the king of France and was so absorbed in geometry that he could not bear the sight of a paintbrush (Chambers, 1970, pp.144–8). Unlike her treatment of individual artists, Isabella's taste in art and its subject matter was by and large uniform. Above all, she valued works depicting allegorical or mythological subjects, replete with classical symbolism, which were intended to allude to her own position as consort. Foremost among the symbols which recur in the works she commissioned for her private apartments are images of stability, moral rectitude and female virtue (Ferino Pagden, 1994, pp.77–82).

Exercise

Look at two paintings from Isabella's *studiolo*: Mantegna's *Pallas Expelling the Vices from the Garden of Eden* and Lorenzo Costa's *Garden of the Peaceful Arts* (Cole, Plates 122 and 123).

1   Identify similarities and differences in the style, composition and subject matter of the two.

2   To what extent might these be attributable to the influence of Isabella's patronage? (Cole has helpful comments on this aspect of the question, pp.164–6.)

Discussion

1   Similarities include size, intended location, medium (though note Mantegna worked in tempera, a mixture of egg yolk with pigment) and subject matter. The iconographic programme, or *invenzione*, of both was devised by the humanist Paride da Ceresara, and both pictures include allegorical figures. The most obvious difference between the two pictures would seem to lie in the slightly awkward composition and manner of Costa's work as opposed to the more fluid style of Mantegna. In the former, the figures seem to float in the imaginary landscape and their relation to each other is poorly defined. Mantegna, on the other hand, sets the scene of his work in a clearly articulated landscape. He also provides useful captions which leave the viewer in little doubt as to the underlying meaning of the allegory.

2 Cole implies that Mantegna, because of his high status at the Mantuan court, was impervious to the demands of his patron and was thus far less likely to find himself constrained by the requirements of his zealous mistress. As a painter in the Albertian mould (i.e. one skilled in the humanist arts), Mantegna could be trusted to devise or interpret *invenzioni*, even if he was not the original author. Costa, on the other hand, 'knew his place', and willingly submitted to the demands of Isabella even if this meant, as in this case, that the finished painting lacked simplicity and balance. Consequently, Costa's *Garden of the Peaceful Arts* is far more difficult to 'read' as a picture. ❖

It is probably fair to say that Isabella's reputation as a patron of the arts has suffered over the years from various degrees of gender stereotyping. Most recently she has fallen victim to the view that she lacked both judgement and taste, and the language frequently used to describe her activities as a collector stress an undiscerning and wilful nature. Depicted as either 'notoriously vain', hopelessly muddled, or irredeemably out of step with contemporary fashion, Isabella is readily dismissed by her critics as unworthy of serious study (Hollingsworth, 1994, p.221; Verheyen, 1971, pp.43, 50). Symptomatic of the general reaction to Isabella as patron is the analysis offered by the art historian Charles Hope of Perugino's *Battle between Love and Chastity*, which he suggests:

> illustrates only too clearly what she had in mind – the pedantic elaboration of a banal allegory, conceived with little or no regard for the distinction between a painting and a text. This attitude seems entirely typical of Isabella's pretentious personality, but whether it reflects the normal outlook of contemporary patrons remains to be seen.
>
> (Hope, 1981, p.310)

In a recent study of Isabella as patron of the arts, Rose Marie San Juan has suggested that such criticisms of the *marchesa* fail to grasp the essential dilemma of Isabella's role as consort and court patron; that her rejection of an art which privileged classical authenticity in favour of one which encouraged didactic readings of ancient mythological stories was part of a wider strategy that was largely forced on her by the constraints of gender and court life (San Juan, 1991). It now appears that Isabella was unique as a female patron of the arts:

> Not only did she collect on a much larger scale than other consorts, but ... she departed from the types of objects – religious painting, decorative arts – usually patronised by women in her position. In acquiring mythological paintings and antique statuary, Isabella d'Este

seems to have been quite exceptional among Renaissance court women.

(San Juan, 1991, p.71)

In attempting to secure such paintings and artefacts, Isabella strayed uncomfortably close to the prescribed boundaries for women at court. The commission and purchase of works of art enabled the *marchesa* to extend her cultural and political networks across Italy and boosted her status at court, particularly during the long absences of her husband. The display of such works also forced attention on the court of the consort and encouraged discussion of the moral virtues associated with the subject matter of these paintings. In the process, Isabella's labours paid off. Her patronage of art and successful entry into what was otherwise considered a man's world 'provided the *marchesa* with a sure way to be taken more seriously, to be more effective in building contacts and to endow her with a successful public image' (San Juan, 1991, p.75). Following the death of her husband in 1519, however, she soon found herself out of step with the new wave of artistic and cultural fashion ushered in by her son, Federico, and his favoured court artist, Giulio Romano.

Giulio Romano and the Palazzo Te

The final stage in the evolution of artistic taste at Mantua is usually associated with the arrival at court, through the agency of Castiglione, of the Roman-born artist Giulio Romano (1492–1546). Giulio began his career as one of Raphael's pupils, working for the pope and other wealthy patrons in Rome (these included the Augsburg merchant and Hapsburg banker, Jacob Fugger). A fine example of his early work is the interior decoration of the Villa Madama in Rome for the future pope, Clement VII (Plate 11). On his arrival in Mantua, Giulio began work on the renovation of a rural villa for the Gonzaga but rapidly graduated to more important commissions. Chief among these was the conversion of the Gonzaga stud-farm on the outskirts of the city into a private pleasure palace for Federico, the son of Francesco Gonzaga and Isabella d'Este. The Palazzo Te was undertaken in two main phases between 1526 and 1534 (Figure 1.28, overleaf). There is little doubt that this building, with its remarkable internal decor, laid the foundations for Giulio's subsequent international reputation (Cole, Plates 124 and 126). It also established him as a firm favourite at the court of Federico Gonzaga. As we have seen, the artistic environment at Mantua was highly competitive. It was not unknown for powerful figures such as Mantegna to have rivals beaten up. Giulio Romano's predecessor, Leonbruno, was replaced partly because it was felt that he was too closely attached to the court of Federico's mother,

Isabella, but also because he was unable to keep pace with the new artistic style associated with the school of Raphael at Rome. The search for security and status was often all-consuming. Mantegna finally achieved the ultimate accolade of a coat of arms and the curious title of 'knight of the gilded militia' (Elam, 1981, p.16). Giulio was equally successful in emulating his illustrious predecessor. Not only was he made a citizen of Mantua for life, but he was also rewarded with several pensions and appointments. As city surveyor, for example, he was placed in charge of numerous public projects, including the construction and refurbishment of Mantua's churches, civic buildings and gateways, and was responsible for every aspect of the city's appearance, from drainage to planning permission. He was also awarded lucrative private commissions. In the eyes of the contemporary biographer Giorgio Vasari (1511–74), Giulio was the epitome of the gentleman artist whose display of artistic *sprezzatura*, like that of the courtier, elevated him above the generality of artisan painters (Vasari, in De Vere, 1996, vol. 2, pp.118–40).

Figure 1.28 Giulio Romano, north and west façade of Palazzo Te, Mantua, 1526–7. Photo: Alinari

There are considerable grounds for claiming that the architectural and decorative medium that Giulio brought to Mantua helped to fashion an international court style. Not only were his designs exported abroad by his associates, but foreign visitors frequently sought to imitate his work. He is, for example, the one visual artist mentioned by name in Shakespeare (*Winter's Tale* 5.2; *Love's Labours Lost* 4.5). One of Giulio's pupils at Mantua, Primaticcio (1504–70), went on to work for the French king, Francis I (1494–1547) at Fontainebleau. Following his visit to Mantua in 1536, the duke of Bavaria, Ludwig X, sought to replicate rooms in the Palazzo Te at his palace at Landshut. Designs were obtained from Giulio, and the duke sent a Dutch painter to study alongside the master at Mantua. Later in the sixteenth century a Mantuan goldsmith, Jacopo della Strada (1507–88), established himself as a dealer in antiques and cultural impresario at several German courts. The interiors he created at the palaces of Munich and Vienna paraphrase compositions by Giulio. Moreover, Strada's drawings of the Palazzo Te, together with an inventory of their contents, provide a valuable source of evidence for the original appearance of Giulio's masterwork.

If Giulio's work at Mantua represented the first stirrings of an international court style, it also coincided with a growing concern on the part of his patrons, the Gonzaga, to cultivate political relations with the rest of Europe. In order to secure and extend their authority in northern Italy, it was vital that they establish firm diplomatic and dynastic links with the great powers currently contending for authority in this war-torn and much disputed part of Europe. As early as 1433 Gianfrancesco Gonzaga (1407–44) had seen the wisdom of this policy when he secured the title of marquis from the Holy Roman Emperor Sigismund, and sealed the alliance with the marriage of his son, Ludovico, to the emperor's niece, Barbara of Brandenburg. Similar concerns prevailed in the early sixteenth century. The young marquis, Federico, who inherited the family title in 1519, was particularly eager to consolidate Gonzaga authority in Italy and to shrug off the mantle of *condottiere*, which he saw as inimical to true princeliness. In order to achieve this, however, he would need to steer a very careful course through the minefield of north Italian politics.

In the pursuit of princely status, Federico realized the great value of artistic patronage and courtly splendour as an adjunct to political success. Influenced from an early age by his cultured mother, Isabella, he set about creating at Mantua a magnificent court that would rival that of any neighbouring prince. Federico bore well the advice of his own ambassador, Baldassare Castiglione, who counselled that those who held princely office must seek great splendour in the outward appearance of their court and person if they wished to be remembered by posterity:

> He should hold magnificent banquets, festivals, games and public shows, and keep a great many fine horses for use in peace or war, as well as falcons, hounds and all the other things that pertain to the pleasures of great lords and their subjects: after the manner of signor Federico Gonzaga, Marquess of Mantua, in our own day, who in this regard seems more like King of Italy than the ruler of a city.

> (Bull, 1976, p.310)

Federico's claim to greatness, and hence his right to assume princely status, was thus affirmed by his patronage of the arts, learning and cultivated leisure. His love of horses, for example, had led him to establish one of the most celebrated studs in Europe. Probably the most important aspect of this dimension to Federico's rule and self-image, however, was his desire to renovate and rebuild the city of Mantua in a style befitting an aspiring prince. The creation of the Palazzo Te was simply one among many building projects undertaken during this period which allowed the city to be used as a suitable backdrop for civic pageantry and the entertainment of visiting dignitaries. In 1530, Federico gained his long-awaited reward when he hosted the reception of the Emperor Charles V and received the title of duke from a grateful overlord. Not surprisingly, this visit was celebrated in lavish style. The emperor was honoured with a grand triumphal entry, designed by Giulio, but the climax of Charles's stay was a visit to the uncompleted Palazzo Te.

Exercise

Read the extract from the report on the festivities at the Palazzo Te in honour of Charles V (Anthology, no. 36). What does the account suggest about the private and public functions of the palace?

Discussion

The Palazzo Te clearly performed a variety of functions, both private and public. On the one hand, the building was the private retreat of a single individual, the marquis, and many of its rooms (the emperor was not shown the whole complex) were reserved for him and his mistress, Isabella Boschetti. On the other, it was large enough to cater for banquets, dancing and parties, which formed an essential element of court life and diplomacy in the early sixteenth century (though note that the accommodation allowed the marquis and his eminent guest to dine apart from the rest of the court in the Sala di Psiche, or Psyche's room). The building, however, had other functions; it was, for example, a place of leisure and sport (tennis). It was also, most importantly, an art gallery. Note in particular the interest of the emperor in Giulio's work and his desire to understand fully the meaning of the decorative programme of the palace. ❖

The ball held in honour of the emperor at the Palazzo Te was the climax of a series of celebrations which were designed as the backdrop to Federico's elevation to the title of duke. We might expect therefore to uncover in the decoration and iconography of the rooms subtle references to the authority and majesty of Federico's overlord, Charles V. There are, however, surprisingly few. In all probability this reflects the awkward situation in which Federico found himself in 1530, given his earlier support for the emperor's enemies in Italy, most notably Florence and the papacy. Of greatest potential embarrassment to the marquis was the explicit reference to his previous service as a *condottiere* in the inscription on the architrave of the Sala di Psiche, the very room in which the marquis and the emperor dined alone in 1530. It read: 'Federigo II Gonzaga, Fifth Marquis of Mantua, Captain General of the Florentine Republic, ordered this place built for honest leisure after work to restore strength in quiet' (Eisler, 1987, p.275; and see Cole, Plate 126). Federico's previous contract with the papacy, which entailed his support for the revived Florentine republic under the Medici, was destroyed by his shrewd and ever alert mother, Isabella, and in 1525 he changed sides to fight alongside the forces of the emperor at the battle of Pavia. The outcome – the collapse of papal secular authority in Italy and the sack of Rome by the imperial troops (1527) – guaranteed Federico's rising star. But the question remained: for how long?

The vicissitudes of north Italian politics dictated a cautious and frequently devious approach to foreign policy, a point well made by Machiavelli's contemporary treatise *The Prince* (see Book 1, Chapter 6). Federico had learned the lesson well and was, temporarily at least, on the right side. The decoration of the newly constructed Palazzo Te suggests that he incorporated such caution into his artistic projects. Not until 1532, and Charles V's second visit to Mantua, did Federico feel sufficiently confident to proclaim his support for the emperor in the iconographical programme carried out by Giulio for the newly refurbished Sala dei Giganti (room of the giants) (see Figure 3.22 and Cole, Plate 124), as well as in other rooms especially designated for the emperor's private use. But even then, as William Eisler points out, 'one is forced to observe that ... there is no direct, unmistakable reference to Charles anywhere in the palace [and Federico's] association with the emperor is referred to only in symbolic terms'. He concludes with the suggestion that:

> In the permanent decorations of a palace, homage was paid to the emperor in a type of code, presumably explained to him in his presence, or to his ambassadors in his absence. Perhaps Federico feared a sudden reversal of Charles' political fortunes, which would transform an explicit apotheosis of the Emperor into an embarrassing reminder of a past mistake.
>
> (Eisler, 1987, p.277)

Cole, citing Vasari, suggests that sympathetic court patronage allowed artists to indulge their mannerist wit to a degree unthinkable in the context of a republic (pp.176–7). The style adopted by Giulio Romano is a case in point since it demonstrates a number of the features associated with the mannerist movement, particularly in the way Giulio subverted the regular order and balance associated with the Renaissance *all'antica* mode of art. In terms of the visual arts, mannerism originated with the followers of Michelangelo and Raphael who were working in Rome in the 1510s. Its chief characteristic, regardless of the specific medium, was the prominence it bestowed on the form of the art work at the expense of its subject matter. Mannerist painters thus sought to 'manner' the latter through the use of a number of devices including disguise, allegory, repetition or complexity. The nature and meaning of mannerism and the reasons for its evolution in this period have been the focus of much debate. Some have seen it as a conscious attempt by a new generation of artists to distance themselves from the straitjacket of Renaissance classicism. This is suggested, for example, in the way in which mannerist painters deliberately flouted the rules of classical art as developed by men like Leonardo. Others, however, have stressed mannerism's continuity with the earlier classicizing tradition. In order to bend the rules and appreciate the deviations and distortions inherent in the new style, the mannerist painter had to possess a sound knowledge of the basic conventions governing classical art. Hence a mannerist work will not only look different from its classical precursor but should at the same time demonstrate an awareness of the conventions it seeks to subvert. Sometimes the element of subversion introduced into a painting was for expressive effect (as, for example, in an attempt to suggest movement); at other times it represented a sophisticated intellectual exercise or joke. But whatever the case, the artist's intention was to undermine the naturalism and classicism of earlier Renaissance art. Interestingly, such developments were not restricted to the field of the visual arts. By the 1530s, Italian music theorists were likewise contrasting the 'perfect art' of composers like Josquin Desprez with the more refined and distorted complexity of the 'New Music' (Maniates, 1979, pp.117–22). Similarly, much Italian poetry of this period is suffused with this kind of rule breaking (Shearman, 1967, esp. pp.145–6, 156–8).

Typically, Giulio Romano's conceits in buildings like the Palazzo Te require a familiarity with Renaissance architectural conventions in order to appreciate how his contradictions work. Giulio had read his Vitruvius and Pliny and knew all about the layout of Roman private houses and villas, which he had seen replicated in Renaissance Rome. Yet his application of this knowledge was always presented in such a tongue-in-cheek way as to suggest a jaunty disregard for the rules of classical architecture. A case in point are the pendulous capstones and the heavy **rustication** of the columns in the loggia of the side entrance to the Palazzo Te, which are deliberate distortions of features that had become part of Renaissance decorative vocabulary (Figure 1.29). Note also that the entrance columns lack capitals, but the main arch is none the less regularly proportioned. In similar fashion, Giulio borrowed his use of grotesque ornament from examples found in Nero's Domus Aurea (Figures 1.30 and 1.31). He also incorporated various forms of classical decoration in the Doric

Figure 1.29 Detail of the side entrance to the Palazzo Te, Mantua. Photo: James Austin

Figure 1.30 View of the cryptoporticus with illusionistic candelabra and figures from the Domus Aurea (Golden House of Nero), Rome. Photo: German Archaeological Institute, Rome, DAI 846497

Figure 1.31 Giulio Romano and assistants, Biagio de' Conti and Girolamo da Pontremoli, decorated ceiling of the vestibule of the Secret Garden, 1531–4, Palazzo Te, Mantua. Photo: Alinari

friezes which adorn the courtyard, but in such a way as to poke fun at convention. A good example of this process is suggested by the way in which the **triglyph** breaks the line of the architrave and appears precariously balanced above every bay (Figure 1.32).

Figure 1.32 A view of the courtyard of the Palazzo Te, Mantua, showing detail of the triglyphs (with three vertical incisions) seemingly breaking through the line of the architrave.
Photo: James Austin.

One possible source for Giulio's humorous and subversive approach to the exterior design of the Palazzo Te is Castiglione's *The Courtier*. In a long dialogue on the virtue of humour at court, Castiglione, a familiar figure in Mantuan circles, contended that 'what we laugh at is nearly always something incongruous, and yet it is not amiss'. The ability to make one laugh 'at the right time and in the right way is greatly to be praised'. According to Verheyen, Giulio's visual jesting mirrored precisely Castiglione's thinking on humour and social decorum (1977, p.48). It also seems to have informed his light-hearted approach to the internal decoration of the Palazzo Te. Whether or not Giulio did manage to achieve a decorous balance in his treatment of the story of Cupid and Psyche here is, however, open to serious doubt. His track record was certainly against him. In 1517, he achieved a certain notoriety in Rome when his pornographic engravings of the classical tale landed his engraver in jail. Some indication of the extent to which he subsequently flouted decorous convention in his depiction of the *Wedding Feast of Cupid and Psyche* in the Sala di Psiche can be gained by comparing these to Raphael's composition of the same subject in the Villa Farnesina in Rome (Paoletti and Radke, 1997, pp. 352–3, 366) (Figure 1.33). It is perhaps only fair to point out, however, that the public prominence of Raphael's version of Cupid and Psyche is in contrast to the private setting of Giulio's depiction. In the seclusion of the palace, semi-pornographic scenes such as those painted by Giulio could, arguably, be deemed to accord with contemporary standards of decorum.

Figure 1.33 Raphael and assistants, *Wedding Feast of Cupid*, 1517, fresco, detail of ceiling of Loggia di Psiche, Villa Farnesina, Rome.
Photo: Alinari-Anderson

In this section we have traced Gonzaga patronage over a period of roughly one hundred years. In that time the Gonzaga proved themselves highly adept at both imitating and initiating new trends in Renaissance art and architecture and, as a consequence, firmly established their court at Mantua as one in the forefront of contemporary fashion. In the first place, their interest in cultural show was stimulated by contact with the Medici and Florentine artistic circles (most notably through Alberti). As they grew in confidence and power, it is increasingly evident that they were capable not simply of following fashion but also of encouraging and introducing innovation in the visual arts. Under Federico, who was educated at the court of the Vatican, the cultural pre-eminence of high Renaissance art at Rome was both emulated and surpassed so as to elevate Mantua to the status of one of the major centres of cultural and artistic production in northern Italy. We have also noted how, throughout the period, the impetus to raise the profile of Mantua in this way was itself closely related to the Gonzaga search for political recognition and status. The arts thus constituted one of the many 'strategies' available to ambitious rulers like the Gonzaga. Doubts about political legitimacy were as likely to be 'quelled by ritual, symbol and ceremony ... as by titles and foreign alliances' (Rodríguez-Salgado, 1997, p.26). For nearly a century the Gonzaga proved themselves consummate masters of this particular art, producing in the process one of the most flourishing centres of artistic creativity in Renaissance Italy.

The court of Matthias Corvinus of Hungary: a case study in reception

In this section we shift our attention to a court outside Italy in order to study more closely the process of cultural diffusion in Europe during the Renaissance. The reason behind the choice of Hungary and the court of King Matthias Corvinus (1458–90) relates to the fact that Hungary provides one of the first examples of a conscious attempt by a non-Italian patron to import Italian culture in its entirety rather than in piecemeal fashion. In the process, Hungary was to act as a mediator of Italian culture to other courts in central Europe, such as that of the Polish king in Cracow. By pursuing these lines of transmission we should achieve a better understanding of one of the key problems in Renaissance cultural history, that of reception. Cultural historians have been much influenced by theories of reception and, for our purposes here, two aspects of this work are of interest. First, the idea that the recipients of Renaissance culture were not simply passive agents in the process of transmission, accepting at face value all aspects of the classical revival. It is now widely accepted that the process of reception was a creative one in which something new was constructed out of the fragments of earlier cultures. In the words of one of the foremost historians of Renaissance culture, 'what artists and writers practised was not so much imitation as transformation' (Burke, 1998, p.7). The second feature of current historical work on reception is the idea of a 'grid' or a 'filter' which allows some but not all of the cultural inheritance of the past to pass through: 'what is selected must be "congruent" with the culture in which the selection takes place' (Burke, 1998, p.8). Though these ideas can, and have, been applied to the general history of the reception of classical culture in Renaissance Italy, they have a particular relevance for a study such as this. Hungary, traditionally envisaged in western historical scholarship as peripheral to the major political and cultural trends in Europe, was in fact one of the first great centres of classical revival outside Italy. It did, however, by virtue of its geographical position and socio-cultural traditions, offer a prospect that was very different from Italy in respect of its receptiveness to the cultural heritage of the ancient world.

Exercise

You may find it helpful to read the extract from C.A. Macartney's 'The foreign kings of Hungary' (Reader, no. 14). ❖

Hungary's close connections with Italy and France began in the fourteenth century when the country was ruled by Angevin kings (originally from Anjou, in France). Diplomatic, humanist and artistic contacts with Italy were continued and expanded during the reign of Matthias Corvinus, coming to a halt only after the disastrous defeat of the Hungarian army by the Turks at the battle of Mohács in 1526. Throughout much of this period the kingdom was ruled by the Jagellonian dynasty who also occupied the throne of Bohemia. Another branch of the family held the crown of Poland. The Jagellonian holdings covered much of central and eastern Europe. During the reign of Matthias Corvinus, Hungary extended over a vast area comprising not only the present-day country but also parts of what are today Poland, the Czech and Slovak Republics, Austria and the Balkan states. The mainstays of the economy were mining and agriculture and, unlike northern Italy, Hungary was not greatly urbanized. With a total population of about 4 million, its largest city, Buda, contained as few as 10,000 inhabitants (Figure 1.34).[15]

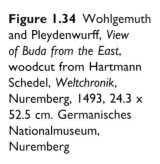

Figure 1.34 Wohlgemuth and Pleydenwurff, *View of Buda from the East*, woodcut from Hartmann Schedel, *Weltchronik*, Nuremberg, 1493, 24.3 × 52.5 cm. Germanisches Nationalmuseum, Nuremberg

[15] The town of Pest, on the east side of the river Danube, was a separate, smaller settlement in the fifteenth century.

Hungary was a predominantly feudal society with a long-established royal court. As many as 25,000 men claimed noble status and aspired to a place in the government of the country through the **diet** of leading magnates who shared power with the king. This relationship was an uneasy and unstable one and created constant tension in ruling circles. Matthias Corvinus, who succeeded to the throne in 1458, was himself descended from the lesser nobility. Under such circumstances, it was not unusual to surround oneself with 'new men', that is, those like oneself who were of lesser blood. One of Matthias's chief goals was the creation of a strongly centralized state in which the demands of the nobility were subjected to the greater need of the king to defend the country from foreign aggression (the Turks and Muscovites). In order to succeed, the king knew that he had to create an efficient and modern form of government, the model for which, in fifteenth-century terms, was provided by the bureaucratic city-states and principalities of northern Italy. Building on contacts between Hungary and Italy that had been established in the fourteenth century, Matthias thus set about providing a suitable education for his state's future politicians and officials.

One of the key figures in this process was the king's chief chancellor and former teacher, János Vitéz (*c.*1408–72). As a humanist, Vitéz was fully conversant with the benefits of a classical education, and under his patronage large numbers of Hungary's finest students were sent to Italy to study under Italian masters such as Guarino of Verona (1374–1460). The result was an efflorescence of Hungarian scholarship:

> In this way a humanist chancellery was created from those who had received the best Italian education, and by now Petrarch himself would not have found fault with the writings that they were producing. Political argumentation in correspondence and orations, laudatory prose and poetry in praise of the king, the urging of Europe's nations to Christian solidarity against the Turks, the rewriting of the history of the nation in the spirit and style of humanism – these were some of the themes of the new humanist literature just being born in Hungary.

> (Klaniczay, 1992, p.166)

In the wake of these developments, humanists from other countries, Italy included, began to visit Hungary, and many settled to study and serve at the Corvinian court. The biggest impetus to this cultural revolution, however, was provided by the marriage of Matthias Corvinus to Beatrice of Aragon (d.1508), the daughter of the king of Naples, in 1476. In the ensuing years, Hungary saw an influx of Italian scholars, architects, artists and writers. These cultural ties with Italy were further sealed by the betrothal of Matthias's illegitimate son, János, to Bianca Maria Sforza, as well as by the growing presence in Buda of an expatriate Italian community of merchants (mostly Florentine) and ambassadors. Contact between the two was also encouraged by the financial and diplomatic support Matthias received from the papacy and the republic of Venice. To many western leaders, Matthias's strong leadership and powerful mercenary army were seen as a vital element in the defence of Christendom against the growing threat posed by the 'infidel' Turks, despite the fact that much of his energy and wealth was expended on an expansionist foreign policy against his Christian and Orthodox neighbours (Mitchell, 1994, pp.118–65, 315–35). Typical of the esteem in which Matthias was held in the west are the sentiments expressed by the Florentine philosopher Marsilio Ficino who, in a letter to the king appealing for his help in stemming the onslaught of Turkish pirates in the Adriatic, described him as a latter-day Hercules (Ficino, 1576, pp.721–2).

In keeping with a number of his contemporaries, including Charles the Bold, the Gonzaga of Mantua and the citizens of the Florentine republic, Matthias was particularly keen to foster the association with Hercules. The ancient hero was an exemplary figure in Renaissance art and letters. Cicero, in his widely read *De officiis*, had presented Hercules as one who chose virtue in preference to leisure and undertook his celebrated labours for public rather than private benefit. In fifteenth-century Florence he was frequently the object of both literary and artistic interest. The Florentine chancellor Coluccio Salutati wrote a Stoic allegorical exposition of the labours of Hercules, while Lorenzo de' Medici had three of the labours painted by Antonio del Pollaiuolo, who also cast small bronzes of the same figure (see Chapter 3, p.192 and Figure 3.13)[16] (Ettlinger, 1972). Representations of Matthias as Hercules permeate the artistic and literary output of his court. At Buda, Hercules appears in manuscripts, small bronze statues and door decorations. A large bronze statue which once stood in the outer courtyard of the royal palace was later taken by the Turks to Constantinople (Istanbul), where it was recorded in a Dutch woodcut (Míko, 1990). Similarly, at Matthias's summer palace at Visegrád, a marble statue of Hercules fighting the Hydra was set on top of a fountain in the courtyard

---

[16] Pollaiuolo (1433–98) designed the drapery for Matthias's throne (Klaniczay, 1992, p.167).

(Figures 1.35 and 1.36). A surviving fragment from excavations at the site seems to represent the same theme (Röll, 1994, pp.126–8).

Matthias's promotion of these allusions to himself as a second Hercules is strongly indicative of the influence of the new learning at the Corvinian court.[17] It would be a mistake to conclude, however, that the king's reverence for ancient literature and learning blinded him to the political necessity of promoting other images of royal power which were starkly at odds with Renaissance iconography. Just as he revelled in the title *Hercules Hungaricus*, so he was equally at home with the idea of himself as a second Attila whose illustrious but 'barbaric' progenitor was lauded in fifteenth-century Hungary as the founder of the nation (see Book 1, Chapter 3 on the revival of national histories in the Renaissance). Not all, or even a majority, of the nobility who served Matthias were able or willing to appreciate the humanist political rhetoric of the myth of Hercules and his defeat of the Hydra (probably associated in learned circles at Buda with the Turks). They were more willing, however, to support a leader who demonstrated close links with their own native histories and traditions. In the wider context of the problem of the reception of Renaissance culture in Hungary, the depiction of Matthias as Hercules is indicative of the syncretic nature of court culture under the king. On the one hand, there is the concrete evidence of Matthias's various artistic and architectural projects, informed throughout with a passion for the new classicism. On the other, there is the conflicting evidence of many of the surviving artefacts and architectural remains which paint a less consistent image of *all'antica* culture in Corvinian Hungary. To cite just one example, the Hercules sculpture at Visegrád, described above, was in a courtyard which was surrounded by an arcade with Gothic pointed arches.

Surprisingly perhaps, Matthias Corvinus never visited Italy, but was an ardent admirer of its architecture and a great patron of its artists and architects (Feuer-Tóth, 1981). Under his direction the Gothic castle at Buda was partly rebuilt in the new *all'antica* style. The Italian Chimenti Camicia, who was in charge of the reconstruction programme, was responsible for the famous hanging gardens of the palace which were based on those at Urbino. Matthias also intended to remodel the city of Buda, for which purpose he commissioned the resident Italian humanist Antonio Bonfini (*c.*1427–1502/5) to compose a Latin translation of Filarete's unpublished treatise on

---

[17] Another minor example, but none the less a telling one, of the king's tendency to favour the trend towards classicizing is suggested by his decision to latinize his surname from Hunyadi to Corvinus. This may also have reflected the need for a 'new man' to assert his legitimate claim to the crown in what was otherwise an unstable polity (Kaufmann, 1995, p.42).

Figure 1.35 View of reconstructed fountain. Visegrád Matthias Museum, Visegrád. Photo: Robert Hack

Figure 1.36 Giovanni Dalmata, *Hercules with Hydra*, detail of Figure 1.35, red marble, 92 × 97 cm. Visegrád Matthias Museum, Visegrád. Photo: Robert Hack

architecture. In an introduction to this work Bonfini described in some detail Matthias's various architectural projects, including his dependence on imported artists, architects and craftsmen (see the extracts from the introduction in the Anthology (no. 34). Bonfini adds the wry comment that although Italian men of letters were also invited to remain in Hungary, they foolishly chose to return home. In doing so, they reaffirmed the view of some foreign observers who depicted Hungary as a cultural backwater, a legacy no doubt of earlier visitors to the country in the early fourteenth century. Matthias, however, strove to reverse this image. Not only did he fund two posts at the Italian University of Pavia, but he also invited to his court some of the most eminent Renaissance scholars of the day, among them Marsilio Ficino. Though the great Florentine philosopher declined the invitation, he did send the king copies of all of his works, some of which were dedicated to him and to Hungarian humanists. In addition, the influence on Buda of Ficino's particular brand of Neoplatonism was guaranteed by the presence at court of one of his closest associates, Francesco Bandini, who established a sub-branch of the Florentine Neoplatonic Academy at Buda during his fourteen-year stay (Klaniczay, 1992, p.167).

As indicated above in the example of the hanging gardens at Buda, there is some evidence to suggest that Matthias's building programme was influenced or shaped by contacts with such important centres of cultural production as Urbino. The humanist confidant of the king, Bonfini, may have played a role in this respect. Born at Recanati, near Urbino, he had earlier served the Montefeltro court (Figure 1.37) and spent much of his time travelling to and from his native land and Hungary. Bonfini's characterization of Matthias as a ruler who embodied the virtues of arms and letters may be indebted to the precedent of Federico da Montefeltro. Moreover, other features of the renovation of the royal palace at Buda incorporated characteristics reminiscent of the ducal palace at Urbino. These include the arcaded courtyard, the library and the hanging garden, which, like that at Urbino, was supplied with water from a concealed cistern (Gerevich, 1971; Kaufmann, 1995, p.43). Ornate Renaissance gardens, in imitation of those described by Pliny the Younger, also feature prominently at the king's summer palace at Visegrád. They were described by a visiting papal legate in 1483 as an earthly paradise. Once again, however, the combination of Gothic backdrop and *all'antica* furnishings (fountains, balustrades and colonnades lined with violets and boxwood) suggests the accommodation of the new style to more established architectural conventions. Moreover, the difficulties implicit in establishing hard and fast evidence of cultural exchange between two such disparate locations as Buda and

Figure 1.37 Justus of Ghent, *Federico da Montefeltro and his Court Listen to a Speech by Antonio Bonfini*, c.1474–82, oil on panel, 130 x 212 cm. The Royal Collection © 1999 Her Majesty Queen Elizabeth II

Urbino is further highlighted by a comparison of internal furnishings in the two palaces (see Figure 1.38, overleaf, and Cole, Plate 57). Though the decoration of the two doorways here is very similar, this may provide evidence of nothing more than the wide distribution of generic forms of *all'antica* decorative motifs and designs which increasingly formed part of a common vocabulary of distinct classicizing in fifteenth-century Europe.

In addition to Urbino, there is some evidence to suggest the influence of Florence and its craftsmen on the Hungarian Renaissance. Vasari, for example, noted that Matthias had 'many Florentines at his court' (De Vere, 1996, vol. 1, p.543) and Lorenzo de' Medici sent the king several works of art as diplomatic gifts. In the parish church of St Mary's, Pest, a Renaissance-style tabernacle, very similar to those designed by Florentine sculptors, suggests an illusionistic sense of receding space (Figure 1.39, overleaf). The inscription, which records the patron, is in Roman capitals and the ornamentation of the **entablature** uses classical motifs which form components of the **cornice** of the Corinthian order. The fantasia of decorative candelabra work on the pilasters can be found in manuscripts of the time as well as surviving in fragments found at other Corvinian sites (Klaniczay et al., 1982, pp.602, 605–6). Similarly, the dolphins, cherubs, festoons, swags and swirling bands can all be found on individual fragments of remains from sites at Esztergom, Visegrád and Buda. One of the few points of difference with Italian work of a similar nature dating from this period is the use of red marble, a distinctive feature of much Hungarian Renaissance sculpture. This, however, provides no clue as to whether the finished work was that of native or foreign artists.

Figure 1.38 Reconstructed doorframe from Buda royal palace. Budapesti Torteneti Muzeum, Budapest

Figure 1.39 Unknown artist, *Tabernacle of Bishop András Nagyrévi*, c.1506, red marble and limestone, 746 x 254 cm. Budapest, Parish Church of the Inner City of Pest. Photo: National Board for the Protection of Historic Monuments Photo Archive, Hungarian Museum for Architecture, Budapest

A much more comprehensive example of Renaissance *all'antica* religious architecture is provided by the funerary chapel of Cardinal Thomas Bakócz (1442–1521) at Esztergom, which has been described as 'one of the purest and most extraordinary examples of Italian architecture outside Italy' (Kaufmann, 1995, p.46) (Figure 1.40).

Attributed to one 'Johannes Florentinus' (fl. 1506–25), it is strongly redolent of Florentine church architecture, as, for example, in the composition of the round arch **pendentive** dome and the juxtaposition of coloured stone against white walls. The white marble altarpiece was imported from Florence. Cardinal Bakócz, one of a number of Hungarian clerics with close ties to humanist circles in Italy, was clearly following the lead provided by Matthias in encouraging Florentine craftsmen to work in Hungary. By the time of his death, however, numerous engineers and stonemasons with Hungarian names were working on similar Renaissance-style projects (Gerevich, 1971, p.118).

The impetus from above for the adoption of *all'antica*-style Renaissance architecture and its various motifs is also evident in the Jagellonian courts in Bohemia and Poland. The Vladislav Hall of the Hradcny Castle in Prague was built by a German architect who had visited Buda. Its Renaissance windows, dating from 1493, contain

Figure 1.40 View of the sepulchral chapel for Archbishop Thomas Bakócz, Cathedral of St Adalbert, Esztergom, 1506–19. Photo: Attila Mudrák

features similar to the classical ornamentation found at the ducal palace in Urbino (Figure 1.41). The Italian architects employed on the extension and refurbishment of Wawel Castle in Cracow borrowed a number of features from Buda Castle where the Polish king, Sigismund I (1506–48), had resided for three years. The role of Buda as a vital 'filter' for Renaissance classicism in central Europe is particularly evident in the case of Cracow where, in the first decades of the sixteenth century, the Polish monarchy set about the transformation of their court in the new antique style. In the early stages of this revival the influence of Hungarian models is everywhere apparent. The internal decoration of Wawel Castle, for example, contains a coffered ceiling with human heads, a feature found originally at Buda. The palace itself was substantially remodelled in the early sixteenth century under the aegis of the Italian architect Franciscus Florentinus, who was summoned from Buda in 1502 to construct a tomb niche for the Gothic funeral effigy of King Jan Olbrecht (1492–1501) in Wawel Cathedral. Another feature of the Polish Renaissance that was similar to the Hungarian experience was the role played by humanist-educated clerics in the 'secondary' phase of reception (the 'primary' phase was essentially royal-led). The Polish cardinal and chancellor Jan Łaski commissioned funeral slabs from Johannes Florentinus at Esztergom in 1516 and built his own tomb in Gniezno Cathedral in imitation of the Bakócz Chapel.

Figure 1.41 View of the exterior façade, Vladislav Hall, Hradcny Castle, Prague, 1493–1502. Photo: Conway Library, Courtauld Institute of Art

The Italian Renaissance style in Poland found its ultimate expression in the tomb commissioned for Sigismund I (1517–33) in Wawel Cathedral, the traditional burial place of Polish kings. It was designed by yet another Italian, Bartolommeo Berrecci, with the support of Italian and Hungarian stonemasons. The chapel itself combines the concept of the triumphal arch with an octagonal drum and high dome reminiscent of the *duomo* in Florence (Figure 1.42). The design of the tomb chapel has been compared to the one Michelangelo was preparing for the Medici in Florence (Kaufmann, 1995, p.56). The distinctive use of red marble, like that used at Esztergom in Hungary, suggests a local accommodation to Italian precepts. Native influence on the design of the tomb is also apparent in the depiction of the 'sleeping king' and his location, 'double-decker' fashion, above his father. These arrangements were rapidly imitated elsewhere in Polish sepulchral art, leading one historian of Polish Renaissance culture to comment that 'in the Renaissance, Poles did not die; they were merely sleeping and dreaming' (Mączak, 1992, p.183; see also Białostocki, 1976, pp. 28–44). The source, however, may well be Italian, as is suggested by the tomb of Ascanio Sforza designed by Andrea Sansovino in Rome (see Figure 1.7).

It would be wrong to conclude from this brief excursion into the diffusion of the Corvinian Renaissance in central Europe that the process was a smooth one. Alongside the introduction of Renaissance fashions in art, architecture, literature and music, native Hungarian culture retained much of its traditional vitality. To some extent this

Figure 1.42 View of Sigismund Chapel, Wawel Cathedral, Cracow, 1517–33. Photo: Andrzej Jaroszewicz/David Williamson, London

was the product of political necessity. If Matthias Corvinus and his fellow Jagellonian rulers in Bohemia and Poland were to retain the support of their nobility (the element of elite society least receptive to the Renaissance in these lands), then it made sense for them to continue to patronise certain elements of the native culture. We have already seen how the Hungarian king adopted a dual persona in appropriating the iconic status of both Hercules and Attila. Numerous other examples of the 'dualistic' nature of culture at the Corvinian court might be cited. The Italian humanist Galeotto Marzio (*c.*1427–*c.*1490) recorded how after dinner Matthias liked to hear songs of love and warlike deeds against the Turks, sung in Hungarian and accompanied by the traditional instruments of harp and zither (Marzio, in Juhász, 1934, p.18). Not surprisingly, many of Matthias's subjects despised foreign ways and customs and equated the *all'antica* style with an alien and hostile culture. Consequently, the survival of Gothic art forms, equated by many with homely Hungarian traditions, continued into the sixteenth century and co-existed alongside the newer styles. This is particularly apparent, for example, in Hungarian panel painting and wooden religious statuary, a feature of late medieval German artistic culture which continued to flourish in centres such as Buda and Cracow.

Exercise

The difficulty of accommodating the new ideas and the vital role of the king in fostering them is neatly exemplified in an anecdote recorded by Galeotto Marzio (Galeottus Martius) in his collection of stories (many of which, it should be stressed, are almost certainly apocryphal).

Read the extract from Marzio's writings (Anthology, no. 35). What does this story suggest about the reception of the Renaissance at the court of Matthias Corvinus?

Discussion

The story suggests three important points. First, the widespread incomprehension felt by the aristocracy towards the book learning of a cleric. Secondly, the role that humanist-educated churchmen like Bishop Miklós Báthory (*c.*1440–1506) played in consolidating and extending Renaissance values in Hungary. And thirdly, the crucial importance of the king as protector and patron of the new learning and arts. In the first instance, the nobles in the council antechamber mock the bishop for reading instead of socializing, the former activity being viewed with particular distaste by the Hungarian aristocracy. Classical literary culture was clearly alien to their way of life. In the second case, Marzio uses the incident as an opportunity to extol the humanist virtues of his prodigy. (Marzio was partly responsible for the young cleric's education, though he also obtained instruction in Italy.) Note in particular how Marzio makes an explicit connection between Báthory's humanism and his subsequent patronage of Italian architects and builders in his diocese of Vác. His residence there is given the aura of a salon where intellectual debate and artistic appreciation are always encouraged. The extract also suggests how Báthory, like Federico da Montefeltro, Alberti and some of the British poets whom you will encounter in Chapter 4, appears to have possessed a heightened sensibility to natural beauty which he associated with classical literature. The third point of discussion focuses on the role of the king as patron and defender of classical learning. Not only does he praise Báthory for spending his spare time constructively, but he does so by recourse to his own knowledge of classical literature (the story of Cato), and so in the process affirms the merit of Renaissance learning. The king is the lynch-pin in the successful transference of the Italian Renaissance to Hungarian soil (though we should also remember the role performed by his wife, Beatrice of Aragon, in this process; see the Anthology, no. 34). ❖

Antonio Bonfini wrote of Matthias Corvinus that 'he strove to transform Pannonia[18] into a second Italy' (cited in Klaniczay, 1992, p.167). Much was achieved in a very brief period, though doubts remain as to the extent of the king's success. During Matthias's lifetime, and that of his successors Ladislav II (1490–1516) and Louis II (1516–26), Renaissance values were increasingly adopted by the clergy and nobility whose churches and palaces were transformed into visible monuments to cultural reform. In addition, whereas in the early stages the process of *renovatio* was dominated by Italian masters, by the early sixteenth century more and more Hungarian craftsmen, fully inducted into Renaissance styles and techniques, were displaying their talents across the country. This movement away from Italy was reinforced by political and cultural developments following the death of Matthias in 1490. In the early sixteenth century Hungary found itself increasingly drawn into the orbit of central European politics, a bond strengthened by the ties of family, marriage and diplomacy. At the same time, a 'cosmopolitan humanist central Europe' was beginning to emerge, an indication perhaps that this region, culturally speaking, could now stand on its own feet without the support of Italian scholars and artists. Increasingly, the dominant voice in central European humanism was no longer Italian, but rather northern European, reflecting the dominant influence of Erasmus (see Book 1, Chapter 3). The precociously 'modern' character of the Hungarian court was, however, short-lived. In 1526, Louis II's forces were defeated and the king killed at the disastrous battle of Mohács.

---

[18] Pannonia was the Graeco-Roman name for Hungary.

The victorious sultan, Suleiman the Magnificent (1520–66), captured Buda and ransacked Matthias's Renaissance palace, destroying in the process the celebrated Bibliotheca Corvina, which contained one of the largest and most impressive collections of Renaissance writings and manuscripts in early modern Europe. The kingdom was subsequently partitioned, not to be reunited for a further 150 years (Klaniczay, 1992, pp.169–70).

Bibliography

ALEXANDER, J.J.G. (1995) *The Painted Page: Italian Book Illumination*, Munich, Prestel.

ANGLO, S. (1990) 'Humanism and the court arts' in A. Goodman and A. MacKay (eds) *The Impact of Humanism on Western Europe*, London and New York, Longman.

ASCH, R.G. (1991) 'Introduction: court and household from the fifteenth to the seventeenth centuries' in R.G. Asch and A.M. Birke (eds) *Princes, Patronage, and the Nobility: The Court at the Beginning of the Modern Age c.1450–1650*, Oxford, Oxford University Press.

BAXANDALL, M. (1988) *Giotto and the Orators: Humanist Observers of Painting in Italy and the Discovery of Pictorial Composition 1350–1650*, Oxford, Clarendon.

BERTELLI, S. (1986) 'The courtly universe' in S. Bertelli, F. Cardini and E.G. Zorzi (eds) *Italian Renaissance Courts*, London, Sidgwick & Jackson.

BIAŁOSTOCKI, J. (1976) *The Art of the Renaissance in Eastern Europe: Hungary, Bohemia, Poland*, Oxford, Phaidon.

BOULTON, D' A.J.D. (1990) 'Insignia of power: the use of heraldic and paraheraldic devices by Italian princes, c.1300–1500' in C.M. Rosenberg (ed.) *Art and Politics in Late Medieval and Early Renaissance Italy 1200–1500*, Notre Dame and London, Notre Dame University Press.

BROWN, C.M. (1997) ' "Fruste et strache nel fabricare": Isabella d'Este's apartments in the Corte Vecchia of the ducal palace in Mantua' in C. Mozzarelli, R. Oresko and L. Ventura (eds) *La corte di Mantova nell'età di Andrea Mantegna, 1450–1550*, Mantua, Bulzoni.

BULL, G. (trans.) (1976) B. Castiglione: *The Book of the Courtier*, Harmondsworth, Penguin.

BULL, G. (trans.) (1999) N. Machiavelli: *The Prince*, intro. A. Grafton, Harmondsworth, Penguin.

BURCKHARDT, J. (1990) *The Civilization of the Renaissance in Italy*, trans. S.G.C. Middlemore, Harmondsworth, Penguin; first published 1858.

BURKE, P. (1998) *The European Renaissance: Centres and Peripheries*, Oxford, Blackwell.

CARDINI, F. (1986) 'The sacred circle of Mantua' in S. Bertelli, F. Cardini and E.G. Zorzi (eds) *Italian Renaissance Courts*, London, Sidgwick & Jackson.

CHAMBERS, D.S. (1970) *Patrons and Artists in the Italian Renaissance*, London, Macmillan.

CHAMBERS, D.S. and MARTINEAU, J. (eds) (1981) *Splendours of the Gonzaga*, London, Victoria and Albert Museum.

CHELES, L. (1986) *The Studiolo of Urbino: An Iconographic Investigation*, Wiesbaden, Ludwig Reichert.

CHRISTIANSEN, K. (1998) 'The view from Italy' in M.W. Ainsworth and K. Christiansen (eds) *From Van Eyck to Bruegel*, New York, Metropolitan Museum of Art and Harry N. Abrams.

COLE, A. (1995) *Art of the Italian Renaissance Courts*, London, Weidenfeld & Nicolson.

CSAPODI, C. and CSAPODI-GÁRDONYI, K. (1969) *Bibliotheca Corviniana: The Library of King Matthias Corvinus, King of Hungary*, Shannon, Irish University Press.

DE VERE, G. du C. (trans.) (1996) G. Vasari: *The Lives of the Most Excellent Painters, Sculptors, Architects*, 2 vols, London, David Campbell.

EISLER, W. (1987) 'Patronage and diplomacy: the north Italian residencies of the Emperor Charles V' in F.W. Kent, P. Simons and J.C. Eade (eds) *Patronage, Art and Society in Renaissance Italy*, Oxford, Clarendon.

ELAM, C. (1981) 'Mantegna at Mantua' in D.S. Chambers and J. Martineau (eds) *Splendours of the Gonzaga*, London, Victoria and Albert Museum.

ELIAS, N. (1980) *The Court Society*, Oxford, Oxford University Press.

ETTLINGER, L.D. (1972) 'Hercules Florentinus', *Mitteilungen des Kunsthistorischen Instituts in Florenz*, vol. 16, pp.119–42.

FENLON, I. (1981) 'The Gonzaga and music' in D.S. Chambers and J. Martineau (eds) *Splendours of the Gonzaga*, London, Victoria and Albert Museum.

FERINO PAGDEN, S. (1994) *Isabella d'Este, Fürstin und Mäzenantin der Renaissance*, Vienna, Kunsthistorisches Museum.

FEUER-TÓTH, R. (1981) *Architecture in Hungary*, trans. I. Feherdy, Budapest, Corvina.

FICINO, M. (1576) *Opera omnia*, 2 vols, Basle, Officina Henricpetrina.

GARZELLI, A. (1985) *La miniatura fiorentina*, 2 vols, Florence, Scandicci.

GEREVICH, L. (1971) *The Art of Buda and Pest in the Middle Ages*, Budapest, Akademiai Kiadó.

GILBERT, C.E. (ed./trans.) (1980) *Italian Art 1450–1500, Sources and Documents*, Englewood Cliffs, NJ, Prentice Hall.

GIORDANO, L. (ed.) (1995) *Ludovicus Dux*, Vigevano, Diakrona.

GOLDTHWAITE, R.A. (1993) *Wealth and the Demand for Art in Italy, 1300–1600*, Baltimore, Md. and London, Johns Hopkins University Press.

HEYDENREICH, L.H. (1996) *Architecture in Italy 1400–1500*, rev. P. Davies, New Haven, Conn. and London, Yale University Press.

HOLLINGSWORTH, M. (1994) *Patronage in Renaissance Italy: From 1400 to the Early Sixteenth Century*, London, John Murray.

HOPE, C. (1981) 'Artists, patrons and advisers in the Italian Renaissance' in G.F. Lytle and S. Orgel (eds) *Patronage in the Renaissance*, Princeton, NJ, Princeton University Press.

HOPE, C. and McGRATH, E. (1996) 'Artists and humanists' in J. Kraye (ed.) *The Cambridge Companion to Renaissance Humanism*, Cambridge, Cambridge University Press.

JUHÁSZ, L. (ed.) (1934) G. Marzio: *De egregie, sapienter, iocose dictis ac factis regis Mathiae*, Leipzig, B.G. Teubner.

KAUFMANN, T. da C. (1995) *Court, Cloister and City*, London, Weidenfeld & Nicolson.

KLANICZAY, T. (1992) 'Hungary' in R. Porter and M. Teich (eds) *The Renaissance in National Context*, Cambridge, Cambridge University Press.

KLANICZAY, T., TÖRÖK, G. and STANGLER, G. (eds) (1982) *Matthias Corvinus und die Renaissance in Ungarn*, Vienna, Amt der Niederösterreichischen Landesregierung.

LA ROCCA, G. (ed.) (1978) B. Castiglione: *Le lettere*, 2 vols, Verona, Mondadori.

LUBKIN, G. (1994) *A Renaissance Court: Milan under Galeazzo Maria Sforza*, Berkeley, Los Angeles and London, University of California Press.

MĄCZAK, A. (1992) 'Poland' in R. Porter and M. Teich (eds) *The Renaissance in National Context*, Cambridge, Cambridge University Press.

MAGNANI, R. (1910) *Relazioni privati tra la corte Sforzesca di Milano e casa Medici 1450–1500*, Milan, S. Giuseppe.

MAIER, I. (ed.) (1971) A. Poliziano: *Opera omnia*, 2 vols, Turin, Bottega d'Erasmo.

MALLETT, M. (1974) *Mercenaries and their Masters*, London, Sydney and Toronto, Bodley Head.

MANIATES, M.R. (1979) *Mannerism in Italian Music and Culture, 1530–1630*, Manchester, Manchester University Press.

MARTINES, L. (1979) *Power and Imagination: City-States in Renaissance Italy*, Harmondsworth, Allen Lane.

MASPES, A. (1890) 'Prammatica per ricevimento degli ambasciatori inviati alla corte di Galeazzo Maria Sforza, duca di Milano', *Archivio Storico Lombardico*, vol. 7, pp.146–51.

MÍKO, A. (1990) 'Divinus Hercules and Attila Secundus', *The New Hungarian Quarterly*, vol. 31, pp.90–6.

MITCHELL, S. (1994) 'The image of Hungary and of Hungarians in Italy, 1437–1526', unpublished PhD thesis, Warburg Institute, University of London.

NORRIS, A.S. (1990) 'The Sforza of Milan', *Schifanoia*, vol. 10, pp.19–22.

PAOLETTI, J.T. and RADKE, G.M. (1997) *Art in Renaissance Italy*, London, Laurence King.

PARAVICINI, W. (1991) 'The court of the dukes of Burgundy: a model for Europe?' in R.G. Asch and A.M. Birke (eds) *Princes, Patronage and Nobility: The Court at the Beginning of the Modern Age c.1450–1650*, Oxford, Oxford University Press.

PERNIS, M.G. and ADAMS, L.S. (1996) *Federico da Montefeltro and Sigismondo Malatesta: The Eagle and the Elephant*, New York, Peter Lang.

RODRÍGUEZ-SALGADO, M.J. (1997) 'Terracotta and iron: Mantuan politics (*c.*1450–*c.*1550)' in C. Mozzarelli, R. Oresko and L. Ventura (eds) *La corte di Mantova nell'età di Andrea Mantegna, 1450–1550*, Mantua, Bulzoni.

RÖLL, J. (1994) *Giovanni Dalmata*, Worms am Rhein, Wernersche Verlag.

ROTONDI, P. (1969) *The Ducal Palace at Urbino: Its Architecture and Decoration*, London, Alec Tiranti; first published 1950, Istituto Statale d'Arte per Il Libro, Urbino

RYKWERT, J., LEACH, N. and TAVERNOR, R. (eds) (1988), L.B. Alberti: *On the Art of Building in Ten Books*, Cambridge, Mass. and London, MIT.

SAN JUAN, R.M. (1991) 'The court lady's dilemma: Isabella d'Este and art collecting in the Renaissance', *Oxford Art Journal*, vol. 14, pp.67–78.

SCHAPIRO, M. (1994) *Theory and Philosophy of Art: Style, Artist and Society: Selected Papers*, New York, George Baziller.

SHEARMAN, J. (1967) *Mannerism*, Harmondsworth, Penguin.

SPALLANZANI, M. and BERTELÀ, G.G. (1992) *Libro d'inventario dei beni di Lorenzo il Magnifico*, Florence, Associazione 'Amici del Bargello'.

SPENCER, J.R. (ed./trans.) (1965) A. Averlino (Filarete): *Treatise on Architecture, Being the Treatise by Antonio di Piero Averlino Known as Filarete*, 2 vols, New Haven, Conn., Yale University Press.

SPENCER, J.R. (ed./trans.) (1966) L.B. Alberti: *On Painting*, New Haven, Conn., Yale University Press.

STARN, R. (1990) 'State as a work of art-again: a comment', *Schifanoia*, vol. 10, pp.11–14.

TREXLER, R.C. (1980) *Public Life in Renaissance Florence*, London, Academic Press.

VERHEYEN, E. (1971) *The Paintings in the Studiolo of Isabella d'Este at Mantua*, New York, New York University Press.

VERHEYEN, E. (1977) *The Palazzo del Te in Mantua: Images of Love and Politics*, Baltimore, Md. and London, Johns Hopkins University Press.

WALSH, R. (1976) 'The coming of humanism to the Low Countries: some Italian influences at the court of Charles the Bold', *Humanistica Lovaniensia*, vol. 25, pp.146–97.

WARNKE, M. (1993) *The Court Artist: On the Ancestry of the Modern Artist*, trans. D. McLintock, Cambridge, Cambridge University Press.

WOODS-MARSDEN, J. (1989) 'How quattrocento princes used art: Sigismondo Pandolfo Malatesta of Rimini and *cose militari*', *Renaissance Studies*, vol. 3, pp.387–414.

WOODS-MARSDEN, J. (1990) 'The Gonzaga of Mantua', *Schifanoia*, vol. 10, pp.27–30.

Anthology and Reader sources

Leonardo da Vinci, extracts from his notebooks: *Leonardo on Painting*, ed. and trans. M. Kemp and M. Walker, New Haven, Conn. and London, Yale University Press, 1989, pp.13–15, 32–4, 37–8, 49–55, 57, 59–61, 63–4, 87, 24, 26, 119–20, 122, 205 (Anthology, no. 31).

Earl Rosenthal, The diffusion of the Italian Renaissance style in western European art: *Sixteenth Century Journal*, vol. 9, no. 4, pp.33–45 (Reader, no. 13).

Michael Baxandall, *Painting and Experience in Fifteenth-century Italy*: Oxford, Oxford University Press, 1988, 2nd edn, pp.36–46 (Reader, no. 10).

Meyer Schapiro, Style: *Theory and Philosophy of Art: Style, Artist and Society: Selected Papers*, New York, George Baziller, 1994, pp.518 (Reader, no. 12).

Vespasiano da Bisticci, Life of Federigo da Montefeltro: *The Vespasiano Memoirs: Lives of Illustrious Men of the Fifteenth Century*, ed. and trans. W.G. and E. Waters, London, George Routledge & Sons, 1926, pp.99–102, 104–11, 113–14 (Anthology, no. 32).

Pliny the Younger, extracts from *Letters and Panegyricus in Two Volumes: Letters, Books 1–7*, ed. B. Radice, Cambridge, Mass. and London, Harvard University Press, 1975, Book 1, pp. 133, 135, 137, 139, 141, 143; English text only (Anthology, no. 42).

Federico da Montefeltro, Letter patent to Luciano Laurana: *The Ducal Palace of Urbino: Its Architecture and Decoration*, P. Rotondi, London, Alec Tiranti, 1969, pp.11–12, trans. for this edn by Dorigen Caldwell (Anthology, no. 33).

Luigi Gonzaga da Borgoforte, A report on the festivities at the Palazzo Te, Mantua, in honour of Charles V: *Cronaca del soggiorno di Carlo V in Italia dal 26 Luglio al 25 Aprile 1530*, ed. G. Romano, Milan, Ulrico Hoepli, 1892, pp.260–8, trans. for this edn by Dorigen Caldwell (Anthology, no. 36).

C.A. Macartney, The foreign kings of Hungary: *Hungary: A Short History*, Edinburgh, Edinburgh University Press, 1962, pp.38–63 (Reader, no. 14).

Antonio de Bonfini, Ten books on Hungarian matters: R. Feuer-Tóth, *Art and Humanism in Hungary in the Age of Matthias Corvinus*, trans. G. Jakobi, Budapest, Academic Press, 1990, pp.123–9, trans. for this edn by Caryll Green (Anthology, no. 34).

Galeottus Martius Narniensis, Concerning the famous, wise and amusing words and actions of King Matthias Corvinus: *De egregie, sapiente, iocose dictis ac factis regis Mathiae ad ducem Iohannem eius filium liber*, ed. L. Juhász, Leipzig, Teubner, 1934, pp.34–5, trans. for this edn by Robert Goulding (Anthology, no. 35).

CHAPTER TWO

Artists at the Sforza court

BY GEORGIA CLARKE, DAVID MATEER, PETER ELMER AND NICK WEBB

Objectives

The objectives of this chapter are that you should:

- compare and contrast the role of patronage in the promotion of different art forms at the court of the Sforza;
- examine the relationship between patron and artist at the Sforza court through the case studies of three leading artists: the architect Filarete; the musician and composer Josquin Desprez; and the multi-talented figure of Leonardo da Vinci.

Introduction

This chapter focuses on three artists who were employed at the court of the Sforza in Milan in the second half of the fifteenth century: the architect-sculptor Antonio Averlino (known as Filarete); the musician and composer Josquin Desprez; and the polymath Leonardo da Vinci. While it is important to remember that these artists did not work exclusively for the Sforza, we shall limit discussion here to the environment of the Sforza court, which we have previously encountered in Chapter 1 as a 'typical' north Italian princely court. In this chapter we are particularly concerned to shed further light on the relationship between patron, client and the various art forms which thrived within the context of the Renaissance court. This will involve further discussion of the wider political significance of cultural production in the late fifteenth century. We shall also explore in more detail the debate – introduced in Chapter 1 – surrounding the extent to which the court actively fostered or discouraged the development of artistic innovation and independence in this period.

During the course of the fifteenth century, Milan, first under the Visconti and then under the Sforza, achieved a growing reputation in Europe as a centre for cultural and artistic creativity. It reached its zenith during the rule of Ludovico Sforza (il Moro), who effectively held power from 1479 to 1500, first as regent and then, from 1494, as duke. Burckhardt, whose assessment of Ludovico was greatly coloured by his promotion and encouragement of 'men of genius' like Leonardo, was clearly of the opinion that the Milanese court was a conducive environment for the cultivation of artistic innovation (1990, p.45). The evidence, however, for such an assertion is ambiguous to say the least. Leonardo, for example, does appear to have escaped the fate of many of his artistic peers in the local guild of St Luke in Florence who were contracted on piecemeal commissions. He certainly seems to have been granted more of a free hand by his Sforza patrons to explore his own interests and to develop his own artistic techniques. However, even he did not enjoy the status of an official court painter in the same way as Mantegna or Giulio Romano at Mantua (see Chapter 1; Welch, 1995, pp.241–68). The case of Filarete is equally ambiguous in this respect. Despite the apparent success of his learned treatise on classical architecture in introducing the ruling family of Milan (and those elsewhere) to the revival of the *all'antica* style, Filarete's own career and the many buildings he planned and built for the Sforza pay testament to the continuing obstacles which artists faced in the Renaissance in attempting to raise the profile and status of their chosen profession. Even when men like Leonardo, Filarete and Josquin Desprez earned a European-wide reputation in their given area, it is not always clear that they acquired at the same time the opportunity to act independently of the wishes of their various patrons. Though it would be wrong to exaggerate the extent to which artistic creativity was stifled by the demands of courtly patrons, we shall need to be alert to this possibility and to pay close attention to the various ways in which the reception of cultural innovation was shaped by factors other than the purely aesthetic.

Filarete and his treatise on architecture

BY GEORGIA CLARKE

The first fifteenth-century treatise on architecture in Italian was written around 1460–4 at the court of Milan by the Florentine artist Antonio Averlino, better known by his preferred name, Filarete (*c.*1400–69). The treatise was originally dedicated to his patron, Duke Francesco Sforza, and was written not only to be read but also to be read out aloud. While it was a discourse intended for noble ears, its use of the vernacular, rather than Latin, meant that its message could reach a wider audience. The treatise opens by setting the scene at a nobleman's meal during which a discussion on architecture arises. Filarete steps forward, as an architect, to set out his ideas on the topic, and cites as his precedents the Roman theorist Vitruvius and Leon Battista Alberti, thereby placing himself firmly in a classical and humanist tradition.

Just as important as the written or spoken word are the illustrations in the text and the act of drawing described in the narrative, which are integral to the nature of the treatise and to the reader's or listener's ability to understand architecture. Filarete introduces his work as one of instruction; he gives it a literary framework of monologues, dialogues, digressions and imaginary excursions and tours around buildings that make up the fictional city of Sforzinda and a port, Plousiapolis (Greek for a 'rich city'). (The name Sforzinda was a piece of courtly flattery comparable to Pius II's contemporary renaming of his home town of Corsignano, as Pienza, after himself.) Neither of these cities was actually built, but a hospital complex described in the treatise, the Ospedale Maggiore, was designed and built by Filarete for the Sforza in Milan (see below, p.106).

Filarete was a noted sculptor. His remarkable bronze doors for St Peter's in Rome (c.1433–45) drew on a knowledge of ancient sculpture and coins to create a rich ensemble telling a Christian story. After he left Rome, in 1448, Filarete seems to have spent some time in Venice before he arrived in Milan in about 1451 to work for the Sforza. Here his work was mostly architectural. Projects included a commission for a new cathedral in Bergamo as well as involvement in the design and construction of a number of major buildings in Milan, most importantly the Ospedale Maggiore.

Filarete did not share the taste in Milan for Gothic architecture, although he did seem to appreciate colour and ornament. He also found it hard to comply with a way of working where multiple masters were appointed to construct a building, preferring instead that clear authority should be given to a single, respected architect. His decision to present his ideas in the form of a long, illustrated treatise may have sprung in part from the difficulties he experienced with local architects, as well as from a desire to be recognized in his profession.

In his treatise Filarete represented himself as a courtier informing and entertaining the lord and his family – thinly disguised versions of the Sforza. This was an attempt to illustrate the argument that a knowledge of architecture should be an element of a noble education. Building itself was to be seen as a creative act involving both patron and architect. It was similar to human conception and birth, in which the patron (father) and architect (mother) produced the building (child) and together ensured that it was 'good and beautiful' (Filarete, in Spencer, 1965, Book 2, 7v–8r). But this was not merely an act of duty, rather:

> Building is nothing more than a voluptuous pleasure, like that of a man in love. Anyone who has experienced it knows that there is so much pleasure and desire in building that however much a man does, he wants to do more ... There is no half way for him: he loves it. He makes it useful and honourable for only two ends. The first for utility and the second for fame, so that they will say it was he [the patron] who made such a beautiful building rise.
>
> (Spencer, 1965, Book 2, 8r)

Exercise

Read the passage below from Filarete's treatise and then consider these issues:

1 Filarete's definition of the relationship between architect and patron;

2 the special role he allows for the architect in this process;

3 the language used in the extract and its wider significance for our understanding of social relations in the Renaissance.

> The building is conceived in this manner. Since no one can conceive by himself without a woman, by another simile, the building cannot be conceived by one man alone. As it cannot be done without a woman, so he who wished to build needs an architect. He conceives it with him and then the architect carries it. When the architect has given birth, he becomes the mother of the building. Before the architect gives birth, he should dream about his conception, think about it, and turn it over in his mind in many ways for seven to nine months, just as a woman carries her child in her body for seven to nine months. He should also make various drawings of this conception that he has made with the patron, according to his own desires. As the woman can do nothing without the man, so the architect is the mother to carry out this conception. When he has pondered and considered and thought in many ways, he then ought to choose what seems most suitable and most beautiful to him according to the terms of the patron. When the birth is accomplished, that is when he has made, in wood, a small relief design of its final form, measured and proportioned to the finished building, then he shows it to the father.
>
> As I have compared the architect to the mother, so he also needs to be the nurse. He is thus both nurse and mother. As the mother is full of love for her son, so he will rear it with love and diligence, cause it to grow, and bring it to completion if it is possible; if it is not he will leave it ordered in such a way that it will not perish because of its incompleteness. A good mother loves her son and with the aid and

knowledge of the father strives to make him good and beautiful, and with a good master to make him valiant and praiseworthy. So the good architect should strive to make his building good and beautiful. As the mother makes every effort to find good masters for her son, so the architect ought to find good masters, masons and all the others needed for the work, if the patron does not prevent him. Without the goodwill of the patron he would be like the woman who can do nothing against the will of her husband; the architect is exactly the same ...

Since [a building] is created through the good offices of the architect, he ought to be loved and honoured as much as is fitting. For this reason the architect ought to exert himself to make it as excellent as he can.

(Spencer, 1965, Book 2, 7v–8r)

Discussion

1 The relationship is clearly one of power, with the patron the guiding force, since the architect is dependent on the patron to pay for a building. But the architect has a considerable part to play, which includes making choices about the design and about what should be presented to the patron – so there is a two-way dialogue. The architect needs to be sensitive to the patron's wishes, but it is the architect's skill and training that determine their interpretation. The presentation of the design to the patron is not the end of the story, for the architect needs to be involved in the process after this, and to ensure that skilled workmen perform their tasks satisfactorily. The architect also needs to be a diplomat, since he must keep the patron 'on side' and not only convince him to build in the way that the architect judges to be right but make sure that he remains interested in the project so that the building is completed. The comment about incompleteness in the extract above acknowledges that this was sometimes a problem; to avoid it happening, the architect must seek to ensure that a building reaches such a state that, even if it does not achieve its intended extent, it can stand on its own and will not become a ruin or be pulled down or altered beyond recognition.

2 It is clear that Filarete does not see the architect merely as the direct 'translator' of the patron's wishes but as someone who can have a significant effect on the final result. The architect is presented by Filarete as needing skill in design, imagination and architectural knowledge, together with the ability to negotiate, persuade and adapt his ideas to those of the individual paying for the building. At the same time the architect and patron are seen as enjoying a mutually pleasurable and satisfying relationship in

101

which the architect should be recognized as a creative figure and not just as an overseer and artisan.

3   The terms in which Filarete characterizes the relationship between architect and patron also reveal something about male–female relations in the Renaissance. They show mutual needs between husband and wife, as well as the importance of mothers both in the nurturing of the unborn child and then, after the child's birth, in its education and guidance. ❖

The architect's role was to make sure that the object of the patron's desire – the building – was designed and completed to the highest possible standards. Like Alberti, Filarete called for the architect to be given due status and recognition in return. This was rare in the fifteenth century. In Milan Filarete himself constantly sought to be so rewarded, but was thwarted and denied the kind of easy access to the duke and his family that the treatise suggests as appropriate. Thus his treatise, with its emphasis on the professionalism of the architect and good design, dedicated first to Francesco Sforza and then to Piero de' Medici (*c.*1465), represented the aspirations of a courtier in its expectation of career advancement. The copy dedicated to Piero, who was by then head of the Medici family, included an additional book describing Medicean buildings which was perhaps produced, as Filarete was leaving Milan in 1465, in the hope of securing patronage from the ruling family of his native Florence.

In 1488 the Florentine humanist Francesco Bandini took a copy of Filarete's treatise to the court of Matthias Corvinus in Buda, where it was immediately translated into Latin by another Florentine – Antonio Bonfini. This made it accessible to a wider, non-Italian audience. In the process, it could be also be argued, the work acquired some of the prestige and authority that attached to the Latin treatises of Vitruvius and Alberti. The continued esteem in which Filarete's treatise was held by sophisticated patrons of the arts who were aware of current trends in architecture and had close connections to Florence is demonstrated by its presence in 1492 in the library of King Ferrante II in Naples. All of these notable and aristocratic patrons owned not just Filarete's treatise but also copies of Vitruvius, which was to be found in a considerable number of Italian and European libraries. Vasari's mid sixteenth-century dismissal of Filarete's treatise as 'mostly ridiculous' was evidently not a view shared by them. The rarity and high status of copies of Filarete – all extensively illustrated – were comparable to Alberti's *De re aedificatoria* (*On Architecture*) (Rykwert et al., 1988) before the latter was printed in 1485.

One of Filarete's main aims in his treatise was to present and explain the new *all'antica* architecture – that is, buildings designed in a manner that drew on and recalled the designs and ornaments of antiquity. In contrast to the current taste for the Gothic style, which he thought was 'barbaric' (Spencer, 1965, Book 8, 58r), Filarete urged modern designers to imitate ancient forms. As a Florentine, it is not surprising that he chose above all to praise the Florentine architect Brunelleschi, who, he said, had 'revived in our city of Florence the antique way of building', noting that 'if it were not the most beautiful and useful [style], it would not be used in Florence' (Spencer, 1965, Book 8, 58r). By way of illustration, he mentioned the newly built Palazzo Rucellai in Florence, as well as the Gonzaga residence at Revere. He also praised Marquis Lodovico Gonzaga, who, he claimed, would not have adopted this style if it were not praiseworthy. As has been seen in Chapter 1, the Gonzaga were at this time employing artists and architects, such as Mantegna and Alberti, who were greatly interested in propagating the principles of classical art and architecture.

This sense of the revival of elegance and its reintroduction into architecture was compared by Filarete to the 'ornate' Italian prose in common use since the 1420s or 30s, which brought it closer to the language of Cicero and Virgil. In Filarete's view it was essential to understand the theories which informed ancient architecture and not merely to try to copy classical forms. Through proper knowledge the errors of the more recent past could be avoided. In adopting such an approach Filarete was clearly dependent on humanist ideas and interests in the formulation of his arguments. Either by himself or with the help of humanist scholars at the Milanese court, Filarete read Vitruvius and other classical authors such as Cicero, as well as Alberti's *De re aedificatoria*.

Some scholars have argued that a number of his ideas, and perhaps the use of the dialogue to deliver them, can be traced back to Greek texts, especially the works of Plato. Since these were not available in translation at this time it seems most likely that Filarete was informed of them by his friend Francesco da Tolentino (1398–1481), called Filelfo, a noted scholar of Greek at the Sforza court. The support of such scholarship by the Sforza led some to applaud Milan as a 'new Athens'. Filelfo may also have been responsible for Filarete's Greek pseudonym, which means 'lover of virtue'. Whatever his sources, Filarete made use of an array of ancient and modern texts on architecture and other subjects to help develop his own theories about the **architectural orders** and connections between architecture and society.

The architectural orders and their use were at the core of classical architecture. Filarete limited himself to the ancient Greek orders –

Doric, **Ionic** and **Corinthian**, an erudite choice stemming from his attachment to Greek literary and philosophical models. In addition, they were also the orders which were clearly defined and discussed by Vitruvius. But to try to identify and understand the orders through texts and the remains of classical buildings was a difficult task for any architect in the fifteenth century. While Filarete understood from Vitruvius that proportion was a key element in distinguishing one order from another, unlike Alberti he did not fully recognize that each order had a distinct form of capital. Filarete also recast Vitruvius's account of the anthropomorphic origins of the ancient Greek orders in a Christian light. (Doric based its proportions on those of the nude male body and lack of decorative ornament, Ionic on the figure and adornments of a woman, and Corinthian on a young girl.) Since Adam was the first man, fashioned in the likeness of God, Filarete thought that his body was the likely model for the first proportioned column. Indeed, he argued that all measurements were based on the human body and thus had an aspect of the divine in them.

Rather than following Vitruvius precisely, Filarete placed Ionic lower than the other two orders instead of treating it as an intermediate form. He stated that all columns were based on male proportions, but that they were differentiated by size – large, medium and small – and by degree of decoration (see Figure 2.1). Accordingly, Doric, which in its ancient form was severe and rugged, in his view was the tallest and also the most ornate. He went to great lengths to expound the details of the proportioning of every element of columns and capitals, adjusting and altering Vitruvius's account to suit his own purposes.

The column, though, was only part of a building and could not stand alone, and Filarete made an analogy between it and a lord who needs supporters. He further argued that the more noble the lord, the more varied and numerous were the supporters he needed, just as the greatest buildings were composed of many components and greatly ornamented. A hierarchy of types of column and, more importantly, of building styles was proposed – Doric, Corinthian and Ionic – and these in turn corresponded to a social hierarchy and order. The smallest and least ornate column (Ionic) he equated with the lowest class, suited to bearing weight, while the highest order (Doric) supported and decorated a building but did not bear so great a physical load as the others.

This proportional theory was also applied to the size and ornament of houses according to rank, starting with the duke's palace, with the bishop's palace only slightly smaller – thus making an equivalence between secular and ecclesiastical authority – and moving down the

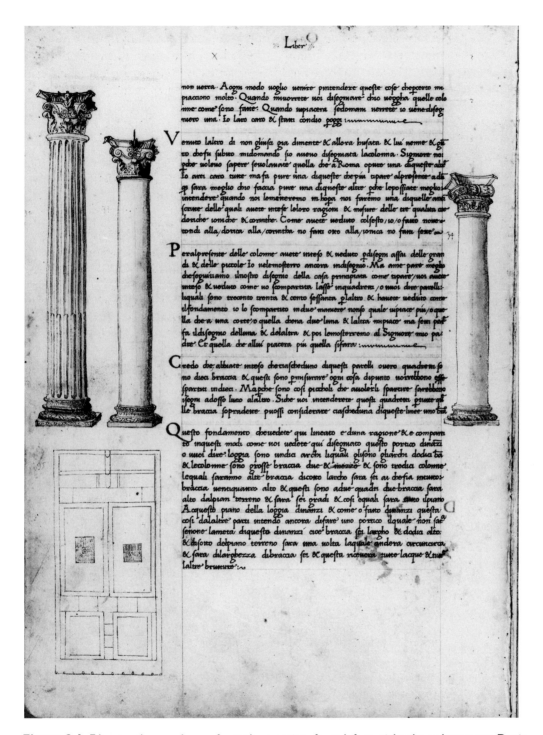

Figure 2.1 Filarete, three columns from the treatise; from left to right the columns are Doric, Corinthian and Ionic. Biblioteca Nazionale, Florence, MS Magliabechianus XVII,30=II.I.140, 57v. Photo: MicroFoto srl

social scale to the houses of nobles or gentlemen, merchants, artisans and the poor:

> There are many qualities in buildings, just as there are among men ... some men are more dignified than others; buildings are the same, according to their use. As men should be dressed and adorned according to their dignity, so ought buildings.

> (Spencer, 1965, Book 7, 48v)

In this, Filarete was following the lead of Vitruvius and Alberti, but the way in which he sought to define and distinguish status through architecture is an important reminder for us of the nature of fifteenth-century society, especially in the context of a court, where, as Filarete noted, even the minutiae of dress were observed and commented on as indicators of position and power.

The Ospedale Maggiore, Milan

High rank and status did not just carry privileges; they also entailed duties. One of these duties, which coincided with the Catholic doctrine of good works, was provision for the poor and needy through charitable foundations. When Francesco Sforza took power in Milan in 1450 a plan was already in place to co-ordinate the administration of Milan's multifarious collection of *ospedali* (hospitals). These, it should be stressed, were not like modern hospitals but were usually ad hoc small-scale establishments organized by lay confraternities which carried out one or more of a number of functions ranging from orphanage to alms house, pilgrims' hostel, soup kitchen and short-stay hospital.

In 1451 the duke decided to continue this project. The intention was to construct a large building which would provide a municipal administrative centre as well as medical wards for sick men and women, lodging for illegitimate foundlings and a place for the giving out of alms. Such a building was intended as a proud statement of Sforza godliness and care for their subjects. In public the enterprise was often presented as a joint effort with the civilian government of the city. One inscription that celebrated the Ospedale Maggiore's foundation, for example, stated that Francesco Sforza and his wife Bianca Maria Visconti were joint patrons with the Milanese people. The duke and duchess were not directly involved in the organization of the project, which was in the hands of a committee of important Milanese citizens, but many of these individuals were intimately connected to the court, and the Sforza retained ultimate control. Cosimo de' Medici in Florence was consulted and promised to send Francesco an 'engineer' (in the fifteenth century the term usually denoted a structural engineer and architect) to help with the design. It has been suggested that this might have been Filarete. However, the foundation and completion of the Ospedale Maggiore was a long, drawn-out procedure, with construction only beginning in 1456.

The importance of the project to the duke is clear from a letter he wrote to his ambassador at the papal court in Rome in 1460 in which he declared that he wanted the hospital finished 'because our people have great expectations and desires to see such a work and also because it will bring great glory to our whole city and to us' (Welch, 1995, p.121). To this end the duke had sought papal permission to take over various religious foundations and obtain ecclesiastical reserves to fund the construction. This was finally granted in 1459, although building work had already begun in 1456 with the donation of land and money by the duke and duchess and with papal approval.

In order that the Ospedale Maggiore should be the most up-to-date and impressive structure possible, in June 1456 Francesco Sforza sent Filarete, 'engineer', and Giovanni di Sant'Ambrogio, 'master builder', to Florence to see and draw a hospital there. This was probably the famous S. Maria Nuova, in which the wards and church formed the sides of a rectangular colonnaded courtyard. Giovanni de' Medici, Cosimo's son, also wrote to Francesco to say that he would send him other plans. While S. Maria Nuova and the equally admired hospital of S. Maria della Scala in Siena may have partly inspired the long form of the Ospedale Maggiore's wards, neither would seem to have been the source for the idea of combining four wards to form a Greek cross, as at Filarete's Ospedale Maggiore. However, two very recently constructed hospitals – one in Pavia (1449–55) in the duchy of Milan to which Francesco Sforza had himself contributed land, and the other in Mantua, begun in 1450 – did have such a plan. The 'beautiful and useful' Milan hospital was to go further than these, for it was to be composed of two sets of Greek cross wards, and its fame ensured that it became a model for others: Bramante, for example, made a plan of it in 1484 for the Venetian republic (Spencer, 1965, Book 2, 79r). Writing in the mid sixteenth century, Vasari said of the Ospedale Maggiore, 'this place is so well made and organised, that I do not believe that there is another like it in all of Europe' (Vasari, in de Vere, 1996, 'Life of Antonio Filarete').

One of the ways in which Filarete introduced clarity and harmony into the construction of the Ospedale Maggiore was through the use of simple dimensions and proportions in its planning, and in the relationship of the various parts of the building to the whole (see Figure 2.2, overleaf). As set out in the treatise, the whole site was divided into three parts: a central rectangular courtyard flanked by

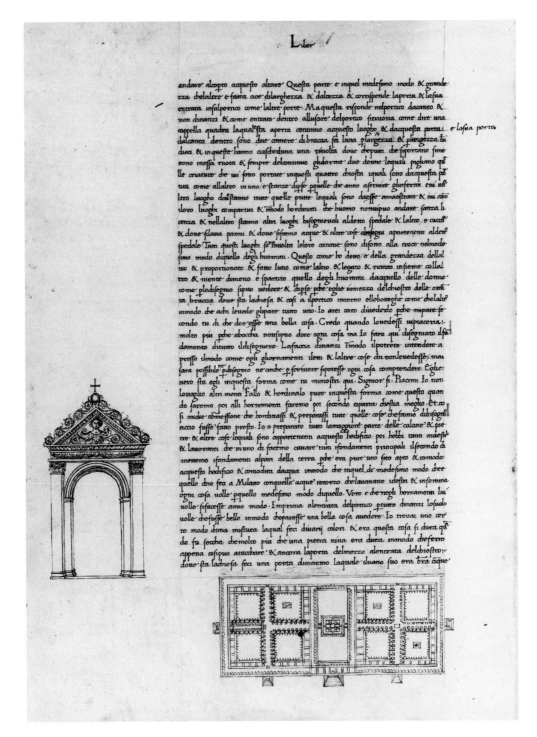

Figure 2.2 Filarete, Ospedale Maggiore from the treatise – plan and elevation together, Biblioteca Nazionale, Florence, MS Magliabechianus XVII,30=II.I.140, 82v (above) and 83v (opposite). Photo: MicroFoto srl

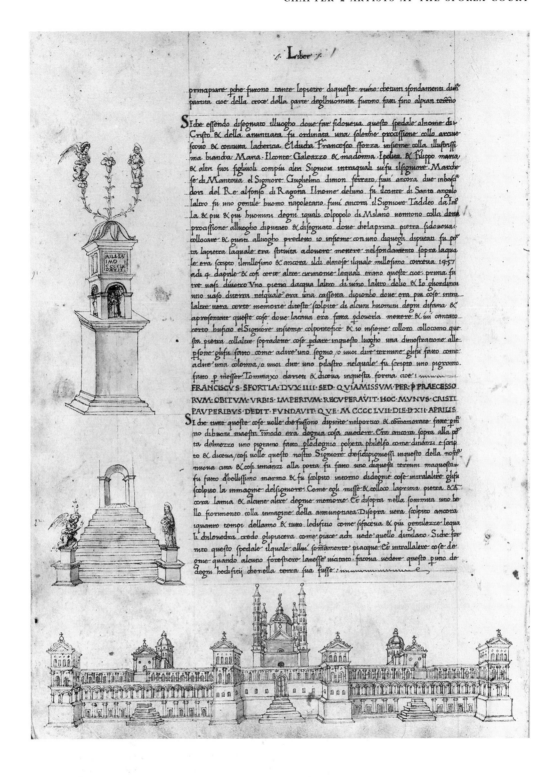

·/· Liber ·/·

ormapiare pche furono tante lepietre diqueste rume chetum isondamenti dum
partita aoe della croce della parte deglihuomin furono fam fino alpian tereno

Siche essendo disegnato illuogho doue far sidoueua questo spedale alnome di
Cristo & della annuntiara fu ordinata una solenne procassione collo arcaue-
scouo & conuira laclerica. Elducha Francesco sforza insieme colla illustrissi-
ma bionda Maria Eleonte Galeazzo & madonna Ipolita & Fileppo maria
& altri suoi figliuoli compiu altri Signori intraquali uisu ilsignore Marche-
se di Mantoua el Signore Guglielmo dimon ferrato suui ancora due imbasca-
dori del Re alfonso di Ragona Ilnome deluno fu ilconte di Santa angelo
laltro fu uno gentile huomo napoletano. fuui ancora el Signore Taddeo da Im-
la & piu & piu huomini degni iquali colpopolo di Milano uennono colla detta
procassione alluogho dipinto & disegnato doue chelaprima pietra sidoueua
collocare & giunti alluogho predetto io insieme conuno diquegli diputati fu po-
sta lapietra laquale era istituita adouere menere nelfondamento sopra laquale era scripto umillesimo & ancora ildi elmese ilquale millesimo correua 1457
adi 4 daprile & cosi certe altre cirimonie lequali erano queste cioe prima fu-
tre uasi diuerso Uno piena dacqua laltro di uino laltro dolio & lo ghordinai
uno uaso diterra nelquale era una cassetta dipinto doue era piu cose intra
laltre uera certe memorie diresto scolpite di alcuni huomini degni disama &
apresentare queste cose doue lacrima era fatta pdouerla menere & in contato
certo busiao el Signore insieme colpontefice & io insieme collo collocamo que-
sta pietra collaltre sopradette cose pdare inquesto luogho una dimostratione alle-
psone ghsu fatto come adiue uno segno io uui dire uno termine ghsu fatto come
adiue una colonna o uui due uno pilastro nelquale fu scripto uno pigramo
fatto p messer Tommaxo dariori & diceua inquesta forma cioe: mmmm
FRANCISCVS · SFORTIA · DVX · IIII · SED · Q VIAMISSVM · PER · P PRAECESSO
RVM · OBITVM · VRBIS · IMPERIVM · RECVPERAVIT · HOC · MVNVS · CRISTI
PAVPERIBVS · DEDIT · FVNDAVIT · Q VE · M · CCCC LVII · DIE · D · XII · APRILIS
Siche tutte queste cose uolle chefussono dipinte nelportico & comemorate fame pri-
mo dibuoni maestri imodo era degnia cosa auedere. Era ancora sopra alla po-
ta dclmezzo uno pigramo fatto plodegnio poheta philelfo come dinanzi esari-
to & diceua/cosi uolle questo nostro Signore chesidipignessi inquesto della nostra
nuoua cita & cosi imanzi alla porta fu fatto uno termini maquesto
fu fatto dbellissimo marmo & fu scolpito intorno didegnie cose intralaltre ghsu
scolpito la immagine delsignore Come egli messe & colloco laprima pietra &
cora lamia & alcune altre degnie memorie. Et disopra nella sommita uno bo-
llo fiorimento colla immagine della annuntiata Disopra uera scolpito ancora
iguanto tempi dellanno & tutto lodisicio come sifaceua & piu gentilezze lequali dilonedra credo glipiacera come piace adni uede quello dumilano Siche for-
mto questo spedale ilquale allui somamente piacque Et intralaltre cose dome quando alcuno forestiero lanesse uisitato facia uedere questo pimo de
degni hodisicii chenella terra sua fusse : mmmmmmm

two squares. These two squares were each subdivided by four arms of a cross – the wards of the hospital. Much of this was translated into the built structure. Filarete thus demonstrated how concerns about proportion that characterized his discussion of the architectural orders were not just theoretical but could have practical and rational applications that created functional as well as graceful buildings. All of the courtyards had porticoes around them on two storeys, thus allowing access to rooms at both ground and first floor level. The left-hand block of wards was for women and the right-hand for men, but only the latter was built in the fifteenth century, so the ideal plan and its neat division of the sexes was not instituted. In the central rectangle it was intended to build a church, and under small domes in the centre of the Greek crosses making up the wards there were also altars, which would have been visible to all those lying in the beds. Spiritual healing and succour was as important a component of the Ospedale as any physical treatment.

Practicality was an essential component of the design. Porticoes meant that all parts of the Ospedale – wards, dispensaries, lodgings for the genteel poor, even the planned church – could be reached under cover. The Ospedale complex was to be a self-sufficient organism with a corn-mill, bakeries, butchers, barbers, laundry, cemetery, etc. The Ospedale's site, next to one of Milan's outlying canals, was a bonus, since supplies could be easily transported and delivered. The site also aided another of the most important aspects of the Ospedale, its sanitary arrangements, to which Filarete devoted much attention. Their design had medieval monastic precedents but they were probably among the most advanced in Europe in the fifteenth century. Latrines were placed between every two beds in the wards, and Filarete devised an ingenious system to ensure that running water fed by the canal and rainwater kept an underground system of sewers flushed and clean. The latrines were also vented to the outside at roof level to make sure that no bad smells lingered. With this attention to cleanliness the Ospedale can perhaps be seen as one of the first 'modern' hospitals. However, although much of this system was built, it did not all work as well as Filarete's description in the treatise suggests it might.

Problems created by rainwater damage from the vents built within the walls may have been one of the causes of Filarete's falling out with the Ospedale's committee, or deputies, and the grounds for criticism by rival Lombard architects and engineers. From the beginning the deputies would have preferred a tried and trusted (Lombard) building master and engineer to have been in control. However, the duke had given Filarete the post, and he supervised work from 1456 or 1457 until he resigned in 1465 when he left Milan. Originally he was given a monthly salary of twelve ducats – commensurate with the status of architect and sole author – but this was considered excessive by the Ospedale's deputies and in 1459 they forced a reduction to eight ducats, which was much closer to Milanese practice for the lesser position of building supervisor. In 1462, as difficulties were encountered in the construction, other engineers and architects were called in for consultation. By this date, too, an additional local architect – Guiniforte Solari – was employed at the Ospedale.

Filarete's plan and overall design, as shown in the treatise, were not completed exactly as he had intended. The parts of the Ospedale that were built in the fifteenth century show how Filarete's Florentine ideas survived, or were mediated or rejected in the context of Sforza Milan. In the case of the external arcade, for example, the lower part is by Filarete, and the upper storey is the work of Solari (see Figure 2.3). In the spandrels of the arches are projecting sculpted busts, and smaller versions set within classical laurel wreaths were placed in a frieze above. These busts and heads had connections to ancient designs and

Figure 2.3 Filarete, Ospedale Maggiore, exterior. (Note that the filling-in of the portico is a later alteration.) Photo: Alinari

to Filarete's schemes elsewhere. The upper storey, however, has pointed Gothic windows (to which Filarete was deeply averse) and a decorative brickwork cornice that derives from medieval Lombard traditions. The pilasters and round-headed openings that Filarete depicted in the treatise are not to be found. The decision must have been in the hands of the Milanese deputies, and consequently Filarete's more classical ideas were only partially fulfilled.

The plan of the Ospedale Maggiore shows an underlying basis in symmetry as well as in geometry, which is also reflected in the function of the Ospedale as a whole. The symmetrical division matches the intended division between male and female sets of wards. Similarly the Greek cross plan of the wards, with their central altars and domes, is a larger version of the Greek cross plan of the central church with its dome, just as the four corner towers on the church can be paralleled with the four corner towers on each of the ward complexes. (See Figure 2.2, fol. 83v, right-hand page.)

Filarete revealed his mathematical ability and skill in setting out the building within disciplined parameters. An interest in proportion was part of his Tuscan background, and can be seen in the work of other contemporary architects and theorists. It was evident, for example, in Brunelleschi's buildings, while Alberti discussed and used proportions as a key element in planning and constructing buildings.

The design was carefully organized to ensure the use of whole numbers and simple proportional relationships. This reflects the influence of classical texts such as those of Vitruvius and the Greek mathematician Pythagoras, as well as Alberti's *De re aedificatoria*, where numbers are set in harmonious relationships with each other. There may also be an argument for suggesting that a more universal set of harmonious relationships was implied here, the duke's buildings reflecting the harmonious nature of the Milanese state under his rule.

The city of Sforzinda

In his treatise Filarete portrayed both the Ospedale and the duke's involvement in it as perfect in every way. Together with many other buildings, it was presented as part of the ideal city of Sforzinda (see Figure 2.4). This was one of the first attempts in the Renaissance to describe in detail the various parts and general organization of a city. In many ways Filarete was merely presenting in codified form what were long-standing practices in the organization of city space. But the vernacular and theoretical context in which he placed his discussion, along with his use of illustrations, made his formulation accessible to contemporaries such as Leonardo, and the architect and treatise writer Francesco di Giorgio.

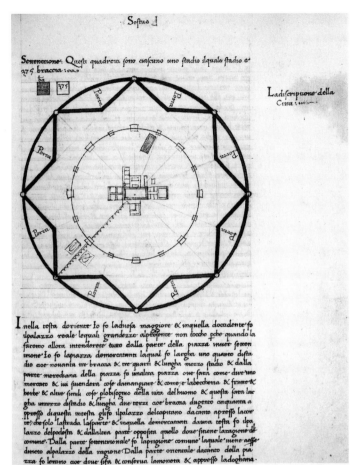

Figure 2.4 Filarete, plan of Sforzinda from the treatise. Biblioteca Nazionale, Florence, MS Magliabechianus XVII,30=II.I.140, 43r. Photo: MicroFoto srl

In Sforzinda, Filarete divided buildings into three groups – public, private and sacred – and then described, often in detail, different sorts of buildings within these broad categories: public offices, various sorts of religious institutions, and types of dwellings, with social rank and status as key factors. The city was defined and protected by strong walls and was fashioned in the image of the prince. After the walls, the first building to be constructed was a castle by the city's perimeter (like the Castello Sforzesco in Milan) – designed by the duke himself because of his military expertise. Not only did this provide a solid defence for the city but it was, of course, a powerful sign of the duke's rule. Filarete enhanced this authority symbolically by giving the castle dimensions and forms which reflected the 365 days and the four seasons of the year – the kind of number symbolism he used elsewhere, perhaps giving a certain 'universal' aspect to his treatise. In the centre of the city was placed a complex of porticoed squares, on and around which most of the public and communal activities of the citizens and their ruler took place.

At the heart of Sforzinda was the main square. On the west side was the ducal palace and to the east the cathedral. On the other sides were shops of silversmiths and cloth merchants. To the north there opened another square, the domain of the merchants, around which were the office of the *podestà* (a judge from another state who was appointed, usually for one year, to oversee justice in a non-partisan fashion), the town hall, the mint and treasury, the customs house, the guild halls, the law courts and prisons, and two churches. South of the main square was another square, which was the site of the main food market (divided and located in different parts according to type of foodstuff). The church at its centre was to be surrounded by the headquarters of the military commander, inns, taverns, baths, a brothel and the offices of the money lenders.

While interconnected, each of the squares had distinct activities and types of building. There was a careful zoning that created a hierarchy of social space: the elite and decorous central square; the high-level economic and political nature of the merchants' square; and the market square, which met more basic human needs and desires. The merchants and workers had their own areas, which were overseen by the forces of law and order, and by implication by the duke himself. The church was omnipresent. Each subsidiary market place in the city was flanked by a parish church, and churches of the religious orders were built beside the main streets. The principal church of the city, the cathedral, sat opposite the ducal palace, showing the inextricable bond between church and state, though where power finally lay was another question – as we saw above, the bishop's palace was only slightly smaller and less ornate than the duke's.

The city centre was connected to its defensive and protective walls, which were built in the form of a circle with an inset eight-pointed star, by eight routes which radiated out from this focal point to the city gates. Half of these routes were intended as paved roads and the others as canals, which enabled goods to be brought in easily and without the need for large numbers of cumbersome carts. The proposal for a canal system was a rationalization of what was actually present in parts of Milan. It also recalled Plato's description of the lost, ideal city and state of Atlantis – an authoritative precedent for the design which would not have escaped the classically erudite reader. The water in Sforzinda also flowed around the main piazza and was used for a magnificent fountain in the middle. In this practical and splendid solution to the organization of the city, Sforzinda and its surrounding territory were constantly connected to the centre of power and government, and thus ultimately to the duke himself.

The duke's authority, the extent of his subtle control and his sense of security were shown by the delegation of duties and powers in Sforzinda. An example of this in Filarete's account was his reference to the appointment of a commissary or administrator, who was to oversee the construction of many parts of Sforzinda, as well as all aspects of the administration of the building sites, from ensuring the supply of materials to the payment of workers. Elsewhere this role was one that was often carried out by the patron himself, or placed in the hands of a committee, but in Milan and Lombardy the custom was to use an administrator for ducal projects. However, Filarete limited the role of this individual in Sforzinda so that he did not in any way encroach on the competency and singular standing of the architect – the man with the ideas. This was not the case on Sforza sites in the duchy itself, where Filarete's authority had often been challenged. Like other incidents in the treatise involving the duke, the duchess and their eldest son, Filarete makes reference to the Sforza and Lombard context, while transmuting such experiences and references into more ideal forms. In Sforzinda, Filarete was proposing a utopian city-state, where architecture reflected a clear social and political hierarchy at the apex of which was the ducal court. This city and its organization were clearly identifiable with Sforza rule.

Filarete's treatise, with his account of the involvement of the duke and his family in the minutiae of the design and construction of the city of Sforzinda, provided the model of the magnanimous prince whose expenditure on his own buildings and on those of the city reflected care for his people – a commonplace of political literature. Yet this was not a tyrant's city; the castle sat on the edge and its role was not that of the permanent residence of the ruler (Alberti had carefully defined cities according to such criteria). Moreover, the buildings and spaces that Filarete proposed for the government of the city, apart from the ducal palace, reflect the sharing of power by different groups in a way that would also be suitable for a republican city. The life-blood of the city – as shown by the prominence of the merchants and markets – was trade and not war. Filarete's treatise in some ways falls into the medieval tradition of *specula principum* (mirrors for princes) – works in which philosophers and scholars sought to guide a prince on the right and just way to rule and in which the beautiful and well-organized city often appeared as a motif.

Once more we find medieval traditions, classical ideas, and contemporary and local customs being combined in a new formulation and presentation – another example of the complicated interaction that created and defined Renaissance culture in this period. This was a time when the figure of the architect as a man of some learning and theoretical grounding, in addition to his practical skills, was beginning to emerge and gain recognition. While Filarete himself may not have been as successful as he had hoped, during the course of the fifteenth century the role of architect was increasingly recognized and valued as a profession. The role came to be distinguished from that of master mason, or carpenter, even if these were trades in which the individual architect might have trained, and in which he often continued to work, just as many architects started out as, and continued to be, artists – most notably painters, sculptors or goldsmiths. By 1500, then, use of the term 'architect' to describe the designer of a building, and to denote someone who was considerably more than an artisan, became more common, and the status of its holder respected by patrons and other professionals.

Music at the Sforza court

BY DAVID MATEER

The Sforza were among the most important patrons of music of their time. Their predecessors in Milan, the Visconti, had supported only a few musicians, the most notable being the composer Jacopo da Bologna (fl. 1340–60). Building on this slim tradition, the Sforza invested heavily in instrumentalists and singers, and employed some of the greatest composers of the Renaissance. The family was in power for less than 50 years, but during that time the musical life of its court ranked with that of the popes in Rome, the Este in Ferrara and the Medici in Florence.

Music at the Renaissance court

Before tracing the rise of music at the Sforza court, it may be useful to examine briefly the ways in which music was integrated into court culture during the period. The forms of music patronage differ fundamentally from those operating in the other arts. The reason for this is that music is essentially a 'recreative' activity. The 'made-to-measure' system, typical of patronage of the visual arts, is rarely encountered in music. In this procedure, the rich would commission a work from an artist or workshop; they would pay the cost of materials, but their relationship to the artist, in theory at least, would last only until the artefact was delivered and the fee was paid. Music, as a performing art, could not easily function in this way, since the commissioned work still required singers and players to translate the composer's intentions into sound. This presupposes the existence of a regularly available group of musicians, one of whom was probably the composer himself. Musical patronage therefore tended to operate under a 'household' system (also seen occasionally in artistic patronage) in which patrons would employ on a more or less full-time basis groups of musicians who would perform for their pleasure.

By the late 1470s, four of these groups of musicians were resident at Milan and other north Italian courts: a body of trumpeters; the wind band (known collectively as the *piffari*); the string and keyboard players who were also the singers of secular music; and the chapel of singers responsible for the performance of **chant** (liturgical melodies) and **polyphony** (part-music) in church services. The chapel of singers might also include an organist. The duties of these ensembles were naturally different. The trumpeters, usually native Italians who numbered between four and twenty, fulfilled a function that was more ceremonial than musical: they sounded fanfares for the proclamation of decrees, played to announce the arrival of courses at banquets, and performed as signal instruments in battle. The *piffari*, often German musicians who played a variety of wind and brass instruments, numbered between three and six. They performed at jousts and in the processions and 'triumphs' of the court. Unlike the trumpeters, they also had purely musical duties, providing music for dances and the *intermedi* – interludes presented between the acts of the classical comedies performed at court; occasionally they joined with the chapel singers in celebrating the mass and offices of the church. The string players, generally two to eight Italian or northern European musicians, also performed at banquets and for the *intermedi*; they too served at court dances and in religious processions, when they would play and sing **laude** (non-liturgical religious songs). The duties of the ducal chapel, which might number from six to thirty members, involved the provision of sacred music in the court chapel or town cathedral. They too might be required to sing at table and to perform in the *intermedi*. The nationality of chapel members varied greatly, the most valued employees coming from the itinerant, mercenary singers of northern Europe: France, the Low Countries, Germany, and sometimes England.

Exercise

Listen now to two pieces that give a flavour of the sort of music these ensembles would have performed. The first is an instrumental arrangement of 'A la bataglia' ('To battle') (Track 1) by Heinrich Isaac (*c.*1450–1517), a Flemish composer who, in the course of an international career, spent some time at the courts of Florence and Ferrara. The second piece, 'Dolores mortis' ('The pains of death') (Track 2), is a *lauda* by Diomedes dating from *c.*1500; notice how the solo voice, which appears almost to declaim the text, is supported by an accompaniment of plain chords only. ❖

At most, the household musicians might number approximately 60 members, although typically there were fewer than this. Their salaries and systems of support differed widely. If they were clerics, as were many members of the chapel and some of the secular singers, then benefices might be made available to provide or augment their salaries. A benefice was, in effect, a gift that customarily took the form of an ecclesiastical post and provided its holder with an income, in return for whatever spiritual duties the office required. Although the right of conferring the overwhelming majority of benefices fell to the pope, the most powerful of the secular lords were often able to influence the dispensation of benefices in their own domains and thus lure the best singers to their courts with the promise of such prizes. If the musicians were laymen, as were most of the secular singers, trumpeters and *piffari*, then other means of support had to be found; the *signori*, for instance, might allow them to exploit the local mineral wealth or present them with land in their territory which they could either work themselves or sub-let to tenant farmers.

Music at the court of Galeazzo Maria Sforza

Before about 1470, courtly patronage of music at the north Italian courts was focused primarily on the forces for instrumental and secular vocal music. In the whole of Italy there were only four centres that maintained groups of singers capable of performing complex sacred polyphony: Savoy, Florence, the papal court and Naples. This situation changed dramatically in the early 1470s with the institution of princely chapels by Galeazzo Maria Sforza (1466–76) at Milan and by Ercole I d'Este (1471–1505) at Ferrara. After succeeding to the duchy in 1466, Galeazzo Maria increased the size and quality of his musical forces and almost immediately enlarged the body of trumpeters to twenty. In 1469, as part of his general interest in pomp, he decreed that half of these were always to travel with him wherever he went; by this year, the number of ducal *piffari* had been increased to at least six. However, the establishment of a princely chapel for the performance of sacred polyphony was perhaps the most significant of all the changes wrought by Galeazzo Maria. He was one of the first north Italian princes to found such an institution, and he did so in direct competition with the equally determined Ercole I. In 1471 they both announced the creation of *cappelle dei cantori* (chapels of singers), and by 1473 the latter had established two choirs, one of fourteen men and another of fourteen German boys. By the same year Galeazzo Maria had also founded two choirs, a **cappella** *da camera* (chamber choir) and a *cappella*, consisting of thirteen and over twenty adult members respectively. We get some idea of the make-up of the Milanese *cappella* from Bernardino Corio – the city chronicler and one of Galeazzo Maria's chamberlains – who reports that 'the duke took great delight in song, for which he kept about 30 northern singers, honourably paid' (Welch, 1993, p.151).

Galeazzo Maria seems to have been particularly taken with music, having studied it in his youth as part of the extensive educational programme devised by his father to prepare him for his inheritance. In 1452, when he was only eight years old, his tutor wrote to Francesco to say that the boy was studying hard and that 'he has begun Latin and is also doing well at learning to sing. He has learned eight French chansons and every day he learns others' (Prizer, 1989, 'Music at the court', p.151). This reference is crucial in two ways. First, it makes clear that Galeazzo Maria was musically literate; this was a necessity for an informed musical patron. Secondly, when combined with the knowledge that he was an avid reader of French books, it shows an early interest in French music and culture; this may in turn partly explain his later determined search for northern singers for his chapel.

It is not clear exactly when Galeazzo Maria conceived the idea for his *cappella*, but in 1469 he invited two singers from the royal chapel of Naples, Antoine Pons and a certain Raynero, to come to Milan, and it seems likely that his decision to begin a *cappella* was closely tied to his building projects, which included a chapel in the Castello itself. By 1471, there is clearer evidence: in October of that year, he sent Raynero and one Aloysio (thought to be the composer Loyset Compère) to northern Europe and England in search of singers. In the following year, he dispatched agents to Flanders, Burgundy and France for the same purpose. However, in his desire to recruit the best musicians, Galeazzo Maria at times succumbed to a certain deviousness. He sent for singers of the court of Savoy and then tried to keep them for himself, initiating an angry correspondence with the Duchess Yolanda of Savoy; but this in no way dissuaded him from sending missions to Naples and Rome to try to entice their singers away. Occasionally, he was the victim of such 'head-hunting', as is clear from the courteous, but cool, tone of his letter to Ercole I, dated 24 July 1476:

> We are certain that your Lordship would neither wish nor permit that any of your singers should steal away any of ours, just as we would shun such behaviour ... but we must advise you that a certain Michele Feyt, a singer of ours, has left our service ...

> (Lockwood, 1981, p.234)

Just at this time we find a 'Michele cantore' admitted to service at Ferrara.

The maintaining of a chapel was an expensive business for Galeazzo Maria and Ercole; recently published figures show that it roughly equalled the total expenditure for the other three groups of musicians, principally because of the number of singers required. So why did they do it? There are three interrelated answers. First, both rulers enjoyed music passionately; Galeazzo Maria confessed that he took 'delight in music and song more than any other pleasure'. Secondly, they were, in accordance with their times, truly devout; to invest in the chapel, therefore, was to invest in the salvation of their own soul. And thirdly, for a prince to support a chapel was a sign that he was illustrious; the ability to retain great musicians said something about the activities of the court, which was regarded as an extension of the ruler himself. The chapel, then, was a visible symbol of splendour and power.

Exercise

The following is a translation of a letter of 5 February 1473 written by Zaccaria Saggio, the Mantuan ambassador at the Sforza court, to his master Ludovico Gonzaga. What does it tell you about the following?

- Galeazzo Maria's personality;
- the conditions at his court;
- his plans for the *cappella*;
- the means he intended to employ to achieve them.

His most illustrious Lordship [Galeazzo Maria] thanks your Lordship greatly for the effort you have made concerning the tenor [Andrea da Mantova, previously in the service of Ercole d'Este]. He wishes very much to have him and says that he pays tenors twelve ducats a month in salary and that he shall do the same for him and that he can come assured that he will be accepted. His Excellency has certainly made a fine beginning with these singers and is spending fabulously for them. He has given to one alone [Heinrich Knoep?] the equivalent of four thousand ducats in a house, land, money, clothing, and so forth and has made him personal chamberlain. He is a young man of twenty-four from Liège in Germany [*recte* the Low Countries] ... He is a tenor and is married. His Lordship has also given other houses in Milan worth seven or eight hundred ducats each and has written to Rome to request the pope to agree that every bishop of his principal cities – Milan, Pavia, Novara, Cremona, Piacenza, and Parma – can confer benefices up to the sum of three hundred ducats for each city specifically for singers in order to have in every city a *cappella* in the cathedral. And he says that, in addition to the three hundred ducats in benefices, he will give the rest necessary for the said singers from his income from those cities. For this he has written most insistently to the [papal] court and says that he wants to sustain music in Italy. And then his Excellency will be able to choose from these *cappelle* the best singers and in this way will have the best chapel of all, and then when he wants to hear a great noise, he will send for all [the singers] and have them shout at once in such a way that their voices will go up to heaven.

(after Prizer, 1989, 'Music at the court', pp.156–7)

The letter seems clearly to demonstrate the lengths to which Galeazzo Maria was prepared to go to establish a position of musical hegemony in north Italy. It is apparent that he was spending a good deal of his time with matters concerning the new chapel. His pursuit of the grandiose – note his quaint conceit of calling all the choirs together for performance *en masse* – verges on megalomania, as does his egocentric belief that he was 'sustain[ing] music in Italy'. This honourable goal was to be achieved by establishing a *cappella*, with singers mostly funded from benefices acquired from the pope (Sixtus IV), in every cathedral within his jurisdiction; the best singers were to be selected from them to serve in Galeazzo Maria's own chapel. The letter mentions the material inducements offered and the enormous salaries paid; indirect reference is also made to the rivalry with Ercole d'Este for the recruitment of singers. ❖

Such extravagance and ostentation were typical of the vainglorious and pleasure-loving Galeazzo Maria, who entertained grand designs of turning his ducal coronet into a king's crown and transforming Lombardy into a royal realm, just as Charles the Bold sought to elevate the duchy of Burgundy to a kingdom. The theorist and composer Johannes Tinctoris, who was employed by Ferdinand, king of Sicily and Naples, must have had Galeazzo Maria in mind when, in the dedication to a treatise on musical proportions written *c.*1472–3, he referred to the dramatic increase in Italian musical patronage during the early 1470s:

> The most Christian princes, of whom, most pious King you are by far the foremost in the gifts of mind, of body, and of fortune, desiring to augment the divine service, founded chapels after the manner of David, in which at extraordinary expense they appointed singers to sing pleasant and comely praise to our God with diverse (but not adverse) voices. And since the singers of princes, if their masters are endowed with the liberality which makes men illustrious, are rewarded with honour, glory and wealth, many are kindled with a most fervent zeal for this study.

(Strunk, 1952, pp.194–5)

Galeazzo Maria seems to have taken the imitation of David seriously. The magnificently illuminated opening leaf of a missal that once belonged to his chapel, now in the Wallace Collection in London, shows him kneeling in prayer in front of a battle scene enclosed by towers which provide the outline of a capital A – the opening initial of the Introit for the first Sunday of Advent, 'Ad te levavi animam meam' (Figure 2.5, overleaf). Traditionally, the kneeling figure of King David appears at this point in the missal, but in the leaf from

Figure 2.5 Cristoforo da Preda, *Galeazzo Maria Sforza at Prayer*, illuminated parchment leaf, with the Sforza coat of arms below. Wallace Collection, M342. Reproduced by permission of the Trustees of the Wallace Collection, London

the Wallace Collection that position has been usurped by Galeazzo Maria, who thus directly identifies himself in the role of the biblical king. In the light of Tinctoris's comments about Italian princes founding chapels after the manner of David, Galeazzo Maria's representation of himself as a second David in his missal is all the more striking. David, of course, is traditionally regarded as the author of the Book of Psalms, and a further comparison between him and Galeazzo Maria arises when we find that in 1473 the latter wrote to the Neapolitan court – a royal court, it should be noted – asking for a copy of the psalms that were sung there, so that he could have them performed at his own court. The incident not only indicates that Galeazzo Maria concerned himself directly with the repertory of his chapel, but is further evidence of his self-identification with David, the musician-king of the Old Testament.

Among the composers employed by Galeazzo Maria were Josquin Desprez, Gaspar van Weerbeke, Alexander Agricola and Loyset Compère. Josquin Desprez (*c.* 1440–1521) is introduced in Book 1 in this series (Chapter 4). He had been in Milan since at least 1459, when he was first recorded as an adult member of the cathedral choir; in 1473, however, he moved to the ducal chapel, where he received a benefice that brought his total income to nearly 160 ducats per year, making him one of the best-paid singers at court. (Food prices from Milan for 1460 show that a single ducat would have bought 130 pounds of bread or 10 chickens.) After Galeazzo Maria's assassination in 1476, Josquin joined the entourage of his brother, Cardinal Ascanio Sforza. Weerbeke (*c.*1440–after 1518), from Oudenaarde in Flanders, was one of the longest serving of the ducal musicians. He was already in Milan in 1472 and served as the master of the *cappella da camera* during its early years. Weerbeke eventually left Milan in 1481 to join the papal chapel, although he returned to the Milanese court under Ludovico il Moro. Agricola (*c.*1446–1506), from the Low Countries, was in Milan by 1471 and served as a member of the *cappella* until June 1474, when he was released from the Sforza service. Compère, from Hainaut, was in Milan much more briefly, during 1474 and 1475, although it is possible that he is the 'Aloysio' sent with Raynero on the 1471 recruiting trip mentioned above.

Josquin Desprez

Josquin was by far the most important member of this group; indeed, for many he was the greatest composer of the age. The sixteenth-century Florentine writer Cosimo Bartoli described him in his *Ragionamenti accademici* of 1567 as a prodigy of nature – 'un monstro di natura' – and, looking back at the recent past, he compared Josquin's achievements in music to those of Michelangelo in painting, sculpture and architecture. Our discussion of contemporary musical trends will therefore focus on his rich and multifaceted output.

Josquin and his colleagues in the ducal chapel combined to create a new 'Milanese' style of musical composition which helped to lay the foundations of the high Renaissance style. This new approach is particularly apparent in their **motets** (sacred vocal pieces in Latin). Their humanistic preoccupation with 'the word' had important repercussions for their musical style:

1   Josquin and his fellow composers took as their starting point the syntax of the text, and sought to reflect the meaning of the words in all aspects of their music;

2   they were concerned not to obscure the text with elaborate melodic lines; their aim was to ensure the comprehensibility of the words, and to achieve this they sometimes allocated just one note to a syllable when setting the text;

3   if this approach is applied to the other (usually four) voices of a composition, the result is a simple chordal style in which all parts move in the same or similar rhythm.

You may find it helpful at this point to examine a motet that Josquin almost certainly wrote for Galeazzo Maria's chapel – *Tu solus qui facis mirabilia* ('You only, who do wonders') (Track 3). The score of the music is provided in an appendix at the end of the chapter, and the text, with a parallel translation, is given below.

Tu solus, qui facis mirabilia;	*You only, who do wonders,*
Tu solus Creator, qui creasti nos;	*You, the only Creator, who created us,*
Tu solus Redemptor, qui redemisti nos	*You only are the Redeemer, who redeemed us with*
Sanguine tuo pretiosissimo.	*Your most precious blood.*
Ad te solum confugimus,	*In you alone we take refuge,*
In te solum confidimus,	*In you alone we place our trust,*
Nec alium adoramus, Jesu Christe.	*And no other do we adore, Jesus Christ.*
Ad te preces effundimus,	*To you we pour forth our prayers,*
Exaudi quod supplicamus,	*Hear our supplications,*
Et concede quod petimus,	*And grant our requests,*
Rex benigne!	*Benign King!*
D'ung aultre amer, nobis esset fallacia;	*To love another [than Christ] would be deceitful;*
D'ung aultre amer, magna esset stultitia et peccatum.	*To love another [than Christ] would be great folly and sin.*
Audi nostra suspiria,	*Hear our sighs,*
Reple nos tua gratia, O Rex regum:	*Fill us with your grace, O King of kings,*
Ut ad tua servitia sistamus cum laetitia in aeternum.	*That we may remain in your service with joy forever.*

What was it like to be employed as one of Galeazzo Maria's musicians? The archival evidence that would help us answer that question is not plentiful; however, an important document has survived that provides a context for compositional activity at the court.

Exercise

The following is a translation of a newly found letter from Galeazzo Maria to Josquin ('Iuschino'). What does it tell us about the relationship between the composer and his master?

To Iuschino the Singer

Iuschino. We hear that you are spending your time writing something other than the work that we have commissioned from you, and you have set aside our business to serve others, in which we complain greatly of you. And we have been of a mind to have you locked up in prison and teach you to be more wise another time, which will happen to you if you do not arrange that the work commissioned from you is expedited without delay. Abiate 15 March 1473 Gabriel [ducal secretary].

(Matthews and Merkley, 1994, pp.446–7)

Discussion

From this document we learn that Galeazzo Maria commissioned music from Josquin in 1473, and that the composer was also writing for other patrons. The duke's angry reaction to Josquin's wilfulness is understandable in the context of the keen competition that existed between Italian courts for the best musicians, and, consequently, the prestige that their compositions bestowed on the patron. Josquin's first duty lay with his employer, the duke, but work for another patron had apparently been given greater priority. In his letter of reprimand Galeazzo Maria gives full vent to the humiliation he feels; its extreme tone leaves no doubt as to the seriousness of the offence and the dire consequences of future obduracy. ❖

Who was the rival patron who so incensed Galeazzo Maria? It is not possible to answer that question unequivocally, but it could have been Ercole d'Este, given their contemporary efforts to outdo each other in the pursuit of musical excellence. Before looking at a work that Josquin definitely *did* write for Ercole, we must outline the course of the composer's subsequent career. Unfortunately, in the decade following Galeazzo Maria's death, the gaps in our knowledge of Josquin's whereabouts become acute. We know he left Milan, at least for a time, for in April 1477 he is listed as a member of the chapel of René d'Anjou, titular king of Sicily and Jerusalem, in Aix-en-Provence; however, he was apparently back in Milan by 1479. Although Josquin was definitely a member of the papal chapel for some months between September 1486 and September 1487, Edward Lowinsky (1976) has produced strong circumstantial evidence that he was in the service, at least intermittently, of Cardinal Ascanio Sforza between 1479 and 1489, and possibly later. Ascanio (1455–1505, cardinal from 1484) was the fifth son of Francesco Sforza and, like his siblings, was probably musical. It may have been through him that Josquin made his first contacts with the court of Ferrara, where Ascanio was in exile in the early 1480s. One of Josquin's Masses – the *Missa 'Hercules Dux Ferrarie'* (Mass 'Hercules, Duke of Ferrara') – was written as a *pièce d'occasion* honouring Duke Ercole I. Because it was not published until 1505 (the year of Ercole's death) and was seen as a tribute by a great composer to a famous patron, it has generally been assumed that the Mass dates from between 1503 and 1504 when Josquin was definitely at the Ferrarese court as chapel master. Recently, however, this view has been challenged by a number of scholars, and the general consensus of opinion now assigns the work to around 1480.

The Hercules Mass is a **cantus firmus** setting, i.e. a pre-existent melody is used as the basis of the new polyphonic composition. Josquin derives the notes of the *cantus firmus* by letting each vowel of the dedicatee's Latin name and title – '*Hercules Dux Ferrarie*' – correspond to one of the **solmization** syllables as follows:

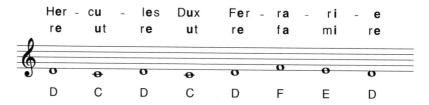

The *cantus firmus* voice – the tenor – uses this eight-note tune three times during each Mass movement or section of a movement, first on *d*, then five steps higher on *a*, and lastly an octave above the original statement, on *d'*. Sometimes the groups of three statements are presented in **retrograde** (backwards) motion and in descending order, on *d'*, *a* and *d*. Look at Figure 2.6 – the first page of the tenor part of the Mass as published by Petrucci; it shows the first three movements of the Mass, i.e. the Kyrie, Gloria (beginning 'Et in terra') and Credo (beginning 'Patrem'). In the Kyrie (first stave) you can see how the eight-note tune in its original form is disposed at three different, ascending levels – at Kyrie (I), Christe, and Kyrie (II). Notice, too, at 'Et in spiritum' near the end of the Credo (halfway along the fifth stave) the notes of the tune are stated in reverse order and the three presentations descend. Lewis Lockwood has suggested that:

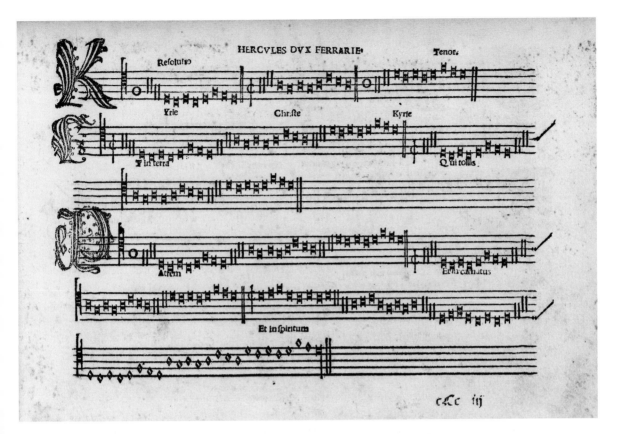

Figure 2.6 Josquin Desprez, first page of tenor part of *Missa 'Hercules Dux Ferrarie'*, from *Liber secundi missarum Josquin Desprez* , 1515, 2nd edn. Venice, Ottaviano Petrucci. British Library k.l.d.(10). Reproduced by permission of the British Library Board

It may not be a complete coincidence that there are twelve complete threefold expositions of the subject in this Mass; the association of its name and this number might well have evoked the mythological Hercules with his twelve labours. If it did, it would have blended perfectly with the glorification of the figure of Hercules in literary and artistic products at Ferrara under Duke Ercole, who never tired of the comparison. A court historian of the mid-sixteenth century actually suggests that the origins of the Estense family line could be traced back to the French royal family and through them to a marriage between the original Hercules and a Celtic princess.

(1984, p.243)

Figure 2.6 also shows that Petrucci provided the tenor part with the opening words only of each Mass section. These verbal **incipits** mapped out the musical terrain for the choir and probably served as reference points during rehearsal. Were the singers expected to complete the liturgical text? If so, how did they fit it to the recurring eight-note melody? No problem arises in the shorter movements like the Kyrie, whose full text consists of only six words – 'Kyrie eleison, Christe eleison, Kyrie eleison'; the tenors could easily have sung these three phrases (respectively of seven, six and seven syllables) to the three statements of the eight-note tune. But what happens in the densely texted movements, like the Gloria and Credo, which have vastly more syllables than the tenor part has notes? The solution proposed by early Josquin scholars, namely that large portions of liturgical text should be omitted to accommodate the music, is unacceptable. The problem would of course disappear if the part was not sung at all but was played on instruments – a theory that has much to recommend it. It seems just as likely, however, that the ducal tenors sang the name and title 'Hercules Dux Ferrarie' in all movements against the liturgical text in the other voices. Such a performance would align the work with a later, sixteenth-century tradition in which double-texted Mass settings were typically compositions written in honour of temporal or spiritual luminaries; one thinks of Palestrina's Mass *Ecce sacerdos magnus* (1554), the tenor part of which has a separate text celebrating the reigning pope. William Prizer believes that if the tenors did sing the syllables of Ercole's name rather than the liturgical text, then:

> we are confronted with a work which explicitly glorifies its patron, a secular lord, within the most sacred context of the Mass, and one which in a certain sense equates the greatness of Ercole with the true religion. This work ... is a revealing instance of the ability of a patron's music and musicians to contribute directly to his self-glorification and magnificence.

(1989, 'North Italian courts', p.141)

Leonardo da Vinci in Milan, 1482–99

BY PETER ELMER AND NICK WEBB

> The colossal outlines of Leonardo's nature can never be more than dimly and distantly conceived.

(Burckhardt, p.104)

For Burckhardt, Leonardo (1452–1519) personified the Renaissance genius (p.104). As heir to that earlier 'universal man', Leon Battista Alberti, he shared a passion for a wide variety of knowledge and learning. And like Alberti, he was a product of the Florentine Renaissance. He trained in the workshop of the Florentine goldsmith and sculptor Andrea del Verrocchio (1435–88), his debt to the artistic environment of the city underlined by his borrowings from Giotto (*c*.1266/7–1337) and Masaccio (1401–*c*.1428) as the principal innovators in painting. Leonardo's precocious ability brought him to the attention of that great connoisseur of local talent, Lorenzo de' Medici, who, in all probability, recommended him to Ludovico Sforza. By 1482 he was in the service of the regent, who eventually provided him with a regular salary and commissions. This marked the start of a long-standing commitment by the artist to the Milanese court – one which was sustained by Leonardo irrespective of who was in power, since he subsequently served Ludovico's French conquerors and their Milanese collaborators, including the aristocratic governor and former renegade, Giangiacomo Trivulzio (see Chapter 1, p.18).[1]

Although there is some uncertainty as to exactly when and how Leonardo entered the service of the Sforza (Cole, 1995, p.93), we do know that he used the occasion of a visit to Milan in 1482 as an opportunity to present his credentials to Ludovico in the form of a letter.

Exercise

Read Leonardo's letter to Ludovico Sforza in the Anthology (no. 38) and comment on the way he prioritizes his artistic credentials.

Discussion

Leonardo presents himself to Ludovico as first and foremost a military engineer. Architecture comes next 'in time of peace'. Sculpture and painting rank a somewhat remote third. The priority Leonardo attached to his prospective skills (as far as we know he had no previous military experience, though his early notes include sketches of siege engines) indicates the greater probability of long-term employment and remuneration which he felt such services might provide. The position of engineer carried with it the chance of a retainer contract as well as higher status. ❖

Towards the end of the letter he adds the comment: 'the bronze horse may be taken in hand'. This refers to the project for an equestrian monument of Francesco Sforza which had first been planned by his son, Galeazzo Maria (d. 1476). In the previous year (1481) Leonardo's teacher, Verrocchio, had sent to Venice a model for a similar equestrian monument for the *condottiere* and erstwhile enemy of the Sforza, Bartolomeo Colleoni. It is highly probable therefore that Leonardo possessed first-hand experience of this type of commission (Figure 2.7, overleaf).

[1] Leonardo briefly left Milan to return to Florence after the defeat of the Sforza at the hands of the French in 1499. In 1506, the new French governor, Charles d'Amboise, petitioned the **Signoria** of Florence to allow Leonardo to return to Milan, where he remained until 1513. Trivulzio, for whom Leonardo designed a commemorative tomb monument, had served as a *condottiere* for Ludovico il Moro before joining and then leading the French forces which overthrew Sforza rule in Milan. Ironically, the monument devised by Leonardo incorporated the imperial imagery that the artist had earlier planned for the ill-fated equestrian monument to Francesco Sforza, discussed overleaf.

Figure 2.7 Andrea del Verrocchio and Alessandro Leopardi, Colleoni monument, 1479–96, bronze, marble, statue, height c.400 cm, height of base (including plinth) c.800 cm. Campo Santi Giovanni e Paolo, Venice. Photo: Osvaldo Böhm

The Sforza equestrian monument

Typically, the Renaissance equestrian statue makes reference to both ancient and medieval artistic motifs. In the ancient world such a monument was most commonly associated with images of imperial authority, whereas in the Middle Ages it recalled knightly chivalry. Free-standing statues of horses and military riders were present in northern Italy during the fourteenth century, most notably those erected to honour the della Scala at Verona and the Visconti of Milan. They were carved in stone and marble and often served as part of a funerary monument. Classical precedents survived and may have acted as models for the Renaissance revival of this particular art form. In the fifteenth century an antique bronze equestrian statue of

Marcus Aurelius, mistakenly believed at the time to be a representation of the Emperor Constantine, stood in Rome. Likewise, the *Regisole*, a memorial to the king of the Ostrogoths, Theodoric, could be found in front of the entrance to Pavia Cathedral (but has since been destroyed). The Sforza commission alluded to by Leonardo in his letter to Ludovico was thus part of a growing trend. During the fifteenth century, three bronze equestrian statues were commissioned from Florentine workshops, one of which, as we have already noted, Leonardo may have been acquainted with through his association with Verrocchio.

Ludovico took up the project for an equestrian statue of his father, Francesco, in the 1480s. Among those he consulted was Lorenzo de' Medici who, in 1484, suggested the names of potential sculptors. Leading candidates included Leonardo's teacher, Verrocchio, who was occupied at the time with the completion of the Colleoni monument in Venice, and the Florentine firm of Antonio and Piero Pollaiuolo (similarly, preoccupied with the tomb of Pope Sixtus IV). Consequently, Leonardo may have been given the commission partly by default, but also because of his earlier training under Verrocchio. Early sketches for the monument date from the mid to late 1480s and show a rearing horse rising above a fallen enemy – a break with classical convention (Figure 2.8). As the project developed, Leonardo's intentions grew even more grandiose. Not only was the

Figure 2.8 Leonardo da Vinci, study for the Sforza monument, c.1485–9, silverpoint on blue prepared paper, 15 × 19 cm. The Royal Collection © Her Majesty the Queen. Royal Library 12358

statue to be twice life-size but the complex nature of the pose placed unprecedented pressure on existing techniques in the casting of bronze. Moreover, doubts as to the viability of Leonardo's project were apparently being entertained by his illustrious patron. In 1489, the Florentine ambassador in Milan, Piero Alamanni, was writing to Lorenzo de' Medici to report that while Ludovico had commissioned 'a very large horse' from Leonardo, he was not confident the sculptor knew how to finish the job. Accordingly, Ludovico requested 'an artist or two, capable of such work'. At this point, Lorenzo wrote to his ambassador at the papal court seeking the temporary release of Antonio Pollaiuolo. The extant drawings by Pollaiuolo (Cole, Plate 74) suggest that Lorenzo was successful. As for the origin or template of Leonardo's original design, seemingly imitated by Pollaiuolo, a number of possible models existed. For example, an image of Francesco Sforza on horseback could be found in a painting in the ducal library at Pavia (Fusco and Corti, 1992).

Just as doubts were being expressed about Leonardo's ability to carry out the commission, the artist seems to have experienced a change of mind, prompted in all probability by his visit to Pavia in 1490. Ostensibly employed to advise on the rebuilding of the cathedral there, Leonardo's attention was drawn to the *Regisole* monument which stood outside the cathedral. Consequently, he returned to the idea of the walking horse which figured in other fifteenth-century designs, most notably that used for the Gattamelata monument in Padua (1447–53)[2] and more recently the Colleoni statue in Venice. A number of drawings and notes from this time testify to Leonardo's close observation of real horses. By 1491 Leonardo was preparing for a one-piece, **'lost wax'** casting of the monument (Figure 2.9, repeated in Cole, Plate 75; note Leonardo's use of mirror writing in this and other diagrams). Two years later a full-scale clay model stood in the Corte Arengo, close to Leonardo's living quarters, while in the same year a replica was displayed during the festivities held to celebrate the marriage by proxy of Bianca Sforza and the Emperor Maximilian.[3] The actual statue, however, was never cast. In 1494 the allocated bronze was reassigned to the production of cannons, and by 1500 the clay model was being used for target practice by French archers.

From the point of view of the patron, the projected monument was part of a wider attempt to legitimize the Sforza claim to power in

---

[2] This is a larger-than-life bronze equestrian statue of the Paduan-born *condottiere* Erasmo da Narni (1370–1443), known as Gattamelata ('tabby-cat', from his mother's name, Melania Gattelli). It was the work of Donatello and stands outside the Santo in Padua.

[3] The religious marriage ceremony took place some months later at Innsbruck.

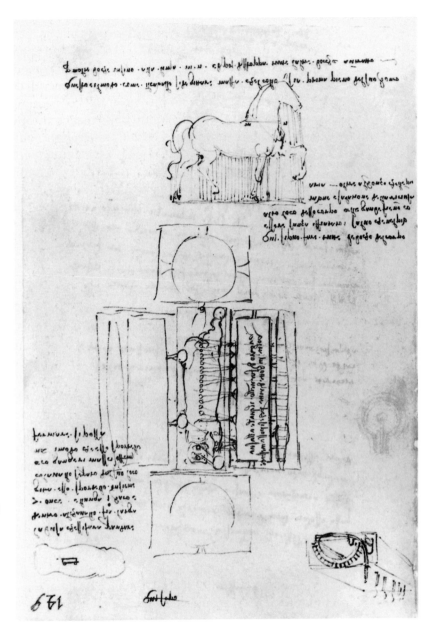

Figure 2.9 Leonardo da Vinci, casting diagram for the Sforza monument, c.1491–3, silverpoint on paper, width 15 cm. Biblioteca Nacional, Madrid, Codex Madrid II, 149r. Photo: Arxiu Mas/ Institut Amattler d'Art Hispanic

Milan. Consequently, it bears comparison with Ludovico's attempt to eulogize Francesco, the founder of Sforza rule, in a popular biography, the *Sphortias* (*Sforziade*), which was originally written in Italian by Francesco Filelfo (see p.103) and was subsequently translated into Latin by the Florentine humanist Cristoforo Landino (1424–98). The monument itself represents a good example of a self-made ruler and usurper utilizing classical forms of sculpture in such a way as to lend strength and legitimacy to the authority of his newly

133

established regime. It also invokes the imagery frequently associated with imperial rule in ancient Rome, and as such may have evoked Ludovico's aspirations to kingship in northern Italy. For Leonardo, on the other hand, the commission provided a valuable opportunity to break away from the constraints of painting and to demonstrate the range of his technical and creative virtuosity. The size and scale of such commissions were not, however, without their problems, as the example here strongly suggests. Painting, on the other hand, was more intellectual, more natural and offered infinite possibilities for illusionary effects. It was also less messy in so far as it did not involve carving or casting (Kemp and Walker, 1989, pp.38–40).

Court painting

A description of Leonardo's working methods appears in one of the *novellas* (short stories) of Matteo Bandello (1485–1561):

> Many a time I have seen Leonardo go to work early in the morning and climb the scaffolding, because the *Last Supper* is somewhat above ground level; and he would work there from sunrise until the dusk of evening, never laying down the brush, but continuing to paint without remembering to eat or drink. Then there would be two, three or four days without his touching the work, yet each day he would spend one or two hours just looking, considering and examining it, criticizing the figures to himself. I have also seen him ... at midday when the sun is highest leave the Corte Vecchia (i.e. the Corte Arengo), where he is working on the stupendous horse of clay, and go straight to the Grazie; climbing on the scaffolding, he would pick up a brush and give one or two brushstrokes to one of the figures and then go elsewhere.

> (Novella 58, in Kemp, 1981, p.180)

In 1497, two years after the *Last Supper* was started, Ludovico, via his secretary, requested that Leonardo complete the projected work on time. Leonardo's mercurial nature and his inability to remain focused on one project at a time frequently exasperated his patrons. For his part, it should be pointed out that he suffered from irregular payment of his court salary and that he was often forced to take on other work in addition to his commitments at court. Working within these constraints, and those imposed by the demands of culturally literate patrons, he none the less, like the musician Josquin Desprez, was able to develop ideas in his chosen medium.

In the field of painting this included an evolving interest in the use of illusionistic perspective and proportion, experimentation with mixtures of pigments, and narrative forms of expression, all of which had been present in his early Florentine work. Some of these interests are clearly present in the *Last Supper* (Cole, Plate 84). Here, for example, one finds a concern for creating a realistic picture space which is integrated with the more overtly symbolic concerns of the painting. Christ occupies the centre of the perspectival scheme which relates to the refectory space.[4] A series of preparatory drawings for the *Last Supper* indicate that such concerns had preoccupied him for some time. They include character studies of individual disciples as well as interrelated groups of figures who are depicted responding emotionally to the unfolding narrative of the scriptural event.

Similarly, it is possible to trace the evolution of Leonardo's artistic ideas in his treatment of the portrait. Two portraits have been generally attributed to him during his stay at the Sforza court: the picture of a musician, now in the Ambrosiana Gallery in Milan, and the *Lady with an Ermine*, a portrait of Cecilia Gallerani, who was the mistress of Ludovico Sforza for ten years prior to his marriage (the ermine or weasel was a common Sforza symbol) (Plate 12; also in Cole, Plate 72). We can follow Leonardo's thinking on the subject of portrait painting through the comments he wrote in his notebooks, some of which are clearly illustrated in the depiction of Cecilia Gallerani. First, he recommends that portraits are produced with low levels of lighting against a dark background in order to give them 'grace through shadow and light'. Secondly, the good painter depicts both the outward appearance of a person and the inner 'motions of the mind', the latter reflected in the posture and physical movement of the sitter. To achieve these effects Leonardo was convinced of the efficacy of the use of oil paint. If successful, the portrait, in Leonardo's view, was a more successful substitute for the real person than poetry (Kemp and Walker, 1989, pp.215, 144–6).

In contrast to Flemish portrait painters or their Italian imitators who sought to focus on naturalistic detail, Leonardo was more selective in the effects he preferred to produce. He carefully related the shape of the mouth to the momentary glance of the eyes, often with the sitter posed at an angle so that the head was turned either to look at the painter or to look out of the picture. This is evident in an early portrait commission, that of Ginevra de' Benci, a Florentine aristocrat, which he completed some time in the late 1470s before he went to Milan (Plate 13). On his return to Florence in 1500 he painted another Florentine aristocrat, the famous *Mona Lisa*. Leonardo's ability to record emotions and his interest in the personality of the sitter were appreciated by the Milanese court, judging by the number of paintings in a similar style attributed to his Lombard followers such as Luini, de Predis and Boltraffio.

---

[4] The systematic nature of Leonardo's use of perspective and proportion is suggested by his discussion of these issues in his notebooks (see the extracts in the Anthology, no. 31; see also Kemp and Walker, 1989).

Look at the portraits of Cecilia Gallerani and Ginevra de' Benci (Plates 12 and 13) and draw up a list of their similarities and differences.

Let's begin with the similarities. They both present young women with high cheek bones, high foreheads and long necks. They both have plucked eyelashes and eyebrows. Their hair covers their ears. Both look consciously posed, although the portrait of Ginevra de' Benci exhibits a more serious expression. The sitters look as if they have been trained in comportment. The design of their dresses is also similar, although Ginevra wears a thin gorget. They are centrally placed and the lightness of their complexions stand out against the dark backgrounds. Both portraits contain allusions to their names: the tree behind Ginevra is a juniper – the same as her name in Italian; Cecilia Gallerani is holding an ermine or possibly a ferret or weasel – the Greek for ermine, *galé*, is probably a pun on her surname, though it might also refer to the common Sforza symbol of the weasel. The use of *imprese* such as these constituted a fashionable parlour game at court, their appearance in the two portraits here being particularly appropriate given the fact that both women were poets.

Now for the differences. The portrait of Ginevra has a painted reverse with the inscription, in Latin, 'Beauty adorns virtue'. The picture has lost a section from the lower edge, which may have shown the sitter's hands. Ginevra's portrait has a landscape background, whereas Cecilia's is set in a dark enclosed space, originally offset by a window on the right. Moreover, the lighting in the latter clearly emanates from the top right and helps to accentuate the twisted pose of the sitter through the diffused light. Ginevra stares directly out at the viewer, but Cecilia glances to her left, thereby allowing the viewer to observe a momentary, faint smile on her face. Compared with the portrait of Ginevra de' Benci, that of Cecilia Gallerani seems to show more interest in the individual character of the sitter. Her dress is a more colourful combination of blue and red, with slashings and a complicated laced sleeve design. ❖

Masques for the Sforza court

The masque combined rhetoric, poetry, music, drama, dance and the visual arts in performances which were at the same time ephemeral court entertainments and serious occasions for political propaganda. Leonardo contributed to at least three such productions during his time in Milan: in 1490, to commemorate the marriage of Giangaleazzo Sforza and the Neapolitan princess Isabella of Aragon in the preceding year; in 1491, following the marriage of Ludovico to Beatrice d'Este; and in 1496, in the production of the *Danaë*, written by the court poet Baldassare Taccone (Figure 2.10). Leonardo exercised his fertile

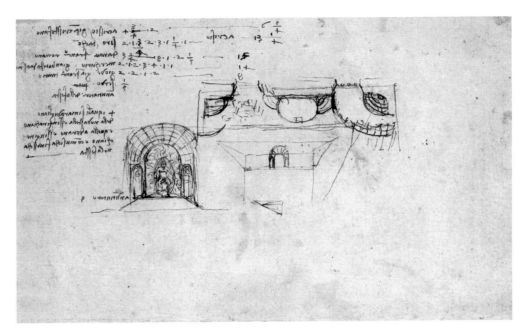

Figure 2.10 Leonardo da Vinci, ground plan and sketch for Taccone's *Danaë* (*Danaë* was performed in Milan on 31 January 1496), pen and bistre. All rights reserved. The Metropolitan Museum of Art, New York. Rogers Fund 1917.17.142.2

Figure 2.11 Leonardo da Vinci, *Youth in a Masquerade Costume*, 1517–18?, pen and ink over black chalk. The Royal Collection © Her Majesty the Queen. Royal Library 12575

imagination both in the design of the elaborate costumes and *fantasie* and in the construction of ingenious stage sets which frequently featured illusionary effects. The evidence of his notebooks suggests that he was deeply interested in the imaginative potential of poetical allegory, and he recorded several designs, sketches and verbal descriptions which may have been intended for such productions (Figure 2.11). Unfortunately, however, nothing else survives beyond these drawings and contemporary descriptions.

Isabella of Aragon had been feted with shows of classical pageantry from the moment she had entered Sforza territory up to the festivities surrounding her wedding in 1489. A year later, *Il paradiso* was performed in her honour, with a script by the court poet Bernardino Bellincioni and visual effects supplied by Leonardo (Cole, pp.103–4). Three days before the performance, invitations were issued to the foreign ambassadors, civic officials and courtiers resident in Milan. Representatives of the papacy, Naples, Venice, Florence and Ferrara attended. The Ferrarese ambassador has left a detailed report of the event. It took place on 13 January in the Sala Verde of the Castello Sforzesco, which had been prepared for the occasion with a 'heaven' decorated with Sforza and Aragonese devices. Along the walls there were tapestries and panel paintings depicting events from ancient history and the deeds of Francesco Sforza. On one side was a sloping platform, mounted by steps, from which the court could view the spectacle. About eight metres away was an 'orchestra' partitioned off by a wooden balustrade. In the middle of the hall was a dais, three steps high and covered in drapes with silver brocade and ducal devices, around which stood the councillors, magistrates and family members of the court.

At one end of the hall, near to the chapel, stood 'paradise'. It comprised a hemispherical 'egg' made of iron girders, its interior formed of gold lines from which were hung a large number of lights. Among the lights were seven boys, representing the seven planets, who circled around a throne in accordance with their heavenly movement. Above them were further representations of the twelve signs of the zodiac, with Jove sitting on the throne. The performance was begun by Isabella and three ladies-in-waiting dancing '*alla napolitana*' in the centre of the room. There followed a series of dances, each performed in national dress, introduced by actors impersonating the ambassadors of Spain, Poland, Hungary, the Grand Turk, the German emperor and the king of France. At half-past midnight, after fireworks, an 'angel' revealed paradise, which up to this point had been covered with a satin sheet. The planets praised Jove for making such a perfect creature in Isabella. Then the ruler of heaven sent Mercury to congratulate Isabella and commanded the three Graces and seven Virtues to serve her well. Apollo then descended to give Isabella a copy of Bellincioni's text of the masque and the troupe concluded with an encomium to Ludovico.

The imaginary world of the masque was intended to convey a series of political messages for the real world. The association of Sforza rule with good government, for example, was readily understood in the astrological references to celestial harmony and the providential rule of the universe by a benign deity. More particularly, the identification of Ludovico with Mercury (identified through his device of the *caduceus* or wand) and not Jove, the ruler of the gods, was intended to obscure the actual power he wielded in the Milanese political universe (see Cole, Plates 71 and 96). Throughout the performance reference is made to the providential and benign nature of Ludovico's rule as regent in Milan, the regency itself legitimated by the presence, both fictional and actual, of important dignitaries from the great powers of Europe. These were difficult years for Ludovico. Not only was his claim to power fragile and easily challenged within Milan, but relations with Naples were strained following the marginalization of Giangaleazzo and his new wife and her entourage at the Milanese court. It was imperative therefore for Ludovico to use every instrument in his power to reassure both Milan and the world of his right to rule as regent, at the same time as reasserting the dynastic claims of the Sforza family and his young nephew, Giangaleazzo. Bellincioni perhaps hinted at the underlying message of the masque when he wrote elsewhere 'If the duke has consummated his marriage/ Moro will protect their patrimony' (Solmi, 1904, p.76).

Temporary architecture and complex machinery for moving scenery were common features of indoor theatricals at this time. Some of the devices used were first developed for the performance of religious drama. Leonardo's stage set and design for the masque of 1490 is not unlike that devised by Brunelleschi for a religious play performed in Florence. During the course of the sixteenth century such theatrical automata became increasingly popular and also became an integral feature of Renaissance garden design.

Exercise

Read the extract from Bellincioni's performance script for *Il paradiso* in the Anthology (no. 39). Comment on the imagery used to depict Isabella of Aragon.

Discussion

Effectively this is a piece of rhetoric – a eulogy designed to elevate Isabella to the status of a goddess. The encomium concentrates on the link between the Neapolitan royal family and the house of Sforza, and stresses her virtuous nature through a comparison with the Graces. Clearly, the format of the piece is entirely conventional – the literary equivalent of the visual representations of virtuous femininity which we have previously encountered in the posthumous portrait of Battista

Sforza, the wife of Federico da Montefeltro (see Chapter 1, p. 54 and Chapter 3, Figure 3.20), and in the self-presentation of Isabella d'Este, as represented in the images she commissioned for her *studiolo* (see Chapter 1, p.64). We might also note that the script of the masque was presented to Isabella in book form, thus providing a keepsake of the occasion as well as a permanent model for such events in the future. ❖

Drawing as a scientific aid

Leonardo's science and its relationship to his overriding concern with the visual image have been the subject of much debate in recent years. The popular image of Leonardo as a scientific visionary ahead of his time is difficult to dispel. Everyone is familiar with his preoccupation with man-powered flight which produced, among other things, spectacular designs for contraptions which prefigure the first crude flying machines (Figure 2.12). It would be a mistake, however, to conclude from Leonardo's vast output of drawings, rough sketches and notes on scientific subjects that he was a scientist in the sense in which we commonly use the term today. Indeed, he was ill equipped to converse with the 'men of science' of his own age.[5] Not only was he a poor reader of Latin (he described himself as an '*omo sanza lettere*' ('unlettered')), but his lack of formal training or university education in the various disciplines of the natural philosopher meant that he was largely unable or unwilling to engage in discourse with contemporary scholars (one notable exception was his collaboration with Luca Pacioli; see below). As far as we know, Leonardo made no attempt to publish or communicate his scientific interests, despite the existence of the printing press. Nor did he seek to exploit his ideas on a range of scientific topics. Instead, his principal concern would appear to have consisted of the personal need to contemplate and describe the natural world in all its rich variety, to glory in the accomplishments of its Creator, rather than to turn such knowledge to practical account.

In the process, Leonardo adopted a highly eclectic approach in his pursuit of knowledge. A disciple of neither Plato nor Aristotle, he none the less cited both extensively in his notebooks and 'treatises'.[6]

[5] It is arguable that the notion of 'science' and the 'scientist' was itself an anachronism in the age of Leonardo. This issue is explored in more detail in Book 3, Chapter 5.

[6] Leonardo would appear to have planned a number of treatises on a variety of subjects including anatomy, painting, hydraulics and mechanics. Whether they were intended for publication or reserved for manuscript is unknown. Some have suggested the latter on the grounds that print technology at the turn of the fifteenth century was incapable of reproducing fair images of Leonardo's complex drawings, which were integral to his written text (Long, 1997, p.37).

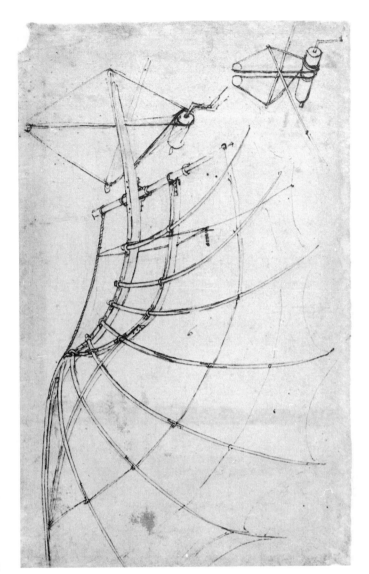

Figure 2.12 Leonardo da Vinci, study for the wings of a mechanical flying machine, early 1490s, pen and ink. Codex Atlanticus, fol. 313r. Biblioteca Ambrosiana, Milan

His high regard for mathematics, for example, was probably indebted to his interest in the revival of Platonism in the fifteenth century. On the other hand, his search for the elusive 'prime mover' in nature – the vital spirit which animated creation – was prompted by his acquaintance with the basic precepts of Aristotelian science. Above all, like Aristotle, Leonardo was an empiricist who borrowed theoretical concepts from ancient sources and utilized them only in so far as they accorded with his own observations. His lack of book learning was in this respect a positive advantage. It enabled him to see the world differently from many of his humanist-educated contemporaries who remained enslaved to the authority of traditional texts. But it would be wrong to exaggerate the extent to which Leonardo's rare skill as an observer of the natural world marked a significant step forward in terms of scientific and technological progress. Unlike Aristotle, Leonardo failed to achieve an over-arching synthesis or general theory based on his many original observations (Ackerman, 1998). His inability to develop an **inductivist** approach to science is evident in the fact that he rarely conducted experiments – the few attested examples are confined to his work in the field of optics, in particular his interest in reflection and refraction. On the other hand, his obsession with mathematical proportion and geometry and his search for geometrical forms in nature made him a curious and acute observer of the natural world. His acquaintance with the celebrated mathematician Luca Pacioli (*c.*1445–1517), for example, who dedicated his *De divina proportione* (*On Divine Proportion*) to Ludovico Sforza in 1498, prompted Leonardo to undertake careful study of the properties of water (see Figure 2.13).

Leonardo's approach to 'science' and scientific investigation is best illustrated by his life-long interest in the human body. For years, he had dabbled in the murky world of dissection, conducting numerous such operations in the later years of his life. While this frequently led him to challenge accepted medical wisdom (e.g. his observation, based on dissection, that 'the confluence of all the senses' occurred in one ventricle of the brain), his observations were for the most part unoriginal and followed the path laid down by ancient experts on the human body such as Aristotle and Galen (discussed in more detail in Book 3, Chapter 5). Consequently, his beautiful drawings and accompanying notes contributed little to new thinking on the subject and were intended, primarily, as 'an exposition of man's role in the natural order of things' (Kemp, 1981, p.124) (Figure 2.14). They were, in other words, part of Leonardo's wider concern with the divine 'first cause'. As such, they were inspired by his desire as an artist to reveal through close study of the movement of the human body the divine nature of mankind and man's relationship to the rest of creation. This is most evident in Leonardo's preoccupation with

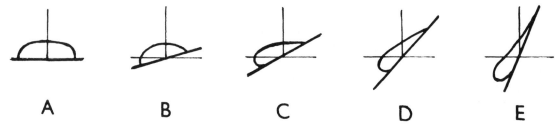

Figure 2.13 Leonardo da Vinci, analysis of a water droplet on a progressively inclined plane. Based on MS I, 90r. Reproduced from Kemp, 1981, p.150

the role of the body in architecture and his debt to the classical theorist Vitruvius, who had posited an analogous relationship between the human body and the ideal building (Figure 2.15, overleaf). The harmonious proportions of the body thus provided a model for the revival of classical architecture and informed much Renaissance thinking on the subject, as we have seen in the discussion on Filarete above. It was therefore no coincidence that when Leonardo submitted his own plans for a new cupola for Milan cathedral he claimed the authority of a 'doctor-architect' who alone was able to restore equilibrium to the various parts of the building (Kemp, 1981, pp.91–151; Schultz, 1982, pp.68–78).

Leonardo as architect

Like many other fifteenth-century architects, including Filarete, Leonardo's architectural training was grounded in practice, notwithstanding his own claim (as in the letter to Ludovico Sforza) to

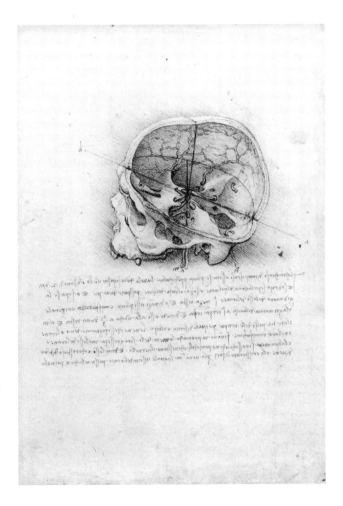

Figure 2.14 Leonardo da Vinci, cross-section of the human skull, c.1489, pen and ink. The Royal Collection © Her Majesty the Queen. Royal Library 19058r

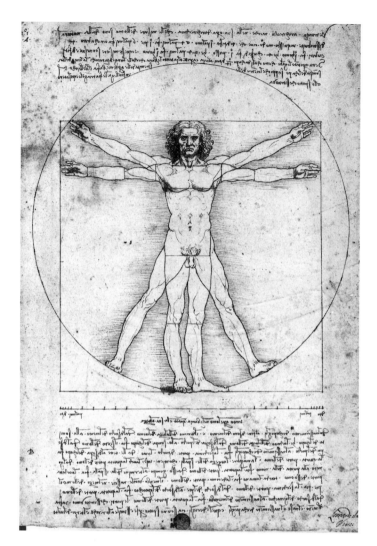

Figure 2.15 Leonardo da Vinci, Vitruvian proportions of the human figure, c.1490, pen and ink, silverpoint, red chalk, wash highlights, 34.3 × 24.5 cm. Accademia, Venice. Photo: Osvaldo Böhm

possess prior knowledge in the theoretical principles of the art of building. Competition for building commissions was hotly contested by men of Leonardo's background, none more so than projects for ecclesiastical buildings which provided both prestige and secure employment. Despite the considerable effort he put into securing such commissions, however, Leonardo would appear to have failed to secure any. A case in point was the competition for a *tiburio* for Milan Cathedral. Leonardo's interest in the project is evident from the fact that between 1487 and 1488 carpenters were paid for a model of his for the projected vault of the *tiburio*. Various other architects were consulted, however, including Luca Fancelli, who was summoned from Mantua to advise on a solution (he subsequently wrote to Lorenzo de' Medici claiming that the cupola looked about to collapse since it lacked 'bones and proportions'). Ultimately, the commission was granted to the local architect-sculptors Giovanni Antonio Amadeo (1447–1522) and Giovanni Giacomo Dolcebuono, who based their design for the *tiburio* on a model by Francesco di Giorgio Martini. Martini, who had worked at Urbino (see Chapter 1, p.47), would appear to have influenced Leonardo's work in this field. Leonardo's annotated copy of Martini's *Treatise of Civil and Military Architecture* testifies to the impact of the Sienese architect on the development of his ideas. Over ten years earlier, in 1490, both men had been actively engaged in the search for a solution to the problem of how to provide a cupola for the transept of Pavia Cathedral. Other lucrative and prestigious commissions included the enlargement of the church of S. Maria delle Grazie in Milan (see Chapter 1, p.34). By 1497 Ludovico Sforza had gathered together some of the 'best architectural experts' in Italy, including in all probability Leonardo and Bramante, to discuss this project. Notes and diagrams from Leonardo's sketchbooks appear to relate to mechanical issues surrounding the distribution of weight in the projected dome for the church. Like his illustrious contemporary Bramante, other sketches by Leonardo attest to his preoccupation with designs for centrally planned churches. In the case of Bramante, this led to his appointment by Pope Julius II as the architect for the new St Peter's.

Leonardo had rather more success in his search for architectural patronage in the sphere of secular urban building. Milan provided plenty of opportunity for him to put into practice his well-developed plans for orderly town planning (see Figure 2.16, overleaf), a preoccupation which coincided with a similar interest on the part of Milan's ruling family, the Sforza. Ludovico Sforza, in particular, wished to enlarge the city and ease overcrowding by the construction of a series of satellite districts in which houses would be built according to orderly and uniform principles. Leonardo was clearly in favour of such planning. In his notebooks he frequently associated orderly town planning with good government. Streets, for example, should be tiered in order to segregate the gentry from the 'lower orders'. One area of Milan where Leonardo was able to put some of these ideas into practice was the district of the Porta Vercellina, close to the restored church of S. Maria delle Grazie. Here, many of Leonardo's wealthy and well-connected patrons and courtiers lived, several of whom were eager to renovate their homes according to the dictates of the revived *all'antica* style. Leonardo drew designs for a number of courtier houses and palaces, and he may even have acted as adviser for the house built for Ludovico's mistress, Cecilia

Gallerani. His work in this field did not cease with the fall of the Sforza. Following his return to Milan in 1506, he designed a suburban villa for the new French governor Charles d'Amboise (d. 1511). He does not appear, however, to have received many secular commissions outside Milan. Though he visited the ducal city of Vigevano in 1494, in company with Bramante, his influence on the remodelling of that city seems to have been restricted to the creation of a labyrinth in the garden of the duke's villa (Pedretti, 1986, pp.32–112, 210–37).

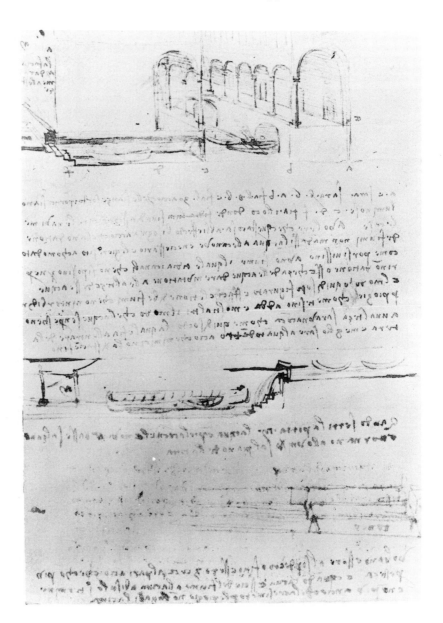

Figure 2.16 Leonardo da Vinci, town planning and canalization studies. Bibliothèque de l'Institut de France MS B, fols 37v and 38r. Photo: Bulloz

One other area of architectural practice in which Leonardo excelled was military construction. Here, the opportunity for innovation came not so much from Ludovico Sforza, for whom he constructed minor fortifications, but during his period of employment with Cesare Borgia in 1502 and with the Florentine republic in the following year (the latter included an ambitious project to re-route the river Arno). Leonardo's interest in military affairs was all-embracing. Apart from the construction of fortifications designed to withstand artillery

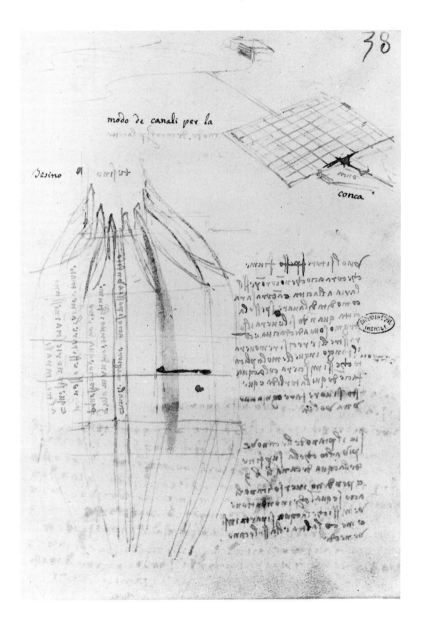

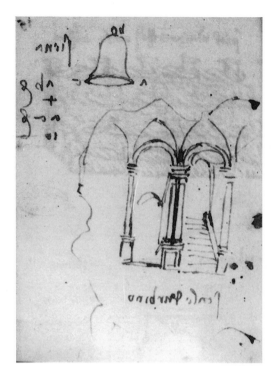

Figure 2.17 Leonardo da Vinci, grand staircase and diagrams of a plinth, c.1502, pen and ink. Bibliothèque de l'Institut de France, MS L, fols 19v and 20r. Photo: Bulloz

attack, he was a prolific 'inventor' of military engines and weaponry, including catapults, crossbows, lightweight bridges and armoured vehicles. He was also, as befits a military engineer, skilled in the drawing of maps and plans of cities.

In the final resort, however, the ascription of specific buildings to Leonardo is often speculative and inconclusive. Among the many works attributed to him, including a palace for the king of France and a villa for the marquis of Mantua, little in the way of solid documentary evidence survives to verify his role as the principal architect. Leonardo's own records are scanty, usually consisting of little more than short annotations or rough sketches and diagrams. While in the service of Cesare Borgia, for example, he drew the grand staircase in the ducal palace at Urbino, which his patron had recently seized, with the accompanying note: 'Steps of Urbino. The plinth must be as broad as the thickness of the wall against which the plinth is built' (Figure 2.17).

Much of Leonardo's work, including his approach to architecture, was characterized by a spirit of innovation and intellectual inquisitiveness which, from a modern vantage point, never ceases to fascinate. His patrons, however, may not have been so easily impressed. Designs for machine guns and submarines were all very well, but their impracticality in the context of Renaissance technology meant that they were of little use to the men who employed Leonardo on a regular basis. In the years to come Leonardo was, however, to stand as an icon for the new artist, one who, in the eyes of Vasari, represented a new phase of artistic achievement in which genius was appreciated by patrons for its own sake (Goldscheider, 1943, pp.9–23). The extent to which Leonardo self-consciously fashioned this identity for himself is open to question. In establishing a reputation as an 'intellectual artist', rather than a skilled craftsman, he was none the less assisted by a number of advantages: the respect he acquired in some courtly and humanist circles; the high status of his family background (in spite of his illegitimacy); and his own self-education. In addition, he could also count on the growing rivalry between powerful patrons who sought to acquire artists of his calibre in order to promote their courts as centres of cultural and artistic excellence. Ultimately, of course, this led to Leonardo's departure for France and the court of the Valois kings, and the initiation of a new chapter in the history of the Renaissance which lies beyond the scope of this particular study (Pedretti, 1986).

Appendix

Josquin Desprez: Tu solus, qui facis mirabilia

Reproduced from Palisca, 1988, pp.113–19

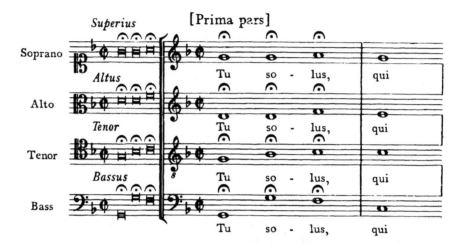

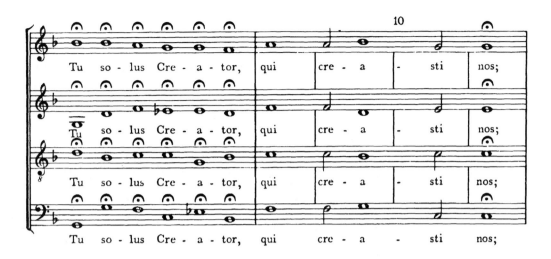

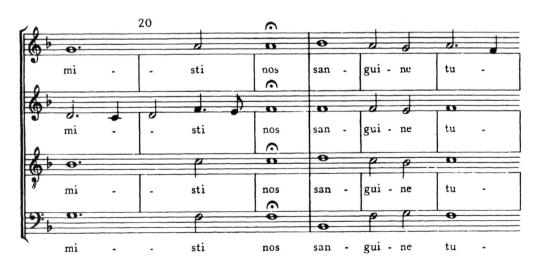

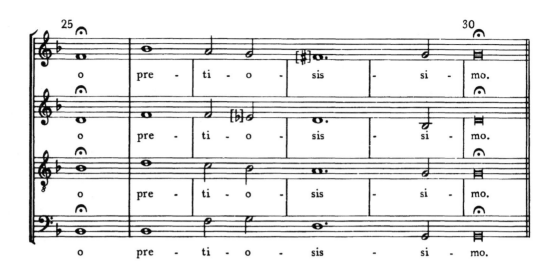

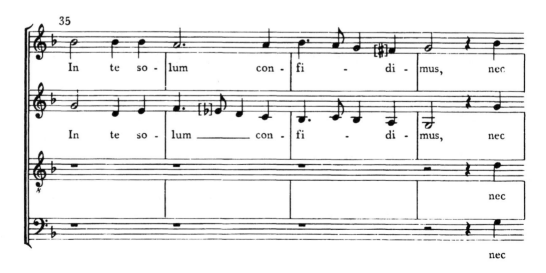

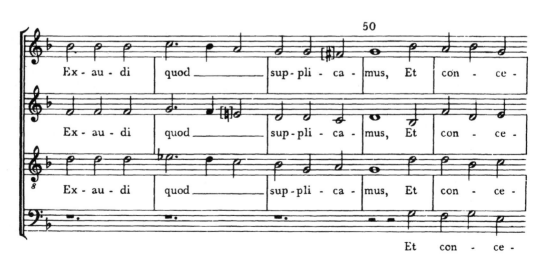

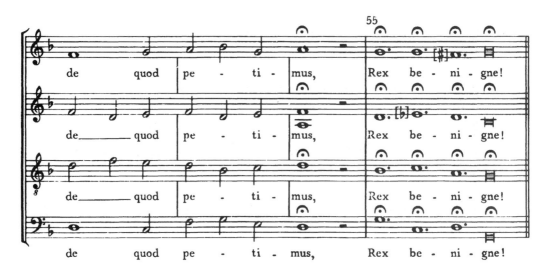

[Secunda pars]

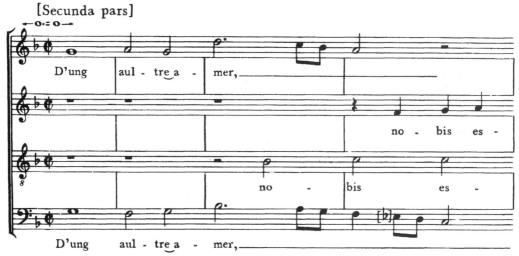

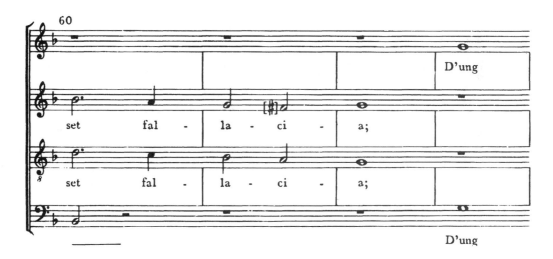

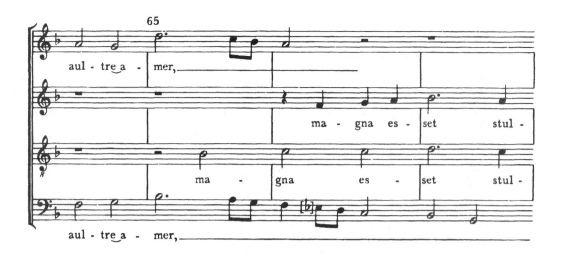

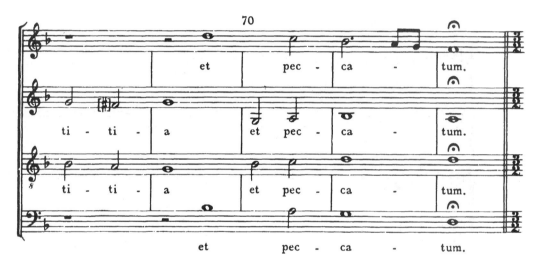

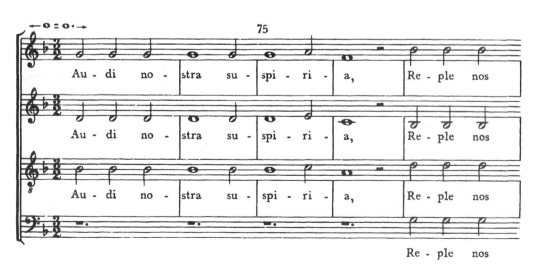

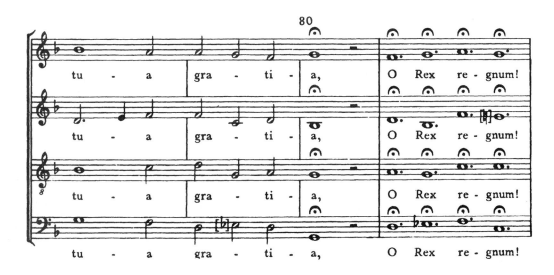

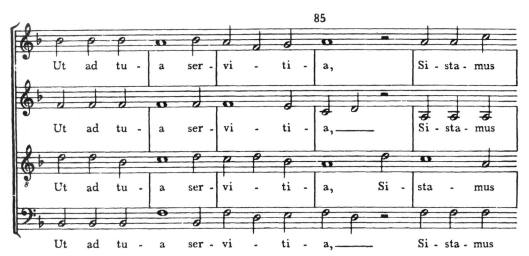

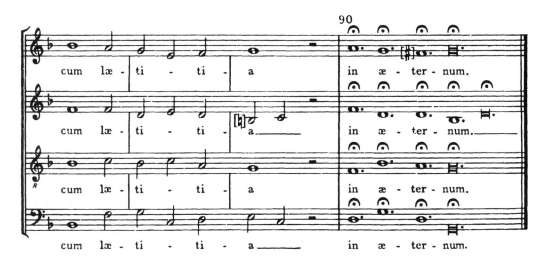

Bibliography

ACKERMAN, J.S. (1998) 'Leonardo da Vinci: art in science', *Daedalus*, no. 127, pp.207–24.

BURCKHARDT, J. (1990) *The Civilization of the Renaissance in Italy*, trans. S.C.G. Middlemore, Harmondsworth, Penguin; first published 1858.

COLE, A. (1995) *Art of the Italian Renaissance Courts*, London, Weidenfeld & Nicolson.

DE VERE, G. du C. (trans.) (1996) G. Vasari: *The Lives of the Most Excellent Painters, Sculptors, Architects*, 2 vols, London, David Campbell.

FUSCO, L. and CORTI, G. (1992) 'Lorenzo de' Medici on the Sforza monument', *Achademia Leonardi Vinci*, no. 5, pp.11–32.

GOLDSCHEIDER, L. (1943) *Leonardo da Vinci: Life and Work*, London, Phaidon.

KEMP, M. (1981) *Leonardo da Vinci: The Marvellous Works of Nature and Man*, London, Dent.

KEMP, M. and WALKER, M. (eds) (1989) *Leonardo on Painting*, New Haven, Conn. and London, Yale University Press.

LOCKWOOD, L. (1981) 'Strategies of music patronage in the fifteenth century: the cappella of Ercole I d'Este' in I. Fenlon (ed.) *Music in Medieval and Early Modern Europe*, Cambridge, Cambridge University Press.

LOCKWOOD, L. (1984) *Music in Renaissance Ferrara 1400–1505*, Oxford, Oxford University Press.

LONG, P.O. (1997) 'Power, patronage, and the authorship of *Ars*: from mechanical know-how to mechanical knowledge in the last scribal age', *Isis*, no. 88, pp.1–41.

LOWINSKY, E.E. (1976) 'Ascanio Sforza's life: a key to Josquin's biography and an aid to the chronology of his works' in E.E. Lowinsky (ed.) *Josquin des Prez: Proceedings of the International Josquin Festival-Conference, 1971*, Oxford, Oxford University Press.

MATTHEWS, L. and MERKLEY, P.A. (1994) 'Josquin Desprez and his Milanese patrons', *Journal of Musicology*, no. 12, pp.434–63.

PALISCA, C.V. (ed.) (1988, 2nd edn) *Norton Anthology of Western Music*, vol. 1, New York and London, W.W. Norton.

PEDRETTI, C. (1986) *Leonardo Architect*, trans. S. Brill, London, Thames & Hudson; first published 1981.

PRIZER, W.F. (1989) 'Music at the court of the Sforza: the birth and death of a music centre', *Musica disciplina*, no. 43, pp.141–93.

PRIZER, W.F. (1989) 'North Italian courts, 1460–1540' in I. Fenlon (ed.) *The Renaissance*, London.

RYKWERT, J., LEACH, N. and TAVERNOR, R. (eds) (1988), L.B. Alberti: *On the Art of Building in Ten Books*, Cambridge, Mass. and London, MIT Press.

SCHULTZ, B. (1982) *Art and Anatomy in Renaissance Italy*, Ann Arbor, Mich., UMI Research Press.

SOLMI, E. (1904) 'La festa del Paradiso di Leonardo da Vinci e Bernardo Bellincione', *Archivio storico lombardo*, no. 31, pp.75–89.

SPENCER, J.R. (ed./trans.) (1965) A. Filarete: *Treatise on Architecture*, 2 vols, New Haven, Conn., Yale University Press.

STRUNK, O. (1952) *Source Readings in Music History*, London, Faber & Faber.

WELCH, E.S. (1993) 'Sight, sound and ceremony in the chapel of Galeazzo Maria Sforza', *Early Music History*, no. 12, pp.151–90.

WELCH, E.S. (1995) *Art and Authority in Renaissance Milan*, New Haven, Conn. and London, Yale University Press.

Anthology and Reader sources

Leonardo da Vinci, Prospective letter of employment to Ludovico Sforza (*c*.1481–2): *Leonardo on Painting*, ed. and trans. M. Kemp and M. Walker, New Haven, Conn. and London, Yale University Press, 1989, pp.251–3 (Anthology, no. 38).

Leonardo da Vinci, extracts from his notebooks: *Leonardo on Painting*, ed. and trans. M. Kemp and M. Walker, New Haven, Conn. and London, Yale University Press, 1989, pp.13–15, 32–4, 37–8, 49–55, 57, 59–61, 63–4, 87, 24, 26, 119–20, 122, 205 (Anthology, no. 31).

Bernardo Bellincioni, Il paradiso: *Le rime de Bernardo Bellincioni, scelta di curiosità lettararie inedite o rare dal secolo XIII al XIV*, ed. P. Fanfani, Bologna, Gaetano Romagnoli, 1876, 1878, vol. 2 (2 vols), pp.218–19; trans. for this edition by Nick Webb, with Tim Benton and Catherine King (Anthology, no. 39).

Music sources

Note: the following sources were used in preparing this chapter, but other sources or versions of the music would be acceptable for your study.

Track 1: Heinrich Isaac, 'A la bataglia', from *A Florentine Carnival: Festival Music for Lorenzo de' Medici*, performed by London Pro Musica, dir. Bernard Thomas, Pickwick CD PCD 825 (1986) Track 11 (4'20).

Track 2: Diomedes, 'Dolores mortis', *Renaissance Music from the Courts of Mantua and Ferrara, c.1500*, Chandos CD Chan 8333 (1984) Track 10 (1'43).

Track 3: Josquin Desprez, 'Tu solus qui facis mirabilia', *Josquin Desprez, Missa 'Hercules Dux Ferrariae', etc.*, performed by the Hilliard Ensemble, dir. Paul Hillier, EMI CDC 7 49960 2 (1990) Track 10 (4'48).

CHAPTER THREE

Fifteenth-century Florence and court culture under the Medici

BY ANABEL THOMAS

Objectives

The objectives of this chapter are that you should:

- understand why Burckhardt regarded fifteenth-century Florence under the Medici as representative of a 'golden age' for Renaissance culture;

- consider Burckhardtian notions of courtly culture and individualism within the context of Medicean patronage of the arts and learning;

- assess, in the light of current historical research, the extent to which Medicean cultural patronage can be considered within the context of a Renaissance court;

- contrast the artistic culture of a republican 'court' with those monarchical and seigneurial courts studied in Chapters 1 and 2 of this book.

Introduction

In a political and social context, the court defined the space inhabited by the prince (the lord of a territory), his consort, household, courtiers, and officials; this space had invisible boundaries which were determined by those who exercised power and influence on behalf of the prince.

(Cole, 1995, p.8)

Chapters 1 and 2 of this book examined how princely and seigneurial courts functioned as important sites of cultural activity in the fifteenth century. This chapter will look at similar processes, but in the context

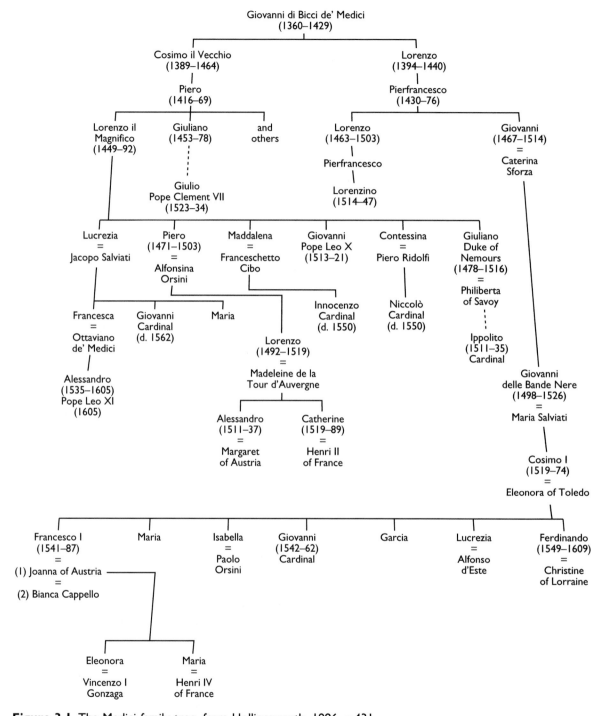

Figure 3.1 The Medici family tree, from Hollingsworth, 1996, p.431

of a republican city-state which, ostensibly at least, precluded the creation of such courts. For much of the second half of the fifteenth century, Florence was effectively ruled by a single family, the Medici, who did in part attempt to emulate the court-based regimes of neighbouring princes. Consequently, one of the central concerns of this chapter is the extent to which the Medici cultivated the courtly arts, as defined by Burckhardt. The chapter will also consider the degree to which patronage of the visual arts reflected the political status quo in Florence, and how, within the context of a republican city-state, the visual arts might also have been used actively to assist in shaping and legitimating the political aspirations of the Medici.

The roots of Medici power in Florence were firmly established in 1418 when Giovanni di Bicci de' Medici (1360–1429) became the banker to the papacy and established the wealth of the family for generations to come (see Figure 3.1). Under his son Cosimo (1389–1464), the family extended its control over the political machinery of the republican city-state to the point at which they were the *de facto* rulers of a city which none the less continued to display the outward trappings of a republican regime. Cosimo and his heirs worked assiduously to maintain their control of the government of Florence through an intricate network of alliances with other patrician families in the city. At the same time, they sought to undermine or dominate those power bases in the city which they considered a threat to their own authority. Ultimately successful in their political machinations (as discussed in Book 1, Chapter 6), the Medici were careful throughout this period to preserve the semblance of the traditional, republican organs of government. Florence thus remained a nominal republic, but in reality it was increasingly governed by the autocratic Medici who strove to emulate the princely rule of neighbouring states until they were forced into temporary exile in 1494.[1]

Throughout this period, and culminating in the so-called 'golden age' of Medicean rule under Lorenzo il Magnifico (1449–92), the arts flourished in Florence. This was not simply the product of Medicean patronage – the city had long held a European-wide reputation as a centre of cultural, literary and artistic excellence. On the other hand, under the guidance of the Medici, Florence's reputation as a cultural centre was undoubtedly enhanced, so much so that ruling princes and nobility from the rest of Italy frequently looked to the city and its craftsmen for artistic inspiration. Artists supported by the Medici

---

[1] A good example of Medicean authority in action, and of the anxieties it provoked, is provided by the aftermath of the Pazzi conspiracy (1478), in which Lorenzo de' Medici was wounded and his brother Giuliano murdered. The conspirators were arrested and brutally murdered. For Machiavelli's account of these events, see the Anthology, no. 26ii.

frequently served as cultural ambassadors, and their work was used as diplomatic gifts. Acutely conscious of their social and political status in fifteenth-century Italy, the Medici were thus well aware of the political opportunities such cultural activity provided. Not only did foreign dignitaries appreciate the aesthetic value of such gifts, but they acknowledged, at the same time, the princely magnificence of the gesture. In this way, the Medici not only maintained the fiction of their domestic status as ordinary citizens of the republic, but they were also able to promote a very different image of themselves in the wider world of international politics and diplomacy.

How they achieved this fine balancing act will constitute one of the main themes of the chapter. In analysing the 'court culture' of Medicean Florence it is thus necessary to pay careful attention to the complex interplay of social, religious and political factors that informed cultural production. Any such investigation, as Burckhardt himself was acutely aware, demands close study of a wide variety of cultural activity in order to reflect the disparate nature of Renaissance culture. Later sections of the chapter, for example, look at the production of medals and coins in fifteenth-century Florence as an illustration of this process, as well as at expressions of art in public display and state ceremonial. It is in this spirit that the chapter argues it is possible to characterize such objects and events as representing the fundamental features of a court culture, even if they were embedded in, and the product of, a political framework which was essentially republican.

Cultural activities in Florence under the Medici

Manifestations of magnificence:[2] notions of authority and power

In his own time and in subsequent ages Cosimo de' Medici was famous for the vast amounts of money he spent on architectural projects both within and around Florence. By the middle of the century he was one of the wealthiest citizens in the city. Pouring money into the construction, restoration and development of ecclesiastical sites such as the Dominican friary of S. Marco and the parish church of S. Lorenzo, as well as into his own private palace in

---

[2] According to the fourth-century BCE Greek philosopher Aristotle (*Nicomachean Ethics* 4.2), *magnificentia*, or magnificence, as a form of conduct somewhere between asceticism and impulsive extravagance, could be seen as a moral virtue in so far as it represented a mean between two extremes.

Florence and villas in the countryside, Cosimo ran the risk of criticism for ostentatious display. Machiavelli, in his *Storie fiorentine*, likened Cosimo's promotion of architecture to that of a king, but noted at the same time that he was careful to avoid appearing grander than an ordinary citizen in his way of life and thereby attracting envy. A powerful defence of Cosimo's patronage of architecture can be found in a contemporary fifteenth-century text, *In magnificentiae Cosmi Medicei florentini detractores* (Against those who disparage Cosimo de' Medici's magnificence), written by Timoteo Maffei, a member of the Augustinian canons (who had directly benefited from Cosimo's munificence when he paid for the reconstruction and decoration of the church and monastery of the Badia at Fiesole). Maffei's text was important for establishing an early use of the term 'magnificence' in reference to Cosimo's virtuous character as a patron.

The concept of magnificence in terms of great expenditure by the rich and powerful was already current during Cosimo's time. Maffei's use of the term was certainly not new. However, in referring to architecture 'wonderfully embellished at the expense of Cosimo de' Medici, that most famous and magnificent man', Maffei sought to combine the magnificence of patronal gesture with magnificence of the mind. In a conscious attempt to defend Cosimo's seeming extravagance and lack of decorum in setting himself above other citizens, Maffei asked his readers to consider Cosimo's selfless virtue in distributing his riches in this manner. Cosimo was deemed 'magnificent' by Maffei for his virtuousness in spending more than he needed to; for providing appropriate monuments for his city; in sum, for presenting to posterity examples of 'divine excellence'. That Cosimo stamped so many of his architectural projects with his own personal insignia could be excused, as this allowed later generations not only to know the name of the person for whom they might pray, but also in their own turn to be inspired to emulate his good deeds.

The accolade 'il Magnifico', by which both Cosimo and Lorenzo de' Medici were known, was not as distinctive during the Renaissance period as it might seem today, and was in fact often used for men of standing. Nor was Burckhardt the first to recognize fifteenth-century Florence as a centre of elevated political thought or a paradigm of court culture in its literary and artistic aspirations, its leaders mentioned in the same breath as 'other princes'. Looking back on the lifetime of Lorenzo il Magnifico from the vantage point of the early sixteenth century, Francesco Guicciardini presented both the city and its virtual ruler in similar terms. He explained in his *Storie fiorentine* (Palmarocchi, 1931) that Lorenzo's name was glorified because during his lifetime 'all the most excellent arts and virtues' evolved in Florence. According to Rubinstein, Guicciardini regarded Lorenzo's position as that of 'a benevolent despot in a republican constitution who had succeeded in increasing his power to a point where its transformation into a **Signoria** might appear imminent' (1997, pp.250–2). Yet, as Rubinstein notes, the official document declaring Lorenzo's son Piero successor in 1492 refers to him not as king or captain but as 'vir primarius nostrae civitatis' (foremost man in our city), a title similar to that of '*Pater Patriae*' (Father of the Fatherland), posthumously conferred on Lorenzo's grandfather Cosimo after his death in 1464.

Although we should remind ourselves that opposition or criticism could be a dangerous activity in Renaissance Florence, and that harsher evaluations of the Medici leaders emerge from private journals of the time, there seems to have been no doubt in Guicciardini's mind that five decades of Medicean power had established a house which was both noble and rich, as well as renowned throughout the whole Italian peninsula. Under the leadership of Cosimo and Lorenzo, and as a result of great virtue or 'strength', the house of Medici had preserved and developed the state, benefiting not only the family's private affairs but also the fortunes of the city. For Guicciardini, the religious, political, moral and artistic culture which existed in Florence at the end of the fifteenth century depended in large part upon the good offices of Cosimo and Lorenzo. Describing the state of the city in Chapter 9 of *Storie fiorentine*, Guicciardini noted how at Lorenzo's death Florence was 'in a highest degree in the state of peace' (Palmarocchi, 1931), its citizens united in spirit. Recording the great flowering of humanistic studies under Angelo Poliziano, and of philosophy and arts under Marsilio Ficino and Giovanni Pico della Mirandola, Guicciardini wrote that the city was 'abundantly full of all kinds of culture', blessed by Lorenzo's patronage and 'infinite liberality'. According to Guicciardini, Lorenzo il Magnifico countenanced no omission of magnificence of any kind in promoting friendship with other princes of his day. He recounted how each day the Florentine population enjoyed spectacles, feasts and novelties and the city basked in the 'highest glory and reputation abroad' for having a government and a leader of 'such great authority'. Indeed, Guicciardini claimed that the Medici-dominated government had such power that no one dared oppose it.

While recognizing Lorenzo's many virtues, Guicciardini also acknowledged a number of less pleasant characteristics, including his pride, cruelty and overbearing authority. Yet, despite such reservations Guicciardini recognized Lorenzo's outstanding achievements and in particular his ability to maintain friendship and status among princes within and outside Italy. According to Guicciardini, Lorenzo wished not only to equal but also to compete with Italy's princes. He also maintained that Lorenzo's authority over the city was so absolute that it seemed as if he had assumed power by magic. Yet Florence under Lorenzo, although blessed by 'all those glories and happiness that can exist in a city', was no longer free. For Guicciardini, disaffected as he finally was with the Medici power base, Florence was free in name only. Nevertheless, he still maintained that fifteenth-century Florence under the Medici constituted a kind of spirit level or balance for the whole of Italy. With Lorenzo's death in April 1492 (and, more specifically, the invasion of the French in 1494), all was thrown into disorder and confusion.

Fame and memory: the cult of remembrance and questions of lineage

Medici power in Florence was effectively established in 1434 with the return from exile of Cosimo, Giovanni di Bicci's son. Cosimo had been banished after conflict with another powerful Florentine citizen, Rinaldo degli Albizzi. Cosimo's father Giovanni is best remembered now for the role he played in establishing the church of S. Lorenzo as a Medici power base by funding the rebuilding of the sacristy. It was Cosimo, however, who consolidated the family's banking fortunes and political position.

Guicciardini relates how Cosimo and Lorenzo were frequently compared in an attempt to establish which was more excellent. Cosimo was deemed more steadfast and judicious, but the magnificence of both was unquestioned. Cosimo's magnificence lay in the fact that he built palaces and churches both inside and beyond the city, perpetuating his fame. Lorenzo, on the other hand, built hardly anything. He began a sumptuous construction at Poggio a Caiano but left it unfinished at his death. Despite this he was renowned for his generosity and patronage. Ultimately, however, Guicciardini believed that Cosimo was the more worthy of praise. It was for Cosimo, not Lorenzo, that a commemorative medal was posthumously struck (Figure 3.2, overleaf), revealing much about Cosimo's claim to later fame and about broader, corporative Medicean aspirations to seigneurial power and authority in fifteenth-century Florence.

In her *Art of the Italian Renaissance Courts* (pp.57–8, 78, 122–3) Alison Cole describes Renaissance medals and the significance of the symbolic details included in them. You may wish to read these sections now, prior to the discussion, below, about the medal made for Cosimo de' Medici shortly after his death. Cole's comments on

Figure 3.2 Posthumous medal, *Cosimo de' Medici*, obverse (Cosimo de' Medici Pater Patriae) and reverse (Florence holding an orb and a triple olive branch), c.1465–9, bronze, diameter 7.5 cm. Samuel H. Kress Collection, 1957.14.839. © 1999 Board of Trustees, National Gallery of Art, Washington DC

medals struck in honour of the Aragonese King Alfonso in Naples, the *condottiere* Sigismondo Malatesta in Rimini, and members of the dynastic court of the Este in Ferrara should help you understand the significance of the imagery in Cosimo's medal. Note what she has to say about the making of medals and their significance as artefacts for exchange and the bestowing of favours within and between Italian courts. Note also the extent to which such practice during the Renaissance period imitated codes of behaviour in the ancient world.

Medals offered great potential for both subliminal communication and overt display. In Renaissance court culture portrait medals were very sophisticated vehicles of political propaganda. In his posthumous medal Cosimo is clearly established through associative symbolism as the rightful temporal ruler of Florence – imbued as he is with the nobility of past imperial authority. The medal depicts on the obverse side an image of Cosimo in profile in the guise of an imperial ruler (although sporting contemporary headgear) and surrounded by an inscription which reads *Magnus Cosmus Medices PPP* (Great Cosimo de' Medici the F[irst] F[ather] of the F[atherland]). On the reverse side is the enthroned figure of a woman in classical robes (identifiable as Pallas Athena – daughter of Zeus, goddess of wisdom and patron of institutions of learning and the arts), circumscribed by the inscription *Pax libertasque publica* (Peace and liberty for the state). The single word *Florentia* (Florence) runs along the base of her throne, a position often reserved in classical medals for titles of power such as IMP/X. She holds in her outstretched right hand an orb, a symbol of royal power. Positioned across her left shoulder is a sceptre-like olive branch, divided into three foliaged sections, which draws on the imperial symbolism of the victor's wreath. Significantly, the triple division of the olive branch is also reminiscent of the device of the three feathers used by Cosimo's son Piero, just as the orb is reminiscent of the *palle* (balls) included in the family coat of arms.

The choice of Pallas Athena for inclusion in Cosimo's medal is most revealing. It reminds us of Athena's rule over Athens and the parallels that may be drawn with Cosimo's own leadership. According to classical mythology, the goddess Athena was awarded the city and the territory surrounding Athens (the region known as Attica) in a contest with the sea god Poseidon. Victory in this contest, which was judged by a tribunal of the gods, depended on one of the two contestants being able to provide the most useful gift for the people of Attica. Poseidon's offering was a great stallion which rose from the ground when he struck the earth with his trident. Athena, however, caused an olive tree to sprout, thus presenting the people with a greater good – a symbol of peace and a real and practical source of plenty.

To the modern mind, such symbolism may seem complex and obscure. To the Renaissance mind, steeped in classical learning, Cosimo's medal offered a number of messages which were concerned in one way or another with the legitimacy of Medicean power and with the glory and benevolence of this particular individual. Through the use of both covert and overt symbolism, Cosimo de' Medici presides over his own subjects in a land blessed by his wisdom and magnanimity. By association he ranks with the rulers of the classical world and in particular with the wise goddess of peace, Pallas Athena. Cosimo is revealed as a new personification of wisdom and liberality bringing peace and prosperity to a new Athens: complex flattery worthy of this sophisticated culture.

It may be no coincidence that Cosimo's medal is similar to one made for the Ferrarese merchant Bartolommeo Pendaglia, who died in 1462 (Figure 3.3, overleaf). Pendaglia's medal, which was made by Sperandio di Mantua, depicts on the obverse the profile of an elderly man with squashed hat and on the reverse a nude male figure (identified by some as the merchant Pendaglia himself, but more likely depicting Emperor Frederick III), seated with outstretched hand holding an orb (or according to others a pearl), his left arm

Figure 3.3 Sperandio di Mantua, *Bartolommeo Pendaglia,* medal, obverse (Bartolommeo Pendaglia, merchant of Ferrara) and reverse (figure seated on a cuirass, holding a globe and a spear), *c.*1462, bronze, diameter 8.4 cm. Samuel H. Kress Collection, 1957.14.705. © Board of Trustees, National Gallery of Art, Washington DC

embracing a spear. His left foot rests on a sack out of which cascade coins. On this side also there is the inscription *Caesariana liberalitas* (the liberality of Caesar), while on the obverse we read *Bartholomaeus Pendalia insigne liberalitatis et munificentiae exemplum fuit* (Bartolommeo Pendaglia, the emblem of liberality and model of munifice). Pendaglia was perhaps the wealthiest individual in fifteenth-century Ferrara. He claimed noble descent, moreover, from one of the retinue of the twelfth-century Emperor Frederick Barbarossa. Bartolommeo himself assumed a key role in the administration of the affairs of the Este, the ruling family of Ferrara, and received considerable rewards of land, villas, livestock and tax exemptions. His wedding in 1452 was graced by a number of dignitaries including Duke Borso d'Este, Emperor Frederick III and King Ladislav of Hungary. The emperor presented the bride with a priceless pearl as a wedding gift, and honoured the occasion and Pendaglia by endowing him with a knighthood.

Not only merchant leaders of the community but also merchant 'prince-aspirants' drew upon similar sources of classical imagery and classically inspired inscriptions in depicting themselves on these relatively small items of exchange. Reference to imperial favour on the reverse of Pendaglia's medal may have played some part in influencing the content or symbolism of medals produced for other contemporary pillars of society. The similarity of design and detail to the medal produced for Cosimo de' Medici is striking.

Exercise

Reread Alison Cole's descriptions of Renaissance medals (her pages 57–8, 78, 122–3) and list any similarities between these and the posthumous medal struck in honour of Cosimo de' Medici.

Discussion

Cristoforo di Geremia's medal of Alfonso V of Aragon (Figure 3.4) shows on its reverse the king in imperial pose seated upon a throne guarded by **sphinxes** and crowned by mythological deities of war. Alfonso is associated through such symbols and the surrounding inscription *Victorem regni Mars et Bellona coronant* (Mars and Bellona crown the victor of the realm) with military prowess and legitimate kingship. Sigismondo Malatesta's castle on the reverse of his medal (Figure 3.5, overleaf) offers, by contrast, concrete evidence of temporal power. It appears to break the constraints of the surrounding inscription with its bristling and castellated walls and towers – an impregnable fortress representing the broader territorial

Figure 3.4 Cristoforo di Geremia, *Alfonso V of Aragon, king of Naples and Sicily*, medal, obverse (Alfonso V) and reverse (Alfonso crowned by Mars and Bellona), 1458, bronze, diameter 7.5 cm. Samuel H. Kress Collection, 1957.14.804. © Board of Trustees, National Gallery of Art, Washington DC

Figure 3.5 Matteo de' Pasti, medal, reverse of *Sigismondo Malatesta* (the castle of Rimini), 1446, bronze, diameter 8.3 cm. Samuel H. Kress Collection, 1957.14.652. © Board of Trustees, National Gallery of Art, Washington DC

Figure 3.6 Pisanello, *Leonello d'Este, Marquis of Ferrara*, medal, obverse (Leonello d'Este) and reverse (lion being taught by Cupid to sing), 1444, bronze, 10.3 cm. Samuel H. Kress Collection, 1957.14.602. © Board of Trustees, National Gallery of Art, Washington DC

power of the leader of Rimini. Leonello d'Este's medal (Figure 3.6), unlike the previous two examples, appealed to the cultured and intellectual through veiled symbolism. Although clearly depicting Leonello in the guise of an imperial ruler on its obverse side, and referring to his familial links with royalty through the inclusion of *GE[ner] R[egis] AR[agonum]* (son-in-law of the king of Aragon), it turns on the reverse to more subtle references to his territorial power. Here we find combined in the rocky terrain – as if in natural symbiosis with the world around – Leonello's own personal insignia of the *stele* (classical funerary pillar) and billowing sail, the eagle of the house of Este and the ferocious or warlike *leone* or lion (a pun on the ruler's own name) tamed (or perhaps civilized) through the peaceful arts of love and music. Pisanello's medal for Gianfrancesco Gonzaga (Figure 3.7) is significant also for the accompanying inscription *Primus Marchio Mantue* (first marquis of Mantua). Thus, imperial associations, territorial possessions and social status are all combined and displayed in this eminently reproducible and exchangeable art form. ❖

Figure 3.7 Pisanello, *Gianfrancesco Gonzaga, First Marquis of Mantua*, medal, obverse (Gianfrancesco Gonzaga) and reverse (Gonzaga riding in a rocky landscape), c.1439, lead, diameter 10 cm. Samuel H. Kress Collection, 1957.14.594. © Board of Trustees, National Gallery of Art, Washington DC

The art of making medals was developed with particular enthusiasm at the Este court in Ferrara by Leonello d'Este's principal medallion maker Pisanello. Leonello d'Este and other contemporaries of the Medici deliberately used the reverse sides of their medals to project an image of their personal circumstances, achievements and aspirations. Sigismondo Malatesta was probably the first Renaissance 'prince' fully to appreciate the propagandistic potential of medal reverses, using them to advertise his military prowess and territorial gains. His decision to include a portrait of his castle both on the reverse of his medal and in the votive fresco painting by Piero della Francesca in the sacristy to his chapel of St Sigismund in S. Francesco (better known as the Tempio Malatestiano) (Figure 3.8) broke with earlier visual traditions and lent political potency to his own personal image.

Figure 3.8 Piero della Francesca, *Sigismondo Malatesta and St Sigismund*, 1451, fresco, 257 × 345 cm. Sacristy, Chapel of S. Sigismondo, Tempio Malatestiano, S. Francesco, Rimini. Photo: Alinari

In Sigismondo Malatesta's case, we can also be sure that such imagery was meant to last and to be handed down to posterity so that future generations might recognize his eminence. We know that countless medals were sunk into the foundations of buildings constructed in and around Rimini during Sigismondo's reign; some 24 have been discovered in the walls of Castel Sigismondo and over 40 in the foundations of S. Francesco. In his *Trattato di architettura* Filarete noted that such practice reflected the contemporary desire for future recognition in the manner of the ancient Romans: 'they will find these things; and through these we will be remembered and recorded ... Just as we have found those things which represent antiquity' (Woods-Marsden, 1989, n.67, pp.400–1; translated A. Thomas, 1999). According to Timoteo Maffei, Sigismondo Malatesta was also liberal in dispensing medals carrying his image to other states. But such liberality was not the disinterested act it might first appear: Sigismondo's medals contained allusions to state and territory that would have resonated deeply with his fellow rulers.

Diplomacy and territorial expansion

During the fourteenth and fifteenth centuries northern and central Italy witnessed a large number of virtually autonomous states competing for territory and resources. Burckhardt claimed that nearly all such states were themselves the result of recent usurpations and that this influenced both foreign and internal policy:

> Not one of them recognized another without reserve; the same play of chance which had helped to found and consolidate one dynasty might upset another: the necessity of movement and aggrandizement is common to all illegitimate powers.

(1990, p.74)

Fluctuating alliances and constant jostling for power fuelled the development of a sophisticated diplomacy in which external affairs increasingly monopolized the attention of ruling groups. There was also an increasing need for embassies, with the exchange of both resident and short-term ambassadors. These diplomats and negotiators were often deeply involved in humanistic studies and renowned for their eloquence. Such training is frequently reflected in the letters and reports they despatched back to their masters (Mallett, 1994).

In this section we will consider the 1459 visit to Florence of Count Galeazzo Maria Sforza, the fifteen-year-old son of Francesco Sforza, duke of Milan. Although the Sforza visit in some sense represented a ritual of foreign relations, cementing a recent alliance between

Florence and Milan, a scheme of some political significance for the entire peninsula underpinned the 1459 exchange of courtly hospitality. Galeazzo Maria had been despatched to Florence to meet Pope Pius II and thereafter to accompany him to Mantua where Pius was to preside over a fund-raising convention to fuel his crusade against the Turks.[3] That Cosimo de' Medici presided over such a meeting with the pope in Florence and acted as host to both parties serves to underline the extent to which he and his family aspired to, and in practice assumed, a courtly or diplomatic role in contemporary affairs. It was not only politically expedient that they should have formed an alliance with the new leader in Milan in 1452 and that they should honour that relationship by playing a significant part in fostering friendship with other powers, but it was also vital that the Medici should be seen to assume such roles and, more to the point, in a manner fitting for an ally of a princely court. The pomp and circumstance surrounding the 1459 visit illustrate the extent to which Cosimo sought to display his own established position among the ruling elite. Nor were these gestures misunderstood by his contemporaries. In his *Commentaries* (Gragg, 1960 and see Anthology, no. 41) Pius noted that Cosimo de' Medici's ascendancy in Florence was reflected in the fact that state affairs were debated at his house.

The 1459 visit was much proclaimed and even more described and discussed in diplomatic dispatches. After a triumphal welcome outside the city walls Galeazzo Maria was escorted to the main government building, the Palazzo della Signoria, subsequently known as the Palazzo Vecchio, to meet officials before repairing to the Medici Palace, the newly completed town house of the Medici (who were his hosts for the duration of his stay). During this visit there were many manifestations of courtly ceremony, both public and private. Publicly there was a joust in the Piazza S. Croce, a dance in the Mercato Nuovo, a hunt in the Piazza della Signoria and a display of arms in the Via Larga, just outside the Medici Palace, during which the young Lorenzo, Cosimo's beloved grandson, was presented as the 'heir-in-waiting' (Cosimo's son, Piero, being the 'heir apparent'). Inside the palace there were banquets, official meetings and special viewings of the rooms and grounds.

The young count's reception and the sumptuousness of the new palace were described in his personal communications back home as well as in accounts drawn up by accompanying court officials and

---

[3] Following the fall of Constantinople in 1453 western Christendom once again felt threatened by the resurgence of the Muslim Turks. There was also a general lack of unity among the courts and a reluctance to support Pius's campaign, which shortly afterwards failed through lack of funding and the pope's own demise in 1464.

local commentators. The internal decorations of the palace received particular attention in the report despatched to Francesco Sforza by Niccolò de' Carissimi da Parma, one of Galeazzo Maria's political advisers and diplomats. All aspects of the 1459 visit, including descriptions of the palace itself and the nature of the Medicean regime, received exultant praise in an anonymous poem, referred to here and elsewhere as the *Terze rime*. These three texts – Galeazzo Maria's personal communications, Niccolò de' Carissimi da Parma's report to Francesco Sforza and the *Terze rime* – reveal much about the language of Renaissance diplomacy. They also illustrate how splendour and magnificent display (which we now recognize to be an essential ingredient of Renaissance court culture) were associated with the new Medici Palace and its owners.

These documents are examined in some detail later in this section, but first, as an introduction to the language of diplomacy and contemporary responses to courtly display, you will find it helpful to read Chapter 1 of Cole, paying particular attention to pages 19 and 23–4.

Now let us see what Pope Pius II thought of his Florentine host in 1459.

Exercise

Read the extract from the *Commentaries* of Pope Pius II (Anthology, no. 41).

Is there one particular theme that Pius pursued in evaluating Cosimo's position in Florentine society?

Discussion

I would suggest that Pius evaluated Cosimo almost entirely in terms of outward display. Pius (perhaps not unsurprisingly, since he was Sienese rather than Florentine, and anyway powerful in his own right) was also more equivocal about Cosimo de' Medici than Guicciardini in his review of the grandeur of the house of Medici. Although indicating some disapproval at the way in which Cosimo had grasped power by eliminating his enemies, Pius was above all critical of Cosimo for presenting himself as something he was not. Through the luxuriousness of his surroundings he presented himself as a king. Although in reality a mere citizen, he set himself up as 'master of the city'. ❖

Clearly, in his private records Pius felt no need to resort to the language of diplomacy. He had no real need to flatter Cosimo through the use of such terms as '*magnificentia*'. Unpicking the language of contemporary fifteenth-century texts helps us to distinguish between flattery and fact.

How does Cole's analysis in Chapter 1 of her book complement your reading of Pius's *Commentaries*?

Think about Cole's analysis of such key terms as *magnificentia* and decorum.

Cole explains (p.19) how extravagance or *magnificentia* was frequently extolled during the Renaissance period in terms of its representation of a goal or virtue. (As noted earlier, such attitudes no doubt reflected Aristotelian explications of personal decorum which could render magnificence a moral virtue rather than a vice of ostentatious display.) Magnificence, as Cole explains, depended on wealth. Wealth accrued as a result of territorial expansion (although not in the case of the Medici, who grew rich through banking). Thus, magnificence reflected political power and stability. Reading further in Cole, you will note that there was a general understanding during the Renaissance period that magnificence should be tinged with decorum: the degree of luxury expressed, whether in the erection and decoration of buildings or in the hosting of state visits, should fit both the individual and the occasion. According to Pius, Cosimo de' Medici's magnificence was not appropriate, since he aspired to a status above his natural rank. The magnificent displays he presented in support of such pretensions were thus indecorous. ❖

Cole concentrates on the term *magnificentia*. Many other terms were, however, indicative of status.

Read the three extracts from contemporary descriptions of the 1459 Sforza visit to Florence mentioned earlier (Anthology, nos. 40i–iii).

What key terms and concepts run through these accounts of Florence under the Medici? How do such terms indicate contemporary views that the house of Medici was, in effect, a court?

Key terms and concepts that recur with some regularity are beauty (or handsomeness), elegance, gracefulness, workmanship, magnificence, scale, value (or cost), display and reception. In addition, certain themes or analogies recur in all these texts. The architectural achievements and interior decorations of the Medici are likened to those of kings and emperors on account of their lavish scale, copious internal spaces and employment of rich material (gold, silver, ultramarine blue, fine marbles and imperial porphyry). Moreover, the secular power of the Medici seems blessed by association with a higher authority, since the spaces of their earthly home are likened to those of paradise. ❖

To what extent are such texts to be interpreted as accurate descriptions and to what extent as diplomatic eulogies? Rab Hatfield describes the language of the *Terze rime* as 'shot through with obligatory commonplaces', 'clichés of eulogistic technique' (1970, 'Some unknown descriptions', pp.237–8). Ernst Gombrich reminds us that 'Exaggeration, *amplificatio*, was a legitimate rhetorical trope' in the Renaissance (1960, p.35). According to Burckhardt, what was desired was the most cultivated humanistic talent, and nowhere were such skills required more than in public speaking, in the orations of ambassadors, in private writing and in diplomatic exchanges. For many, therefore, the descriptions of the Medici Palace in the *Terze rime* would seem to have little basis in fact; rather, they served as explanations of status and reflections of social decorum. The Medici Palace is a **topos**, a suitable subject for eloquent discourse. Hatfield draws our attention to similar language used in references to the Medici church of S. Lorenzo in the *Terze rime*, claiming that these are conventional descriptions, established forms of **ekphrasis**, rhetorical techniques. So in the description of S. Lorenzo we find references to the ceiling of 'fine gold, of ultramarine blue and full of roses shining like the morning stars', of a church 'so marvellous and so joyful that whoever attentively admires it seems to be dazzled, because throughout it seems that sun is there', and:

> there are so many gentle and handsome carvings of porphyry, of glass and various marble, that I don't know of anything worthy to which I might compare it ... think now of how the church, which really represents a paradise, will be when it is appointed as is planned.
>
> (translated A. Thomas, 1999)

The references to magnificence, kingship and royal power are relevant to our question concerning the extent to which the house of Medici was seen as a princely court. As Hatfield notes, the Medici Palace was an emblem of Cosimo and his family which in terms of decorum was measured against not merely Florentine but also international standards. Small wonder therefore that in all these texts the concept of magnificence, scale and value (or cost) dominates. Decorum appropriate to nobles rather than to bankers dictates the choice of those spaces in which members of the Sforza retinue are entertained. Galeazzo Maria refers, on his arrival at the house of the 'magnificent' Cosimo, to the height of the walls, to the worth of the books, to the chests of inestimable workmanship and value, and to the priceless silver. The author of the *Terze rime* describes the palace as 'full of marvels' that 'cost and [are] worth more than a city'; to a chapel that is 'so ornate that it has no like in all the universe'; to Piero's chamber covered with tapestries, and with 'rich hangings of gold, silver and silk', prepared 'in a manner worthy of an emperor and queen' and of an overall cost of 'a hundred thousand florins net'.

A recurrent theme in these texts concerns display and reception. The guests are received and honoured by their Medici hosts through reception committees, great banquets and street festivals. They are also expected to view and respond to their hosts' domain. Niccolò de' Carissimi refers to the 'tour' of the palace and especially its 'noblest' parts. The young Galeazzo Maria, while lingering over the richness of gilded ceilings, offers further insights into the hierarchy of space within the Medici Palace. We learn much from this about distinctions between public and private spaces during the Renaissance. Galeazzo Maria, for example, was invited into a private chapel for his audience with Cosimo de' Medici. Other members of the entourage were allowed access only to the more public 'state' rooms.

The author of the *Terze rime* takes us through the palace and its surroundings as if on a guided visit. Although we may now dismiss much of the description as eloquent diplomacy and artificial rhetoric, Niccolò de' Carissimi suggested, significantly I think, that his own 'lord', Francesco Sforza, would not only wish to match such magnificence but should, if at all possible, endeavour to erect something even 'worthier', because:

> given your magnanimity and greatness of mind, you too would want to do something worthy – and not only equal to this but surpassing it if that were possible.

(translated A. Thomas, 1999)

Niccolò de' Carissimi's reference to such an endeavour as '*qualche cosa degna*' (something worthy) indicates worthiness not only in terms of real monetary value but also as an appropriate and dignified reflection of the patron himself. The element of competition is also significant. It was one thing to keep up with, or aspire to, the state of kings and princes, but these individuals themselves had constantly to readjust their own positions, making sure not only that they were still perceived as worthy of their established or recognized status, but also that they were upwardly mobile within this hierarchy. Cosimo's display created diverse ripples within the princely community.

References to the beauty (or handsomeness), elegance, gracefulness and workmanship (or mastery) of the Medici Palace and the fact that its contents were so great that it was almost impossible to believe or describe them, raised Cosimo and his family to the realms of the courtly milieux. The house of Medici was seen not only to be comparable with higher ranks but also to threaten the pecking order. Pope Pius II hinted at Cosimo's desire for upward mobility when he recorded his amassing of great wealth 'worthy of Croesus' and the construction of a palace 'fit for a king'. Guicciardini recognized the extent to which the grandeur of the house of Medici impressed the citizens of Florence and courtly spheres beyond that city when he spoke of the displeasure of Lodovico Sforza (Francesco's younger son, and brother to Galeazzo Maria) in the face of Lorenzo de' Medici's wish not only to equal but also to compete with Italy's princes.

Niccolò de' Carissimi's report reveals much about the significance of symbolism in diplomatic exchanges and manifestations of courtly display. He describes how Galeazzo Maria and his company were conducted on a tour of the palace between two audiences with Cosimo de' Medici. In the garden they found newly planted grass in the form of the Sforza snake and Cosimo's personal heraldry, presumably the Medici *palle* and Cosimo's motto, '*semper*' (always). No visual evidence remains to prove the references to Sforza and Medici emblems entwined in friendship in the newly established topiary of the Medici Palace gardens. However, the concept of a symbolic unity designed visually to extend and expand through natural growth with the passage of time indicates at the very least something about the political expectations of the two families. It must also surely indicate something about Medicean hopes concerning their own evolving position within courtly spheres.

In Niccolò de' Carissimi's account Cosimo is represented as the key player in the construction and decoration of the Medici Palace and as the orchestrator of political diplomacy during the visit. The *Terze rime* suggests, however, that Cosimo's son Piero assumed a key role in preparing the palace for the courtly visitors. Surviving internal decorations in the Medici Palace indicate that several members of the family assumed significant roles in constructing this paradigm of court culture well before Cosimo's death in 1464. Moreover, they took care to mark such contributions with their own personal *imprese* or heraldic devices, thus establishing personal claims within their own familial space.

Diplomatic symbolism

There is little doubt that *imprese* of this kind were used consciously to establish distinctions in rank and patronage. Thus, in Benozzo Gozzoli's frescoes in the Medici Palace chapel, Cosimo is distinguished as head of the family by the inclusion of the Medici *palle* on his horse's caparison (see Plate 14, which shows part of the east wall of the chapel). These help identify the key personalities, Cosimo and Piero, as well as members of their personal retinue. Identification of contemporary portraits can play a key role in assisting our understanding of the political symbolism of such fresco cycles.

Some 30 or so recognizable portraits have been tentatively identified in the courtly retinue of Cosimo and Piero de' Medici. As Cristina Acidini Luchinat (1990, p.363) suggests, the inclusion of portraits of famous or well-known men was inextricably linked with the fifteenth-century development of humanistic studies based on the example of ancient Rome. Yet, as she reminds us, studies of Gozzoli's frescoes in the Medici chapel have frequently downgraded the significance of the portraits there, other than those in the front row of the cortège which depicts leading members of the Medici family and 'princely' contemporaries such as the young Duke Galeazzo Maria Sforza, the middle-aged Sigismondo Malatesta (see Figure 3.9) and, as we shall see, the painter himself.

Figure 3.9 Benozzo Gozzoli, *Duke Galeazzo Maria Sforza and Sigismondo Malatesta*, detail, east wall of the Medici Palace chapel, 1459, fresco. Palazzo Medici-Riccardi, Florence. Photo: Alinari

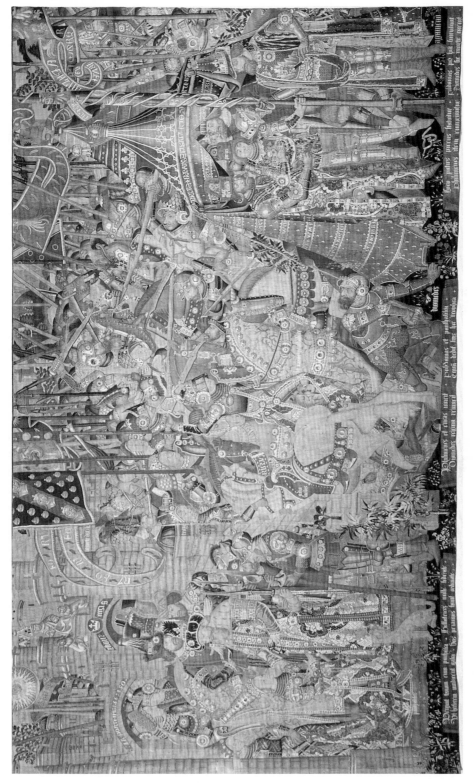

Plate I Workshop of Pasquier Grenier, Tournai, *Penthislea Joins Priam: The Amazons Issue from the Dardanid Gate; the Arming of Pyrrhus*, from a cycle of tapestries on the Trojan War, 1475, wool and silk, 416 × 737 cm. Victoria and Albert Museum. Reproduced by courtesy of the Trustees of the V & A

Plate 2 Benedetto da Milano and workshop, *The Twelve Months of the Year, January*, after designs by Bramantino, c.1509, wool and silk, 285 × 320 cm. Castello Sforzesco, Milan. Photo: Saporetti

Plate 3 Hugo van der Goes, altarpiece for Tommaso Portinari, c.1473–9, oil on panel, 253 x 586 cm. Uffizi Gallery, Florence. Photo: Scala

Plates 4 and 5 Illuminator Attavante degli Attavanti, illuminated title pages of first volume of the Bible, 1489–90, 365 x 532 mm, unfinished. Biblioteca Medici-Laurenziana, Florence, Plut. 14, MS Cod. 17, fols 1v and 2r

Plate 6 Leonardo da Vinci and Giovanni Ambrogio de Predis, *Madonna of the Rocks*, 1483–6?, oil on canvas, 197 x119.5 cm. Louvre, Paris. Photo: RMN–Gérard Blot/Jean

Plate 7 Anonymous, *cassone* panel front
showing Dukes Galeazzo Maria and
Giangaleazzo Sforza as dukes of Milan, and
Ludovico Sforza as the duke of Bari, 1480–95,
tempera on walnut, 43 x 189 cm. Castello
Sforzesco, Milan. Photo: Saporetti

Plate 8 Justus of Ghent, *Inauguration of the Eucharist*, oil on panel, 228 x 328 cm (above), and its predella, Paolo Uccello, *The Profanation of the Host*, tempera on panel, 42 x 351 cm (opposite). Palazzo Ducale, Urbino. Photo: Scala

Profanation of the Host sequence (1) woman redeems her cloak at the price of a consecrated Host;
(2) attempted destruction of the Host; (3) Host restored to the altar; (4) execution of the repentant woman;
(5) Jew and his family are burned; (6) angels and devils dispute over the woman's corpse.

Plate 9 Detail of the *studiolo* in the Palazzo Ducale, Urbino. Photo: Scala

Plate 10 Pietro Perugino, *Battle between Love and Chastity*, 1505, oil on canvas, 160 x 191 cm. Louvre, Paris. Photo: RMN–R.G. Ojeda

Plate 11 Raphael and assistants, interior of Villa Madama, Rome, 1516–24. Photo: Scala

Plate 12 Leonardo da Vinci, *The Lady with the Ermine* (Cecilia Gallerani), *c.*1483, oil on canvas, 55.25 x 40 cm. Czartoryski Museum, Crakow. Photo: Bridgeman Art Library, London/New York

Plate 13 Leonardo da Vinci, Ginevra de' Benci, c.1471, oil on panel, 38.8 x 36.7 cm. Ailsa Mellon Bruce Fund. National Gallery of Art, Washington DC

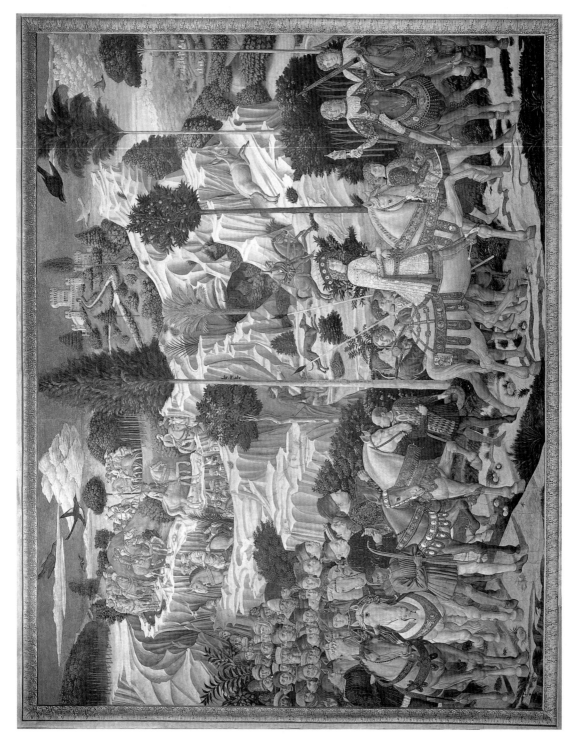

Plate 14 Benozzo Gozzoli, *The Medici Family*, east wall of the Medici Palace chapel, 1459, fresco. Palazzo Medici-Riccardi, Florence. Photo: Scala

Plate 15 Benozzo Gozzoli, *Cortège of King Melchior*, detail, west wall of the Medici Palace chapel, 1459, fresco. Palazzo Medici-Riccardi, Florence. Photo: Scala

Plate 16 Gentile da Fabriano, *Adoration of the Magi*, completed 1423, panel, 173 x 220 cm. Uffizi Gallery, Florence. Photo: Scala

Plate 17 Paolo Uccello, *Battle of San Romano*, c.1445, tempera on panel, 182 × 322 cm. Uffizi Gallery, Florence. Photo: Scala

Plate 18 Paolo Uccello, *Battle of San Romano*, c.1445, tempera on panel, 182 x 320 cm. Reproduced by permission of the Trustees of the National Gallery, London

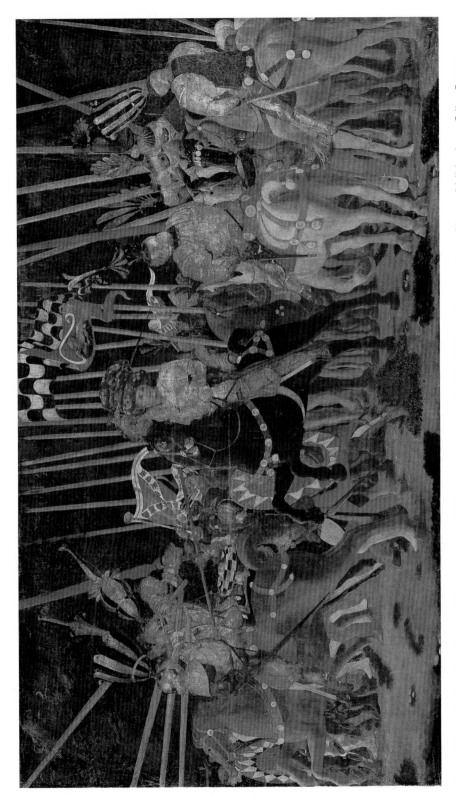

Plate 19 Paolo Uccello, *Battle of San Romano*, c.1445, tempera on panel, 182 × 316 cm. Louvre, Paris. Photo: RMN – Jean-Gilles Berizz

Plate 20 Fra Angelico and Fra Filippo Lippi, *Adoration of the Magi*, c.1445, tempera on panel, diameter 137.2 cm. Samuel H. Kress Collection. © 1999 Board of Trustees, National Gallery of Art, Washington DC. Photo: Richard Carafelli

Plate 21 Piero Pollaiuolo, *Galeazzo Maria Sforza*, 1471, tempera on panel, 65 x 42 cm.
Uffizi Gallery, Florence. Photo: Scala

Plate 22 *The Tazza Farnese*, second century BCE, sardonyx agate cameo, diameter 21.7 cm (inner disk 15.7 cm). Museo Archeologico Nazionale, Naples. Photo: Scala

Plate 23 Sandro Botticelli, *Man with a Medal*, 1474, tempera on panel, 57.5 x 44 cm. Uffizi Gallery, Florence. Photo: Scala

Plate 24 Sandro Botticelli, *Adoration of the Magi* (the Lami altarpiece), c.1475, tempera on panel, 111 × 134 cm. Uffizi Gallery, Florence. Photo: Scala

I would argue that both the inclusion and the positioning of individual figures in the retinue following Cosimo and Piero offer significant insights into the kind of courtly diplomacy surrounding the house of Medici during the early Renaissance. Many of the individuals identified by Acidini Luchinat were not only officials of the Medici bank but were also affiliated to the Medici family through marriage. One such example on the east wall is the figure second from the end in the second row, directly behind Cosimo, whom Acidini Luchinat suggests is Giovanni di Francesco Tornabuoni, son-in-law to Cosimo and brother-in-law to Piero, as well as factor (merchant) in the Medici bank in Rome (see Plate 14). Another individual positioned prominently in the cortège of the aged King Melchior on the west wall (see Figures 3.10 and 3.11, overleaf, and Plate 15) has been identified as Bernardo Giugni, a great friend of Cosimo and several times 'ambassador'. In the row behind him, again in prominent profile, is Francesco Sassetti, previously director of the Geneva and Lyons branches of the bank and, at the time of the painting of the frescoes, only recently recalled to Florence as vice director-general. Next to Sassetti stands Agnelo Tani, director of the Bruges branch.

In effect, therefore, we are presented with a roll-call of Medici supporters and high-ranking employees who are intimately associated with the family's affairs while at the same time acting as ambassadors in cities abroad, amassing information and sending back reports from their various centres of activity. Moreover, according to Acidini Luchinat, Gozzoli himself assumes a key role at various stages of the Magi's progress towards the new-born child depicted in Filippo Lippi's altarpiece of the *Adoration of the Magi*. (Fra Filippo Lippi, who produced a number of decorations for the Medici Palace, is considered in greater detail later in the chapter.) Acidini Luchinat argues that Gozzoli is depicted no fewer than three times: first (Figure 3.12), on the east wall, gazing directly out at us from the third row behind Cosimo and Piero, and identified by the inscription on his hat; secondly (Figure 3.11), in prominent position on the west wall, with raised hand in salutation, in the immediate foreground; and thirdly (Figure 3.11), again on the west wall, looking back at us as Melchior's cortège turns the corner, winding its way through the ravines of the mountainous countryside. Thus, the painter himself appears to direct our gaze and control our viewing of the depicted scene.

Figure 3.10 Benozzo Gozzoli, *Cortège of King Melchior*, west wall of the Medici Palace chapel, 1459, fresco. Palazzo Medici-Riccardi, Florence. Photo: Alinari

Figure 3.11 Benozzo Gozzoli, detail, *Cortège of King Melchior* (see Figure 3.10 and Plate 15), showing: 1 Bernardo Giugni, 2 Francesco Sassetti, 3 Agnelo Tani, 4 Benozzo Gozzoli, 5 Benozzo Gozzoli (two portraits). Photo: Scala

Figure 3.12 Benozzo Gozzoli, *Self-portrait*, detail, east wall of the Medici Palace chapel (see Figure 3.9 and Plate 14). Photo: Alinari

'Courtly' artefacts: the role of the patron and the artist

In this section we will examine some aspects of fifteenth-century patronage against the background of Medicean 'rule' and fifteenth-century Florentine artistic expertise. We will first analyse the extent to which Medicean taste and artistic preference may be described as 'courtly'.

The Medicean reputation for 'princely' munificence has persisted through several centuries of historical analysis. Burckhardt noted that the Medici 'paid for charities, public buildings and taxes from 1434 to 1471 no less than 663,755 gold florins, of which more than 400,000 fell on Cosimo alone' (p.69). There were subtle changes, however, in the pattern of Medici patronage as the affairs of the Medici bank declined during the fifteenth century, and later members of the family were both less inclined and financially less able to indulge in costly projects. In his pioneering study of the early Medici as patrons of art Gombrich (1966) maintained that there was a clear division in matters of patronage between Cosimo de' Medici and his two sons Piero and Giovanni– distinctions that may have resulted in part from the comparative prestige of individual projects. Cosimo was renowned in his own time for his costly and prestigious architectural foundations and endowments, as our discussion of magnificence above has shown. His son Piero is now better known for his patronage of smaller artefacts such as panel paintings, glazed terracotta ware, illuminated manuscripts and medals.

Gombrich argues that Cosimo deliberately left negotiations with painters and other 'interior decorators' to his sons. It may be significant that painters were less highly esteemed than architects or sculptors during the early Renaissance. Thus, Piero's involvement in 'minor' artistic matters may reflect a hierarchy within the family as much as individual taste. There is certainly a great deal of evidence to support Piero's involvement in commissions for painted altarpieces and items of furniture long before his father's death in 1464. There is, for instance, the letter sent by Domenico Veneziano to Piero in 1438 in which the painter asks to be considered for the commission of the new high altarpiece in the church of S. Marco; this, despite the fact that Piero at that date had barely turned 20, and Cosimo had assumed control of the architectural development of that site. A few years later, in 1441, another artist, Matteo de' Pasti, wrote to Piero in respect of the commission to paint the triumphs of Petrarch, one of which has been identified as the painted panel of *The Triumph of Fame* on a *cassone* (a large chest), now displayed in the Davanzati Palace.

But the most famous correspondence of all is that which took place between Benozzo Gozzoli and Piero concerning the fresco decoration in the new Medici Palace chapel.

Gozzoli's frescoes reveal much about the personal taste of Piero il Gottoso (Piero the Gouty) and his preference for the rich artistic style so favoured by noble contemporaries in the Burgundian court of northern Europe. Indeed Gombrich suggests that Piero's business dealings with Burgundian and French banking customers played an important part in fashioning his own preference for the International Gothic style – an artistic style prevalent throughout northern Europe during the fourteenth century and noted for its emphasis on rich surface decoration and courtly imagery.

Clear parallels can be drawn between the Medici chapel frescoes and other 'courtly' art works such as tapestries and illuminated manuscripts, especially those produced for wealthy and powerful patrons like the duc de Berry. Cole indicates (pp.21, 50, 119–21, 130) that the International Gothic was also favoured among the Italian courtly milieu. Benozzo Gozzoli's brand of International Gothic displayed in the Medici chapel frescoes was heavily dependent on that practised by Gentile da Fabriano, who is often regarded as the chief exponent of the International Gothic style in early fifteenth-century Italy. Gentile da Fabriano played an important role in importing his 'courtly' style to Florence during the early 1420s, after catering at an earlier stage in his career for aristocratic and courtly patrons in the north-east of the peninsula. He died in Rome in the late 1420s, and by this date a simpler, more statuesque style based on rational rules of perspective and realistic modelling in light and shade was being established in Florence under the influence of Masaccio's Brancacci chapel frescoes in the Carmelite church of S. Maria del Carmine.

Gentile da Fabriano's altarpiece of *The Adoration of the Magi* (Plate 16), which was painted for the noble Strozzi family in 1423 and placed in their family chapel in S. Trinità in Florence, is not only richly embellished with gold and exquisite details of flora and fauna, but also includes identifiable portraits of the Strozzi family in the Magi's retinue. The style of the Medici chapel frescoes may have been determined as much by imitation of that Strozzi milieu as by reflection of 'courtly' environments elsewhere. The political implications of such local imitation are significant. In commissioning their own version of the Adoration of the Magi to decorate the walls of their newly constructed family chapel, and in choosing an artist capable of imitating Gentile da Fabriano's style, the Medici revealed two significant aspirations. By adopting imagery of this kind, they wished to imply that they were equal to the Strozzi in terms of their social position within early Renaissance Florentine society; and they also wanted to establish that they had similar tastes, that they belonged to the same cultural milieu. In adopting the International Gothic style favoured by such wealthy and 'aristocratic' families as the Strozzi, and by associating themselves with the company of kings, the Medici gained social as well as political status.

There is another aspect worthy of our consideration. In serving his Medici masters with such fare, Benozzo Gozzoli was continuing a trend established in Florence some three decades earlier. In many respects his work in the Medici chapel was out of step with what is now considered to have been the avant-garde style of his time. Renaissance taste was clearly governed to a large extent by patronal expectations. In imitating Strozzi taste, the Medici were making a statement about their own political and cultural aspirations, but practical realization of these depended on the availability of artists capable of working in that particular artistic style. We should perhaps give greater consideration, therefore, to the extent to which preference for the International Gothic in Italian aristocratic spheres was fostered by, or dependent on, the ability of the artists themselves to work in that way.

Had Benozzo Gozzoli not been able to satisfy Medicean demands in returning to the *retardataire* style of rich detail and gold embellishment, the frescoes in the new Medici Palace chapel might well have presented a very different face to the enquiring gaze of later generations and our own historical assessment of early Medicean taste. It is worth remembering that Gozzoli had previously created a much more sober 'Giottesque' style in frescoes carried out for Franciscan patrons in Montefalco and Viterbo. He was thus not necessarily the most obvious choice for the Medici, who were intent on displaying a different kind of artistic style. The finished look of a work of art depends on both the expertise of the artist and the expectations of the patron. Such symbiosis underpinned the endurance of the International Gothic style in later fifteenth-century Florence. It is, moreover, clearly reflected in Medici commissions for the interior decorations of their new palace, ranging from manuscript illuminations to tapestries and panel paintings.

While Gozzoli's frescoes illustrate a Medicean preference for a richly decorative style during the middle years of the fifteenth century, other records reveal an even earlier taste for elaborate tapestries. Many such works were sold in the markets of the Netherlands, and it was to these sources that Medici patrons directed their artistic agents. In 1448 the Medici agent Fruoxino wrote from Bruges to Giovanni, the brother of Piero il Gottoso, describing his efforts at the fair in

Antwerp to buy suitable tapestry hangings for the new Medici Palace. These tapestries were presumably required for a pre-defined space since Fruoxino was particularly anxious to ensure that their style, content and size were appropriate. He had rejected one set depicting the exploits of Samson because of its inappropriate imagery and because it was somewhat too large, although richly worked. Another set illustrating the story of Narcissus was also rejected, because it was insufficiently rich in workmanship, although appropriate in terms of subject matter and measurements. And so he had come away empty-handed. To a certain extent this taste for tapestry set the Medici apart from other wealthy burghers in Florence, since such artefacts were enormously costly. Both the desire for and the purchase of tapestries placed the Medici firmly in the cultural milieu of their courtly neighbours. Tapestries were for princes rather than merchants.

It has often been argued that the wealthy Davizzi, owners of what is now known as the Davanzati Palace, were restricted by cost to the fictive painting of wall hangings as an alternative to the purchase of woven ones. Evelyn Welch (1997, p.293) suggests, however, that tapestries were taken down in summer as a precaution against excessive heat, and that painted versions on the underlying walls reflected their decorations while offering cooler surroundings. It may also have been the case that there were clearly defined hierarchies not only between the rich and the poor but also among the various echelons of the wealthy. Some kinds of wealth allowed for the purchase of tapestries; others did not. Contemporary records concerning the purchase of tapestries, and valuations of such artefacts contained in inventories of the Medici palaces, reveal that they cost more than their painted equivalents and that, unlike paintings, they maintained their value, possibly even increasing in worth over time.

Reconstructions of courtly space

The agent Fruoxino rejected the tapestry hangings depicting the struggles of Samson not only on account of their size but also because of the emphasis in their figural content on dead bodies. This may indicate consideration of the function of the room in which these tapestries were to be displayed. The reference to dead bodies no doubt concerns that part of the Old Testament story where Samson was first bound with cords by his own people and then handed over to the Philistines. Samson's cords, we are told, loosened like burning flax and he subsequently slaughtered a thousand Philistines with an ass's jawbone before sinking down to the ground to slake his thirst and rest. Although one could draw some links between such imagery and Cosimo's own history – in being exiled from Florence, but returning to overcome local adversaries there – this was not necessarily the image Cosimo or other members of his family sought to promote, once reinstalled in Florentine society. Indeed, from what we know of the fifteenth-century (and later) decorations of the Medici household, emphasis was on models of support for the Medicean cause rather than heroic personal resistance in the face of overwhelming odds. Depictions of military campaigns fought on the Medici's behalf, and reflections of their own dignified and courtly status – expressed through depictions of members of the family in company with royalty or engaged in diplomatic exchanges – were the order of the day.

Benozzo Gozzoli's Medici chapel frescoes serve to convey both support for the house of Medici and the royal-like dignity of its individual members. Similarly, Paolo Uccello's painted panels of the *Battle of San Romano* (Plates 17–19), while depicting a comparatively minor skirmish between Florence and Siena, glorify the exploits of Niccolò da Tolentino, a key supporter of Cosimo de' Medici prior to Cosimo's exile in 1433. Although there is still uncertainty concerning the original site of these panels, and whether they were first commissioned for the old Medici house and completed only subsequently for the new palace, it seems clear that they were displayed in a prominent and 'public' position for a significant period of time. In the following section I offer a reconstruction of the room in which these and other panels were displayed at the end of the fifteenth century – '*la chamera grande terrena detta Chamera di Lorenzo*' (the large ground-floor room known as the room of Lorenzo).

The furnishings of the Medici Palace

According to Giorgio Vasari, famous for his *Lives of the Artists* (Bull, 1971), and a useful source of anecdotal information, the rooms in the new palace were divided up in a way which was not only useful but also most beautiful ('Life of Michelozzo'). On the ground floor there were two courtyards with magnificent loggias on to which opened reception rooms, bedrooms, antechambers, studies, closets, stove-rooms, kitchens, wells, and both secret and public stairways. The 'large room' on the ground floor, referred to above, which was described as 'living quarters during the summer period', was situated in the north wing on the garden side. Another room, described as the 'large room of Lorenzo' (as opposed to the 'room of Lorenzo' on the ground floor) – presumably used during the winter months – was situated on the first floor next to the Sala Grande or audience hall.

After Lorenzo il Magnifico's death in 1492 an inventory of the contents of the Medici Palace was drawn up. This inventory was subsequently copied in 1512 at the request of Lorenzo's grandson Lorenzo di Piero de' Medici. During the intervening years the Medici had been expelled from Florence and their palace ransacked. Lorenzo di Piero was no doubt interested in establishing among other things the extent of the damage wrought during those years. This must certainly have been of interest also to other members of the family who returned to live on the Via Larga at that date.[4] As Guidotti notes (1990, p.248), the 1492 inventory is unusual in systematically detailing, room by room, the contents of the palace. But inventories of movable goods are by their nature incomplete, since they rarely note wall decorations such as frescoes. Moreover, a copy of an earlier document may well contain errors and omissions. Nevertheless, the 1512 version of the 1492 inventory serves as a useful tool for reconstruction of 'courtly' space. It also offers insights into contemporary evaluations of 'courtly' decorations. Interestingly, valuations set against tapestries and brocade hangings frequently ran into hundreds of florins, whereas painted panels, like marble reliefs and sculptures, were, by comparison, deemed worthy of only a handful of florins. Of even greater significance, perhaps, was the value placed on elaborately carved woodwork, and the extent to which this material governed the look of the fifteenth-century courtly room. On occasion in contemporary descriptions more attention is paid to the nature of the woodwork than to the painted panel it surrounds or supports. This was certainly the case in references to the siting and display of the *Battle of San Romano* panels.[5] We know that Uccello's paintings were displayed in Lorenzo il Magnifico's chamber on the ground floor of the Medici Palace by the end of the fifteenth century, since the 1492 inventory refers to six panel paintings with gilded frames (with an overall value of 300 florins) which hung above wooden panelling. In three of these panels there were battle scenes, in another a battle between dragons and lions, and in the remaining two panels a 'story of Paris' (presumably the Judgement of Paris) and a hunting scene. The inventory notes that the hunting scene was painted by Francesco Pesello and implies that the other five panels were all produced by Paolo Uccello. Uccello thus emerges as a key figure in the painted decoration of that room.

[4] Both the old Medici house and the new Medici Palace were on the Via Larga.

[5] As you can see from the captions to Plates 17–19, these three battle scenes by Uccello are now individually displayed in the Uffizi Gallery, Florence, the National Gallery, London, and the Louvre, Paris.

Numerous attempts have been made to establish the original hang of the *Battle of San Romano* paintings in an attempt to reconstruct the dimensions of the room in which they were first displayed, and to confirm once and for all that they were indeed produced for the room later known as Lorenzo's summer room. Comparatively little attention, however, has been paid to the other decorations that are known to have been in that room, or to the room's actual use, apart from its convenience as cool summer quarters close to the refreshing air of the garden. The combined length of the panel paintings that hung above the wooden panelling in this summer room is noted in the 1492 inventory as some 23 metres. Even if divided between four walls, this indicates a room of considerable size. In reflecting earlier traditions of tapestry decorations and courtly tastes, the depiction of a hunting scene, and even a battle between dragons and lions, indicates that the chamber was a 'courtly' space suitable for one aspiring to 'princely' status. The inclusion of the 'story of Paris' suggests that it could also have served another purpose. If that scene did indeed depict the dilemma of Paris referred to above, the room may have assumed some legal or political function. It was quite common for bedrooms to be used for matters of state. The Camera Picta at Mantua is one such example (see Chapter 1, p.39). Perhaps Lorenzo's 'summer room' also served as an audience room. The dual public/private nature of Lorenzo's chamber is in fact supported by references to a long, narrow bench almost five and a half metres long which was positioned below the wooden wall panelling. There were also chandeliers around the room, perhaps to throw light on the various decorations. Such elaborate lighting offers further evidence that entertaining, and possibly business, was carried out here.

The 1492 inventory notes that the wooden panelling contained a chest or wardrobe with seven shelves, and that it was interrupted in two places by doors. Along part of its length there was a further chest some eight metres long. These descriptions of seating areas and storage spaces suggest that the room could have served as an audience chamber as well as a bedroom. The measurements of the wooden fittings themselves indicate that there was sufficient seating for a considerable number of people. Moreover, the wardrobe or dresser set into the wooden panelling offered expansive shelving space for the display of the porcelain ornaments that are also listed. This, combined with the sumptuously decorated woodwork and narrative paintings displayed above, would have rendered the room both formal and stately.

It is perhaps significant, also, that the same chamber contained a painting of *The Adoration of the Magi* by Fra Angelico and two portrait heads of Federico da Montefeltro (duke of Urbino) and Duke

Galeazzo Maria Sforza, the latter painted by Piero Pollaiuolo. The Fra Angelico painting has been identified as that attributed to both Angelico and Fra Filippo Lippi in the Washington National Gallery of Art (Plate 20), and the portrait of Galeazzo Maria as that in the Uffizi Gallery in Florence (Plate 21). The portrait head of Federico has not so far been identified. No indications are given as to the positioning of these images. Perhaps they were inserted into the wooden wall panelling or displayed on one of the shelves of the dresser, although the latter seems less likely, since the inventory specifies that a variety of porcelain vases were on view there.

The assembling of wise men and the offering of gifts and learned counsel as depicted in Fra Angelico's painting, combined with references to contemporary examples of power and authority, would not have been lost on any company gathered in that room. In a study of the paintings of the Medici Palace, Maria Grazia Ciardi Dupré dal Poggetto (1992) has also considered implications of ownership and display. She suggests that the painting of Federico in the ground-floor chamber could have been sent to the Medici as a sign of personal esteem (p.139). On this analysis the exchange of painted portraits assumes a currency of power and propaganda similar to that of medals. The propagandistic nature of Pollaiuolo's portrait is discussed in greater detail below. For now, I would argue that the display of such images in close proximity to scenes associated with victory, judgement, royalty and courtly pastimes reflected the function of the room itself and contributed to its magnificence. It was through rooms such as these that the young Galeazzo Maria Sforza and his retinue were guided by their Medici hosts in 1459. It was decorations and furnishings of this kind that Niccolò de' Carissimi urged Francesco Sforza to emulate and surpass.

Piero il Gottoso is often described as the first member of the Medici family to turn his attention to the collection and display of small items such as illuminated manuscripts, gem stones, tableware and medals. Indeed his *studiolo*, or private study, is presumed to have set a new model for connoisseurship. But Piero was not the first to display precious objects in the small space of a study. An inventory drawn up in 1417–18 of the old palace belonging to Giovanni di Bicci, Cosimo's father, records ceramics, goldwork, precious metalware, gem stones and crystals in Cosimo's *scrittoio*, or writing chamber. While some of these items may later have formed the basis of Piero's own collection, the distinguishing feature of later inventories – such as those drawn up between 1456 and 1464 – is the degree of richness and extreme refinement of the golden artefacts, silverware, jewels and semi-precious goods acquired by that date. The elaborate nature of many of the goods cited in Piero's possession prepares us for the splendour of his son Lorenzo.

The next exercise considers the courtly nature of some of the furnishings associated with the Medici Palace. In preparation for this exercise you will find it helpful to read Cole's descriptions of some of the objects displayed in the courtly space of Isabella d'Este's apartments in Mantua (pp.160–8).

Cole refers to Isabella d'Este's 'insatiable desire' for antique works, including cameos and bronze and painted works '*all'antica*'. While referring to *grisaille* (monochrome) images (probably produced for Isabella's *studiolo*) 'painted to look like Roman reliefs of polished stone against a background of veined marble', Cole also draws our attention to the portrait medal in a diamond-studded frame and an onyx cameo of the third century BCE which Isabella displayed in her *grotta* – one of the areas set aside for the specific purpose of display in her suite of rooms in the ducal palace at Mantua.

We can draw close comparisons between the objects owned by Lorenzo de' Medici and those acquired and displayed by Isabella d'Este. Many of the items listed as '*beni mobili*' (movable objects) in the Medici inventories were clearly for display rather than for everyday use. While illuminated manuscripts served a devotional purpose, and elaborately painted *deschi da parto* (birthing trays) and beakers fashioned from semi-precious gem stones were on occasion used to carry food and drink, the small bronze statuette, the bronze relief and the dish made from an antique cameo were certainly not put to such practical purposes. Small and precious items were, instead, appropriate for mounting in cabinets or erecting in display areas such as *studioli*. Depictions of heroic exploits drawn from antiquity made appropriate exemplars, moreover, in reflecting the struggles and triumphs of contemporary political life. Displayed within a 'courtly' space such images promoted the present while representing the past.

Exercise

Listed below are three of the artefacts in the 1492 inventory. They are shown in Figures 3.13 and 3.14 and in Plate 22. What characteristics, in your opinion, do they have in common?

- *Hercules and Antaeus*, Antonio del Pollaiuolo (small bronze originally in the study of Lorenzo il Magnifico, now in the Museo Bargello, Florence), height *c.*45 cm.

- Bertoldo di Giovanni, *Battle between the Romans and Barbarians* (bronze relief executed for the Medici Palace, now in the Museo Bargello, Florence), *c.*92 x 37 cm.

- The Tazza Farnese (valued at 10,000 florins) (second-century BCE cameo acquired by Lorenzo il Magnifico, now at Naples in the Museo Archeologico Nazionale), diameter 21.7 cm (inner disc 15.7 cm).

Figure 3.13 Antonio del Pollaiuolo, *Hercules and Antaeus*, *c.*1475–80, bronze, height *c.*45 cm. Museo Nazionale del Bargello, Florence. Photo: Scala

Figure 3.14 Bertoldo di Giovanni, *Battle between the Romans and Barbarians*, *c.*1480, bronze relief, *c.*92 × 37 cm. Museo Nazionale del Bargello, Florence. Photo: Scala

Discussion

All these items are comparatively small in size. Bertoldo's relief, the largest of the three, measures only *c*.92 x 37 cm. They are all made from comparatively expensive material, two fashioned from bronze and the third a sardonyx cameo. All three are concerned in one way or another with classical antiquity. The Tazza Farnese is an original item from that age. Lorenzo acquired this cameo from Pope Sixtus IV, who had himself acquired it from his predecessor Paul II, a renowned collector of antiquities and precious objects. All three objects also deal with heroic exploits – Hercules in his battle of physical strength against the giant Anteaus, the Romans in their repelling of the barbaric hordes from the north, and the Tazza Farnese with its allegory of the Egyptian princess Cleopatra. ❖

The Tazza Farnese has been identified as the 'flat dish made out of sardonyx, chalcedony and agate which is decorated with several figures and on the outside a head of Medusa', listed in the 1492 inventory as being in the study next to the antechamber which was adjacent to Lorenzo's chamber on the first floor of the Medici Palace. This was presumably the small treasure house purpose-built by Piero il Gottoso for his ever-expanding collection of medals and other exquisite examples of gold and silverware. Bertoldo's relief is recorded as being in the small room behind the 'large room' (probably an audience chamber) on the same floor. Dal Poggetto (1992, pp.154–5) suggests that Pollaiuolo's bronze statuette may be identified with the one recorded as being in the 'room of Monsignore [my Lord] now used by Giuliano [duke of Nemours, youngest son of Lorenzo]'. She suggests that this room originally belonged to another son of Lorenzo, Giovanni (the future Pope Leo X), and possibly prior to that to Giovanni, son of Cosimo. Such observations, as Dal Poggetto frequently reminds us, must alert us to the difficulties of drawing clear-cut conclusions concerning ownership and display, even from primary source material such as inventories. It is significant, nevertheless, that at least two of these objects can be traced with some certainty to comparatively confined spaces. We know, moreover, that the 'room of Monsignore' opened on to a diminutive chapel in which there was a small altarpiece by Fra Angelico, depicting once again one of the Medici's most favoured scenes, an Adoration of the Magi.

Miniature items fashioned from precious materials and based on classical themes were accorded great and ever-growing value during the second half of the fifteenth century. Noting that Isabella d'Este was 'anxious for fame and prestige', Cole indicates (p.161) that one route to this and to a reputation for magnificence lay in Isabella's nurturing of classical connoisseurship. In many ways Isabella and contemporaries such as Lorenzo set the fashion for art collecting in the sixteenth century. In Cole's last chapter ('Continuity and adaptation', pp.171–9) she reminds us that similar attempts at nobility underpinned later collections where individual items were displayed not just for the pleasure of viewing or as representations of status, but also as expressions of individual taste. The late fifteenth-century Neapolitan writer Giovanni Pontano considered that magnificence derived from wealth, and personal 'splendour' was reflected through a person's possessions. Splendour was expressed in private refinements. Goldthwaite (1993, p.249) reminds us that Pontano presented the gem collection of the duc de Berry as a prime example of such splendour. It is, moreover, significant that for Pontano distinctions in splendour depended on the nature of the materials from which such possessions were fashioned. The fact that the dresser in the ground-floor chamber of the Medici Palace displayed porcelain, as opposed to terracotta or pewter, indicates a high degree of refinement. References to gold, silver and porphyry in descriptions of the 1459 visit offer further evidence of splendour. The growth of splendour in the house of Medici is nowhere more obvious than in the lists of their possessions compiled at various dates throughout the fifteenth century and in the years prior to their removal to the 'royal rooms'[6] of the Palazzo Vecchio in 1540.

Patronage as a cultural tool

The Compagnia dei Magi

Patronage was indeed one of the chief instruments of Medici policy during the century when they had no legal title of authority.

(Gombrich, 1966, p.35)

So far we have discussed the extent to which contemporary descriptions liken the Medici Palace to a royal abode and its owner to a sovereign. The Medici expressed their interest in being associated with royalty and in particular with the three wise kings, or Magi, in a number of ways. Their predilection for painted scenes of the Adoration of the Magi is one reflection of this, but there is another association with royalty which merits consideration. From perhaps even the time before his expulsion from Florence in 1433, Cosimo de' Medici was a member of the lay confraternity known as the Compagnia dei Magi – the Company of the Kings. This confraternity, which was renowned for its elaborate pageantry, congregated at S. Marco, the

---

[6] The title given to these apartments by Duke Cosimo I in a personal letter of that year (quoted in Bulst, 1990, p. 123).

church endowed by Cosimo before his greater involvement in the construction and decoration of S. Lorenzo. Each year on the feast of the Epiphany (6 January) the company's brothers decked themselves out in the apparel of the three Magi and their retinue. With great pomp and ceremony they then paraded through the city, finishing up at S. Marco where they celebrated the birth of Christ and offered gifts in a festive tableau containing the Christ child in a manger. The visual resonance with the imagery in the Medici chapel frescoes and the numerous depictions of the Adoration of the Magi commissioned by the Medici is clear.

We know that Cosimo himself took part in several of the Compagnia dei Magi processions, since we are told that on one occasion in 1451 he wore a fur cloak and on an earlier occasion a gown of gold. Membership of the company offered more than 'princely' elevation in the Epiphany procession. As more members of the family joined, the Medici assumed an increasingly significant voice in the company's affairs, and ultimately in the affairs of the neighbourhood bordering and surrounding S. Marco. Lay confraternities, as well as constituting close-knit groups of religious devotion, were also often involved in the social welfare of their neighbourhood, offering financial assistance to the needy and making appropriate arrangements for the sick, the dying and the dead. Membership endowed individual members with power, both temporal and everlasting. The political implications of a confraternity being monopolized by a particular family are clearly reflected in the Dominican friar Savonarola's decision in 1494 to abolish the Compagnia dei Magi, and to appropriate the meeting house at the side of S. Marco which had been constructed with Medici funds (and which was no doubt also furnished and decorated at Medici expense and according to Medici taste). With the expulsion of the Medici in 1494, and Savonarola's own elevation in the friary which had previously housed both Cosimo's private cell (including a wall fresco depicting the Arrival and Adoration of the Magi) and a library full of books bestowed by the Medici, Savonarola was clearly anxious to eradicate the last vestiges of that family's power.

In describing the Compagnia dei Magi's annual Epiphany procession, Rab Hatfield draws our attention to the aesthetic, ideological and above all political implications of involvement in such a company:

> This was not simply a quest for aesthetic gratification, but the fulfilment of a set of didactic, psychological and symbolic needs. The brothers' vicarious adaptation of their lives served to make the holy patrons more accessible and real. It was an 'imitatio', a way for the brothers to become better Christians by assuming the virtues of the Magi. And it permitted a manner of ostentation that was inadmissible

in normal life. In their confraternity under the sanction of traditional forms of devotion the brothers – including the Medici – might do no less than pose as Lords. And in the 'Festa' they carried that pose before the people.

(1970, 'The Compagnia dei Magi', p.143)

Benozzo Gozzoli in effect recreated the Compagnia dei Magi's procession on the walls of the Medici's private chapel. In his analysis of Gozzoli's fresco of *The Journey of the Magi*, Gombrich (1966) draws our attention to the fact that Cosimo and Piero de' Medici and other members of their 'courtly' retinue, including Gozzoli, follow the Magi as if in attendance on, and in witness of, their splendour. They assume significance through physical proximity to these royal individuals. The inclusion of individual portraits of the Medici family and their close business and social acquaintances in the retinue of the Magi was both a visual record of public display and a discreet reflection of private aspirations. In many ways the Gozzoli frescoes may be seen as reflecting the political reality of Medici supremacy while maintaining the myth that they were on the same social level as other members of the ruling elite in mid-fifteenth century Florence.

Portraiture

Portraits can be enunciations of cultural display rather than of private subjectivities; they can be readable as ideological apparatuses rather than as aesthetic units reporting referential truth; as a medium of exchange between art and society, object and viewer, sitter and artists, patron and artist, sitter and spectators (frequently including the posing subjects themselves), in a rich conversation of overlaid, even competing and conflicting voices, rather than as singular objects with one universalized and static, authoritative interpreter. Portraits themselves performatively shape their world and are not passive reflectors of simple, pre-existing appearances.

(Simons, 1995, pp.264–5)

Before the next exercise you will find it useful to turn to Burckhardt's section 'Despots of the fourteenth century' (pp.27–34), to remind yourself of the ideal picture of a prince of the fourteenth century as relayed by Petrarch. Consider Burckhardt's own comments concerning the duties of such princes to maintain the urban fabric and encourage the arts, as well as the tyrannical power which seemed to go hand in hand with such cultural exploits.

Exercise Look now at Burckhardt's description of Federico da Montefeltro, starting on page 46 in his section 'The greater dynasties'.

What in your view are the characteristics which, according to Burckhardt, reveal Federico as a 'brilliant representative of the princely order'?

Discussion   Burckhardt was impressed by the fact that Federico, despite earning his keep as a mercenary soldier and therefore being an individual of questionable morality, nevertheless chose to spend the money he earned on his own city and territory. A careful and compassionate leader, Federico was loved and esteemed by his subjects; his state and court were a 'work of art and organization'. ❖

I would argue that some of these characteristics are reflected in the portrait of *Federico da Montefeltro and Son Guidobaldo* which was painted by Pedro Berruguete (see Figure 3.15). Federico, in a mixture of military and stately dress (proclaiming his profession as a mercenary soldier and his present state as courtly ruler of Urbino), is shown seated before a lectern, engrossed in the contents of a learned volume (evidence perhaps of his early training in humanistic studies at the Gonzaga court in Mantua). His small son Guidobaldo, decked out in elaborate pearls and brocade, stands beside him in formal pose, sceptre in hand, looking out of the painting as if engrossed in something beyond the picture's time and space.

This painting, which was probably originally displayed in Federico's study, where he is known to have conducted diplomatic business, is significant both as a statement of familial legitimacy and in terms of its associative symbolism with other princely courts. The fact that the young Guidobaldo stands holding a sceptre which carries the inscription '*Pontifex*' (pontiff or sovereign), in imitation of his father's similar gesture when raised to ducal rank by the pope in 1474, probably reflects Federico's dynastic claim to rule over Urbino and its territory. Federico's authority to rule papal vicariates is transferred through the symbol of the sceptre and its inscription to the future rule of his son. Guidobaldo's own pose and gaze seem to imply expectation of this future state.

The fact that Federico is also shown wearing the robes of the Order of the Ermine, an honour bestowed on him by King Ferdinand of Naples in 1474, is a deliberate reflection, according to Cecil Clough (1992), of Federico's long-standing relationship of mutual friendship and protection with the Aragonese court. This order of chivalry had been established by King Ferdinand in 1465 and, according to Clough, was intended to unite those loyal to him and his dynasty in lavish ceremonial proclaiming his pre-eminence as ruler of Naples. King Ferdinand was no doubt aware that such princely investment of chivalric worth also forged significant friendships beyond his realm.

Figure 3.15 Pedro Berruguete, *Federico da Montefeltro and Son Guidobaldo*, 1475–8, oil on canvas. Ducal palace, Urbino. Photo: Alinari

Only a year after the investiture of Federico da Montefeltro, Ferdinand bestowed a similar honour on Ercole d'Este, the ruler of Ferrara to the north-west of Urbino. Such 'threading' of alliance through the peninsula established powerful chains of defence as well as support for dynastic claims to power. Many such alliances were further strengthened through betrothals and marriages. It is significant that when Berruguete painted this portrait, Federico's son Guidobaldo was already betrothed to Lucrezia, King Ferdinand's youngest daughter. Although the marriage contract was broken after Federico's death in 1482, this depiction of the ruler of Urbino and his future heir offers potent evidence of courtly 'affiliations' and future expectations expressed in Renaissance portraiture. It also illustrates how 'princely' patrons of the period sought to invest their painted images with complex layers of symbolism in support of such claims.

Botticelli, 'court artist' and portrait painter of the Medici

In the time of the elder Lorenzo de' Medici, Lorenzo the Magnificent, truly a golden age for men of talent, there flourished an artist called Alessandro.

(Vasari, in Bull, 1971, p.224)

In his *Lives of the Artists* Vasari, who was closely associated with the grand ducal court in the sixteenth century, was eager to emphasize the role of the earlier Medici in promoting the arts. Vasari describes how Lorenzo de' Medici patronized the young artist Sandro Botticelli, who had been trained in the workshop of Filippo Lippi, the artist favoured by Lorenzo's grandfather Cosimo. He suggests that Botticelli received training as a goldsmith prior to his apprenticeship as a painter to Lippi. According to Vasari, Lippi became a close friend of Cosimo de' Medici and was offered accommodation by him in the Medici Palace. Lippi certainly produced the altar painting of the *Adoration of the Christ Child* for the Medici Palace chapel, and it seems likely from contemporary descriptions that it was in front of this image that the young Sforza was offered a private audience with Cosimo during his 1459 visit to Florence. Lippi was also responsible for the painted lunettes of the *Annunciation* and *Seven Saints* (Figures 3.16 and 3.17) (now in the National Gallery in London) which are thought to have been commissioned by Cosimo's son Piero il Gottoso or Piero's cousin, Pierfrancesco di Lorenzo di Giovanni di Bicci de' Medici. Such connections with the Medici may well have contributed substantially to Lippi's subsequent success in other fields. Vasari mentions the little scenes painted by him and sent by Cosimo as a gift

Figure 3.16 Filippo Lippi, *Annunciation*, late 1450s, tempera on wood, 68.5 × 152 cm. Reproduced by permission of the Trustees of the National Gallery, London

Figure 3.17 Filippo Lippi, *Seven Saints*, after 1456, tempera on wood, 68 × 151.5 cm. Reproduced by permission of the Trustees of the National Gallery, London

to Pope Eugenius IV, thereby earning Lippi the favour of the pontiff himself. It may also have been through Medicean channels that Lippi received the commission to paint frescoes in the cathedral at Prato. According to Vasari, it was through the personal mediation of Cosimo that Lippi was asked to execute his last great work – the fresco cycle in the apse of the cathedral at Spoleto. Botticelli's early workshop association with Lippi may well have brought him favour with Cosimo and his heirs. His early expertise in setting and mounting precious jewels may even have brought him to the attention of the Medici household before his relationship with Lippi.

Botticelli is best remembered now for the series of pagan mythologies he is thought to have painted for Lorenzo il Magnifico and other members of the Medici family during the 1470s and 1480s. The most familiar of these is perhaps the *Primavera*, although equal pride of position is given in the Uffizi Gallery in Florence to the *Birth of Venus* and *Pallas and the Centaur* (Figure 3.18). *Pallas and the Centaur* is most frequently cited in discussions of classical influence and Neoplatonism at the Medicean 'court'. Although at one time thought to have been painted for Lorenzo il Magnifico and at another time presumed to be the jousting standard painted by Botticelli for Lorenzo's brother, Giuliano de' Medici, it seems more likely that this painting was commissioned by a younger cousin of the family, Lorenzo di Pierfrancesco de' Medici. A painting fitting its description appears in the inventory of Lorenzo di Pierfrancesco's palace on the Via Larga in 1498 and was later hung together with the *Primavera* and the *Birth of Venus* in the Medici Villa di Castello which had originally been purchased for Lorenzo di Pierfrancesco.

It has often been argued that *Pallas and the Centaur* closely reflects Medicean culture under Lorenzo il Magnifico in meshing classical Platonic theory with the Neoplatonism of Marsilio Ficino, one of Lorenzo's closest advisers. The classical undertones of the painting are clear. Pallas Athena is entwined in sprigs of olive and appears to tame the brute sensuality of the centaur through gentle restraint as opposed to the force of her arms. In this, she represents Platonic theories which elevate the cultivation of the soul over the physical body. She also assumes a pose found in classical reliefs. Her morally elevating qualities are clearly associated with the house of Medici since her dress is liberally sprinkled with the Medicean symbols of clusters of diamond rings. There are clear resonances here with Cosimo's posthumous medal. But the symbolism in the painting is even more explicit. Pallas Athena is not merely associated with the house of Medici; she metamorphoses into a symbol of the house itself. Some have proposed connections with specific political events, for example that Pallas Athena's nobility in tempering the centaur reflects Lorenzo's successes in dealing with local opposition and his papal and princely neighbours. Others have suggested that the painting served as moral guidance to the viewer, and in particular to the young patron Lorenzo di Pierfrancesco. Thus, in overcoming bestial instincts with reason and chastity, he is encouraged to follow

Figure 3.18 Sandro Botticelli, *Pallas and the Centaur*, 1482, egg tempera, 207 × 148 cm. Uffizi Gallery, Florence. Photo: Alinari

the guidance offered in classical philosophy, as well as the guidance offered by his Medici relations. Despite conflicting interpretations, the work clearly constitutes both an internal 'Medicean' view and a vehicle for external propaganda. Commissioned from within the Medici family, it offers specific evidence of the reflections they wished to see held up to them in their 'hall of mirrors'.

I want to concentrate now on two less familiar paintings by Botticelli, since I believe these illustrate much about the way in which the Medici were viewed from beyond the walls of their own palaces. The two works I have chosen offer broader insights into Botticelli's position as artist to the Medici 'court', and into the contributions made by other patrons of Botticelli to the courtly aspirations of the Medici family. The first work is Botticelli's painting of the *Man with a Medal* (see Plate 23). Before considering the symbolism of this late fifteenth-century Florentine portrait in terms of courtly culture, I would like you to consider the way in which it is designed and painted. To help you do this, I ask you to look at Botticelli's painting in relation to a very similar portrait painted by Hans Memling, a contemporary Netherlandish painter.

Exercise

Compare Botticelli's *Man with a Medal* (Plate 23) with the *Portrait of a Man with a Roman Coin* by Hans Memling (Figure 3.19), and list the points of similarity. Then contrast the two portraits, listing some ways in which they are dissimilar.

Figure 3.19 Hans Memling, *Portrait of a Man with a Roman Coin*, unknown date, parchment on wood, 22 × 29 cm. Koninklijk Museum voor Schone Kunsten, Antwerp. Copyright ACL

Discussion

Both portraits depict a young man in half length looking out at the spectator and holding a medal as if to present it to the viewer. Both individuals are dressed in sober dark clothing laced at the neck and showing the wrinkled cloth of white underclothing at the neck. Both wear tall beret-like bonnets and are set against a landscape background with a distant view of water, fields, trees and mountains. The main difference between the two is the greater scale of the medal in the Botticelli painting. It is perhaps significant also that Botticelli's youth presents the medal with both hands, as if in a deliberate gesture of display. In contrast, Memling's youth seems hardly aware of the small coin which is squashed rather ignominiously in the lower right-hand corner. There seems to be a greater element of performance or theatricality in the positioning of Botticelli's figure and in the suggested movements of his body. His assertive pose against the extensive landscape background suggests an association bordering on ownership. ❖

Botticelli's painting is frequently compared with that of Memling in attempts to illustrate the influence of Flemish painting on late fifteenth-century Florentine art, and the extent to which symbolic details were inserted as a means of identification. The Memling coin has, in fact, been identified as a *sestertius* (a silver roman coin) and depicts the Roman Emperor Nero. This, combined with the palm tree in the right-hand foreground, has led some historians to suggest that the young man depicted by Memling may have been Italian, a member of the Palmieri family and with a first name deriving from Nero. There are remains of laurel leaves at the lower edge of the picture (not shown), indicating a possible connection also with a name such as Lorenzo or Allori (in Latin Lorenzo is *Laurentius*, or 'laurel-growing').

For our purposes the two portraits are probably most interesting in the context of cultural display. Nothing is known of the circumstances surrounding the commissioning of either of the paintings, although Botticelli's portrait is known to have been in the collection of Cardinal Carlo de' Medici, son of Grand Duke Ferdinando I, during the early seventeenth century. In the early eighteenth century it was identified as a portrait of Piero, Cosimo's son. This identification was subsequently disputed and many alternative names have been suggested, including various other members of the Medici family, Giovanni Pico della Mirandola and Botticelli's brother Antonio. Burckhardt proposed that it might even depict the maker of the medal, who is thought to be Niccolò Fiorentino. While a positive identification has yet to be made, I would argue that there can be little doubt there were close ties between this sitter and Cosimo de' Medici or his family. To this extent, therefore, we may identify him as a 'courtier' of the Medici.

Although we do not know whether Botticelli's painting was commissioned by a member of the Medici family, I would suggest that its content clearly proclaims support of the Medici regime. The connection with the Medici, and in particular with Cosimo, is made clear by the fact that the young man (who is shown in almost frontal view as if turning towards us in that moment) balances in both hands, and holds forward, as if for inspection, a stucco and gilt replica of Cosimo's medallion. The obverse view is tendered, which leaves no doubt as to the identity of the individual commemorated here. The youth engages us with steadfast gaze, in silent but forthright testimony of his allegiance to the individual depicted on the medal. The size and position of the medal appear to give it prominence equal to the youth who holds it. To this extent, we might argue that Botticelli's portrait is as much an 'ideological apparatus' as a subjective depiction of reality. There is, indeed, a rich exchange of information between sitter and viewer concerning status, association and allegiance. It is, for example, significant that the youth is shown in semi three-quarter view as if emphasizing his corporeal reality, while the deceased Cosimo is portrayed in flattened profile. Yet Cosimo's living power is suggested through the realistic portrayal of individual details. Despite the imperial profile, Cosimo is shown wearing contemporary fifteenth-century costume. This depiction of the 'Father of the Fatherland' is, moreover, strategically positioned at the level of the young man's heart. Perhaps Botticelli meant to indicate Cosimo's personal power or authority over this individual even after death.

Rather than assessing this portrait in terms of a specific personality we would do better, in my opinion, to consider it against the abstract notion of 'a figure representing a courtier', although it probably does depict a contemporary individual. I believe we learn more about cultural expectations in this period if we regard it as a depiction of an ideal courtier – one of many images produced in support of Medicean power, just as Cosimo's medal was one of many distributed to a large number of now unidentifiable friends and supporters of the Medici cause. We could, for example, argue that Botticelli's 'courtier' constitutes a comment on, or reflection of, the Medici regime – comparable to Baldassare Castiglione's claim that *The Book of the Courtier* was intended as an ideal portrait of the court of Urbino.

Leon Battista Alberti's 'book' on painting, *De pictura*, produced first in Latin in 1435 and then in the vernacular (*Della pittura*) in 1436, had an immense influence on both patrons and artists. It combined mathematical theory with artistic practice. Patricia Simons (1995) reminds us that, for Alberti, portraiture was not just a matter of depicting individual fame or physiognomic accuracy. It served rather to illustrate the worthiness of painting or the artist's expertise in presenting the viewer with a recognizable image. For him, portraiture rendered the absent present. Through portraiture subjects were reminded of their sovereign's power. A portrait such as Botticelli's *Man with a Medal* would have communicated specific messages concerning power and status, for it is concerned not only with the dignity of office conferred on Cosimo through representation in a posthumous medal, but also with this unknown individual's own position in Medicean society. Portraits such as these contributed to the artificial construct or concept of a Medicean 'court'.

Simons (1995) analyses the role assumed by portraits in constructing an exemplary world of stability and elitism. She also reminds us of Burckhardt's argument that political circumstances fundamentally shaped the development of individualism: the state is a construct born of 'reflection and calculation'. Botticelli's portrait is a constructed image of individual allegiance towards a particular 'master', yet it also reflects Burckhardt's Renaissance or 'modern' man.

In his section 'The development of the individual' Burckhardt suggests that it was during the Middle Ages that 'Man was conscious of himself only as a member of a race, people, party, family or corporation', whereas during the Renaissance 'man became a spiritual individual' (p.98). At first sight, Botticelli's 'courtier' would seem in Burckhardtian terms to belong to the former age, since he so obviously displays a talisman which connects him with a particular section of Florentine society. But we could also argue that, for Burckhardt, such a portrait might also have reflected the quintessential characteristics of the Renaissance. While Botticelli's man is aware that the viewer views him and his medal, he is aware, too, of his own significance in presenting the medal to the viewer, at the same time as engaging with individual viewers through direct eye contact. According to Burckhardt, despotism:

> fostered in the highest degree the individuality not only of the tyrant or *condottiere* himself, but also of the men whom he protected or used as his tools – the secretary, minister, poet and companion.

> (p.99)

He argues that individuality was born from political flux:

> the more frequently the governing party was changed, the more the individual was led to make the utmost of the exercise and enjoyment of power.

> (p.100)

207

Thus, Botticelli's portrait may be viewed as a positive assertion rather than as a negative illustration of servility. This individual is no mere 'subject' advertising his master's largesse through the dispensation of medals. He is empowered by association with that 'master' and his positive espousal of that master's cause. In his chapter 'Education of the *cortegiano*' Burckhardt describes Castiglione's courtier as the 'ideal man of society'; an individual who educated himself as much for his own sake as for the sake of court society; 'the court existed for him rather than he for the court' (p.246). The inner impulse which inspired him was directed 'not to the service of the prince, but to his own perfection' (p.246). Such descriptions seem not inappropriate to Botticelli's *Man with a Medal*.

Botticelli's portrait was clearly painted after the death of Cosimo de' Medici, since we know that the medal itself was a posthumous production. Yet Botticelli's involvement in this work could indicate that he was associated with the family even before the interest shown in him as a young man by Lorenzo il Magnifico. Piero Pollaiuolo's portrait of Galeazzo Maria Sforza (Plate 21) was, however, certainly produced during Lorenzo's period of power and on the occasion of a second visit to Florence in 1471 by Galeazzo Maria, who had succeeded his father as duke of Milan in 1466. Like Botticelli's portrait, this work offers further insights into portraiture as an 'ideological apparatus'. Alison Wright suggests that Pollaiuolo's portrait was commissioned by Lorenzo de' Medici to demonstrate the continuing alliance between Florence and Milan, and in confirmation of Galeazzo Maria's support both for Lorenzo's position within Florence and for Florence's position within the peninsula (1993, pp.67–8). Significantly, Galeazzo Maria refers to Lorenzo as the new *signore* when describing the purpose of his visit to the Milanese ambassador Sacramoro as a method of strengthening his ties with the new ruler.

Wright argues that Galeazzo Maria's 1471 visit to Florence also served as useful 'self-publicity' for him. In laying his seal of approval on Lorenzo's new position he advertised the fact that he was a suitable ally. Recognition of another imbued the bestower himself with significance. Galeazzo Maria was once more lodged in the Medici Palace, and during this visit delivered a speech to the Signoria in which he confirmed the ratification of the newly formed league between Milan, Florence and Naples, and offered Milanese military support to the Florentine state. Clearly, this occasion assumed in more overt fashion the political undertones of the 1459 visit. The portrait commissioned from Piero Pollaiuolo in commemoration of this visit, and subsequently displayed in the Medici Palace, depicts Galeazzo Maria in three-quarter view, dressed in a garment decorated

with the *fleur de lys* of France (perhaps originally made in connection
with an intended visit to France in the company of his French wife,
Bona of Savoy). In one hand Galeazzo Maria carries gloves; the other
hand gestures out of the picture, as if making a point or
communicating with an interlocutor. Wright (1993, p.73) doubts that
this portrait formed part of a **diptych**, like that of Federico da
Montefeltro and his wife Battista Sforza (Figure 3.20). The 1492
inventory of the Medici Palace describes this as a single panel
hanging next to the portrait of the duke of Urbino in the large
ground-floor chamber. Wright suggests that portraits of this kind
reflected the 'simultaneously personal and familial nature' of
Medicean alliances (p.73). She also argues that Galeazzo Maria's
costume may have been construed by onlookers as deferential to the
Medici dynasty, rather than as advertising his own affiliations with
France, since the symbol of the *fleur de lys* had been incorporated in
the Medicean armorial device in 1465. Regardless of the precise
meaning of such symbolism, there can be little doubt that this
portrait served as a visual reminder of a powerful alliance to those
seeking audience with the Medici.

Figure 3.20 Piero della Francesca, *Battista Sforza and Federico da Montefeltro*, 1472, tempera on panel,
47 × 33 cm. Uffizi Gallery, Florence. Photo: Scala

Cultured taste and cultural exchanges

So far in this chapter we have concentrated on identifying characteristics of courtly culture based on representation and display. We have looked at the significance of titles given to and assumed by various members of the Medici family, and the extent to which such titles established the dynastic legitimacy of their regime. We have also considered the courtly status accorded to them through contemporary descriptions of their grandiose palace and the sumptuous quality of its internal furnishings. Detailed analysis of Cosimo de' Medici's posthumous medal and Botticelli's *Man with a Medal* has also introduced us to the complexities of symbolism in Renaissance portraiture and to a range of interpretations of these images. In his unpublished 'Introduction to the aesthetics of the arts', written mainly between 1851 and 1863, Burckhardt conceded that art 'likes to conclude a mysterious alliance with those objects that it can assimilate', that art glorifies 'the most dear and most sacred that every period has venerated' (Sitt, 1994, p.231), and most significantly, that art historians should:

> no longer look for one idea in a work of art, to be considered a key that could be expressed in language, because we know that the work of art is of an exceedingly complex nature and origin.

(p.236)

Considerations such as these have established Burckhardt as a cultural historian. Yet they should also alert us in our own studies to the complexity of art-historical interpretations.

While Botticelli's *Man with a Medal* has allowed us to analyse the extent to which declarations of allegiance to political powers may be embedded in Renaissance portraiture, it may equally serve as testimony to the courtly taste for Flemish painting which existed during that period. As our analysis has shown, the composition itself is strongly suggestive of a painting by Hans Memling. The positioning of the figure against a distant landscape view is also reminiscent of many other paintings by Flemish artists. When Bartolommeo Fazio, historian and secretary to Alfonso V of Naples, wrote *De viris illustribus* in 1456 he included two Flemish painters (Jan van Eyck and Rogier van der Weyden) among the four artists he considered the most able of his time. The taste for Flemish tapestries, painting and music was well established in Italian court circles by the end of the fifteenth century. Fazio describes paintings by Rogier van der Weyden at the Aragonese court and at the court of the Este in Ferrara. Medici inventories reveal that such works were also prized in Florence. Federico da Montefeltro, we are told, sent for Justus of Ghent because he could find no painters of equal stature in his own country. The famous double portrait (Figure 3.20) painted for Federico by Piero della Francesca which, like Botticelli's *Man with a Medal*, positions the half-length figures against a distant landscape, offers further evidence of contemporary interests in the realism of texture and light developed by Flemish painters.

Ciriaco of Ancona, when shown a painting by Rogier van der Weyden in Leonello d'Este's private apartments, praised particularly the minute detail of the landscape. Piero's landscape reflects similar interests; the artist may even have known the painting by Jan van Eyck owned by Ottaviano Ubaldini della Carda, nephew and counsellor to Federico da Montefeltro, and described by Bartolommeo Fazio in *De viris illustribus* as containing in the background 'mountains, groves, hamlets, and castles, carried out with such skill you would believe one was fifty miles distant from another' (Baxandall, 1971, p.107).

Art-historical analysis of Piero's double portrait has concentrated also on the implications of territorial legitimacy in the depiction of the landscape background. While many have noted similarities with the countryside around Urbino, others have been even more specific in suggesting that the townscape behind Battista represents the city of Volterra, which was crushed with great ferocity by Lorenzo de' Medici (with Federico's help) in 1472. Botticelli's own employment of a distant river landscape, while clearly reflecting Flemish conventions, might also contain similar references to power and authority by association with the figure depicted there.

Federico's own preference for Flemish art was no doubt fostered as much by political and diplomatic exchanges beyond the Alps as through his links with courtly circles inside Italy. In 1476 he is known to have acquired a series of tapestries from Tournai which were identical to the series owned by the duke of Burgundy. Shortly afterwards a similar set was bought (perhaps even on Federico's advice) by Ferdinand of Aragon in Naples. Federico was certainly closely involved with the royal family in Naples, but he also established close cultural links with the Medici in Florence. Indeed, as you will see from your reading of Cole (pp.67–90), many aspects of the palace at Urbino derived from Florentine designs and craftsmen. The famous *studiolo* (see Figure 1.23 and Plate 9) was probably inspired directly by Piero de' Medici's small study in the new Medici Palace, but long before the construction of this room Florentine sculptors and architects were despatched to Urbino to assist in the construction of Federico's new palace. Cole (p.73) indicates that Federico may even have turned to Cosimo de' Medici for advice concerning 'the best Florentine artisans'.

To some extent, therefore, we may view the exchange of artists between centres of power during the Renaissance in terms of diplomatic currency. There is no doubt that Florentine artists influenced the early style of court art at Urbino, but they also fulfilled an ambassadorial role. Botticelli's employment in the Sistine Chapel is frequently viewed in terms of a peace offering between Lorenzo de' Medici and Pope Sixtus IV on the cessation of hostilities following the 1478 Pazzi uprising in Florence. Lorenzo's personal negotiations with the Aragonese court in Naples played a crucial part in bringing that war to an end. The reinstatement of diplomatic relations was reflected in the exchange of artistic expertise.

Establishing a Medicean mythology

Botticelli's role in the making of myths: the Lami altarpiece of the *Adoration of the Magi*

The second of the two paintings by Botticelli considered in detail here is the *Adoration of the Magi* (Plate 24) which was painted for the late fifteenth-century Florentine money broker Guaspare di Zanobi di Lami. Like Benozzo Gozzoli's frescoes in the Medici Palace chapel, this painting is renowned for the fact that it contains recognizable portraits of various members of the Medici family. Here, however, Cosimo de' Medici is not portrayed following the royal retinue; he has himself assumed the role of Melchior, the oldest of the kings. Moreover, his two sons Piero and Giovanni assume the characters of Melchior's regal companions, Balthazar and Caspar. This painting thus offers a potent illustration of the ascendancy of the house of Medici. As I hope the following discussion will show, it also serves as a visual confirmation of this family's claim to dynastic legitimacy and the right to rule.

Sixteenth-century reports describe the Lami altarpiece of the *Adoration of the Magi* as one of Botticelli's most admired works. Indeed Vasari suggests that it was known far beyond the confines of Florence, and claims that it was this painting which brought Botticelli to the attention of Pope Sixtus IV and earned him the commission to paint in the Sistine Chapel. Originally situated on the Lami family altar in the church of S. Maria Novella in Florence, it was no doubt more accessible than the Medici mythological paintings which subsequently brought Botticelli such fame.

It might seem curious to us that this painting contains so many Medici portraits when it was clearly not commissioned by a member of that family. Nor does there seem to be any evidence that the patron, a relatively insignificant member of Florentine society, had any close connections with the inner Medicean circle. We do know, however, that as a money broker he must have belonged to the same guild as that favoured by the Medici, and he must at least, therefore, have had some business dealings with them. What then is the purpose of including such a 'gallery of the great' in his own family altarpiece?

One answer must surely be that in commissioning such a work Lami made clear his allegiance to the Medici family and his personal support for them in their aspirations towards princely authority and power. The fame of the Lami altarpiece derives in great part from its association with Medici rule. Like Botticelli's *Man with a Medal*, it seems to reflect various degrees of courtly deference. Moreover, in this painting we can with greater certainty identify the 'courtier'. Guaspare Lami is portrayed among the royal retinue, but not, as one might expect, in the guise of his royal namesake Caspar – as mentioned above, the likeness here is of Giovanni de' Medici, the younger son of Cosimo. Guaspare himself is depicted as the elderly man in the middle foreground who is distinguished by the fact that he looks out at us as if to catch our attention.

In many respects the Lami *Adoration of the Magi* is reminiscent of the lunette of *Seven Saints* (Figure 3.17), which Filippo Lippi painted a generation earlier as part of the interior furnishings of the new Medici Palace. Thought to have been commissioned by Cosimo's son Piero or his cousin Pierfrancesco di Lorenzo de' Medici, this lunette, like the Lami altarpiece, appears to trace the Medici family's lineage back to a central source of power. In the case of the Lippi painting the central figure of St John the Baptist is not the patron saint of the commissioner, but rather that of the head of the family, Giovanni di Bicci de' Medici. St Peter Martyr, in contrast, sits at the far right-hand side of the composition opposite St Francis. St Peter rests his head on his hands as if listening to St Anthony Abbot who is seated next to him. Yet rather than turning towards St Anthony, as Francis on the other side appears to do towards his neighbour Lawrence, Peter looks out at us. This Albertian device[7] does in fact concentrate our attention on the three central figures of John the Baptist, Cosmas and Damian. We are encouraged to view Giovanni di Bicci not only as the head of the family but also as the source from which other members of the family (by association) received dynastic legitimacy.

[7] Alberti, in describing the art of history painting (*istoria*) in *De pictura*, advises painters to place one figure at the side of their composition who gestures towards the scene while engaging the viewer with his eyes, as if to invite them into the painted space.

This complex symbolism is continued in the Lami *Adoration of the Magi*. As noted above, Cosimo de' Medici, the perceived source of power handed down to the later generations of the family, is portrayed in the visage of the old King Melchior, and his son Piero appears as the middle-aged King Balthazar. Lorenzo and Giuliano, Piero's two sons, are placed at either side of the composition as if leading groups of courtiers towards their dynastic core. In addition, the portraits of Poliziano and Giovanni Pico della Mirandola have been identified among the crowd at the right – 'courtiers' to the biblical kings and to their own master Lorenzo de' Medici. Guaspare Lami is literally displaced by his Medici masters. Yet, in looking out at us and gesturing with his right hand, he encourages us to view the scene with him, and, like him, to recognize the Medici dynasty and its 'royal' associations. It is perhaps no coincidence that the painting of the Lami altarpiece finally found its way into Medici possession. Although it is not clear when this happened, the painting was certainly displayed in the house of Antonio de' Medici (son of Francesco I and Bianca Cappello) during the early seventeenth century. Even at that later date it apparently assumed a significant role as witness to the legitimacy of the earlier Medici dynasty.

In conclusion, there is one further element in the Lami altarpiece portraits which brings to mind Simons's argument, as already quoted (p.197), that portraiture constitutes:

> a medium of exchange between art and society, object and viewer, sitter and artists, patron and artist, sitter and spectators (frequently including the posing subjects themselves).

> (1995, p.265)

One of the standing figures to the right seems (like Lami) to be physically detached from the crowd. He stares out at the viewer as if to engage our attention, while at the same time drawing significance to himself in his role as arbiter between the real world and the painted scene. This figure has traditionally been identified as the artist Sandro Botticelli. There is thus a complex mesh of exchange. Contemporary individuals displace the traditional figures of the biblical scene; the house of Medici metamorphoses into royalty; the patron is displaced from his traditional depiction in the guise of his patron saint, yet by association remains embedded in the scene of adoration, legitimately linked through Caspar, his royal namesake. Physically liberated from that figure he, like the artist, can turn to engage with us. Both patron and artist seek to control our gaze.

How 'courtly' were the Medici 'court' artists?

Secular dynastic courts had regard to the fact that a servant had served the ruler's ancestors honourably and faithfully.

(Warnke, 1993, p.123)

None of the artists employed by the early Medici can be viewed strictly in the sense proposed by Warnke, since none of them was truly emancipated from his guild or trade background as a result of such patronage. It is quite clear, however, that later artists and historians such as Vasari, who was closely involved with the grand ducal court in the sixteenth century (and who had a vested interest in establishing his own honourable lineage), wished to imbue the earlier generation of artists with courtly status.

In many of the 'Lives' Vasari stresses the role of the early Medici as protectors of their artistic protégés. Cosimo, for example, not only acted as host in offering bed and board, but also mediated on behalf of his artists with patrons elsewhere. Donatello was clearly a favoured tenant of the Medici, since the tax return filed in 1433 by Cosimo and his brother Lorenzo di Giovanni de' Medici mentioned a house with a courtyard which was let to the sculptor at the peppercorn rent of five florins a year. This property, which consisted of three buildings, was probably used as a workshop by Donatello, and may even have been offered as an inducement to persuade him to return from Rome in order to continue work on the pulpit of the Sacred Girdle in Prato, a project in which Cosimo had some personal interest. Other contemporary documents describe how, at a later date, all the buildings on this site were destroyed in order to build the new palace next to the old Medici dwellings. Thus Donatello had, in a real sense, worked under the eye of his Medici patrons. Although he was not accommodated within their own palace – an honour that Vasari tells us fell later to the painter Filippo Lippi – his artistic activity must have been closely enmeshed in Medicean affairs.

According to the fifteenth-century bookseller and commentator Vespasiano da Bisticci, Cosimo even gave clothes to Donatello – an action defined by Warnke as one of the 'benefits in kind' for artists at court (1993, p.128). Vasari also notes Cosimo's role in protecting and furthering the future prospects of artists employed by him. Cosimo is said to have arranged for Donatello to receive property and land, thus providing for the artist in his old age, and to have recommended both Donatello and his erstwhile partner Michelozzo to his son Piero for future employment. Vasari ('Life of Donatello') tells us that Donatello's inheritance was subsequently exchanged for a regular monetary pension from Piero and that 'Donatello was more than satisfied with this arrangement and, as a friend and servant of the Medici family, he lived carefree and happy all the rest of his life' (Bull, 1971, p.187). Donatello is not the only fifteenth-century artist to be described as servant and friend to their Medici patron. Vasari uses similar terms for Michelozzo, Filippo Lippi and Andrea Castagno. He also tells us ('Life of Botticelli') that Botticelli was looked after by Lorenzo il Magnifico because he had worked for him in the past (Bull, pp.227–8).

Despite Botticelli's fame in comparison with, for example, his lesser-known contemporary Neri di Bicci, I would argue that he should not be considered merely in terms of his service of an elite. I do not think it was the case that he was constantly engaged (as later artists such as Vasari clearly were) in massaging his own and his master's importance. Nor do I think it is helpful to lay too much emphasis on Botticelli's service or allegiance to the house of Medici. The workshop practice of fifteenth-century painters was to a great extent market-driven. Patrons certainly influenced the look of finished works of art through strict contractual stipulations, and artists no doubt benefited from previous associations and patronal networks in continuing to receive the commissions necessary to the well being of their trade. But none of the individuals dealt with here can truly be described as a court artist, dependent on his master for personal fame and physical welfare. Donatello, Lippi and Botticelli were clearly close to the Medici, and according to Gombrich (1966, p.56) the late fifteenth-century sculptor Bertoldo may even have been a kind of 'valet de chambre', but Neri di Bicci's business arrangements and working activity were very likely no different from those of Botticelli in the service of the Medici or other patrons faithful to that house. Like his contemporaries, Botticelli carried out the business of the day. His association with the Medici has resulted in too much stress being placed upon his 'courtly' artistic practice, and this has distorted the nature of his ongoing, 'run-of-the-mill' work.

Just as later ages may have misinterpreted or over-emphasized Botticelli's 'courtly' status, so considerations of Lorenzo il Magnifico's role as patron of 'court' art probably require revision.

Exercise

Consider the following quotes – all from Gombrich's essay on the early Medici as patrons of art (1966) – and explain how you think these help us disentangle the myth of Lorenzo il Magnifico.

> The idea of Lorenzo offering his support to the cause of art as such which so appealed to later generations would probably have left him cold.

(p.36)

Yet Lorenzo de' Medici was clearly aware of the role his patronage of the arts could play in establishing power and pre-eminence when writing in a memorial to his sons 'I find we have spent large ... I think it gave great lustre to the state'.

(p.38)

The very name of Lorenzo the Magnificent has come to stand for posterity as the embodiment of princely magnificence ... it comes as a shock of surprise to realize how few works of art there are in existence which can be proved to have been commissioned by Lorenzo.

(p.52)

Fastidious men make difficult patrons and Lorenzo had come to think of himself as an arbiter of taste and was so regarded by others.

(p.54)

Discussion

Gombrich employs here a number of themes which underpin much of our own enquiry in this chapter. Most of these, I would argue, must play a key role in our assessment of the contribution to 'courtly' art made by various members of the house of Medici during the fifteenth century.

I would draw your attention particularly to the following:

- individual support for and patronage of art;
- the role of patronage in establishing power and pre-eminence;
- the extent to which spending large amounts of money affected the way in which the individual or governing family was viewed;
- how princely magnificence could also constitute a yardstick for taste.

Gombrich rates Lorenzo less highly than Cosimo or Piero as a patron of the arts. Indeed, he seems to suggest that Lorenzo gave little 'active' support to the arts, although he was clearly well aware that his standing and status were affected by such patronage. He was, moreover, aware that spending large amounts of money affected the way in which his role in government or the city itself was viewed. Burckhardt's later coining of the phrase 'the state as a work of art' seems to bear direct relation to this. Our consideration of Pontano, above, should also help us understand what Gombrich means by such terms as 'embodiment of princely magnificence'. Given his position of power, Lorenzo must have imposed a certain criterion or standard of taste on others. Yet, as our examination of the 1492 inventory has indicated, much of the splendour with which Lorenzo surrounded himself was probably inherited from his father and grandfather, and was not actually commissioned or acquired by him personally. ❖

Medici self-fashioning

Io non sono signore di Firenze, ma cittadino con qualche auctorità, la quale mi bisogna usare con temperanza et iustificatione. (I am not Lord of Florence, merely a citizen with some authority, which I must use carefully and with justification.)

(letter from Lorenzo de' Medici to Pierfilippo Pandolfini, 1481, in Mallett, 1990, p.100; translated A. Thomas, 1999)

One wonders to what extent Lorenzo had this in mind when planning his prestigious new villa at Poggio a Caiano. Work began on its construction around 1485 on the site of a farm he had acquired in 1474. This project, lauded by the contemporary poet Poliziano in his Latin poem 'Ambra', in which Lorenzo is described as the 'glory of the Muses', remained unfinished at Il Magnifico's death in 1492. Its completion and entire decoration thus fell to Lorenzo's heirs. Yet, according to Vasari in the 'Life of Giuliano da Sangallo' (the architect responsible for the initial stages of the work there), the villa and its design depended entirely on Lorenzo's own *capriccio* or extravagant whim. It must serve therefore as a potent example of late fifteenth-century Medicean self-fashioning.

The decoration of the great hall was ordered by Lorenzo's son Giovanni, by then Pope Leo X. Responsibility for work on site rested with Giovanni's cousin, Cardinal Giulio de' Medici, and the husband of Giovanni's niece Francesca, Ottaviano de' Medici. Mary Hollingsworth describes the imagery at Poggio a Caiano as 'a type normally associated with established ruling dynasties ... an audacious choice for the display of Medici prestige' (1996, p.246).

Andrea del Sarto's *Tribute to Caesar* (Figure 3.21), which was painted in fresco in the great hall at Poggio a Caiano in 1521, is curiously suggestive of an Adoration of the Magi. A number of classically robed figures stand and kneel around and in front of the seated figure of Caesar. The figure immediately in front of Caesar gestures back down the steps to other figures carrying and leading forward gifts of animals, including sheep and birds. Such details remind us of the booty presented by subject towns in the wake of Roman conquests. Indeed the references here are drawn from the imagery of Roman triumphal processions. Yet the *Tribute to Caesar* also contains references to contemporary events. Clearly distinguished in the middle background is the figure of a giraffe, standing in profile as if in imitation of the nearby statue of a classical goddess. The giraffe offers an overt reference to the underlying agenda in this depiction of Roman political history. This exotic beast was offered in homage to Lorenzo de' Medici by the sultan of Egypt and presented in person to

Figure 3.21 Andrea del Sarto, *Tribute to Caesar*, 1521, fresco. Poggio a Caiano. Photo: Scala

him by Egyptian ambassadors in 1487. Lorenzo himself is thus insinuated in the portrait of Caesar. Even more significantly, this imagery implies that, like Caesar, Lorenzo enjoys the attention and respect of states far beyond his own.

According to Kate Lowe, by 1512 when the Medici returned by force of arms to rule in Florence, they represented:

> a form of hereditary, family rule which at best could be characterized as benevolent tyranny ... which had developed elaborate and highly successful networks of political patronage and dependency.
>
> (1993, p.258)

219

During their exile the Medici had acquired a new status in affairs outside Florence and even beyond the bounds of the peninsula itself. With the election of Lorenzo il Magnifico's son Giovanni to the papacy in 1513, the family descending from Cosimo il Vecchio was set to expand its honorific titles and dynastic links into the most exalted of spheres. But it was another branch of the family, that descending from Cosimo's brother Lorenzo, that gave rise to the grand ducal court of Cosimo I (1519–74) in the middle of the sixteenth century.

The grand ducal period is beyond the scope of this chapter, but we would do well to remember that Vasari's *Lives of the Artists* was written for Grand Duke Cosimo, and, as Cole reminds us in her final chapter (p.176), much of Vasari's language, and thus our own impression of fifteenth-century courtly culture, was influenced by the writings of one of his own contemporaries, Baldassare Castiglione. Castiglione is best remembered now for his written 'portrait' of the court of Urbino in the early sixteenth century, and for the evidence we find there concerning the nature of courtly pursuits and the character of the Renaissance courtier. In her last chapter Cole describes a new artistic quality, '*terribilità*', which she says represents a new kind of court art associated with the 'awesome' power of sixteenth-century popes and princes. In many ways Giulio Romano's decorations in the Palazzo Te, at Mantua (Figure 3.22), represent this 'triumphalist' move away from the less agitated imagery and more covert symbolism of fifteenth-century decorative schemes. Yet I would argue that 'triumph' was a concept already deeply embedded in earlier court culture, and perhaps nowhere more personally implied than in the external and internal decorations at Poggio a Caiano.

Moreover, the internal frescoes and particularly the one I have chosen to discuss in some detail here, the *Tribute to Caesar*, clearly continue the Medicean traditions of self-fashioning noted throughout this case study in their emphasis on dynastic legitimacy and a personal relationship with the classical world. Contemporary and recent events concerning Medicean rule are camouflaged in the depiction of heroes of ancient Rome, but there can be no doubt that the frescoes at Poggio a Caiano served to emphasize the magnificence of the house of Medici and confirm its position in history.

In concluding his epilogue 'Piero di Lorenzo and the fall of the regime', Rubinstein (1997, pp.270–1) traces the changes made to the Medicean system of government in the wake of Piero de' Medici's flight from the city in November 1494. In December of that year a law was introduced ratifying the abolition of Medici councils. In their stead was established the Great Council, which in Rubinstein's words remained 'the foundation of the republican constitution until 1512'.

Figure 3.22 Giulio Romano, details from the Sala dei Giganti frescoes, 1532–4. Palazzo Te, Mantua. Photos: Alinari

Yet the room built to house this great new governmental body – the Sala del Cinquecento – was subsequently remodelled by Cosimo I in order that, as Mary Hollingsworth notes, it should 'give visual expression to the changed nature of power' (1996, p.270). It was here that Vasari covered the walls and ceilings with scenes of Florentine history and Cosimo's own territorial victories and power. It was here that he inserted a painted panel of *Cosimo I Studying the Plans for the Conquest of Siena* (Figure 3.23) in a composition which in many ways reflects that painted by Berruguete so many decades earlier at the court of Federico da Montefeltro. Like Federico, Cosimo I is dressed in courtly clothes and accompanied by items of armour. Yet here the similarities cease. No young heir is positioned at his side holding symbols indicating dynastic legitimacy. Cosimo is instead surrounded

Figure 3.23 Giorgio Vasari, *Cosimo I Studying Plans for the Conquest of Siena*, 1563–71, oil on panel. Ceiling of Sala del Cinquecento, Palazzo Vecchio, Florence. Photo: Scala

by classically garbed figures suggestive of Roman deities and philosophers. No longer in contemplative pose, imbibing the wisdom of literature, Cosimo leans forward against his desk and plans the submission of the city shown in the form of a model. Above him hover two cherubs holding sprigs of laurel or olive – the one in the hands of the cherub immediately above Cosimo fashioned in the form of a victory wreath. Rich in symbolism and offering varying layers of interpretation, this sixteenth-century depiction of a courtly ruler depends heavily on the imagery of the past. Although Cole refers to the shattering of the confidence of fifteenth-century princely courts (p.172), the cultural ambience nurtured under the early house of Medici combined with their own conscious self-fashioning clearly contributed to the establishment of the sixteenth-century grand ducal court in Florence, and in particular to this portrait of Grand Duke Cosimo I.

'Renaissance self-fashioning' is the key phrase in Stephen Greenblatt's seminal essay on Renaissance literature (1980). This term has assumed a central position in New Historicist scholarship, and is particularly relevant not only to Burckhardt's views concerning individualism during the Renaissance period but also to our own consideration of the 'courtly' aspirations of the house of Medici. Reflecting on the New Historicism, John Martin reminds us that such scholarship is based on the reading of texts as 'cultural artifacts or practices' which reflect the 'specific cultural, social, and political contexts' in which they are produced (1997, p.1313). You may feel that we have adopted a similar approach here in our consideration of works of art and contemporary fifteenth-century records. Greenblatt's own assertion on this point might strike you as something of an understatement:

> the simplest observation we can make is that in the sixteenth century there appears to be an increased self-consciousness about the fashioning of human identity as a manipulable, artful process.
>
> (in Martin, 1997, p.1314)

Our consideration here of the self-conscious display and representation adopted by the early Medici must surely indicate manipulation of appearances at a considerably earlier date. In conclusion, I would draw your attention to an extract from Michael Mascuch's *Origins of the Individualist Self*, inserted into John Martin's own survey:

> individualism is a multidimensional phenomenon, an amalgam of practices and values with no discernible centre. A variety of forces – social, economic, political, intellectual – contributed to its making, each

one of which was paramount at some time or another, either separately or jointly with others. Thus, a single account of individualism cannot possibly represent its development, its contours, its functions.

(Martin, 1997, p.1312)

I suggest we should bear this in mind when drawing our own conclusions concerning the extent to which a court culture existed under Medici rule in fifteenth-century Florence.

Bibliography

ACIDINI LUCHINAT, C. (1990) 'Medici e cittadini nei cortei dei Re Magi: ritratto di una società' in G. Cherubini and Giovanni Fanelli (eds) *Il Palazzo Medici Riccardi di Firenze*, Florence, Giunnti Gruppo Editoriale.

BAXANDALL, M.(1971) *Giotto and the Orators*, Oxford, Oxford University Press.

BULL, G. (trans.) (1971) G. Vasari: *The Lives of the Artists: A Selection*, Harmondsworth, Penguin.

BULST, W.A. (1990) 'Uso e trasformazione del Palazzo Mediceo fino ai Riccardi' in G. Cherubini and G. Fanelli (eds) *Il Palazzo Medici Riccardi di Firenza*, Florence, Giunnti Gruppo Editoriale.

BURCKHARDT, J. (1990) *The Civilization of the Renaissance in Italy*, trans. S.G.C. Middlemore, Harmondsworth, Penguin; first published 1858.

CLOUGH, C.H. (1992) 'Federico da Montefeltro and the kings of Naples: a study in fifteenth-century survival', *Renaissance Studies*, vol. 6, no. 2, pp.113–72.

COLE, A. (1995) *Art of the Italian Renaissance Courts*, London, Weidenfeld & Nicholson.

DAL POGGETTO, M.G.C.D. (1992) 'I dipinti di Palazzo Medici nell'inventario di Simone di Sragio della Pozze: problemi di committenza e di arredo', *Lorenzo il Magnifico. Politica, Economia, Cultura, Arte*, Florence, Pacini Editore, pp.131–62.

GOLDTHWAITE, R.A. (1993) *Wealth and the Demand for Art in Italy 1300–1600*, Baltimore, Md. and London, Johns Hopkins University Press.

GOMBRICH, E. (1966) *Norm and Form*, Studies in the Art of the Renaissance, London, Phaidon.

GRAGG, F.A. (trans.) with GABEL, L.C. (1960) *The Secret Memoirs of a Renaissance Pope: The Commentaries of Pius II*, London, George Allen & Unwin.

GREENBLATT, S. (1980) *Renaissance Self-fashioning: From More to Shakespeare*, Chicago, University of Chicago Press.

GUIDOTTI, A. (1990) 'Gli arredi del Palazzo nel tempo' in G. Cherubini and G. Fanelli (eds) *Il Palazzo Medici Riccardi di Firenze*, Florence, Giunnti Gruppo Editoriale.

HALL, J. (1974) *Dictionary of Subjects and Symbols in Art*, London, John Murray.

HATFIELD, R. (1970) 'Some unknown descriptions of the Medici Palace in 1459', *The Art Bulletin*, no. 52, pp.232–49.

HATFIELD, R (1970) 'The Compagnia dei Magi', *Journal of the Warburg and Courtauld Institutes*, no. 23, pp.107–61.

HOLLINGSWORTH, M. (1996) *Patronage in Sixteenth-Century Italy*, London, John Murray.

LOWE, K.J.P. (1993) 'Patronage and territoriality in early sixteenth-century Florence', *The Society of Renaissance Studies*, vol. 7, no. 3, Oxford University Press, pp.258–71.

MALLETT, M. (ed.) (1990) *Lorenzo de' Medici: Lettere*, vol. 6, Florence, Giunti-Barbera.

MALLETT, M. (1994) 'Ambassadors and their audiences in Renaissance Italy', *Renaissance Studies*, vol. 8, no. 3, pp.229–43.

MARTIN, J. (1997), 'Inventing sincerity, refashioning prudence: the discovery of the individual in Renaissance Europe', *American Historical Review*, vol. 102, no. 5, pp.1309–41.

PALMAROCCHI, R. (ed.) (1931) F. Guicciardini, *Storie fiorentine dal 1378 al 1509*, Bari, G. Laterza e Figli.

RUBINSTEIN, N. (1997, 2nd edn) *The Government of Florence under the Medici (1434 to 1494)*, Oxford, Clarendon; first published Oxford University Press, 1966.

SIMONS, P. (1995) 'Portraiture, portrayal, and idealization: ambiguous individualism in representations of Renaissance women' in A. Brown (ed.) *Language and Images of Renaissance Italy*, Oxford, Clarendon, pp.263–311.

SITT, M. (1994) 'Jacob Burckhardt as architect of a new art history', *Journal of the Warburg and Courtauld Institutes*, vol. 57, pp.227–42.

SPENCER, J.R. (ed.) (1966) L.B. Alberti: *On Painting*, New Haven, Conn., Yale University Press.

WARNKE, M. (1993) *The Court Artist: On the Ancestry of the Modern Artist*, trans. D. McLintock, Cambridge, Cambridge University Press; originally published in German as *Hofkünstler. Zur Vorgeschichte des Modernen Künstlers*, Cologne, DuMont Buchverlag, 1985.

WELCH, E. (1997) *Art and Society in Italy 1350–1500*, Oxford History of Art, Oxford, Oxford University Press.

WOODS-MARSDEN, J. (1989) 'How quattrocento princes used art: Sigismondo Pandolfo Malatesta of Rimini and *cose militari*', *Renaissance Studies*, vol. 3, no. 4, pp.387–414.

WRIGHT, A. (1993) 'A portrait for the visit of Galeazzo Maria Sforza to Florence in 1471', 'Piero de' Medici and The Pollaiuolo', offprint from *Piero de' Medici il Gottoso (1469–1459)*, Berlin, Andreas Beyer and Bruce Boucher.

Anthology and Reader sources

Niccolò Machiavelli, The Pazzi conspiracy: *Florentine History*, trans. W.K. Marriott, London, J.M. Dent, 1912, pp.1–3, 317–18, 321–9 (Anthology, no. 26ii).

R. Hatfield, Three accounts of the visit of Galeazzo Maria Sforza to the Medici Palace, Florence (1459): letter from Galeazzo Maria Sforza to his parents; diplomatic despatch from Niccolò de' Carissimi da Parma; and the *Terze rime*: 'Some unknown descriptions of the Medici Palace in 1459', *The Art Bulletin*, 1970, no. 52, pp.246, 232, 247–8; trans. R. Hatfield with revisions for the Anthology by Anabel Thomas (Anthology, nos. 40i–iii).

Pope Pius II, On his visit to Florence and the hospitality of Cosimo de' Medici (1459): *The Secret Memoirs of a Renaissance Pope: The Commentaries of Pius II*, trans. F.A. Gragg with L.C. Gabel, London, George Allen & Unwin, 1960, pp.105–10 (Anthology, no. 41).

CHAPTER FOUR

Britain's Renaissance of letters

BY CERI SULLIVAN[1]

Objectives

The objectives of this chapter are that you should:

- develop skills in analysing literary texts;
- learn about the technical aspects of Renaissance verse, and its range of topics and styles;
- reflect on the accommodation of classical and continental models by British writers;
- think about the interrelationship of the political and literary spheres.

Early modern or Renaissance?

For Burckhardt, one of the attributes of the Italian Renaissance was a self-conscious enthusiasm about language, as is described in Book 1 of this series. He argued that the development of political systems in Florence and Venice, based on the prince and the state, required the support of certain types of individual. Humanist educational techniques enabled the emergence of these talented public thinkers and administrators. Similar political and cultural changes also occurred in Britain, but later. The one and a half centuries covered by the Tudor and Stuart reigns are usually defined as the British Renaissance, from the accession of Henry VIII in 1509 to some point in the mid seventeenth century (often the emergence of the Commonwealth in 1649 after the Civil War, or the restoration of the monarchy in 1660). Historians see in this period the start of a distinctively 'modern' consciousness, and give it the title 'early modern'. Put crudely, their debates are structured around four issues: the move from the medieval subsistence economy to a market economy, and the growth of global commerce; the effects of increasing urbanization; a developing recognition of the social depth at which political debate existed, in both elite and popular circles,

[1] This chapter was originally planned by Margaret Healy, of the University of Sussex, whose helpful suggestions I have adopted.

counter-balanced by a centralization of power at court; in learning, a shift in the certainty with which knowledge of the natural and divine orders was spoken of, yet also, in Burckhardt's terms, a 'great and general enthusiasm for antiquity'. The Renaissance, as a specifically literary concept, resides within the area of 'early modern'; it is a self-labelling 'rebirth' of learning, stimulated by direct contact with classical forms and ideas and applied to the new conditions of public life through the mediation of Italian humanists.

The geo-political area from which the poetry discussed here is drawn needs some explanation. Wales was not legally united with England until 1536, although the administration of the principality had been carried out by adherents to the English crown since the late thirteenth century. Moreover, although James VI of Scotland succeeded Elizabeth I to become James I of England and Wales in 1603, Scotland and England remained separate countries – in constitution, government, law, economy and culture – until 1707 (with the exception of a brief period during the 1650s). England undertook the colonization of Ireland in the sixteenth century by means of open warfare, economic attrition and the plantation of English settlers. Thus the concept of a united British Isles was a creation; more myth than reality, it was useful to a self-defined centre and to those at its margins who identified with that centre. While James used the term 'Britain' at significant moments, such as his first speech to the English Parliament which addressed his hope of union, its application by others was frequently confined to the Welsh, or the original inhabitants of the island, the ancient Britons. Thus, while this chapter deals with poetry from all four nations, it uses 'British' with reservation. Here it signifies those people who aligned themselves with the new forms of English nationalism – of which the Renaissance is, in part, an expression – rather than all those who lived in these islands.

If Burckhardt was alert to the political element in the cultural revival of antiquity, some of his readers were not. Nineteenth- and early twentieth-century literary critics narrowed down the definition of the 'Renaissance' to court poetry's use of classical and European genres in a personal vein. They focused on the figure of the poet who spoke lyrically of his feelings, not of his political position. C.S. Lewis, for example, dealing with verse from what he called the 'golden' period of the later sixteenth century, describes it as a poetry which eschewed any reference to a local situation and expressed 'the emotions in which all men are alike ... [using] a learnable technique, soon leading to a standard of workmanship which earlier poets had hardly even attempted' (1954, p.480). The sonneteers, his prime example of 'golden' verse:

> wrote not to tell their own love stories, not to express whatever in their own loves was local and peculiar, but to give us others, the inarticulate lovers, a voice. The reader was to seek in a sonnet not what the poet felt but what he himself felt, what all men felt.

(p.491)

Lewis is not concerned with the theatricality and self-promotion in Renaissance literature in English, its dialectical and political aspects, nor with its ability both to manipulate and to hear from the marginal figures any cultural centre will produce. All criticism is the product of the issues that preoccupy its writers; Lewis – writing in 1954 – does not see Renaissance literature from the cultural perspective of the late twentieth and early twenty-first centuries, with their concerns for women, the disaffected, New World inhabitants and the poor. Just as our modern interest in the construction of the self in a public sphere allows us to create particular readings of selected poems, so commentators in years to come will distinguish our concerns in our readings of the poems, and in our readings of the work of Lewis and Burckhardt.

The following discussion considers a number of poems from *The Penguin Book of Renaissance Verse 1509–1659*, selected and introduced by David Norbrook (1993), as well as associated poems and prose extracts from the Anthology. It asks if and how these pieces accommodate classical and Italian forms and ideas, how they are parodied or varied to throw attention on their formal features, and how they are mingled with native popular and medieval genres. Initially, the chapter takes examples of two genres accounted typically 'Renaissance', the pastoral and the Petrarchan, and discusses why these modes may have been selected – a competition for patronage, a display of fashion and talent, a desire to comment on social and political situations of the time. Having established some of the formal features of Renaissance verse, it discusses how this poetry copes with contemporary political, economic and religious topics. The chapter then turns to the question of whether a distinctively Renaissance aesthetic can be inferred from the poems, and concludes with a case study of an estate poem by Ben Jonson.

Norbrook's Appendix 4 contains a biography for each British author dealt with here, and Appendix 1 is an index of poems according to genre. Sections of this chapter which discuss Renaissance politics and aesthetics are closely tied in to Norbrook's introduction.

Reading the pastoral and Petrarchan modes

Christopher Marlowe's 'The passionate sheepheard to his love' first appeared in print in 1599 in an anthology of love poetry, *The Passionate Pilgrim*. This volume included **sonnets** by William Shakespeare, and was sufficiently popular to have been reprinted twice by 1613. The poem had circulated widely in manuscript before printing, and had been attributed to Sir Philip Sidney and to Raleigh. It inspired a reply by the latter which was printed with Marlowe's poem in *Englands Helicon* of 1600, a collection of pastoral poetry which showcased the most fashionable authors of the day (Helicon is the mountain in Greece where the Muses were said to reside). The two poems continued to be popular: William Corkine's *Second Book of Ayres* (1612) contains an instrumental piece entitled 'Come live with me and be my love', and as late as 1653 Izaac Walton's *Compleat Angler* features a milkmaid who sings Marlowe's poems to her mother, who in turn replies with Raleigh's prudent verses; both songs are praised by the listening fishermen as 'old fashioned poetry but choicely good'.

Exercise

Read Marlowe's 'The passionate sheepheard to his love' (Norbrook, no. 98) and Raleigh's 'The nimphs reply to the sheepheard' (Anthology, no. 43). What are these poems about? What tone do the poets take?

Discussion

A first reading of the two **lyrics** is likely to produce a sense that they are sweet, twittering irrelevancies (Lewis calls them poetry in its 'innocent' condition, including 'all that is naturally delightful'). The poems flow through the mind, leaving dainty images of gentle dalliance on sunlit afternoons. The countryside exists to provide pleasures for a shepherd whose only employment is to produce posies of verse and flowers for his fair mistress. Even the rivers and birds sing madrigals, part-songs, with the shepherd's pleas. The deliberately artless method of description adopted, of simply listing the rural delights – beds of roses, a cap of flowers, a belt of straw, May morning dances – delicately articulates them. They appeal to the senses: the fragrance of amber and blooms, the vivid colours of coral and gold, the softest wool, the murmur of water.

In Marlowe's poem the beauty of the shepherdess is assumed from the natural beauty in which the swain wishes to envelope her, her clothes acting as a **synecdoche** (a part which represents the whole) for her body. The shepherd is improbably well spoken, using regular iambic tetrameters in rhymed quatrains (Norbrook's Appendix 2 gives a brief description of metres and stanzaic forms used in the poems). The world the poem creates is wholly artificial. Real sheep would sully the grass, winter freeze the fantasy, and work interfere with the careful cultivation of the art of love.

Raleigh's poem is equally coy, where a nymph sighs back her wistful refusal. Winter will come, the flowers will fade, and even the loving heart will turn sour towards the beloved. Raleigh's verse inverts the theme of *carpe diem* (or 'seize the day', a tag from one of Horace's odes), where mistresses are urged to take their pleasures while they can. Even when pragmatism reasserts itself, it does so with regret: the nymph uses the same verse form as Marlowe's shepherd; she repeats the delights he listed, and assures him that if youth could last, then so would their love. The poem is in the conditional mood – it begins 'If all the world and love were young' – prompting readers to reply 'but they aren't', as they listen to the 'pretty pleasures'. The fantasy is exposed, but its impossibility is regretted. To read the poems in this way is to see them as amusing and charming; to go beyond such a reading it is necessary to know something of the classical and continental referents used by Marlowe and Raleigh. ❖

The audience for these poems was well versed in the pastoral mode, which Tudor literary historians thought originated with the Greek writer Theocritus, who worked in Alexandria in the third century BCE. His poetry was translated into English by Joseph Barnes in 1588, and shows the concern for art above content or, to be more precise, an understanding of artfulness as the content of this mode – which is a feature of Elizabethan lyric verse. Theocritus's shepherds engage in singing matches, where love is merely an occasion for verse, rather than caring for their sheep. However, it was the first-century BCE Roman poet Virgil whom most Renaissance readers knew best from their school days. Robin Sowerby (1994) has described how, in the peace which followed the fall of the Roman republic in 31 BCE and the accession of Augustus Caesar as 'first citizen', poets heralded the transformation of the Roman state. Augustus was celebrated for re-edifying Rome, and for strengthening its moral tone through the enactment of legislation encouraging family life and curbing excessive private wealth. It was said that he appealed to traditional Roman values. Foremost among these Augustan poets were Virgil and Horace. They took on a public role in proclaiming the newly rediscovered aspirations to virtue, in verses of the highest refinement. Moreover, they saw:

good art [as] the product of a good life in which self-examination and knowledge of the world are equally vital. The refinement of language with which Virgil has always been associated [was] also the expression of a refinement of sensibility and spirit.

(Sowerby, 1994, p.42)

Virgil's *Eclogues* (strictly, the Latin form of a Greek word meaning 'a choice' of small poems, but used by Renaissance writers to stand for 'pastoral' by association with Virgil's subject matter) were translated, parsed and examined by boys in their last two years of grammar school. Eclogue 5, for example (Anthology, no. 44), shows the competition within the pastoral to exhibit poetic talent. In this poem Menalcas and Mopsus take a brief holiday from work in order to lament the death of a fellow shepherd, Daphnis, and to celebrate his deification. The springtime setting of the *locus amoenus* (pleasant place) where the shepherds relax is contrasted with the work of husbandry they must do, the changing seasons, and death. The pastoral mode is inherently wistful, and it moves easily between the details of the realistic scenery and their symbolism. The shepherds compete in praising each other's songs, in looking forward to other occasions of mournful ritual, and in making the countryside an altar to Daphnis's charms.

While Virgil remained the most important influence on British writers of pastoral, both in the original and in translation (there were at least eight English translations of the *Eclogues* printed before 1634), continental models were also available. Five writers of epic pastoral romances and plays – Jacopo Sannazaro, Jorge de Montemayor, Ludovico Ariosto, Giovanni Battista Guarini and Torquato Tasso – influenced poems such as Edmund Spenser's *Faerie Queene* (published in two parts, in 1590 and 1596), and romances such as Philip Sidney's *Arcadia* (published in 1593). (Norbrook, nos. 14, 32, 64, 80–2, 181 are selections from these poems.) Sannazaro's Latin eclogues, and in particular his Italian *Arcadia* of 1504, have slight narratives which deliver the reader into points in the landscape where shepherds are singing. Montemayor's *Diana* of 1559 influenced Spenser, who may have read the Spanish original, as Sidney did, or one of the French translations. The Italian Ludovico Ariosto's *Orlando Furioso* of 1535 was frequently republished with allegorical commentary (Norbrook, no. 341 is a contemporary translation of a portion of the poem). The pastoral mode was not confined to verse and romance. Giovanni Battista Guarini's play *Il pastor fido* (*The Faithful Shepherd*) of 1589 and the pastoral dramas of Torquato Tasso, such as the *Aminta* of 1573, were frequently imitated in Britain. Tasso was a court poet at

Ferrara under Alfonso II d'Este, until a recurrent mental disorder made it necessary for Alfonso to confine him between 1579 and 1586. The *Aminta* was followed by a highly successful religious epic, *Gerusalemme liberata* of 1581, which described the conquest of Jerusalem by Crusaders. Within eleven years sections of this were turned into plays for the English stage, and a translation into English appeared in 1594 (Norbrook, no. 342 gives an extract from another translation of 1600). Guarini succeeded Tasso as court poet at Ferrara and later took up the same position at Florence and Mantua. *Il pastor fido* was printed in Italian in London in 1591 and translated into English in 1602. Thus, English writers and readers of the pastoral were fully conversant with its conventions from classical and contemporary European antecedents. *Englands Helicon* has over a hundred poems on a similar theme, so the interest which the pastoral held for its audience was not its novelty.

Burckhardt will have prepared you to read such pastoral lyrics as unmediated pictures of the heart; more recent literary criticism, however, views them as self-interested and competitive exercises.

Exercise

Read the biographies of Raleigh and Marlowe in Norbrook's Appendix 4. Given the poets' lifestyles, what is unexpected about the two poems you read in the previous exercise? Where does the humour of the verse lie?

Discussion

The spectacle of two Elizabethan men of action pretending to be nymphs and shepherds writing amorous verses to each other should make us pause. Marlowe was a former government spy who had been arrested for coining and had subsequently become a writer of blood-and-thunder dramas in the new medium of the public theatre; Raleigh was a soldier, one of the first Europeans to explore Virginia and Guyana, and an ambitious courtier. The two poems are self-regarding, not merely in re-using an old form and answering each other, but also in being 'about' nothing except seduction of the reader; aesthetic delight is placed before any reference to reality. (Ben Jonson's ironic complaint about Guarini's pastorals, that the shepherds spoke as well as the author, is pertinent here.) It is in the poems' emphasis on conventionality that their subtle variations of form become apparent and significant. Dinner jackets are conventional: it is slight changes in the width of the lapels or the set of the sleeve which demonstrate an eye for fashion. Such varying depends for its effect on a knowledgeable audience, one which is able to recall the original, and can make quick comparison between the two. ❖

In producing these verbal pictures Marlowe and Raleigh demonstrate their easy mastery over the form. Burckhardt's influential figure of the Renaissance man, '*l'uomo universale*', gives such talents only to 'the private man, indifferent to politics, and busied partly with serious pursuits, partly with the interests of a dilettante' (Burckhardt, 1990, pp. 101, 99). This display of effortless superiority was labelled as *sprezzatura* (careless grace) by Baldassare Castiglione's *Il libro del cortegiano* of 1528 (translated into English by Sir Thomas Hoby as *The Book of the Courtier* in 1561). The courtier was advised to work hard in private to acquire accomplishments but never to allow such effort to appear when using them. Marlowe and Raleigh show their intelligence to their peers in producing small things with grace and ease, allowing the inference that they could cope with great things with equal facility. Contrary to a Burckhardtian reading, these poems can be read as a politically interested display of their authors' learning, wit and ability. (Similar uses of the pastoral can be seen in Norbrook, nos. 174, 191, 216–17.) But pastoral was not simply a way in which witty writers, desirous of career advancement, could advertise their abilities; as we shall see, Edmund Spenser's *Shepheardes Calender* employs it as a vehicle for social commentary. Yet in another revision of Marlowe's original by another ambitious courtier poet, John Donne, we are confronted by the same problem: why is the poet recycling this particular poem?

Exercise

Read John Donne's 'The bait' (Anthology, no. 45). There is a manuscript version of this poem but there are no details of its circulation before Donne's death. It was printed posthumously in 1633 in an edition of his collected poems.

What is the relationship between this poem and the poems by Marlowe and Raleigh?

Discussion

Sir Izaac Walton's Angler notes that Donne wrote 'to show the world that hee could make soft and smooth verses, when he thought them fit and worth his labour'. While Donne certainly shows a deft command of the pastoral, making the natural landscape a jewel-bright realm of pleasure, he also demonstrates a poetic competitiveness. Marlowe's gentle romance is here made explicitly erotic – fishes nibble a naked woman and his scene is sardonically recast. With a shudder of disgust the poet contemplates the brutal reality outside the literary fantasy: the deflationary details of the freezing angler, the sharp shells, the action of catching and killing a fish. **Hyperbolic** (overstated) reasoning takes the place of Marlowe's lists of sensual delights, as Donne argues that the woman's radiance will eclipse both sun and moon. The conclusion triumphantly turns on itself in what was called a **conceit**, a deliberately far-fetched comparison between two dissimilar things, which draws attention to the wit of the poet in bringing the two images together so powerfully. Here, the woman herself becomes a bait to all fishes, including the goggling, love-struck poet. Taking over a previously used form in order to reverse its meaning (as well as the representation of the masterful poet) is a witty way for Donne to appropriate part of the former generation's fame. Moreover, readers like yourself, who are able to recollect Marlowe's verse, are complimented on being one of an elite number who can see the point of Raleigh's poem, and Donne's riposte. ❖

Another writer whose work at this time relied on an elite audience was George Buchanan. He was born in Stirlingshire, and studied at the Universities of St Andrews and Paris; he became a professor at the Collège de Guyenne, Bordeaux, where Michel de Montaigne was one of his pupils. In 1547 he became a lecturer at the University of Coimbra in Portugal. He was imprisoned several times for satires on the Catholic church. Around 1561 he returned to Scotland and professed himself a Protestant. He was appointed keeper of the privy seal of Scotland and in 1570 tutor to the four-year-old James VI of Scotland, a post he held until 1578. He became the centre of a Scottish humanist circle – the English court was only one of several focuses for the new learning in Britain. His 20-volume *Rerum scoticarum historia* (Matters from Scottish history) was published in 1582 and became the standard work on the subject throughout the seventeenth century. His Latin poems and Psalm paraphrases were widely famed as models of pure style. Henri Etienne, the Parisian printer and scholar, deemed him 'easily the first of the poets of our age'. He was acquainted with members of the Pléiade group of writers: Du Bellay, for instance (see p.276, below), rendered Buchanan's first elegy and an ode into French.

Exercise

Read Buchanan's 'Calendae Maiae' (Norbrook, no. 175) and think about the following issues:

- the depiction of the landscape;
- the relationship between this poem and the English pastorals;
- Buchanan's choice of Latin rather than English;
- the use of both classical and biblical allusion – Buchanan's reference to Lethe and to God's 'last flames'.

Discussion

Buchanan's pastoral is more strictly classical than the previous three poems examined: the Graces dance in a ring (as they do in *The Faerie Queene*, Norbrook, no. 348); the loss of the golden age described by Hesiod and Ovid – where time once stood still, and justice, peace and plenty ruled the earth – is lamented; the Hesperides or Isles of the Blessed beckon, which the dead reach after a voyage over the Lethe, the river of forgetfulness. The conditional mood of the three English poems is maintained here: the *locus amoenus*, representing the golden age, has gone from the earth, but may come again. However, two features distinguish this poem from those by Raleigh, Marlowe and Donne: the use of Latin, and the Christian classicism. By writing in Latin Buchanan was not making a special point, as he would have done if he had chosen the vernacular. Scholarly writing, public debate and political business were conducted in Latin, the *lingua franca* of Europe. To a much greater extent than today, learned and powerful people saw themselves as part of a European community with a shared language and interests, worshipping in a universal church. Buchanan was addressing a wide audience of elite readers, and though he circulated his poems in manuscript, not print, his own career shows how texts travelled among the learned in Europe. Secondly Buchanan feels no strain in referring both to the Christian Last Judgement, when the earth will be consumed by fire, and to the classical Isles of the Blessed. Christian doctrine and pagan theology are here not mutually exclusive; rather, the classical vision is re-used as a metaphor for the Christian reality. Time and again in Renaissance verse, classical writings are 'purified' for Christian use by reading them figuratively. Even classical erotica, such as Ovid's poems on the arts of love, are 'saved', with some ingenuity (for example, the love of Christ for the soul or his church). The capacious generosity of spirit in Renaissance verse, its accretive – even greedy – appreciation of other cultures' forms and ideas, is one of its joys. ❖

One of the major figures who allowed later writers to treat pagan materials in this way was the poet Francesco Petrarca (1304–74). Burckhardt describes how the Italian reception of Petrarch's work focused on his historical and philosophical commentaries, his support for the revival of classical learning, his role in the discovery and preservation of antique remains, both textual and archaeological, and his neo-Latin poetry (p.137). For British writers, however, it was Petrarch's vernacular *Canzoniere* ('songs', also called *Rime sparse* or 'scattered rhymes') that were of greater interest. They became the primary models for amatory poetry in the Renaissance. The sonnet form was not unknown in Britain before this: Chaucer, for instance, translated Petrarch's Sonnet 132 into three seven-line stanzas. It was only in the sixteenth century, however, that Petrarch's sonnets were widely emulated, as a result of a debate in Italy over which dialect should be used in public affairs, scholarship and literature. In *Prose della volgar lingua* (Italian prose) of 1524 by the Italian humanist Pietro Bembo, the fourteenth-century Tuscan of Petrarch's sonnets was set out as the model for Italian poetry. Bembo's appeal to the authority of Petrarch – combined, of course, with the inherent interest of the sonnets' themes – helped ensure Petrarch's popularity in the courts of Italy.

The *Canzoniere's* 317 sonnets, 29 canzoni, 9 sestine, 7 ballads and 4 madrigals largely form a sequence in which Petrarch explores his experience of lifelong unrequited love. While some of the poems are on religious and political themes, the majority are concerned with the extreme emotions precipitated by Petrarch's obsession with the idealized figure of the beloved, Laura. In Sonnet 190 (see the Anthology, no. 46) he uses a white hart which appears before him at dawn in a grove of laurel to suggest Laura's purity, her golden attributes and her precious value. (The laurel, the dawn and the gold, all of which in Italian can be used to play on the sound of the name *Laura*, appear repeatedly in many other poems as metaphors of Laura herself – they not only sound like her, they *are* her.) Here her inaccessibility is emphasized by the message and the material of the jewelled collar around the hart's neck (diamonds cannot be scratched or affected by other stones, so are a symbol of chastity). The collar uses Christ's warning to Mary Magdalene when he appeared to her at the sepulchre after his Resurrection, '*noli me tangere*' ('do not touch me', John 20.17). The hart's sudden disappearance – referring to Laura's death – sends her to heaven's 'Caesar', God (compare Buchanan's conflation of Christian and classical motifs). Some Renaissance readers would have received this vision through a Christian Neoplatonic understanding of the immanence of God in creation. As Book 1 discussed (Chapter 5), Plato's *Phaedrus* describes the soul's growth at the sight of the beloved. The fifteenth-century Florentine philosopher Marsilio Ficino, in his commentary of 1469 on Plato's *Symposium*, described the function of physical beauty in raising the contemplation of the lover up to the beauty of the beloved's soul, and then on to the Divine Form which created that soul in its own likeness. Castiglione echoed this in the fourth book of *The Courtier*, through a character named after and modelled on Pietro Bembo, himself the author of a dialogue which explores Platonic love, *Gli Asolani* (The lovers of Asolo) of 1505 (see the note in the Anthology, no. 16). English Neoplatonic poets later took up this conceit. In Philip Sidney's *An Apology for Poetry*, printed in 1595, lyrical songs and sonnets are allowed 'in singing the praises of the immortal beauty, the immortal goodness of that God who giveth us hands to write and wits to conceive'. Poetry is praised for depicting that 'unspeakable and everlasting beauty to be seen by the eyes of the mind, only cleared by faith'.

The central situation of Petrarch's sonnets is the separation of the humbled, passionate poet and his untouchable mistress. Michael Spiller comments on their presentation of a lover whose 'varying style' between weeping and discoursing, vain hope and grief, marks:

> the first time in European literature that such instability, both psychic and rhetorical, is announced as the principle of a work of poesis ... It is the brevity of the sonnet which makes this possible here ... enclosing the narrated experience in a box that is discontinuous with other boxes.

> (1992, p.49)

The Italian form of the sonnet is a poem of fourteen lines, with a turn in meaning between the first eight-line unit (the octave, which is often broken into two quatrains) and the last six lines (the sestet). In Sonnet 190, for instance, the poet's desire for the vision is rebuked by the stern injunction on the hart's collar. The turn in the sonnet demonstrates Spiller's 'instability of the psyche and of the tongue' (p.48), as does the contrast in tone and theme between different sonnets in a sequence.

Certain conventional topics spring from the fixed and frustrated position of the sonneteer. He meditates on the brief encounters he has with the woman – his first sight of her, their first quarrel, their first kiss. He recreates her in his imagination, dwelling on her virtues and beauties, part by part. He passes sleepless nights, cries out with passion, cannot behave with courtesy, sense or social propriety, even in situations which have nothing to do with his love (for English instances of these, see Norbrook, nos. 57, 59, 74, 90, 92, 120–2, and a sonnet by the Scottish poet Mark Alexander Boyd, Norbrook, no. 78). In *The Arte of English Poesie* of 1589 George Puttenham describes 'in what forme of poesie the amorous affections and allurements were uttered' to convey the pains and pleasures of the inconstant emotion:

> the poore soules sometimes praying, beseeching, sometime honouring, avancing, praising, an other while railing, reviling, and cursing, then sorrowing, weeping, lamenting, in the ende laughing, reioysing, & solacing the beloved againe.

> (Smith, 1937, vol. 2, p.47)

So formalized was the position of the Petrarchan lover that Shakespeare's *As You Like It* was able to make teasing reference to the marks of a man in love, who had:

> a lean cheek ... a blue eye and sunken ... an unquestionable spirit ... a beard neglected ... your hose should be ungartered, your bonnet unbanded, your sleeve unbuttoned, your shoe untied, and everything about you demonstrating a careless desolation.

(3.2.363–71)

Compare, too, Sir John Davies's guilty sonnet on love 'The sacred muse that firste made love devine' (Norbrook, no. 93).

Chastity, cruel circumstance, then death keep the poet alone, in a perpetual state of desire. Petrarchan sonnets are predicated on a dynamic in which the woman to whom the poems are addressed is permanently chaste, while the poet-lover is in a continual state of arousal. This erotic frustration in the face of chastity leads to poetry: as Nancy Vickers tartly remarks, the words of a Petrarchan sonnet 'affirm absence by their presence' (Abel, 1982, p.105). The description of the woman substitutes for herself; the poem only exists because the poet's suit has been unsuccessful. It is a verbal monument to his erotic failure.

Petrarchan models underpin certain sonnets of Sir Thomas Wyatt. His work circulated in manuscript during his lifetime, and was published posthumously in *Tottels Miscellany* (1557), an anthology of new forms and fashionable verse similar to *Englands Helicon*. Wyatt undertook diplomatic missions in France, Italy, Spain and the Low Countries on behalf of Henry VIII, and was appointed ambassador to the court of Charles V of Spain in 1537. While travelling, he took the opportunity to translate and adapt poems in some of the modish literary forms on the Continent.

Exercise

Read 'Who so list to hount' (Norbrook, no. 54). Where is the turn in Wyatt's sonnet? How does the tone of his poem differ from Petrarch's?

Discussion

Wyatt has preserved Petrarch's form: the sonnet is divided into an octet and a sestet, marked by the repetition of 'who list her hount' at the point at which the poet himself gives up the chase. Puttenham praises Wyatt for:

> having travailed into Italie, and there tasted the sweete and stately measures and stile of the Italian Poesie ... greatly pollished our rude & homely maner of vulgar Poesie from that it had bene before.

(Smith, 1937, vol. 2, p.62)

Wyatt has extended the messages on the white hind's collar to refer to Christ's differentiation between the taxes which must be paid to the earthly authority and the duties owed to the heavenly; otherwise the poem's setting is the same as Petrarch's. Wyatt uses both Petrarchan diction – flowers, gold, diamonds, burning love – and biblical and proverbial registers ('catch the wind').

The whole tone, however, is changed: the 'touch me not' hart is no longer a vision of divine purity which can only ever be glimpsed briefly here on earth, and for which the poet must long. Since Wyatt gives up the chase in disgust, his hart must have offered at least a chance of capture, an earthly beauty who has rejected his advances. The concentration is on the poet, not on his vision (indeed C.S. Lewis noted sardonically 'how very disagreeable it must be for a woman to have a lover like Wyatt' (1954, p.229)). ❖

The poem is sometimes held to refer to Wyatt's entanglement with Anne Boleyn, before she became the mistress, then the wife, of the king. (Wyatt was arrested on suspicion of adultery with Boleyn, when Henry replaced her with Jane Seymour.) Read with this knowledge, the poem shows not only a cynical weariness with the courtship game, but also a wary understanding of the poet's position in a different sort of courtship: Britain's 'Caesar' would not want his game caught. Similar tones can be distinguished in other poems by Wyatt, and by Alexander Scott (Norbrook, nos. 54–5, 58).

Exercise

Read Sonnet 1 from Philip Sidney's sonnet sequence *Astrophil and Stella* (Norbrook, no. 65). ❖

Written around 1582, the sequence circulated in manuscript and was eventually printed posthumously in an unauthorized version in 1591. Composed of 108 sonnets and eleven songs, it deals with the love of Astrophil for the chaste – or disdainful – Stella, identified by puns within the text as Penelope Devereux, daughter of the earl of Essex, who married Lord Rich in 1581.

Burckhardt allows that the sonnet may be used for 'personal reminiscence' or political commentary, but foregrounds the solipsism and sensibility of the form: 'the world of Italian sentiment comes before us in a series of pictures, clear, concise, and most effective in their brevity' (p.201). He praises Dante, for instance, for the:

> unflinching frankness and sincerity [with which] he lays bare every shade of his joy and sorrow, and moulds it resolutely into the strictest forms of art ... Subjective feeling has here a full objective truth and greatness, and most of it is so set forth that all ages and peoples can make it their own.

(p.202)

The publisher of Sidney's poems in 1591 was equally anxious to give the impression that Astrophil speaks from his heart, moving the reader to pity and gentle laughter. He employed the pamphleteer Thomas Nashe to write a preface describing the sequence as a 'tragicomody of love ... performed by starlight ... The argument cruell chastitie, the Prologue hope, the Epilogue dispaire' (Smith, 1937, vol. 2, p.223). Sidney's first sonnet appears to be a cry from the heart for simplicity and sincerity in love poetry. Astrophil is desperate to impress Stella with his passion-strangled verse.

Our next task will be to examine the central position given to rhetoric in the literature of Renaissance Britain. As the syllabus from Eton shows (see the extract in the Anthology, no. 47), grammar school boys up to the age of thirteen or fourteen received an education which focused on making them verbally dextrous. The system of education followed lines laid down by classical pedagogues, such as Quintilian in his rhetorical handbook *Institutio oratoria* (On the training of the orator). Latin, the core of the scheme of classes, was taught by translation – at first of sentences composed by the master and then of portions from classical writers. Texts would be turned from Latin to English, then back to Latin again, with the focus first on the grammatical construction of each sentence before more complex rhetorical analysis began.

Rhetorical handbooks used by sixteenth-century British schools followed the classical division of rhetoric into five parts. First, the orator gathered together ideas for his speech, a procedure known as *inventio*. This was achieved either by referring to manuals of logic through which he 'processed' his topic (asking himself what were its precedents and antecedents, analogies, causes and effects, accidents and essentials, and so on) or by referring to stores of common wisdom, points which past orators had found helpful when discussing similar cases (also called commonplaces, *loci communes*, or *topoi*). 'Inventing', or finding, material in this way meant that some of what was collected proved irrelevant to the speech in question. Thus the next stage in composing a speech, known as *dispositio*, was to select what was useful and arrange it according to the effect the orator wished to produce on the audience – a subtle opening, perhaps, or a rousing peroration which closed the speech with an emotional appeal. The material that had thus been found and arranged was then clothed with words, the stage known as *elocutio*, which selected diction, including **schemes** (patterns of sound, such as repetition and rhyme) and **tropes** (turns in meaning, such as metaphor and synecdoche) to create a high or low style, adorned or plain. (The Anthology (no. 48) gives a relatively truncated list of schemes and tropes from a manual which was widely used in Tudor schools, the

Rhetorica ad Herennium, traditionally but erroneously attributed to Cicero. Renaissance commentators on rhetoric produced lists which were frequently augmented; the *Thesaurus rhetoricae* (1559) by Giovanni Battista Bernardi, for instance, gives around 5,000 rhetorical terms (Vickers, 1990, p.269).) Last came memorizing the speech and delivering it, stages on which the Elizabethan grammar school did not concentrate. Boys would be encouraged, when translating passages, to note their grammatical and rhetorical features, picking out the forms of *inventio* used and *topoi* appealed to, and noting the details of *elocutio*. Richard Lanham has described the effects of this training:

> start your student young. Teach him a minute concentration on the word, how to write it, speak it, remember it. Stress memory in a massive, almost brutalizing way, develop it far in advance of conceptual understanding ... Require no original thought. Demand instead an agile marshaling of the proverbial wisdom on any issue ... Let him, to weariness, translate, not only from one language to another, but from one style to another ... Make this intense training in the word ... the only path to wealth and honor.
>
> (1976, pp.2–3)

Exercise

Bearing in mind what you have just read, look again at Sidney's Sonnet 1. Does the poem allow for a more cynical reading than that suggested by Nashe's preface? Look particularly at how the poem dramatizes its own composition.

Discussion

The effects of Sidney's education are evident. He initially uses the scheme of **gradatio**, described by the *Rhetorica ad Herennium* as the repetition of a word or phrase which leads the reader on to the next stage of the argument (here, pain–pleasure, pleasure–reading, reading–knowledge, knowledge–pity, pity–grace). The effect is to sweep him or her into agreeing with the poet's conclusion, without realizing that the organization of sounds has made this seem inevitable. Astrophil is trying to write a poem which will affect Stella in a similar way, using the approved method of imitation. 'Oft turning ... leaves' from the classical and Italian models of love poetry – or possibly even from his commonplace book, where he has noted phrases which were effective in other poems – Astrophil 'studies' for material to speak about his love, and for metres ('feet' or metrical units) to adorn his poem. The painful picture of a dull scholar, 'beating' himself to learn, provokes the reader to laughter at his expense; it is some distance from our admiration of Burckhardt's sensitive and impassioned writer. Even Astrophil's Muse is sharp with the silly lover: he must speak what he feels.

Modern-day readers, brought up on novels which claim to reveal the inner lives of their characters, receive lyric poetry as though it embodies the **Romantic** ideals of originality and sincerity. We respond to an authorial self who appears to be speaking directly and passionately to each of us, as solitary readers who empathize with the poet's pain. Yet although Sidney's first sonnet appears to endorse this reader–writer relationship, in the Muse's comment there is room to read the purpose of the sonnet sequence differently. ❖

Sidney treats the protestations of love poets more ironically than Puttenham (see p.238, above):

> truly many of such writings as come under the banner of unresistible love, if I were a mistress, would never persuade me they were in love; so coldly they apply fiery speeches, as men that had rather read lovers' writings (and so caught up certain swelling phrases ...), than that in truth they feel those passions ...

> (Shepherd, 1973, pp.137–8)

While Astrophil's first sonnets appear to focus on his love, the degree of artistry they employ in staging a repetition of the failure of art to win his mistress, and their concentration on varying the conventions of the sonnet, suggest Sidney's competitive and humorous attitude to the form. The sonnet's structure, an unsuccessful attempt by Astrophil to express his love followed by a retreat to sincerity, is used in the following five sonnets in the sequence. Such a move must arouse suspicion, given that Astrophil's inability to speak of his devotion is repeatedly re-presented by him, in sonnet form, using the full range of rhetorical devices. (See another instance of this in Norbrook, no. 68.)

Exercise

Read Sidney's Sonnet 9 (Norbrook, no. 67), and look at the contemporary woodcut of the sonnet lady – Figure 4.1 (overleaf).

How does the verse form of the sonnet mirror its argument? What does the woodcut suggest about the attitude of the sonneteer towards his beloved?

Discussion

The sonnet is in the form of a **blazon**, a part-by-part praise of the woman's body. The Petrarchan diction used, of gold, pearls and marble, makes Stella's hair, teeth and cheeks into things which are no longer part of a flesh-and-blood woman but rich, exotic spectacles to be gazed at. The blazon enabled the poet to display his art in far-fetched comparisons, and consequently it became a popular form; there are blazons, for instance, by Spenser and Campion (Norbrook, nos. 84, 131). The woodcut shows how conventional this overstatement became: the beloved's eyes radiate darts of love; her

Figure 4.1 *The Blazon*, from Charles Sorel, *The Extravagant Shepherd*, 1654, London. Bodleian Library, University of Oxford, Douce

complexion is of lilies and roses; her hair entangles the heart of the poet; her breasts are like globes. Sidney's poem is an ironic comment on poetic hyperbole, as in its emphasis on those features which 'endure' the name of cheeks. ❖

Sidney's sequence is sometimes read as a comment on his exclusion by Elizabeth from the centre of power; he was never given a noteworthy public post. In this interpretation the sonnet sequence becomes a meditation on the failure of patronage, a protest against the impotent position in worldly affairs in which the queen keeps him. Those who dote on an unresponsive but powerful woman are mocked. Certainly the woman is given no voice in *Astrophil and Stella*, apart from a few faint negatives (see Norbrook, nos. 65–72). Instead, as Nancy Vickers notes, she is fragmented into scattered words controlled by the poet (Abel, 1982, pp.96–9). A blazon can be a defensive manipulation of a superior woman and an aggressive proof of the poet's intelligence, as well as a doleful lay of love.

Let's look at a radically different presentation of the erotic subtext, in Sir John Davies's parodic poem 'Faith (wench) I cannot court'. Davies trained as a lawyer. Like many of the young men at the Inns of Court, he was searching for patronage as well as fitting himself for a legal career. Several of his longer poems were designed to catch the eye of a possible patron, or work himself back into favour (he was expelled from the Middle Temple for rowdy behaviour on one occasion). This poem appeared only in the first two editions of his *Epigrammes and Elegies*, which were published anonymously, with no date and false information about where they were printed. It was not included in further editions of Davies's work after the bishop of London ordered the public incineration of such 'lewd and satiric' poems in 1599.

Exercise   Read Davies's 'Faith (wench) I cannot court' (Norbrook, no. 94). ❖

Davies deliberately deflates the self-conscious affectation of Petrarchan lovers, doubting the sincerity with which they 'oyle' their 'saints'. He uses low diction ('fiddle', 'buss', 'wench'), and acts out their follies ('ay me forlorne'). The poem is structured around the man's, rather than the woman's, denial. He refuses to render the services a mistress could expect, and offers instead one that she would not – copulation is too rudely real for the whining lover of the sonnet sequences. Moreover, since the reader must fill in the hole (note the parallels to the parentheses in the first line), 'he' must become privy to – and part of – the wench's undoing. The poem's reader must read as though he or she is male, or the poem will remain incomplete. The tone which Davies takes with his readers can be compared with that of Montaigne, 'a highly unconventional, unliterary, and downright colloquial style' (Book 3, Chapter 8). Of course, the shock at which Davies aims depends on a reader's thorough grounding in the Petrarchan conventions in the first place. (Other assaults on romance, by Nashe and Donne, can be found in Norbrook, nos. 95–6.)

Exercise   Read Lady Mary Wroth's Sonnet 23 (Norbrook, no. 143). ❖

Wroth was the daughter of Robert Sidney, viscount L'Isle (the addressee of 'To Penshurst'), and the niece of Sir Philip Sidney and his sister Mary, the countess of Pembroke. Mary, too, was a writer. She translated the Psalms with her brother, as well as some of Petrarch's poetry and a French neoclassical play. (See Norbrook, nos. 336–8, and for comment on this, Norbrook, no. 31.) Wroth was befriended by Queen Anne, wife of James I, in the early years of his reign. She fell from favour when she contracted an adulterous liaison with her cousin William Herbert, with whom she had two children. (See Figure 4.8, the Sidney family tree.)

Wroth's sonnet sequence, *Pamphilia to Amphilanthus*, used two characters from her prose romance *Urania* and was published with this work in 1621, though written much earlier. In both sequence and romance she was following the example set by her uncle's *Astrophil and Stella* and *Arcadia*, effectively writing a part for herself in the family's literary self-identity. The response to *Urania*, which included certain thinly veiled portraits of members of the court, was hostile. Edward Denny, baron of Waltham, for example, who appears in *Urania* as a brutal figure, wrote an abusive poem to Wroth:

> Hermophradite in show, in deed a monster
> As by thy words and works all men may conster
> Thy wrathfull spite conceived an Idell book
> Brought forth a foole which like the damme doth look ...

He advised her to 'leave idle bookes alone/ For wise and worthyer women have writte none' and, referring her to the conduct of her aunt, the Countess of Pembroke, told her she should 'redeem the time with writing as large a volume of heavenly lays and holy love as you have of lascivious tales and amorous toys; that at the last you may follow the example of your virtuous and learned aunt' (Roberts, 1992, pp.31–5).

Exercise

On the basis of your reading of Wroth's sonnet, what restrictions do you think there may have been on the female sonneteer?

Discussion

The poem at first sight seems to be based on the conventional sonnet *topos* of the lover's disinclination for company, and his withdrawal into himself. But in this poem the speaker is female, not male. Everything around the speaker Pamphilia – hunting, hawking, conversation, music – is converted into material to meditate on her love. Secrecy is important. She must stay 'free from eyes', though not, as is the case with male sonneteers, in order to enjoy the company of her lover; this is not a public declaration of love which could circulate among readers other than the mistress. Wroth's sequence as a whole makes little reference to other people; unlike, for example, *Astrophil and Stella*, it seldom mentions other courtiers or Pamphilia's friends. Where Sidney varies Astrophil's obsessive voice by provoking the reader to laugh at the trembling narrator, Wroth appears to take the sonnet's conventions seriously. As a woman she may not speak publicly of her love for fear of being thought immodest or mad, as Denny's rebuke indicates (see also Norbrook, no. 144). Pamphilia can only suffer in silence. Yet love need not be seen as the sole inspiration for Wroth's verses. Helen Hackett comments that:

> if the love poems of male courtiers can be seen as metaphorical expressions of the frustrations of a courtly career, Wroth's verse, too, can be seen as laments not only for erotic disappointments but also for exile from royal favour and courtly success. They are infused with the imagery of the courtly life and its opposite, pastoral retreat.
>
> (Wilcox, 1996, p.183) ❖

To sum up: the two major Renaissance modes you have looked at, the pastoral and the Petrarchan, self-consciously display their artistry and their Italian and classical heritage. A Burckhardtian reading of them is open to you, where the poet speaks to the reader, heart to heart. Yet a more cynical reading is also possible, where the poem's circumstances of production and reception are part of its meaning, and its designs on the reader are uncovered.

Political, economic and religious poetry

The examples of the Petrarchan and pastoral modes you have looked at do not make overt political references. What happens when early modern verse deals directly with such subjects? This section looks at some examples of poems on matters of state: the perfect form of government, praise and the monarch, the growth of London, the management of a patron and the repeated changes in religion in Britain. In the process, it will also allow you to widen your experience of early modern literary genres such as the epigram, the ballad, the eclogue, the satire, metaphysical verse and the emblem.

Exercise

Read Norbrook's discussion of 'Rhetoric, poetry and philosophy' in his introduction (pp.51–60).

What, in Norbrook's view, is the relationship between poetry and politics?

Discussion

The thrust of Norbrook's argument is that:

> Poetry and rhetoric were not just inferior supplements to philosophy or theology but were media on the very cutting edge of intellectual inquiry, capable of taking on and even surpassing abstract discursive thought.
>
> (p.53)

For many poets, poetry was a component of the active life, rather than an activity distinct from that life:

> [Poetry's] devices of formal distancing – parody, allusion, irony, genre, metre – helped to form an imaginative distance from the everyday discourses of public life which could facilitate political and intellectual independence. Constructing a golden world could be a means of criticizing the given world.
>
> (pp. 12–13)

Poets do not merely debate political issues, they are a part of what the German social theorist Jürgen Habermas has termed 'the public sphere', an idealized discursive space in which all citizens are free to discuss issues affecting society. (Habermas locates the rise of this in the eighteenth century; other commentators detect it earlier.) Norbrook argues that poems 'do not simply reproduce discourses but transform them through their own particular resources of genre and language, and may then have *a reciprocal influence on received discourses*' (p. xxviii; emphasis added). ❖

In contrast, writing in 1860, Burckhardt reads Italian verse through a Romantic aesthetic. The definition of the poet provided by William Wordsworth in 1800 is typical of nineteenth-century discussions of art. Poetry for him was 'the spontaneous outflow of powerful feelings' (de Selincourt, 1944, p. 387):

> [A poet] is a man speaking to men ... endowed with more lively sensibility, more enthusiasm and tenderness, who has a greater knowledge of human nature, and a more comprehensive soul, than are supposed to be common among mankind.
>
> (p. 393)

In a similar vein, Burckhardt argues that Petrarch's work gives:

> pictures of the inmost soul – descriptions of moments of joy and sorrow which must have been thoroughly his own ... His verse is not in all places equally transparent; by the side of his most beautiful thoughts stands at times some allegorical conceit, or some sophistical trick of logic, altogether foreign to our present taste ... [Yet such poems are] documentary proof of the widest knowledge of the movements of the human heart.
>
> (pp. 203–4)

The effect of this Romanticism on perceptions of Elizabethan poetry was felt in the selection made by anthologies compiled after Burckhardt. Norbrook's preface describes how the changing shape of the Renaissance as an evaluative concept was reflected by these: 'the preference was for what C.S. Lewis termed "golden" poetry, the courtly and pastoral verse of the high Elizabethan period' (p.xxiii). As he points out, only a few literary historians resisted this bias and made available 'early English poetry which illustrated public struggles as well as private sensibilities ... popular religious individualism and protest ... the downrightness of popular verse on sexual matters' (p.xxiv). Most, however, continued to focus on the courtly lyric. This apolitical approach was underpinned by the development in the 1940s of the school of New Criticism, which focused on the text as an object in itself, a set of verbal structures whose meaning was to be constructed without reference to the social or biographical context. Yet:

> this conservative reading of English Renaissance culture inevitably generated a reaction. Critics variously labelled 'new historicists' or 'cultural materialists' have insisted that poetry does not transcend its age but is closely bound up with structures of social power; they have argued that the formation of a restricted canon of great poetry functions to defend the status of a social elite, relegating to the margin the voices of those who do not qualify as sufficiently literary.

> (p.xxv)

Burckhardt's honesty as a critic, in admitting that what he read was not always 'sincere', allows for some negotiation between his position and later commentary. The conceits and tricks of logic he criticizes are the very things which twentieth-century criticism now considers to be central to Renaissance literature. Such poetry is now seen as using rhetorical techniques to intervene in 'political' situations. The poet's discursive abilities in these areas are exhibited to his peers and to possible patrons. He stages himself, writes himself into an elite circle of the linguistically dextrous. The critic most closely associated with this New Historicism, Stephen Greenblatt, calls this 'Renaissance self-fashioning', returning to Burckhardt to explain how:

> the transition from feudalism to despotism, fostered a radical change of consciousness ... [so that princes and poets] were cut off from established forms of identity and forced by their relation to power to fashion a new sense of themselves and their world: the self and the state as works of art ... The chief intellectual and linguistic tool in this creation was rhetoric, which ... was the instrument of a society which was already deeply theatrical.

> (1980, pp.161–2)

Exercise

Read Sir Thomas More's epigram 'Quis optimus reipublicae status' (Norbrook, no. 3). ❖

This poem was printed with More's collected epigrams in 1520; both come from the period before More was appointed Master of Requests and privy councillor in 1517. Its title echoes part of the full title of More's *De optimo reipublicae statu deque nova insula utopia* (*Concerning the Best State of a Commonwealth and the New Island of Utopia*) of 1516. The *Utopia* was also written in Latin (the first English translation was published in 1551) and was prefaced by commendatory letters from eminent European humanists. Its first part presents a debate on authority and the law in Britain; its second describes an imaginary island whose inhabitants hold all things in common and who are governed by elected officials.

Exercise

In reading discursive verse there are three firm questions to be asked:

1   what are the issues?

2   what does the author want you to think?

3   how does he or she argue for this?

So, in this epigram, what are the arguments given for and against collective government?

Discussion

More argues that moderation is produced by the compromises necessary in collective government, so that a senate is more likely to be ruled by good counsel than by strong personalities. Rational choice rather than blind chance governs the selection of its members, and the regular change of leadership under an elected system ensures that the current incumbents in office will be careful, for otherwise they will be removed. ❖

The question of what constituted the best form of government had been debated since Plato's *Republic*. Interest in such issues was revived in Italy in the fifteenth and sixteenth centuries. It was a topic of deep interest to commentators such as Machiavelli, as the republics and city-states sought to legitimate their rule, and as servants of these new states worked out roles for themselves. More answers specific arguments raised by the fourth-century BCE Greek orator Isocrates, whose *To Nicocles*, printed in Paris in 1509, was translated into Latin by Erasmus in 1516.

Exercise

How does the form of More's epigram relate to the concept of *inventio* (see above, p.241)?

Discussion

The epigram is set out as though More is studying for what to say on one side of a debate. As described in the previous section, the ability to compose such an exercise – known as a theme – was a part of grammar school training in *inventio*. More allows his invisible opponent an objection – that factional politics can produce weak leadership – but overcomes it by suddenly reframing the question.

Up to these last few lines, he has been appealing to topics from the branch of oratory known as **deliberative rhetoric**, which attempted to persuade the audience that a proposal was either praiseworthy or possible. When he meets a point which cannot be answered (whether or not a country should elect a senate) he moves suddenly from whether it is praiseworthy to whether it is possible. If the 'you' of the debate can decide to give authority to one structure or another, then that reader is already in the position of election. Thus he or she is 'forced' to conclude that if this debate is possible – and it must be, since she or he is engaging in it – then elected authority must be praiseworthy. ❖

This debate, by someone deciding whether or not to become a privy councillor, demonstrates some of the difficulties humanists had in relating to the court. As Book 1 in this series has shown in its discussion of *otium* and *negotium* (Chapter 6), they took to heart Cicero's belief in education as a preparation for the *vita activa*, the active life in public affairs as a senator or a lawyer:

> since ... we are not born for ourselves alone, but our country claims a share of our being, and our friends a share ... we ought to follow Nature as our guide, to contribute to the general good by an interchange of acts of kindness, by giving and receiving, and thus by our skill, our industry, and our talents to cement human society more closely together, man to man.

> (*De officiis* I.7.22)

Trained in the newest linguistic techniques, able to accumulate material on any question swiftly and produce an opinion to be acted on, humanists were the perfect advisers and administrators for the new courts. Yet while their classical training urged them to engage with the centres of power, the republicanism which their Roman mentors revered posed problems in the service of a monarch.

More does not argue that kings are necessarily tyrants; indeed, in 1509 he wrote coronation poems which welcomed the new monarch. He does, however, argue for a role for debate and advice in public life, using a dialectical form for the poem which allows the reader some choice. Such Utopian discussions operate ironically, allowing a distance to develop between the ideal form of government presented and the real situation in the country at the time. More's epigram is dialogic both in the matter it discusses and in the way in which it provokes the reader to decide on the best form of government.

The editor of More's *Epigrammata*, Beatus Rhenanus, praised the author for the way he adapted his models. A collection of epigrams made in the tenth century, of poems composed as far back as the first century BCE (the *Greek Anthology*), is cited by Rhenanus as the model for the epigram. This 'must have wit combined with brevity; it must be lighthearted, and then it must end promptly with a witty point' (Miller et al., 1984, pp.73–5). More, Rhenanus commented, had exceeded the achievements of the contemporary Italian epigrammatists, Giovanni Pontano and Michele Marullo (a Greek *émigré* to Italy), in his easy metre and unforced diction. He was also to be praised for adapting the form to political debate, and for abandoning the *Greek Anthology's* eroticism.

Exercise

Read George Puttenham's 'Her Majestie resembled to the crowned piller' (Norbrook, no. 16). ❖

Puttenham was the nephew of Sir Thomas Elyot, the author of *The Boke Named the Governour* (1531), a popular Henrician text which described the ideal (largely humanist) education of a prince or nobleman's son. While Elyot was patronized by the king, Puttenham was less successful, and he remained a minor landowner. This poem was published in the second book of *The Arte of English Poesie* (1589), which dealt with 'proportion' in rhyme, metre, verse forms and the physical layout of a page. Puttenham notes of proportion that:

> it is said by such as professe the Mathematicall sciences, that all things stand by proportion, and that without it nothing could stand to be good or beautiful.

> (Smith, 1937, vol. 2, p.67)

The 'ocular representation' he gives of Elizabeth's virtue is designed to embody her qualities of 'stay, support, rest, state, and magnificence' (p.101). She is described in the form of a classical Doric column, where the 'pedastall or base' is of the same diameter as the 'chapter or head', with an unornamented capital which does not distract from the beauty of the column's proportions. Puttenham asks the reader to build up an understanding of the conceit (Elizabeth will be, very deliberately, 'resembled' to a pillar) by reading upwards: her immortal fame rests on her steadfast virtues. The poem, then, is a visual pun.

The praise which Puttenham lavishes on his queen may appear to be exaggerated, part of an attempt to claim attention. It was argued earlier that the mechanisms of patronage at a continental court required the aspiring courtier to reflect back the court's own preferred image. So Puttenham argues that patterned poems, like

'Her Majestie resembled to the crowned piller', perform a courtly function; they show:

> not onely more art, but serveth also much better for briefenesse and subtiltie of device; and for the same respect are also fittest for the pretie amourets in Court to entertaine their servants and the time withall, their delicate wits requiring some commendable exercise.

> (Smith, 1937, vol. 2, p.95)

That *sprezzatura* is essential to the courtier's art is clear. What might be less clear are the political reasons why **panegyric** was encouraged. Erasmus's dedicatory letter in his *Pangyricus* to Philip, archduke of Austria, published in 1504, notes that his:

> preference for plain speaking made him feel a certain distaste for all this kind of writing, to which Plato's phrase 'the fourth subdivision of flattery' seems especially applicable ... But there is certainly no other method of correcting princes so effective as giving them an example of a good prince for a model, on the pretext of pronouncing a panegyric.

> (Levi, 1986, p.7)

Positioning himself as an unofficial adviser to the queen, Puttenham holds up to Elizabeth a mirror of the ideal prince, though her own reign at this point was not characterized by concord and peace, engaged as England was in bitter war with Spain and its dependent territories in Europe and the New World (the Armada sailed in 1588, a year before *The Arte* was published).

Exercise

Read Fulke Greville's Sonnet 78 from *Caelica* (Norbrook, no. 26). ❖

Greville was a schoolmate and close friend of Philip Sidney. This sonnet was probably written after Sidney's death in 1586, but it was not published until Greville's works were collected posthumously in 1633.

Coming fresh from Petrarch, this sonnet looks unfamiliar. Greville criticizes the courtier's flattery: insubstantial flatterers sell vanities, trifling matters, to the prince in return for being borne up to high positions. In such cases, the 'place' is the man; there is no more to him. Moreover, 'these follow Princes veines,/ And so, by pleasing, doe corrupt them too'. Greville uses commercial, sporting and scientific vocabularies to destroy traces of a courtly register. The proverbial tags of wisdom (commonplaces or *sententiae*) were printed in italics. The effect is one of plain speaking by a friend to the commonwealth. (For a similar, acerbic, use of the sonnet by the Scottish author Alexander Montgomerie, see Norbrook, no. 23.) Greville's biography of Sidney is preoccupied with such unworthy court favourites:

> now let princes vouchsafe to consider, of what importance it is to the honour of themselves and their estates to have one man of such eminence [as Sidney]; not only as nourisher of virtue in their courts or service, but besides for a reformed standard.

> (Rees, 1973, pp.143–4)

Yet, as this life also makes clear, Greville turned to poetry precisely because the queen did not call on him to act in official business; Sidney, using his own unemployment to write *Astrophil and Stella* and the *Arcadia*, was in a similar position according to Greville (see the Anthology, no. 49). A disavowal of flattery at court could be a plea for position: it was tactful advice to the monarch.

Exercise   Read Donne's 'To Sir Henry Wotton' (Norbrook, no. 228). ❖

This originally circulated in manuscript and was not published until Donne's poems were collected posthumously in 1633. The poem is addressed to a close friend who was at Oxford with Donne. Both sailed on expeditions to sack Cadiz with the earl of Essex in 1596 and to hunt Spanish treasure ships off the Azores with Raleigh in 1597. While Donne and Wotton went on to secure advantageous posts, the former as secretary to Sir Thomas Egerton and the latter as an agent for Essex, the parallels between their careers ended when Donne, to Egerton's disapproval, married a niece of Egerton's wife. Donne was swiftly deprived of his post. He moved, with a growing family, to the small village of Mitcham, in Surrey, and into a long period of semi-employment involving a search for further patronage. Wotton meanwhile continued to rise up the ladder, as a successful lawyer and diplomat.

The poem was written around 1597/8 as part of a debate in the Essex circle about the relative virtues of town or country. This was a hoary topic, whose revival at this point was in part due to the rapid growth of cities and towns in Britain. In particular, London's population doubled to around 200,000 people between 1500 and 1600. The rise was almost entirely due to immigration from the countryside, connected with business at the major law courts, in government offices and in commercial enterprises. Moreover the court, located near London, attracted people of rank, and in turn they pulled in their own clients, in a long chain of influence. Much was made of the monstrous growth of the city by moralists, social theorists and economists. (See Norbrook, no. 186 for a satire on London by

Everard Guilpin, also discussed with reference to *The Merchant of Venice* in Chapter 5.) Yet Donne does not follow the traditional line that a retreat to the plain and honest country life is virtuous (see Wyatt's and Sidney's poems on this, Norbrook, nos. 223, 181). Rather, the country is a desert, where man declines into brutish incivility; the city produces grasping men, dead to humanity; the court produces vain and hollow spectacles, and men who are slaves to the whims of princes. You cannot hope to escape from the faults of the latter two places by dwelling in the former: all three produce lust, covetousness and pride, and 'men are spunges', sucking up evil from their circumstances. Wotton is advised to dwell in himself by travelling between the places, since it is 'continuance [which] maketh hell'.

The form of the verse letter gives the impression that Donne and Wotton are both free agents in a literary circle, able to choose their vocations (it mirrors Greville's Sonnet 78 in its tone and implied authorial position). The situation, of course, was quite different: Donne, considered a failure at this point, had to work hard at maintaining his early contacts. After the assertion that 'letters mingle Soules', Donne proceeds to show why he was a contact worth keeping. There is an ease and breadth in the references used to make a banal point about society which suggest the reader's attention should be held by the author's *copia* and fluency in the most fashionable areas of learning, and by his supple way of arguing, rather than by what he is saying. (When collecting his works, Donne said, with typical *sprezzatura*, that it took more effort to write to recipients of his verse and ask for copies than it did to write the poems.) He deals in Platonic concepts (that the breath contains the soul, thus kisses mingle it, and thus, to the sceptical, letters can bear the soul more surely), topographical allusions to the new areas being explored (the poles) and to the results of the grand tour (the political depravity of the Italians, German religious divisions, French sexual scandals), natural history (the remora, the snail, the torpedo, sponges and cork), proverbial wisdom, and Galenic and Paracelsian medicine.

Burckhardt suggested that this fluency of reference to the latest scientific and geographic knowledge, the determination to observe the natural world, was characteristic of 'Renaissance man':

> when once the veil of illusion was torn asunder, when once the dread of nature and the slavery to books and tradition were overcome, countless problems lay before them for solution ... [Dante, for instance, takes images] from reality, whether in nature or in human life, and uses them, never as mere ornament, but in order to give the reader the fullest and most adequate sense of his meaning.

(pp. 187–8)

255

Yet Donne is not concerned to give full and adequate counsel to Wotton. Instead, he points proudly to his deliberate paradoxes ('O knottie riddle'), carefully qualifies his logic ('as habits, not borne'), tactfully reverses the advice he is giving ('I rather doe/ Say o'er those lessons, which I learn'd of you') and plays on his own name. He produces a verbal distance from his subject with his conceits and puns. This style, dubbed '**metaphysical**' in John Dryden's contemptuous dismissal of Donne, concentrates on the writer's ability to produce abstruse and ingenious argument.

Donne claims the status of Renaissance poet not because he uses the golden age diction of loves, doves, gold or gazes (see Thomas Carew's elegy on Donne, below), but because he mingles classical and new learning without distinction, in order to reach the preferred conclusion. (You may want to read the Welsh poet Henry Vaughan's 'Cock-crowing' (Norbrook, no. 301), which refers to hermetic philosophy, alchemy and the Bible with quite different effect. Vaughan is also described as a metaphysical poet, but his poems are devotional rather than argumentative or self-displaying.)

Turning to religion, Burckhardt thought that Italian Renaissance politicians and scholars were unconcerned with confessional matters:

> their powerful individuality made them in religion, as in other matters, altogether subjective ... they feel themselves able to make good out of the plastic resources of their own nature, and therefore they feel not repentance.

(pp.312–13)

The gradual infiltration into England of Protestant concepts during the reign of Henry VIII (1509–47) was simultaneous with the English Renaissance in letters. While the assertion that the two movements were causally related is a contentious one, there are features of both which are evident in the literature of the period. A change in the theology of salvation affected the devotional forms used. The Catholic church stressed God's justice: the human will was free to co-operate with divine grace, and thus earn merit. The Protestant position emphasized God's omnipotence: he ordains who is to be saved and who damned, even before they exist. It had no place for the mediation between God and the soul, central to the sacraments administered by a Catholic priest. Each individual was to scrutinize his or her own soul for signs of election, and learn God's purpose by reading his word. This interest in the individual soul, in education and in reading the Bible and other texts in the vernacular, is common to both the Renaissance and the Reformation in Britain.

The next six poems to be examined deal with aspects of Catholic and Protestant devotion, the scepticism created by the repeated changes in faith which the state endorsed, and the practical difficulties of conforming.

Edmund Spenser's *The Shepheardes Calender* was published in 1579 and proved extremely popular; five editions had been brought out by 1597. Its dedication to Sidney, the nephew of the earl of Leicester, brought Spenser into Leicester's client circle and allied him with its Puritan and nationalist leanings. The *Calender* consists of twelve eclogues, combining political allegory and aesthetic competition. It is prefaced by a dedicatory epistle signed by 'E.K.' and an anonymously written description of 'the general argument of the whole booke'. Each month has a woodcut representing its matter (see Figure 4.2, 'Maye'), a brief 'argument' about this, either by E.K. or by Spenser, the verses themselves, a verbal emblem or motto for each speaker, summing up the subject, and extensive annotation on the text, presumably by E.K. (see the Anthology, no. 50, which gives these from 'Maye').

Maye.

Ægloga Quinta.

Figure 4.2 'Maye', Aegloga Quinta, from *The Shepheardes Calender*. Reproduced from *The Works of Edmund Spenser, a Variorum Edition, the Minor Poems*, Part I, 1943, Baltimore, Md., Johns Hopkins University Press

Exercise

Read Spenser's eclogue 'Maye' (Norbrook, no. 182) and its emblems and annotations (Anthology, no. 50). Consider the questions below and jot down any ideas that occur to you. Review your notes when you have read the text that follows this exercise.

- How does this eclogue's use of pastoral compare with that of Marlowe and Raleigh?

- What arguments does Palinode offer about the pastors of the true church?

- What is the relationship between the different parts of the eclogue (its woodcut, emblems, notes and the verse itself)?

- How does E.K. present Spenser? ❖

This eclogue uses a familiar mode of pastoral: Palinode's uncomplicated desire to celebrate with music the springtime beauty of the countryside recalls the singing contests in the *locus amoenus* described by Marlowe. In the vision of Henry VIII and Elizabeth's mother, Anne Boleyn, who brings back the may blossom, Spenser infers a not-quite-lost golden age in Britain which reflects glory on its present sovereign. Piers, however, takes a different view of contemporary political and religious issues. Pastors play 'while their flockes be unfedde' (l.44); they live like the laity, content merely to enjoy the pleasures God has sent. He cites with approval the insistence by Algrind (Edmund Grindal, archbishop of Canterbury) that churchmen should not accumulate wealth to leave to their family; in the past, 'nought having, nought feared they to forgoe' (l.110). Moreover, it was when pastors first began to look for worldly position that papistry infected the church. Though Palinode dismisses these criticisms as envy, Piers is not convinced, and the eclogue ends with a fable of how the credulous can be seduced from the right path.

The *Calender* uses figures from earlier anti-church satire (for example, John Skelton's work, Norbrook, no. 247) which was adopted by Elizabethan radicals to attack the Protestant hierarchy. In 1590 Spenser's work was translated into Latin by John Dove, who praised its dedicatees for being Algrinds and Pierces, not Palinodes (Norbrook, 1984, p.67). Spenser repeats contemporary arguments about the attitude which the Church of England should take towards sensual pleasures, including art. Piers represents them as papist snares which could tempt the unwary Protestant from the safety of the reformed fold. Norbrook argues that Palinode is accused of 'aestheticizing politics by appealing to ideas of Merrie England in order to justify clerical privilege' (1984, p.72). You should, however, beware of attributing complete victory to Piers's arguments, as E.K. does in commenting on his emblem:

> Piers thereto strongly replyeth ... what fayth then is there in the faythless. For if fayth be the ground of religion, which fayth they dayly false, what hold then is there of theyr religion.

Though the Reformation in Britain had been confirmed by Elizabeth's succession, the iconoclasm associated with extreme Puritan views was not generally accepted. The legitimacy of what was later to be called 'the beauty of holiness', the appeal to the passions to rouse a congregation's devotion, was still an issue. Palinode's argument, that it is natural to use what God has given, is powerful, instanced as it is by the delicate descriptions of maying. His blunt commonsense conclusion, that there is no point in being miserable if it is not necessary, could leave the debate about devotional methods open in the reader's mind.

Puttenham also describes pastoral in political terms:

> the Poet devised the *Eglogue* long after the other *dramatick* poems, not of purpose to counterfait or represent the rusticall manner of loves and communication, but under the vaile of homely persons and in rude speeches to insinuate and glaunce at greater matters, and such as perchance had not bene safe to have beene disclosed in any other sort, which may be perceived by the Eclogues of *Virgill*, in which are treated by figure matters of greater importance than the loves of *Titirus* and *Corydon*.

> (Smith, 1937, vol. 2, p.40)

This was a view of pastoral also expressed by one of Spenser's models, Baptista Spagnolo Mantuanus (commonly known as Mantuan, 1447/8–1516). While a student at Padua he wrote ten neo-Latin eclogues in the 1460s which, refashioned and annotated, were used as a school text throughout Europe under the title *Bucolica*. The earliest English edition was published in 1523. Helen Cooper views Mantuan's eclogues as a retrospective of medieval pastoral, being both didactic and realistic. In them, winter exists, love fails, women are inconstant, poets are not patronized, towns are corrupt places; only in heaven will the shepherd find the true pastoral (Hamilton et al., 1990, p.452, and see Norbrook, no. 174 for a similar eclogue by the Scottish poet Alexander Barclay). Piers shows a similar impatience with idealizing pastoral; he labels Palinode's Henrician idyll as foolish escapism, and returns to his criticism of the church.

The Shepheardes Calender blends verbal and visual elements into a sophisticated structure, where each part modifies the inferences a reader should draw. The book is intriguing as a material object, offering the reader both the literary stimulation of Spenser's poetry and the visual appeal of the illustrative woodcuts. The twelve woodcuts, one for each month, enhance the idea that this is a calendar of the year. Each has its zodiacal sign, a vignette of traditional country life in the relevant season, and a reference to the content of the eclogue in question. In 'Maye' merrymakers dance in the centre of the woodcut (see Figure 4.2), while the fable of the wolf and the kid, which Piers goes on to tell, is illustrated in three episodes in the background; the two shepherds stand in discussion; sunlight glints off a church behind. E.K.'s argument directs the reader to a two-fold understanding of the eclogue: as a political allegory which argues against moderation in ecclesiastical reform, and as a moral tale concerned with the temptations of the flesh and the promptings of the spirit. His commentary is ambiguous. Sometimes it sheds light on the doctrinal terms in the shepherds' allusive statements ('meant of the Pope, and his Antichristian prelates, which usurpe a tyrannical dominion in the Churche' (see the Anthology, no. 50)). At other times references to the contemporary situation in Britain are tactfully – or humorously – flattened, in both commentary and eclogue (Algrind is simply 'the name of a shepherd').

E.K. is assiduous in pointing out Spenser's use of archaic English, in low **register** ('ycladd', 'buskets', 'thilke') and high ('faitours', 'miscreance'), and his inclusion of native rustic characters and words ('sopps in wine', 'sicker', 'tway'). Spenser is twice compared to the great national poet, Chaucer (as he is in the *Calender's* dedicatory letter by E.K.). Andrew Hadfield has commented on the 'reinvention' of Chaucer:

> by poets such as Spenser, as a proto-Protestant, [and also] as part of the vernacular tradition against which the courtly poets of the 1580s and 1590s were reacting in attempting to establish an English poetic style based on Italian and French models.
>
> (1994, p.4)

E.K. commends Spenser's appropriation of classical names and myths to the English situation in his notes on 'great Pan' and 'greate Atlas'. A casual parallel is also drawn between 'Tully's' (another name for Cicero) report of Sardanapalus's epitaph, the earl of Devonshire, and the homely proverb cited by Palinode. E.K. carefully picks out a flower of rhetoric offered by Spenser, a **syncope** or elision of words, and annotates the newest terms English had acquired from the continent, such as 'jouissance'.

The verbal emblems offered are similarly full. The emblem is said by Puttenham to be a 'wittie sentence or secrete conceit', which must be 'unfolded or explained by some interpretation'. It may be 'in word or in mute show', but its purpose is the same: 'to insinuat some secret, wittie, morall, and brave purpose presented to the beholder, either to recreate his eye, or please his phantasie, or examine his judgement, or occupie his braine, or to manage his will' (Smith, 1937, vol. 2, pp.106, 112). Spenser attributes to the homely English shepherds two phrases in Greek (said to be from Theognis). The two elements of this rather ambiguous ascription mirror the lack of closure in the eclogue's debate. Spenser's complex interweaving of different parts of the text uses the new print techniques to tease a variety of readers into constructing their own positions on the issues he raises; 'Maye', in structure and techniques, is dialogic (compare More's epigram, and the extract from William Browne's *Britannia's Pastorals*, Book 2, Norbrook, no. 37). The political aspect of the *Calender* appears to contrast with the overtly self-referential pastoral of Marlowe, Raleigh and Donne. The poem did, however, have a bearing on Spenser's career. He had been with Leicester's household for only a few months when the poem appeared. As a discreet intervention in the question of church discipline on the side of Grindal and the low church tradition, it appealed to the Leicester circle. The *Calender's* easy movement between political commentary and highly wrought poetry promoted an image of Spenser as an intelligent, shrewd and well-read man who could be trusted to compose verse on the right side. It proved a successful piece of self-advertisement – in 1580 Spenser was sent to Ireland as secretary to the lord deputy.

A poet whose work led to a very different end was Anne Askew. She was executed in 1546, ostensibly for her heretical views on the Catholic Mass. Her interrogators, who included members of the privy council, covertly desired to implicate certain high-ranking courtiers, since Askew was connected with the Protestant reading circle of Henry VIII's sixth wife, Katherine Parr. Her examinations (a portion of which is given in the Anthology, no. 51) were printed by John Bale, a Protestant cleric and polemicist. His work was incorporated into the hugely successful *Actes and Monuments* by John Foxe (popularly known as the Book of Martyrs). This was first published in English in 1563 (an early version had been published in Latin in Strasburg in 1559, the material having been collected to demonstrate the bloody nature of the Marian persecution of Protestants). The Book of Martyrs went through five successively enlarged editions before the end of Elizabeth's reign. Given the isolated position that England held among the mainly Catholic countries of Europe, it was understandable that Foxe's work was viewed as a national epic as well as a martyrology. In 1571 the privy council ordered that the book be displayed for public use in every cathedral church and in the homes of chapter clergy. In this way, Askew became an icon of Protestant endurance in the face of papist tyranny.

Exercise

Read Anne Askew's 'Balade' (Norbrook, no. 248). What are the major differences between Askew's and Wroth's presentations of themselves in their poems?

Discussion

Askew uses a popular form, the ballad, which was not influenced by the new learning. (Compare Norbrook, no. 250 for similar devotional verse from the Catholic position.) She speaks largely through biblical reference: she is protected by the armour of God and the shield of faith (Ephesians 6.11–18); she journeys through the valley of death among foes but Christ takes her part (Psalm 23); she asks for help and receives it (Matthew 7.7); she has more enemies than there are hairs on her head (Psalm 40).

Elaine Beilin has described devotional writing as a way for women to find a voice without transgressing the social conventions which required a chaste silence from them (Hannay, 1985, pp.77–91). When Christ speaks through her, regardless of her sex, Askew has no right to keep quiet:

> not oft use I to wryght
> In prose nor yet in ryme
> Yet wyll I shewe one syght
> That I sawe in my tyme.

Addressing Askew's captors, Bale portrays her ability to overcome what were deemed to be inherent weaknesses in her sex (irrationality, ignorance, physical frailty) as proof of the divine strength which upholds her, and thus, of the righteousness of the cause for which she is martyred:

> Ryght farre doth it passe the strength of a yonge, tendre, weake, and sycke woman ... to abyde so vyolent handelynge ... Thynke not therfor but that Christ hath suffered in her, and so myghtelye shewed hys power, that in her weakenesse he hath laughed your madde enterpryses to scorne.

> (Beilin, 1996, p.129)

The victim, after all, is only a martyr if she dies for a just cause; otherwise she is simply an obstinate heretic and traitor. Bale exhibits Askew's ability to confound her examiners (in part by substituting relevant biblical references for her own answers) as an extraordinary gift from God. Her inherent weakness must be stressed to make this point – Bale is no proto-feminist. In comparison, Wroth deals with a secular topic, love, in a high register, using a Renaissance genre, the sonnet. Her focus is her own subjectivity; rather than using the authoritative voice of the Bible, she speaks in her own voice of herself. While both Askew and Wroth see themselves as 'tendre, weake' women at the mercy of a stronger power, Askew makes this the very point of her victory. However, it is not necessary to interpret the poet's position solely in terms of gender. ❖

Askew takes an orthodox Protestant position, emphasizing the words 'righteousness' and 'faith'. Her salvation will come from God's election of her as one of his saints, rather than from any merit derived from her own exertions. The martyr's sincerity became a matter of some urgency for those readers who looked for confirmation that God was allied with the reformed church in the miracles of constancy which the Protestant martyrs exhibited during their sufferings.

Askew shows extensive familiarity with the Bible and a strong sense of her own position, but it would not be appropriate to describe her work as Renaissance verse. She shows no interest in calling attention either to the language or the form she is using (one habitually used for homely subjects), or to herself as an artist. Indeed, by appropriating the language of a divine text, she is removing herself from the position of 'author'.

Figure 4.3 *The Order and Manner of the Burning of Anne Askew*, from John Foxe, *Actes and Monuments*, 1596. Bodleian Library, University of Oxford, S3.19.Th, p.1130

Read Donne's sonnet 'Batter my heart' (Norbrook, no. 259). ❖

Donne came from a Catholic family (his uncle, Jasper Heywood, was leader of the Jesuit mission to reconvert Britain, and his brother died during a term of imprisonment for sheltering a priest). He converted to Protestantism in his twenties, and his retirement at Mitcham ended when he became an Anglican divine at the insistence of James I, who prevented his preferment in secular employment. This sonnet was written after that conversion. Donne ended his life as dean of St Paul's, and the poem was printed posthumously in 1633.

Contrast the doctrinal positions and tone of Askew's 'Balade' and Donne's 'Batter my Heart'.

Donne's sentiments are far from the calm trust in God's 'stronge power' expressed by Askew. The poem expresses the darker side of Protestantism; Donne rails because he can do nothing to save himself. The Thirty-nine Articles (defining the doctrinal position of the Church of England, repeatedly revised and enlarged in number since the adoption by Convocation of Ten Articles in 1536, and published in their final form in 1563) express this impotence starkly: 'we are accounted righteous before God, only for the merit of our Lord and Saviour Jesus Christ by Faith, and not for our own works or deservings' (Article 11). Betrothed by original sin to Satan, Donne demands to be penetrated by God (compare Norbrook, no. 257). His reason is powerless to help him, and his will is naturally bent towards sin. The violence of Donne's imagery (town walls battered down, imprisonment, rape), the imperative tone he uses towards the Almighty, the way he genders himself as a passive female waiting to be saved, all indicate desperation. Beyond the flurry of demands, most frighteningly of all, there is silence from an impassive God (compare George Herbert's affectionate colloquies with God, Norbrook, nos. 280, 282, 285). The sonneteer's assertion 'I love you', which you have hitherto seen used as a playful assertion of aesthetic or intellectual values, here is bellicose. ❖

Henry Constable moved in the opposite direction from Donne. He started as the agent of Elizabeth's secretary of state, Sir Francis Walsingham, in Scotland and Paris. Constable converted to Catholicism in 1590 and spent most of the rest of his life on the Continent. During a brief visit to Britain in 1603 he was imprisoned for his religion. His Petrarchan sonnet sequence *Diana* was published in 1590, though his spiritual sonnets, written after his conversion, remained in manuscript until the twentieth century.

Exercise	Read Henry Constable's sonnet 'To St Mary Magdalen' (Norbrook, no. 254). What comparisons can be made between the authorial personae of this sonnet and Donne's?

Discussion	Constable's spiritual sonnets parallel those of Donne in concentrating on feminine experience. Of the seventeen sonnets, Constable devotes four to the Virgin Mary, four to Mary Magdalene, and two to other female saints. The Magdalene provided a symbol of repentance and ecstasy for the Counter Reformation. While Constable pre-empts Donne's eroticism in desiring to lie 'like a woman spowse' in 'sweete conjunction' with God, his tone is one of joyous submission to such love. In its openness to physical experience the poem celebrates the Incarnation. ❖

There had been an earlier vogue for spiritualizing the themes and topics of Petrarchan verse in Italy, as in Girolamo Malipiero's *Il Petrarca spirituale* of 1537. In his spiritual sonnets Constable produces a sacred parody: the conceits and overstatement of the secular sonneteers can be used without irony when describing the divine. As Puttenham says, 'we can not exhibit overmuch praise, nor belye [God] any wayes, unlesse it be ... by scarsitie of praise' (Smith, 1937, vol. 2, p.30). Both Donne and Constable proudly display a style full of conceits, a fashionable genre, and a concentration on the lyric voice of the sonneteer. The rigidity of the sonnet form proves flexible enough to express Constable's devotion and Donne's anxiety, as the earlier discussion of the genre indicated.

Exercise	Read Donne's 'Show me deare Christ' (Norbrook, no. 261). ❖

The importance and difficulty of deciding between the faiths are made evident in this impatient demand to be told how Christ would have Donne act. Donne was reported to have left notebooks showing he had read through over 1,400 authors in the process of conversion to the Protestant church. Despite this effort, John Carey notes, his poetry 'reveals the lasting disorientation his apostasy entailed', placing him in a church where justification by faith alone promoted 'ceaseless, agonized introspection' in its members, as they attempted to determine if they had been saved (1990, pp.16, 43). Donne needs God to intimate that his decision was right; he cannot reason his way to this conclusion, although he 'assays' his faith by his reading. The Protestant anxiety about gaining an inner assurance of the truth is clear in this action – personal apostasy may not be the only explanation for the dilemmas Donne explores in the Holy Sonnets. The sonnet lays out the two options, and asks how a true church can be lost and found: 'sleepes she a thousand, then peepes up one yeare?' Given Christ's promise to support his church so that it would never founder, which church can claim his authority? (Donne tussles again with the question in his 'Satyre 3', Norbrook, no. 256.)

In giving the doctrinal choice female allure, Donne creates a verbal emblem of the problem. This technique of creating what Sidney calls a 'speaking picture' (the remark can be traced back to Plutarch's *Moralia*) is used by Renaissance poets to move the reader's emotions. These visual allegories are not simply ornamental amplification: they are meant to strike the reader with their vivid summary of the position. The final image – a universal church, open to all – also conveys Donne's desperately ambiguous feelings towards this church, a spouse 'who is most trew, and pleasing to them then/ When she is embrac'd and open to most men'.

Exercise

Which other poems have used the technique of the speaking picture?

Discussion

Spenser's shepherds, Sidney's blazons, Wyatt's white hart are all speaking pictures. In using an emblem – albeit verbal – these poems produce a physical manifestation of a complex situation. ❖

Sir John Harington's epigrams were published in 1618, when a certain scepticism about the importance of the earlier heated disputes over religion (exemplified by the accounts of the martyrs) was less dangerous than in Elizabeth's reign.

Exercise

Read Harington's 'A groome of the chambers religion' (Norbrook, no. 255). What differences can you see between Donne's and Harington's attitudes to religion?

Discussion

Deciding between the churches had practical as well as devotional consequences. Donne's own conversion from Catholic to Protestant could be construed as an opportunistic manoeuvre, designed primarily to gain advancement. Harington's satire links position at court and pliability in religion, using mock deference to the king ('sure he may ... /Conforme himselfe in lesse then ten days warning'). Burckhardt considered that 'the development of the individual' sprang from a freedom that was itself the result of the balance of power between church, state and culture. Harington's epigram suggests that the courtier had no need to wait for this equilibrium to occur: adroit manipulation within the court could create such a space. In Donne's poem the concision of the sonnet is used to focus on the decision that had to be made after extensive reading. In Askew's verse, the glory of martyrdom is demonstrated. In Harington's epigram, however, the wit lies in its pointed refusal to take the subject of conversion seriously. His epigram is deliberately flaccid, in contrast to Donne's intensity; a mere earthly king needs to be pleased (see also the extract from Robert Wild's 'Alas poor scholler, whither wilt thou goe', Norbrook, no. 295). ❖

Print, education and the state

The texts we have examined so far suggest that a reappraisal of Burckhardt's model in relation to poetry may be needed. In this section we shall look in more detail at how the state relied on humanist courtiers and administrators, the role of education in the development of the Tudor state, and the impact of such changes upon the individual reader in the reformed polity.

An underlying theme of sixteenth-century English history is the preoccupation of the ruling dynasty with its own illegitimacy. The establishment of the Tudor dynasty in 1485 owed more to military victory than it did to heredity, and the anxiety this created in governing circles was reflected in much of the literature of the period. Shakespeare's history plays, in particular *Richard II* and the two parts of *Henry IV*, pay eloquent testimony to the general fear of political disorder and concern over the succession at the end of the century.

Nevertheless, it is now well established that during the sixteenth century government in England underwent a remarkable transformation. As the administrative capacity of the centralized state grew under the control of the Tudors, so too did the demand for loyal and well-educated courtiers and bureaucrats. The Tudor court was thus a site of unprecedented opportunity for men of talent and learning. It was also the venue for a variety of court spectacles, pageants and cultural displays, all of which provided the insecure Tudors with powerful imagery which underlined their right to rule.

One aspect of this cultural policy was the crown's representation of itself as patron and defender of learning. For instance, when James I presented a copy of his collected works to the Bodleian Library in Oxford (translated into Latin for the sake of posterity), building work on the Tower of the Five Orders (Figure 4.4, overleaf) was halted to allow for the insertion of a seated statue of the king handing over the book, flanked by a grateful, kneeling figure representing the university, and Fame with a trumpet. The poems in Norbrook's selection were often products of this 'virtuous' courtly circle.

Figure 4.4 Tower of the Five Orders, seen from the Bodleian quadrangle, Oxford. Photo: A.F. Kersting

What role, then, did education have in this circulation of human and physical resources (Greenblatt (1980) calls this 'social energy')? We know that it became increasingly important for the ambitious to qualify for a place in the state. The ability to write, or to select and employ one's own writers, contributed to political success. The education system itself evolved in order to produce these new state servants. Petty (first) school education, where reading, writing and some arithmetic were taught, grew apace in this period. In addition, many grammar schools were opened or expanded, both at the top end of the market for the sons of the elite, such as Winchester and Eton, and at the local level, where schools were created by clerical or (after the Reformation) lay benefactors across the country. In Cambridgeshire, for instance, approximately one-fifth of the villages had a schoolmaster licensed continuously from 1570 to 1620; with the exception of two sparsely populated areas, nearly all children were within walking distance of a master (Spufford, 1981, pp.19–20). The result was a discernible growth in adult male literacy, though precise figures are impossible to substantiate. Recent research suggests that literacy levels varied markedly according to gender, social station and geographical location. We can, however, assert with some confidence that for the 'middling sort' (yeomen and lesser gentry in the countryside, merchants and professionals in the towns) the ability to read and write was becoming the norm during the course of the sixteenth century (Cressy, 1980).

Likewise the two universities in England – Oxford and Cambridge – were undergoing expansion to fulfil the new demand for places. Increasingly, those who attended were the sons of the nobility, gentry and 'middling sort', only a minority of whom proceeded to a traditional post in the church. A trend developed for endowing colleges, a process which gave the colleges independence from the university authorities and allowed new syllabuses to be adopted. In particular, lectureships were set up in Greek, Latin, rhetoric and moral philosophy, supplementing the traditional curriculum which remained largely dependent on Aristotelian logic and canon law.

The role of printing and the support given to writers in the spread of learning were important factors. Persons of rank and importance were expected to support authors, sometimes by cash in return for dedications, more often by assistance in the search for positions. In return the influential man (it was usually a man) received poetry which enhanced his own status. The production and consumption of poetry at court was as much a sign of importance as feasts, masques, tilts and processions. The new fashionable forms being imported into Britain were part of a 'conspicuous consumption of artifice', where the ability to purchase ornament, verbal and physical, denoted a person who could afford to 'waste' his time and resources on such luxuries.

Exercise

Use Woudhuysen's notes to the Norbrook poems dealt with so far to see which poems circulated in manuscript and which in print (pp.759–849). Can you align the method of circulation with the purpose of the verse or the rank of the poet?

Discussion

The method of circulation frequently reflects or draws attention to a writer's professional or amateur status. Marlowe, for example, was a professional, in contrast to the self-proclaimed amateurs of the Sidney circle. Most poems circulated in manuscript; they were sent to their dedicatees, and copied and recopied by readers into personal commonplace books. Given that the poems were designed for specific readers, putting them into print was not necessarily the most profitable way of gaining support. (By analogy, plays were written for specific acting companies, and were only published after they no longer attracted audiences, in order to prevent rival companies putting them on stage.) Print was probably regarded as too general a medium given the specific audience for poems which were written in expectation of patronage; it might circulate an undesirable image of the writer (for instance, most of Donne's poems were collected by his son and published after his death; only his sermons and devotional writings were published during his lifetime). It could even be seen as the medium used by the lower ranks, provoking what J.W. Saunders called 'the stigma of print' (1951, p.139). ❖

None the less, the economies of scale that printing possessed over manuscript production encouraged a tripling in the number of printers in England from 1500 to 1550. In a study of books printed in each year Philip Rider lists the 50 or so books printed in 1500, mostly statutes, law books and devotional material. There were more than 400 issues produced in 1600 alone, on a variety of subjects (Pollard and Redgrave, 1991, pp.333, 364–5). As Martin Davies notes, books were imported into Britain as well as printed here. The older centres of manuscript production, the universities and religious houses, were superseded. Unlike manuscript production, the regularity of the book trade allowed printing to proceed on a speculative basis (Davies, 1996, pp.47, 53). Lisa Jardine has sketched the changes in the use of books which the shift from manuscript to print involved:

> the scribally produced manuscript was unique (the pagination of each copy would be different); the printed book for the first time allowed two readers to discuss a passage in a work they were both reading by referring to the precise page on which it occurred. Consistent pagination also made it possible for author or editor to provide an index ... The comparatively effortless production of multiple copies meant that printed books could disseminate knowledge much more rapidly, widely and accurately than their handwritten antecedents. The dramatically lower price of the printed book also made written material available for the first time to a large, less privileged readership.
>
> (1996, p.177)

None the less, both manuscript and print continued to flourish into the seventeenth century.

By the end of the sixteenth century, those who had been only to petty school, or could read only English, were also able to gain access to classical ideas and genres in translation. H.S. Bennett estimates that about 200 editions of Latin and Greek texts appeared in the second half of the sixteenth century. Given an average print run of about 750 copies, he speculates that there were some 150,000 copies of classical works circulating at this time (1965, pp.102–4). Since the population of England and Wales did not rise much above four million by the end of the century, and there were restrictions on literacy according to gender and rank, translations from the classics appear to have been available to a fair proportion of the reading population. Interest in Greek drama and poetry was minimal. The most popular works were those by historians such as Tacitus and Livy, orators such as Cicero and Quintilian, Roman tragedians such as Seneca, comic playwrights such as Terence, and Augustan poets such as Ovid and Virgil (all appeared on the grammar school syllabus). In the dedicatory letter to Henry, prince of Wales, which prefaces George Chapman's version of Homer's *Iliad* (published in full in 1611) the production of translations is described as a national duty:

> How much then, were this kingdomes maine soule maim'd,
> To want this great inflamer of all powers
> That move in humane soules? All Realmes but yours,
> Are honour'd with him.

> (Chapman, 1969, sig.2v)

It was patriotic to bring the riches of other nations to swell Britain's learning. In 1598 Francis Meres was sufficiently confident of native talent to produce 'a comparative discourse of our English poets with the Greeke, Latine and Italian poets':

> as Theocritus is famoused for his *Idyllia* in Greeke, and Virgill for his *Eclogs* in Latine: so Spenser their imitator in his *Shepheardes Calender* is renowned for the like argument, and honoured for most exquisit wit.

> (Smith, 1937, vol. 2, p.316)

Like the Renaissance culture in the rest of Europe, then, the Renaissance in Britain was characterized by the reading, absorption and transformation of classical texts and ideas.

In the face of such copious printed material the technique encouraged by the grammar schools for dealing with texts was pragmatic (see, for example, the extract from the Eton syllabus in the Anthology, no. 47). Rebecca Bushnell describes the humanist's problem:

> by 1586 William Webbe feared for his whole country weighed down with 'innumerable sorts of English books, and infinite fardles of printed pamphlets, wherewith this country is pestered, all shops stuffed, and every study furnished' ... No teacher believed that every man could read everything, so books, like any other kind of commodity useful to a busy gentleman, needed to be consumed prudently and profitably.

> (1996, p.119)

The stress on using the fruits of one's reading led some busy men of state to employ others to read for them. Such facilitators – often employed as secretaries to great men, as Spenser, Donne and Wotton were – would harvest the important aspects of texts which were necessary for the business in hand, or simply those texts which were talked about or recently published. Book 1 in this series has debated whether the spread of humanism across Europe was dependent on its presentation of knowledge as a commodity (Chapter 3). In Britain, too, reading, just as much as writing, had a political and social use which was very far from the silent absorption for private pleasure with which elite literature is now read.

To become versed in classical and continental forms was a sound career move, a fact evident to every schoolboy. On this point, however, Joan Kelly-Gadol has questioned whether women can fairly be said to have had a Renaissance in Britain (see also Book 1, Chapter 3):

> the humanist programme was designed above all as a qualification for entry into the public world: since women were denied a public political identity, their education was sharply circumscribed.

> (Norbrook, p.47)

Since exceptionally well-educated women were also those whose works survive today, it is hard to judge the general level of female education at this time; yet while women and men may have read for different social purposes, the way they read, gathering useful precepts or information, was similar. Humanism was used to serve Christian values, so an emphasis on female piety required some learning in biblical and doctrinal texts.

Exercise

Read the extracts from Siôn Phylip's 'Yr wylan' ('The seagull'), Sir David Lindsay's 'The complaynt of the comoun weill of Scotland' and Eochaidh Ó Heóghusa's 'On Maguire's winter campaign' (Norbrook, nos. 180, 4, 33).

On the basis of your reading so far, do these texts strike you as sharing the Renaissance values of poets like Sidney and Spenser? If not, what aesthetic principles do they embody?

Discussion

These poems – like that of Askew – are not concerned to follow Renaissance rules of art. Phylip's poem is written in a traditional Welsh verse form, in *cywydd* (with rhyming couplets, each line being seven syllables long), and using *cynghanedd* (internal rhyme and alliteration). The extract from Lindsay's verse looks back to medieval satires on court vices (a parrot advises the king). The language which Ó Heóghusa (pronounced O'Hussey) uses to lament the sufferings undergone by Maguire in his rebellion against British forces in Ireland is in itself a nationalist gesture. These are only a few examples of literature written and printed in the period, in English, Scots, Gaelic and Welsh, which is not part of the Renaissance of classical learning. They are not necessarily partisan. 'The Renaissance' was an irrelevant concept for countries or ranks of people who preferred native languages and styles, or who were simply unversed in the new learning. ❖

Norbrook's Renaissance in Britain tails off in the mid seventeenth century, during 'an intellectual reaction against rhetoric, a growing quest for a transcendent rational truth to whose discovery language was a hindrance more than a help' (p.xxix). An image of this is provided by the publication of a history of the Royal Society by the dean of Westminster, Thomas Sprat, in 1667. The Royal Society was set up in 1660 to co-ordinate investigation into the natural world through a process of scholarly collaboration, taking as its example the Italian Accademia della Crusca founded in 1582, and the Académie Française which received a charter in 1635 from the French crown. Sprat described the society's

> constant Resolution, to reject all the amplifications, digressions, and swellings of style: to return back to the primitive purity, and shortness, when men deliver'd so many *things*, almost in an equal number of *words*. They have exacted from all their members, a close, naked, natural way of speaking ... bringing all things as near the Mathematical plainness, as they can: and preferring the language of Artizans, Countrymen, and Merchants, before that of Wits, or Scholars.
>
> (Cope and Jones, 1959, p.113)

Sprat, of course, is describing the society's aims, not necessarily how its members actually spoke! None the less, this resolution to dismiss Erasmian verbosity is one sign of how rhetorical skills were no longer considered to be vital to serve either learning or politics by the 1660s.

Concepts of poetry

Poetry, of course, was not the only genre which was marked by a Renaissance aesthetic. Sidney and Wroth also wrote prose romances modelled on the works of the Spaniard Montemayor; Marlowe's thundering dramas for the public stage drew on popular chapbooks and Seneca's tragedies; and More produced many prose dialogues. Yet, as the century progressed, increasing numbers of published tracts and poems argued about poetry's form and function. This section describes five major debates about literature: concepts of mimesis or imitation, didacticism, the belatedness of the Renaissance in Britain, nationalism and the rejection of artifice.

Exercise

Read the extracts from Sidney's *An Apology for Poetry* (1595) and Puttenham's *The Arte of English Poesie* (1589) in the Anthology (nos. 52 and 53). What role do these writers reserve for poetry?

Discussion

Both men are replying explicitly to contemporary criticisms of poetry and implicitly to Plato's description of poetry as a degeneration from the ideal. In Book 10 of the *Republic* the artist's work is considered to be a second-rate copy of the real thing, itself a mere shadow of an ideal, incorporeal form. In Plato's *Ion* the poet is said to be seized with a poetic madness, where, he claims, the gods speak through him – a state which Plato thinks inferior to the rational approach of the philosopher. Such tracts as Stephen Gosson's *Schoole of Abuse* of 1579 (ironically, dedicated to Sidney) draw on these Platonic attitudes to argue that poetry in general, and theatre in particular, is composed of lies. Moreover, it is socially destructive. It rouses illicit passions and encourages seditious meetings among disaffected citizens and apprentices. Sidney and Puttenham take their answers from Seneca, Quintilian and Aristotle. Poetry is god-like: it is superior to other arts, both scientific and mechanical, because it creates new forms and ideas. While other arts are restricted to the natural order as given, Sidney argues that:

> the poet, disdaining to be tied to any such subjection, lifted up with the vigour of his own invention, doth grow in effect into another nature, in making things either better than Nature bringeth forth, or, quite anew, forms such as never were in Nature ...

> (Shepherd, 1973, p.100)

The poet is divinely inspired, a 'vates' or prophet, a title which could be (and was) applied even to God. This stance is a new departure from simply considering the poet as an imitator of nature (the basis for Plato's criticism of poetry). For Renaissance Neoplatonists, the poet imitates the ideal, not the real. Moreover, they regard the 'divine instinct' with approval: poets create new worlds and imitate the divine; the example of David's Psalms is used to affirm God's approval of the use of poetry.

The social role of poetry is stressed by both Puttenham and Sidney. Drawing on Horace's *Ars poetica* and Cicero's *De oratore*, Puttenham explains how poets were 'the first priests, the first prophets, the first legislators' (Smith, 1937, vol. 2, p.6). Cicero praises eloquent speech:

what other power could have been strong enough either to gather scattered humanity into one place, or to lead it out of its brutish existence in the wilderness up to our present condition of civilization as men and as citizens, or, after the establishment of social communities, to give shape to laws, tribunals, and civic rights?

(*De oratore* 1.8)

More specifically, the poet is seen as the man most able with language. Horace uses the myths of Amphion, who played the lyre so well that stones arranged themselves into the walls of Thebes, and Orpheus, who tamed wild beasts with his music, to show how poetry regulates chaos and civil conversation can create harmony in society. These stories are repeated by Puttenham and Sidney.

The idea of the active life, of 'well doing and not of well knowing only', as Sidney puts it, has been discussed earlier in this chapter in relation to More's poem. Sidney links this to poetry using the Horatian formulation of '*movere, docere, delectare*' (moving, teaching and delighting). 'Poets would either profit, or delight,/ Or mixing sweet, and fit, teach life the right', in Jonson's translation of Horace's *Ars poetica*, published in 1640 (Parfitt, 1988, p.366). For Sidney, poetry is a 'sugared pill', teaching complex philosophy in delightful language, or a way of moving the will of the reader to do the right thing:

> this purifying of wit, this enriching of memory, enabling of judgment, and enlarging of conceit ... is to lead and draw us to as high a perfection as our degenerate souls, made worse by their clayey lodgings, can be capable of.
>
> (Shepherd, 1973, p.104) ❖

However, not all defences of poetry were reliant on Neoplatonic arguments.

Exercise

Read Shakespeare's Sonnet 74 (Norbrook, no. 112). ❖

The first 126 of Shakespeare's sonnets, published in 1609, nominally address his love for a young man; the remaining sonnets are addressed to a young woman. Many of the sonnets, however, use this love as an occasion to meditate on issues of philosophic importance: time, mortality and the self. In this sonnet the poetry is used to provide the beloved with a memorial of the poet. Repeated legal images of arrest for debt (life has only been a loan) are interwoven with phrases reminiscent of the burial service in the Book of Common Prayer ('earth to earth, ashes to ashes, dust to dust'). The

Christian contempt for the dead body as the 'pray of wormes' is supported by religious and poetic consolations: 'My life hath in this line some interest'. Earlier in the sequence the young man is urged to defy time by extending his 'line' through procreation. Elsewhere, however, the poet uses his verse to immortalize the loved one's youth and beauty in the face of time's onslaught (see Norbrook, nos. 104, 109). The sonnet has now lost its Petrarchan connotations; the golden age diction of loves, doves and roses in Sidney or Marlowe is replaced by a metaphysical colloquialism which deals with abstractions, moving the reader to accept death because of the value placed on poetry.

The means by which the poets clothed their inspiration are not neglected in the treatises on poetry. Writing is regarded as a craft which must be painstakingly practised. The mimesis of other poetry, as well as of the ideal or real, was an important element in the poet's training (and indeed, as the Eton school syllabus suggests, in general education). Art was, in part, 'a certaine order of rules prescribed by reason, and gathered by experience'. The principal neo-Latin literary theorist Julius Caesar Scaliger (1484–1558) published his *Poetice* in 1561, in which he classified and defined a large number of poetic genres. Puttenham's treatise is a vernacular example of how the novice writer (and reader) was trained in the forms that were available to him. Puttenham carefully links the poet as craftsman with the poet as creator; the poet imitates what he has thought of, 'the true and lively of every thing which is set before him, and which he taketh in hand to describe'. Decorum is kept when the style and the subject are in harmony.

Norbrook talks about the sense of belatedness to which the Renaissance poet was subject, 'of the need to repeat what had been said before' (p.9). Certainly Gosson, Sidney and Puttenham pit classical authorities against each other when debating aesthetics. The ethos of each classical authority, as much as what they say, is used (a practice known as 'stuffing the margins'). Yet the growth of a national confidence is also evident. The theorists defend the ability of English to appropriate rather than be overwhelmed by the treasures rediscovered in ancient texts. In Paris a group of humanist poets calling themselves the Pléiade had expressed a similar confidence in the French tongue. Notable among them was Joachim Du Bellay (*c.*1522–60), who, in two sonnet sequences, depicted a period when the glories of ancient literature would be rebuilt in France. Spenser and Sidney were highly influenced by Du Bellay, and Spenser translated part of his work (Norbrook, no. 335). With Sidney, Spenser formed part of a group of young poets eager to discuss the new ideas about poetry, and in particular verse forms which were modelled on classical metres. They named the group after the ancient Greek council, the Areopagus.

Exercise Read the extract from Richard Stanyhurst's translation of Virgil's *Aeneid* (Norbrook, no. 333). ❖

Although Stanyhurst (1546–1618) was born in Dublin, he was educated in Oxford. Like Buchanan, he wrote a history of his country, *A Plain and Perfect Description of Ireland*, but unlike Buchanan this work was sufficiently English in viewpoint to be incorporated into a popular English history book, the *Chronicles* (compiled by a team under Raphael Holinshed, and published in London in 1577).

Stanyhurst's translation of the *Aeneid* uses dactylic hexameters, i.e. six feet per line, where each foot is composed either of a long syllable followed by two short ones (a *dactyl*), or of two long syllables (a *spondee*). The fifth foot was almost always a *dactyl*, and the sixth could be either a *spondee* or a *trochee* (long–short). For example, lines 32 and 33 scan as follows:

Hēē scōrnes|thēse rās|cāl tāme|gāmes, bŭt ă|sōundĕr ŏf|hōgstēers,
Ōr thēe|brōwnyē|līon tōo|stālck frŏ thĕ|mōuntĕn hĕ|wīsshĕth.

Notice how Stanyhurst uses a revised spelling to mark the metre, doubling the vowels to indicate length where appropriate: compare 'Hee' with 'he' and 'thee' with 'the'.

Exercise Look through the variety of translations Norbrook provides (nos. 332–45). Note the range of works English absorbs into itself – poems by Virgil, Homer, Ovid, Lucan, Horace, Ariosto, Tasso, Du Bellay, Du Bartas, as well as the Bible. Are British Renaissance writers justified in feeling belated, even derivative? ❖

Puttenham argues that it is possible for the English language to rival Greek and Latin in expressiveness:

> if th'art of Poesie be but a skill appertaining to utterance, why may not the same be with us aswel as with them, our language being no lesse copious, pithie, and significative then theirs, our conceipts the same, and our wits no lesse apt to devise.

> (Smith, 1937, vol. 2, p.5)

English need not be overwhelmed by foreign words and ideas. Samuel Daniel, in his *Defence of Ryme* (printed around 1603), swaggers:

all our understandings are not to be built by the square of *Greece* and
Italie. We are the children of nature as well as they; we are not so
placed out of the way of judgement but that the same Sunne of
Discretion shineth uppon us; we have our portion of the same virtues
as well as of the same vices ... All their Poesie, all their Philosophie is
nothing, unlesse we bring the discerning light of conceipt with us to
apply it to use.

(Smith, 1937, vol. 2, pp.366–7)

Spenser urges British poets to emulate the way the life of Rome is
revived in continental writings, and Sir John Harington admits to
'honest theft' from them (Norbrook, nos. 335, 349). Authors such as
More and Buchanan expected to 'export' their work to European
audiences. While it is true that, as Joseph Loewenstein says, 'lagging
behind 125 years of *editiones principes* [first editions of classical texts],
seventeenth-century English humanists assert themselves within a
Republic of Letters increasingly devoted to scholarly corrigenda
[corrections]', it is also true that scholarly effort was increasingly
refocused from classical texts on to native ones (1996, p.272).
Grammars of the English language were produced, as were editions of
authors such as Chaucer and Skelton (Norbrook, nos. 1, 247, 307,
346), and examples in literary argument were drawn from native as
well as classical authors. Loewenstein notes that whereas the double
translation method from Latin to English and back is recommended
in the mid sixteenth century as a way of improving the pupil's Latin,
by the early seventeenth century it was being practised to improve the
scholar's English (1996, p. 275).

Exercise

Read Thomas Carew's 'Elegie upon the death of ... John Donne'
(Norbrook, no. 365). This was published with other elegies from
friends and admirers in Donne's collected works in 1633.

For what in particular does Carew praise Donne's poetry?

Discussion

Carew (pronounced 'Carey') deals with the same topic as
Shakespeare – the ability of poetry to 'contain' the dead – but he
has to cope with Donne's own poetry in doing so. Donne prides
himself on the originality of his verse, on thinking issues through
from first principles, on maintaining a sceptical independence, on
expressing himself in plain diction and with vigour. Carew
compliments Donne for ridding British poetry of 'The lazie seeds/
Of servile imitation' – such as Puttenham recommended – by using
his own invention (the rhetorical term here taking on its present
connotation of originality). He chides poets of the previous reign
who confined the poetic *furor* to 'A mimique fury'. Now Donne is
dead that golden age style will return, Carew sighs; in will come the

references to gods and tales from Ovid's *Metamorphoses*; in will come amplification to 'swell the windy Page' (Carew here ironically exemplifying his own fear). He praises plain diction over the elevated Ciceronian style, arguing that the lazy adoption of Latin and Greek forms into English has harmed both those languages. In fact, as Loewenstein points out, the plain style was equally derivative:

> an anti-Ciceronianism that originated on the Continent during the late sixteenth century, in the work of Marc-Antoine Muret, Justus Lipsius and Michel de Montaigne [was imported]. These men, by precept and example, promoted a shift from Cicero to Silver Latin prose models: to Tacitus for his tense condensations and to Seneca for his casual, non-compulsive symmetries and to both for their shortened periods. The interest in brevity and point has many analogues in other areas of late Renaissance aesthetic practice – in the vogue for emblems, in the poetry of wit with its demotion of scheme and promotion of trope (and its preference for metaphor over simile), in the generalized social practice of the gnomic remark, in the enthusiasm for epigrams.

> (1996, p.284)

Carew says that moral teaching will go on; 'The Pulpit may her plaine,/ And sober Christian precepts still retaine' (ll.11–12). However, Donne's ability to move the hearer is lost: 'the flame/ Of thy brave Soule, that shot such heat and light,/... Did through the eye the melting heart distill;/ And the deepe knowledge of darke truths so teach' (ll.14–19).

The classical elegy, exemplified for the Renaissance by Ovid's *Amores*, is defined less by its subject than by its metre (alternating pentameters and hexameters, that is, lines of five then six feet). Used for lamenting the lover's trials, it came to be associated with all forms of mourning. Commenting on Roman practice, Puttenham says that it was:

> a peece of joy to be able to lament with ease, and freely to poure forth a mans inward sorrowes and the greefs wherewith his minde is surcharged ... sorrowes that the noble Poets sought by their arte to remove or appease, not with any medicament of a contrary temper, as the *Galenistes* use to cure *contraria contrariis*, but as the *Paracelsians*, who cure *Similia Similibus*, making one dolour to expell another, and, in this case, one short sorrowing the remedie of a long and grevious sorrow.

> (Smith, 1937, vol. 2, pp.49–50)

Carew carefully distinguishes between the extended elegy and its tailpiece: he ends the poem with a brief epitaph suitable to be engraved on a tomb, which memorializes Donne as poet and priest.

Yet Donne is not the only poet to be celebrated in the poem. Carew, after all, is producing an elegy which he says cannot be written unless Donne's talents live on. His is the poem which will commemorate Donne; it is Donne's tombstone. To prove that he is subject to Donne's 'universall Monarchy of wit', Carew re-uses Donne's own phrases in this elegy: for instance, the 'masculine persuasive force' of 'To his mistresse' (Norbrook, no. 96) becomes 'masculine expression' here, and 'nor ever chast, except you ravish mee' of 'Batter my heart' becomes 'committed holy Rapes upon our Will' (contrast Askew's adoption of biblical texts). Carew has forced Donne to join him in writing his own elegy; in doing so Donne has implicitly accepted Carew's claim to be his successor, something which the poem explicitly denies. A second area of contradiction opens up when the poem's desire to go beyond servile imitation of the classics is expressed in the metre which Marlowe chose when translating the *Amores* (heroic couplets, that is, couplets that rhyme and are in iambic pentameter, where each foot is an iamb, containing first an unstressed then a stressed syllable). Carew also uses classical topoi such as the triumphal crown of bays, the death of the arts on the demise of the beloved (remember the laments of Virgil and Theocritus), the casual references to Delphos and Prometheus, Apollo and the *flamens*. The paradoxical attempt to shed artistry from art is bound to fail; Carew, very cleverly, makes this the motivating force of the poem. ❖

George Herbert was a poet who adopted a radically different perspective on the role and purpose of poetry. He was appointed as the public orator at the University of Cambridge in 1620 and twice represented Montgomery in parliament. Changing direction, he was installed as a canon of Lincoln Cathedral in 1626, and thereafter devoted himself to his duties in the church, becoming rector of Bemerton in 1630. Herbert's 'retreat' from the court and Cambridge to follow a vocation in a rural parish can be contrasted with the way Donne's court career was resurrected when he entered the church. His poems were published posthumously in 1633 as *The Temple*, after he had enjoined a friend to burn them if they did not 'turn to the advantage of any dejected soul'.

Read Herbert's 'Jordan' (Norbrook, no. 281). ❖

The poem's title in a manuscript containing early versions was 'Invention'. In *The Temple* it is the second poem to be entitled 'Jordan'. It is a play on the conceited and plain styles. In the first two stanzas Herbert mimes a happily obtuse poet, determined to give his best in describing God, and fussily rejecting words which do not – quite – capture the Almighty's essence. The rhetorical training of the poet is evident in his determination to say the right things with 'trim invention', using the well-turned *elocutio* of 'quaint words', and metaphors which trope or curl the plain sense. The presumption of this weaving of the 'self into the sense' is comically debunked when a 'friend', God, speaks: 'There is in love a sweetnesse readie penn'd:/ Copie out onely that, and save expense'. Overtly the plain style is being praised: any other style would not be decorous, it would concentrate on form rather than sincerity. The poem refers back to Herbert's letter of advice to his successor as public orator at Cambridge: 'perfect speech, as in a perfect man, is foursquare – serious, elevated, transparent, concise'.

Like Carew's poem, however, this is a stylized rejection of Renaissance art. Its title is a metaphor referring to the river which the Israelites crossed when they entered the Promised Land, later interpreted as a 'type' or foreshadowing of Christ's institution of baptism. It stages a play where God speaks through a Herbert who knows, though he pretends not to, how the poem will end. It is built on paradox, since at the climax of the poem's sincerity, when God speaks, he produces a sacred parody of the first sonnet of *Astrophil and Stella*, 'look in thy heart and write'. Moreover, as A.D. Nuttall has sardonically commented, Herbert has already performed the whole manoeuvre of giving up poetry in the first Jordan poem; no one can cross the Jordan twice (1980, p.15; see also Norbrook, no. 284).

Ben Jonson and the humanist poet-scholar

This section is a detailed reading of how Ben Jonson used 'To Penshurst' to create a place for himself as the guardian of Augustan values. After reading it you may want to analyse Aemilia Lanyer's 'The Description of Cooke-ham' (Norbrook, no.189), asking yourself what position Lanyer, as a female poet, claims for herself in the estate (the discussion of Wroth and Askew may help here).

Jonson was born in 1572, the posthumous son of a clergyman. He was educated at Westminster grammar school under William Camden, the antiquary and historian, whom Jonson praised for his 'sight in searching the most antique springs' and for his 'weight, and authority' (Parfitt, 1988, p.39). Camden inspired Jonson with a reverence for, and knowledge of, the classical writers which marked all his future writing. After school Jonson worked in his stepfather's business of bricklaying, saw military service in Flanders, acted with a company of strolling players, and finally was taken on by Philip Henslowe, a theatre proprietor, to write plays for the Lord Admiral's Men. His major plays, including *Volpone*, *The Alchemist* and *Bartholomew Fair*, introduced a new form of comedy, one set in an urban environment and dependent on pace, wit, satire and quickly sketched, strongly flavoured characters. He was imprisoned several times: for killing a fellow actor in a brawl in 1598, and for writing satiric plays which the privy council felt were seditious (the lost play *The Isle of Dogs* of 1597, and *Eastward Hoe* of 1605). Jonson converted to Catholicism during his first period of imprisonment, but returned to Protestantism twelve years later. After 1605 he was employed by the court to write masques (courtly dramatic entertainments which both idealized and admonished their aristocratic audiences), and produced much poetry which served the same function. The foremost proponent of the classical style in architecture at this period, Inigo Jones, was employed to design the stage machinery and costumes for these masques. Jonson's friends included Shakespeare, Donne and Carew. By the time of his death in 1637 he had come to be regarded as the unofficial 'poet laureate' for the court. In 1616 he was the first British poet to publish his own collected drama and poetry in folio. (This format folds each printed sheet of paper once, giving two large pages which can be bound into an imposing volume. In contrast, popular chapbooks or plays were published in quarto or octavo, where the paper was folded twice or three times to create smaller, cheaper volumes.) The folio format, like the heavy annotation which Jonson provided for his text, was a style of publishing hitherto reserved for classical dramatists and poets. The choice of this format was therefore a declaration on the part of Jonson that his works were not simply evanescent crowd-pleasers. Jonson's interest in the physical appearance of his work is comparable with Spenser's self-conscious presentation of *The Shepheardes Calender*. By contrast, during his lifetime Shakespeare's plays were published only in the cheaper quarto format – usually without his involvement. The folio edition of Shakespeare's works (1623) appeared seven years after his death. Unlike Jonson, Shakespeare seems not to have taken any great interest in preserving his work for posterity.

Penshurst Place, in Kent (Figure 4.5), was nearly three hundred years old in 1611, when Jonson is presumed to have written the poem. The Great Hall (Figure 4.6) had been built by John de Poultney, four times lord mayor of London; the whole household was expected to eat, sleep and shelter in here. In 1393 Sir John Devereux was licensed to fortify the house, and enclose it with a wall and towers.

Figure 4.5 Penshurst Place, Kent, from the south. Photo: A.F. Kersting

Figure 4.6 The Great Hall, Penshurst Place. Photo: A.F. Kersting

In 1552 Edward VI granted Penshurst to Sir William Sidney, one of the new men brought to prominence by the Reformation. The Sidney fortunes continued to flourish: his son, Sir Henry Sidney, was appointed lord deputy of Ireland and lord president of the marches of Wales by Elizabeth, and married Mary Dudley, the sister of the earl of Leicester (see Figures 4.7 and 4.8, the Dudley and Sidney family trees). As the family became more established, the house was adapted. Henry added the western range and the gatehouse front at some point in the decade after 1575. When his first son, Philip, was killed in battle against the Spanish at Zutphen in 1586, his younger son, Robert, inherited the house. Robert, who was knighted for bravery at Zutphen, in turn became lord president of Ireland. He was out of favour with Elizabeth towards the end of her reign, but James's accession saw an improvement in his relations with the monarch. He was created Baron Sidney of Penshurst in 1603, viscount L'Isle in 1605, and the first earl of Leicester in 1618. Robert continued to adapt the house to mirror the family's increasing influence, adding state rooms, new stables, an improved orchard and the Long Gallery in 1618. Unusually for an adapted medieval house, the Great Hall retained its central hearth in 1611 (as it does now, Figure 4.6). However, plans to extend the deer park – a move which would have attracted the king, an enthusiastic hunter, to the house – fell through in the face of the financial problems which dogged Robert. His marriage to Barbara Gamage, while successful in personal terms, brought him little wealth. His correspondence in the 1600s is full of plans to alleviate his uncertain financial position but also shows his understanding of the need to compete for status, and hence to spend. Both Elizabeth and James were prepared to visit houses where the magnificence of their entertainment paid a compliment to their credit. 'To Penshurst' is presumed to have been written after May 1611, when an orchard wall of 'countrey stone' (l.45) was erected, and before November 1611, when Prince Henry died (l.77).

Jonson's entry into the loosely Protestant faction of the Pembrokes and Sidneys coincided with his return to the Protestant church. Working against the proposed alliance with Catholic Spain which James favoured, the Pembroke faction supported the Protestant alliance in France, and, in a clandestine manner, the Dutch struggle against the Spanish. The Pembroke group were successors of the militant Elizabethan Protestants, who hoped that Henry, the prince of Wales, could be persuaded to provide a lead against James's foreign policy.

Jonson served as tutor to Robert's son, William, and was patronized by the countess of Pembroke, the sister to Robert and Philip. His collection *The Forrest* (published 1616) includes poems to Sir Robert Wroth, Sir William Sidney and the countess of Rutland (Philip's daughter).

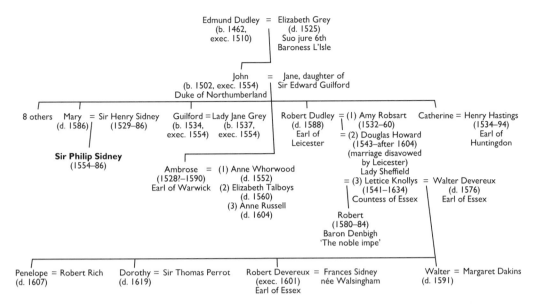

Figure 4.7 The Dudley family tree, from Duncan-Jones, 1991

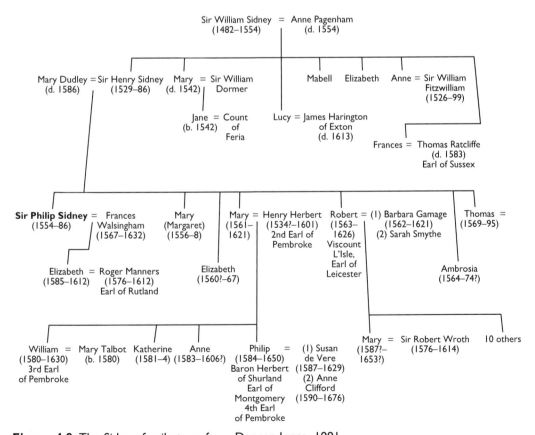

Figure 4.8 The Sidney family tree, from Duncan-Jones, 1991

Read Jonson's 'To Penshurst' (Norbrook, no. 190) and consider the following questions, which form the basis of the remainder of this section:

- how does Jonson present Penshurst in this text?

- how are native and classical customs mingled (use Norbrook's Appendix 3 and the footnotes to the poem)?

- how does the poet 'repay' his patron?

- what is his attitude to Sir Robert Sidney? ❖

'To Penshurst' is initially structured around a negative comparison: the house is a Gothic pile. It is unlike the Tudor and Stuart prodigy houses, built by the newly rich and powerful to display their great wealth in costly ornament and grandiose scale. Penshurst does not have the black marble chimney places or pillars, the burnished and gilded roofs, the banqueting houses or spy towers (lanterns), the magnificent stairs or courts of these new houses. Figure 4.9 shows nearby Knole, built by Robert Cecil (and rumoured by the Essex faction to be financed partly by a Spanish pension), which had a lantern, courts and chimney pieces of touch-stone (see also Figures 4.10 and 4.11).

Figure 4.9 Knole House, Sevenoaks, from the air. Photo: Aerofilms Limited

Figure 4.10 The Great Staircase, Knole. Photo: © Crown copyright. RCHME. National Monuments Record

Figure 4.11 The Cartoon Gallery, Knole. Photo: © Crown copyright. RCHME. National Monuments Record

Figure 4.12 The west front of Burghley House, Stamford. Photo: A.F. Kersting

Burghley House (Figure 4.12) and Theobalds were built by Robert's father, Sir William Cecil (later Lord Burghley, Elizabeth's lord treasurer). These houses were far larger than the owners' households required (Theobalds, for instance, extended over five courts), and were built in part to welcome the monarch. Cecil commented sardonically to the lord chancellor, Sir Christopher Hatton, who erected Holdenby, that 'God send us both long to enjoy her for whom we both meant to exceed our purses in these' (Ford, 1992, p.67). Penshurst had its own share of classical buildings: the south front of the north range boasted a classical loggia from 1579, one of the first to be built in England. The overall design of the house, however, included styles from three centuries. It had grown according to the uses the household made of it – uses which included, of course, demonstrations of the family's consequence.

Jonson, as both former bricklayer and student of the classics, mingled practical experience and ancient allusion in the poem. The construction of Gothic buildings was an accretive process. While each building was produced to a rough plan, this was modified as the work progressed, as either materials or people with particular skills became available. The new Renaissance styles were very different; travel introduced many landowners to these continental practices, which adapted classical principles. In 1611 part of the treatise by the Italian architect Sebastiano Serlio (1475–1552) appeared in English as *The First Book of Architecture Made by Sebastian Serly*, translated, significantly, from Italian into Dutch and then into English. It was dedicated to Prince Henry and laid out the new neoclassical principles of design in a folio of over 400 pages of elevations, sections and detailed drawings of ancient buildings. Serlio drew on the only surviving classical treatise on architecture, written by the first-century Roman architect Vitruvius. Such architecture was built to a plan, and functioned according to formal canons which took little notice of the local conditions. Design with order and proportion was proposed; any ornament was to reflect this restraint. Inigo Jones's sketchbook from 1614 comments that the plan must be produced first, with consideration being given to utility; only then should the building be adorned. 'Ye outward ornaments oft [ought] to be solid, proporsionable according to the rulles, masculine and unaffected' (Lloyd, 1931, p.97). Sir Henry Wotton (the addressee of Donne's verse letter) published *The Elements of Architecture* in 1624; in it he compared elements of buildings he had seen on his travels as a diplomat, and claimed Vitruvius as his 'principall master'. Wotton, like Jones, was not in favour of ornament for its own sake – good building must have regard to 'COMMODITIE, FIRMENESS, and DELIGHT' (Lloyd, 1931, pp.87–8). He criticized the crazed Gothicism of the British decorative style. Jones himself probably influenced architectural fashion as much by his collaboration with Jonson on the masques as with his buildings: he left 450 drawings of designs for masques and only 80 of buildings. Moreover, the audience for the masques consisted of those who could build such houses: Anne of Denmark patronized Jones and Jonson, and even acted in their masques. So Jonson praises the Gothic style of Penshurst here in *classical* terms. It is a 'pile', but orderly and built for use. Its age allows him to present the Sidneys as one of the ancient families of the realm, though they had merely acquired, not created, both the house and the way of life it suggested, an idyllic feudal estate, peopled by contented tenants.

In Jonson's vision classical and native rural deities mix in the Kent estate. Satyrs and fauns dance around trees, where more prosaic local lovers have graffitied their burning passions, inspired perhaps by Philip's sonnets. The Horae, presiding over the three seasons of the classical year, here provide protection for homely garden produce. The Penates (Roman household gods) are present to welcome the monarch. Nature offers herself up willingly – the *sponte sua* ('of its own accord') *topos* – as though this were the golden age. In contrast to the ornamental aspect of the prodigy houses the estate enjoys the use of the four elements: air, water, earth and fire (in wood). Jonson integrates Martial's praise of Faustinus's villa into the English landscape, so that Penshurst has no:

> unprofitable expanses of broad acreage laid out in idle myrtle plantations, unwed planes [without vines], and clipped boxwood, but rejoices in the true, rough countryside. Corn is tightly crammed in every corner and many a wine jar is fragrant with ancient vintages ... All the crew of the dirty poultry yard wander around, the cackling goose and the spangled peacocks ... the painted partridge, the speckled guinea fowl ... nor does the country caller come empty-handed. He brings pale honey with the comb and a cone of milk ... Strapping daughters of honest tenant farmers present their mothers' gifts in wicker baskets ... Nor does a greedy table keep back victuals for tomorrow; there is food for all, and the sated servant never envies the tipsy diner.
>
> *(Epigrams* 3.58)

The sting at the end of Juvenal's satire against Crispinus (a fishmonger who rose to high office by flattery) is lost. Taking a turbot to the imperial presence, Crispinus urges the emperor to:

> 'prepare to eat a turbot saved to adorn your reign – /It insisted on being caught'. Most palpable flattery, yet/The imperial plumage rose: there is nothing godlike power/Will refuse to believe of itself in the way of commendation.
>
> *(Satires* 4.68–9)

Instead, Jonson produces what Alastair Fowler (1994) calls 'hyperbolic banter': in comparing the natural order with a fallen human civilization, Penshurst becomes both the classical *locus amoenus* and the Christian Eden.

The social order is similarly depicted as harmonious. Richard Dutton points out that the flora and fauna of the estate are part of an organic hierarchy, where every element knows and accepts its place below the king (1983, p.111). Moreover, as Fowler notes, the estate poem has as its model Virgil's *Georgics* rather than the pastoral *Eclogues*. The topoi used by Virgil – and Jonson – stress the productive aspect of the land and the workers on it: all members of the estate labour on the land (even the lord and lady of the house are supervisors of the labour of others); the landscape is fertile and responsive to the efforts of the owner; retirement to the country produces a healthy and sober life where each rank aids the others; the traditional ways of life are praised. Fowler rebuts Raymond Williams's suggestions that the poem demonstrates an 'insatiable exploitation of the land and its creatures', where 'this natural order is simply and decisively on its way to table'.

He believes that this interpretation misses the poem's sense of hospitable duty towards the needy, and the need for the upper ranks to display such wealth (1994, p.3). The goods which the tenants bring are not feudal rents paid in kind, for in Kent such dues had long since been commuted to cash payments; rather, they are gifts expressing the tenants' love and respect for their lord.

One symbol of this harmony, in which Jonson conflates life and literature, is the communal meal which the household enjoys daily in the Great Hall. This was an old-fashioned practice by 1611, but one kept up in Penshurst at Robert's orders. Jonson praises the 'liberall board' where 'the same beere, and bread, and self-same wine,/ That is his Lordships, shall be also mine'. William Drummond, an Edinburgh landowner and scholar whom Jonson visited in 1618/19, reported one conversation they had on the topic:

> being at the end of my lord Salisbury's table with Inigo Jones, and demanded by my lord why he was not glad, 'My Lord', said he, 'You promised I should dine with you, but I do not', for he had none of his meat; he esteemed only that his meat which was of [the lord's] own dish.

> (Parfitt, 1988, p.469)

Martial also describes a feast he was at, where the less favoured guest ate separate dishes from the host: 'you take oysters fattened in the Lucrine pool, I cut my mouth sucking a mussel ... Why do I dine without you, Ponticus, when I'm dining with you' (*Epigrams,* 3.60). Both life and poem have been moulded by Jonson's reading.

Dutton argues that 'To Penshurst' instructs by praising, putting the onus on the dedicatee to deserve its praises, and on the reader to compare the actual with the ideal (1983, p.83). He notes that Jonson gives warning of his didactic purpose in:

> the negatives and comparatives ... with which he qualifies his comments. Behind all this lies an attitude to language itself, an assumption that it is a precision instrument, a divine gift, and to be respected as such by both parties in its interchange.

> (p.83)

A number of hints are given by such discriminating praise. Since the estate is beautiful enough, for instance, Robert need not spend more on it. The poem reinforces the king's injunctions to landowners in 1614 that they should spend more time on their estates, in part to restore authority to the country areas.

Contemporary commentators bemoaned the noblemen's ambition at court, their impoverishment caused by frequent litigation, their magnificent houses and plain miserliness: chance guests could no longer rely on being welcomed in by the lords of the great houses they passed on their travels. Robert was not at Penshurst as often as the poem would suggest; his duties at court as chamberlain to Queen Anne's household prevented this. Thus, tactfully proffering advice, Jonson eulogizes old-fashioned hospitality as it declines. The virtue in an Epicurean withdrawal to the land, and the maintenance of the feudal hospitality represented by the Penshurst Great Hall, are central to the way Jonson represents Robert to himself (compare Donne's poem to Wotton). Robin Sowerby sees an echo of Book 2 of Horace's odes, which 'contrasts the vanity of riches and "proud ambitious heaps" with the contentment of a modest life on his Sabine farm', and points out that in *The Poetaster* of 1601, where Jonson deals with the relationship between patron and client, he takes on the identity of Horace:

> The identification is with the poet as guardian and upholder of civilized values through the proper exercise of his art in which the lyric vocation is but a part ...

> (1994, p.152)

Nor were Jonson's contemporaries neglected. Stella Revard notes that Jonson's use of Martial and Horace as models resulted in his rereading of neo-Latin Renaissance poets such as Politian and Sannazaro:

> Jonson certainly knew many of the Neo-Latin imitations of Horace's Epode 2 ... The country estate poem ... becomes popular among the humanist poets of the fifteenth and sixteenth centuries ... Pontano [for instance] urges Sannazaro to come to Baiae ... Du Bellay imagines leaving Paris to return to the countryside and to grow old there.

> (Brady and Herendeen, 1991, p.152)

Certainly the poem allows Jonson to establish a more equal relationship with the Sidneys, where both sides give something. Their positions as guest and host are reversed, as Robert walks through the building Jonson has erected in his praise, composed of classical topoi and native topography. It is perhaps worthwhile to note that in 1607, when Cecil handed over Theobalds to James I, Jonson wrote an entertainment for the occasion. His work is literary real estate.

Jonson claimed to maintain a critical independence from the ancients, as demonstrated in this extract from *Discoveries* (compare Daniel, pp.277–8, above):

> I know nothing can conduce more to letters, than to examine the writings of the ancients, and not to rest in their sole authority, or to

take all upon trust from them ... For to all the observations of the ancients, we have our own experience: which, if we will use, and apply, we have better means to pronounce. It is true they opened the gates, and made the way, that went before us; but as guides not commanders ... Truth lies open to all; it is no man's several.

(Parfitt, 1988, pp.378–9)

The poem appears to provide evidence of such judiciousness, where well-made plainness and bold didacticism are as classical in derivation as English golden age work by Spenser and Sidney.

A British Renaissance?

This chapter has argued that the British literary Renaissance was one of generous accommodation of medieval and contemporary genres, themes and motifs to a revival of classical and neoclassical forms. Some writers at the time saw the concept of a 'Renaissance' as a flattering piece of self-definition. Daniel argued, in 1603, that it was:

a touch of arrogant ignorance to hold this or that nation Barbarous, these or those times grosse, considering how this manifold creature man, wheresoever hee stand in the world, hath alwayes some disposition of worth, intertaines the order of societie, affects that which is most in use, and is eminent in some one thing or other that fits his humour and the times.

(Smith, 1937, vol. 2, p.367)

Yet Thomas Campion, in a treatise on poetics of 1602, talks of how:

learning, after the declining of the *Romaine* Empire and the pollution of their language through the conquest of the Barbarians, lay most pitifully deformed till the time of *Erasmus*, *Rewcline* [Reuchlin], Sir *Thomas More*, and other learned men of that age, who brought the Latin toong again to light, redeeming it with much labour out of the hands of the illiterate Monks and Friers.

(Smith, 1937, vol. 2, p.329)

As Loewenstein argues, the neoclassical ideal was a discriminating habit of mind, 'with its alternation between censorious inspection of the present and studious review of the past' (Loewenstein, 1996, p.269). It was because writers like Campion were able to historicize the classical past, and see its forms and values as separate from their own, that they were able to compare and arrogate them, not belatedly, not slavishly, but deliberately and self-consciously.

Bibliography

ABEL, E. (ed.) (1982) *Writing and Sexual Difference*, Brighton, Harvester.

BEILIN, E. (ed.) (1996) J. Bale: *The Examinations of Anne Askew*, Oxford, Oxford University Press.

BENNETT, H.S. (1965) *English Books and Readers 1558–1603*, Cambridge, Cambridge University Press.

Book of Common Prayer (1968) London, Eyre & Spottiswoode.

BRADY, J. and HERENDEEN, W.H. (eds) (1991) *Ben Jonson's 1616 Folio*, New York, Associated University Presses.

BURCKHARDT, J. (1990) *The Civilization of the Renaissance in Italy*, trans. S.G.C. Middlemore, Harmondsworth, Penguin; first published 1858.

BUSHNELL, R. (1996) *A Culture of Teaching: Early Modern Humanism in Theory and Practice*, Ithaca, NY, Cornell University Press.

CAREY, J. (1990) *John Donne: Life, Mind and Art*, London, Faber & Faber.

CHAPMAN, G. (trans.) (1969) Homer: *The Iliads of Homer*, Amsterdam, Da Capo.

COLE, A. (1995) *Art of the Italian Renaissance Courts*, London, Weidenfeld & Nicholson.

COPE, J.I. and JONES, H.W. (eds) (1959) T. Sprat: *History of the Royal Society*, London, Routledge & Kegan Paul.

CRESSY, D. (1980) *Literacy and the Social Order: Reading and Writing in Tudor and Stuart England*, Cambridge, Cambridge University Press.

DAVIES, M. (1996) in J. Kraye (ed.) *The Cambridge Companion to Renaissance Humanism*, Cambridge, Cambridge University Press.

DE SELINCOURT, E. (ed.) (1944) W. Wordsworth: *The Poetical Works*, vol. 2, Oxford, Clarendon.

DUNCAN-JONES, K. (1991) *Sir Philip Sydney, Courtier Poet*, London, Hamish Hamilton.

DUTTON, R. (1983) *Ben Jonson to the First Folio*, Cambridge, Cambridge University Press.

FORD, B. (ed.) (1992) *The Cambridge Cultural History of Britain: Sixteenth-Century Britain*, Cambridge, Cambridge University Press.

FOWLER, A. (1994) *The Country House Poem*, Edinburgh, Edinburgh University Press.

GREENBLATT, S. (1980) *Renaissance Self-fashioning: From More to Shakespeare*, Chicago, University of Chicago Press.

HADFIELD, A. (1994) *Literature, Politics and National Identity: Reformation to Renaissance*, Cambridge, Cambridge University Press.

HAMILTON, A.C. et al. (eds) (1990) *The Spenser Encyclopedia*, Toronto, Toronto University Press.

HANNAY, M. (ed.) (1985) *Silent but for the Word: Tudor Women as Patrons, Translators and Writers of Religious Works*, Kent, Ohio, Kent State University Press.

JARDINE, L. (1996) *Worldly Goods*, London, Macmillan.

LANHAM, R. (1976) *The Motives of Eloquence: Rhetoric in the Renaissance*, New Haven, Conn. and London, Yale University Press.

LEVI, A.H.T. (ed.) (1986) Erasmus: 'Panegyricus' in *The Collected Works of Erasmus*, vol. 27, trans. B. Radice, Toronto, University of Toronto Press.

LEWIS, C.S. (1954) *English Literature in the Sixteenth Century Excluding Drama* , Oxford, Clarendon.

LLOYD, N. (1931) *A History of the English House*, London, Architectural Press.

LOEWENSTEIN, J. (1996) 'Humanism in seventeenth-century English literature' in J. Kraye (ed.) *The Cambridge Companion to Renaissance Humanism*, Cambridge, Cambridge University Press.

MILLER, C.H., BRADNER, L., LYNCH, C.A. and OLIVER, R.P.(eds) (1984) T. More: 'Epigrams' in *The Complete Works of St Thomas More*, vol. 3, part 2, New Haven, Conn. and London, Yale University Press.

NORBROOK, D. (1984) *Poetry and Politics in the English Renaissance*, London, Routledge & Kegan Paul.

NORBROOK, D. (1993) *The Penguin Book of Renaissance Verse: 1509–1659*, ed. H.R. Woudhuysen, Harmondsworth, Penguin.

NUTTALL, A.D. (1980) *Overheard by God: Fiction and Prayer in Herbert, Milton, Dante, and St John*, London, Methuen.

POLLARD, A.W. and REDGRAVE, G.R. (1991) *A Short-title Catalogue of Books Printed in England, Scotland, and Ireland 1475–1640*, vol. 3, ed. K.F. Pantzer and P.R. Rider, London, Bibliographical Society.

PARFITT, G. (ed.) (1988) B. Jonson, *The Complete Poems*, London, Penguin.

REES, J. (ed.) (1973) F. Greville: *Selected Writings*, London, Athlone Press.

ROBERTS, J. (ed.) (1992) M. Wroth: *The Poems*, Baton Rouge, Louisiana State University Press.

SAUNDERS, J.W. (1951) 'The stigma of print: a note on the social bases of Tudor poetry', *Essays in Criticism*, vol. 1, pp.139–64.

SHEPHERD, G. (ed.) (1973) P. Sidney: *An Apology for Poetry*, Manchester, Manchester University Press.

SMITH, G.G. (ed.) (1937) *Elizabethan Critical Essays*, vols. 1 and 2, Oxford, Oxford University Press; first published 1904.

SOWERBY, R. (1994) *The Classical Legacy in Renaissance Poetry*, London, Longman.

SPILLER, M. (1992) *The Development of the Sonnet: An Introduction*, London, Routledge.

SPUFFORD, M. (1981) *Small Books and Pleasant Histories: Popular Fiction and its Readership in Seventeenth-century England*, London, Methuen.

VICKERS, B. (1990) *In Defence of Rhetoric*, Oxford, Clarendon.

WILCOX, H.(ed.) (1996) *Women and Literature in Britain, 1500–1700*, Cambridge, Cambridge University Press.

Anthology and Reader sources

Walter Raleigh, The nimphs reply to the sheepheard: *Englands Helicon*, ed. H. Macdonald, London, Routledge & Kegan Paul, 1949, p.193 (Anthology, no. 43).

Virgil, Eclogue 5: *The Eclogues*, trans. G. Lee, Harmondsworth, Penguin, 1984, pp.63, 65, 67 (Anthology, no. 44).

John Donne, The bait: *The Complete English Poems of John Donne*, ed. C.A. Patrides, London, J.M. Dent, Everyman, 1985, pp.93–4 (Anthology, no. 45).

Francesco Petrarch, Sonnet 190: *Petrarch and Petrarchanism: The French and English Traditions*, New York, Barnes & Noble, 1980, pp.68–9 (Anthology, no. 46).

T.W. Baldwin, The Eton syllabus: *William Shakespere's Small Latine and Lesse Greeke*, Urbana, University of Illinois Press, 1944, vol. 1, pp.353–8 (Anthology, no. 47).

Figures of diction, from *Rhetorica ad Herennium*: trans. H. Caplan, London, Heinemann, 1981, pp.333–43 (Anthology, no. 48).

Fulke Greville, from *The Life of the Renowned Sir Philip Sidney: Selected Writings of Fulke Greville*, ed. J. Rees, London, Athlone Press, 1973, p.148 (Anthology, no. 49).

Edmund Spenser, the Argument, Embleme and Glosse from 'Maye': *The Works of Edmund Spenser*, ed. E. Greenlaw, C.G. Osgook, F.M. Padelford and R. Heffner, Baltimore, Johns Hopkins Press, 1943, pp.46, 55–8 (Anthology, no. 50).

John Bale, extract from *The Examinations of Anne Askew*: ed. E. Beilin, Oxford, Oxford University Press, 1996, pp.110–13, 124–7 (Anthology, no. 51).

Philip Sidney, from *An Apology for Poetry*: ed. G. Shepherd, Manchester, Manchester University Press, 1973, pp.100–8 (Anthology, no. 52).

George Puttenham, from *The Arte of English Poesie*: *Elizabethan Critical Essays*, ed. G.G. Smith, Oxford, Oxford University Press, 1937, vol. 2, pp.3–9 (Anthology, no. 53).

CHAPTER FIVE

The London stage

BY RICHARD DANSON BROWN

Objectives

The objectives of this chapter are that you should:

- further your understanding of the literary Renaissance in Britain through analysing the London stage;

- explore social contexts underlying the Elizabethan theatre through a detailed study of *The Merchant of Venice*;

- explore the literary contexts for comedy in the sixteenth century in order to develop your sense of the complex traditions manipulated in Shakespearean drama;

- develop your appreciation of the literary innovations generated by Shakespearean comedy through an analysis of the key roles and locations in *The Merchant of Venice*;

- analyse the play as a Renaissance drama.

Your first task if you are not familiar with the play will be to read *The Merchant of Venice*.

Introduction: dialogues with the dead

Stephen Greenblatt begins his book *Shakespearean Negotiations* by explaining what first motivated his study of Renaissance literature. He says, quite simply, that he 'began with the desire to speak with the dead' (Greenblatt, 1988, p.1). This is probably a fantasy we have all had in one form or another. Wouldn't it be marvellous if we could ask a person from the past why they had done or said a given thing that now seems inexplicable? Why did Queen Elizabeth I never marry? How many thousands of critical problems might be finally tidied away if we could have just half an hour with Shakespeare? Christopher Marlowe's *Doctor Faustus* (*c.*1588–9) exploits precisely this fantasy when, through black magic, Faustus conjures up a spirit in the form of Alexander the Great to entertain the emperor, Charles V.

But criticism can't provide this kind of magic; it isn't a literal form of time travel. Greenblatt mischievously suggests that 'literature professors are salaried, middle-class shamen' who enable a dialogue between living students and dead cultures to take place through the paradoxical medium of 'textual traces'. The paradox, or tension, (which Greenblatt rather overstates) is between our desire for dialogue with the dead and the literary constructs to which we look for that dialogue: we 'seek the living will of the dead in fictions, in places where there was no bodily being to begin with' (1988, p.1). When Faustus presents the emperor with a symbolic show of Alexander defeating Darius, and Charles tries to embrace the 'renowned Emperor' he thinks he sees, Faustus quickly reminds him that 'These are but shadows, not substantial'. Even a dramatized shaman, then, is unable to produce the 'bodily being' of the past. He can simulate the wart on the neck of Alexander's paramour, but he cannot actually allow the emperor the dialogue with Alexander which would 'satisfy [his] longing thoughts at full' (*Doctor Faustus* 4.1.102–15; line references are from Bevington and Rasmussen, 1995).

Nevertheless, literature and the other kinds of artistic and historical record this book explores give us the opportunity to stage an interactive dialogue with the past, rather than the dumb show provided by Faustus. Shakespeare won't literally answer us, but through our interrogation of his texts we can refine our understanding of him and his culture, and ultimately of ourselves and of our own historical moment. Let's put it like this. Though the search for the past in 'textual traces' may well be 'paradoxical', it is unlikely to be as one-dimensional as Emperor Charles's experience of the unresponsive shadow of Alexander the Great. Complex literary texts generate responses in us which motivate us to enrich our understanding of the individuals and cultures which generated them. In this way, our reading of the past – however paradoxical or problematic – has a chance of achieving a three-dimensionality lacking in Faustus's party piece.

In this chapter we shall be attempting to engage with the London stage at the end of the sixteenth century through one of Shakespeare's most celebrated plays, *The Merchant of Venice*. As you will discover, despite its familiarity *The Merchant* is a highly complex play, providing audiences and readers with a dizzying array of challenges and problems; I suggest that these difficulties are central to its long-lasting appeal. This chapter will allow you to draw your own informed conclusions about the play, but I also hope that you will be prepared to acknowledge the difficulties of ever making up your mind definitively about *The Merchant*.

Exercise

To give you a preliminary sense of the play's complexity, I'd like you to reread 1.1.1–56. When you've done this, try to write a short paragraph explaining why you think Antonio is unhappy. Then read the remainder of the scene. What support can you find in the second half of the scene for your original answer?

Discussion

The play opens with an enigma that is never fully resolved. Antonio tells his friends Salarino and Solanio that he doesn't know why he is 'so sad', or how he became unhappy. They give him three interpretations. Perhaps he's worried about his argosies (merchant ships) miscarrying on the high seas; perhaps he's in love; or else, in Solanio's contorted logic, Antonio is sad because he is not merry. When Bassanio, Lorenzo and Graziano enter, the conversation is broken off (this is a play of many interrupted conversations), never to be resumed. Yet Antonio's melancholy makes the audience acutely interested in this rich merchant. Why should he be so miserable? What's going on in this opening exchange?

Though Antonio's sadness is never conclusively explained, most critics make the assumption that it is connected with his feelings for Bassanio. When at the end of the scene (ll.113–85) Antonio and Bassanio discuss Bassanio's project for wooing Portia, Antonio asks 'tell me now what lady is the same ... that you today promised to tell me of' (1.1.119–20). Antonio, in other words, already knows about Bassanio's interest in Portia and may well be disturbed about the potential loss of his closest friend. This is a plausible explanation of Antonio's sadness; you may not have been convinced by his brief brushing aside of Solanio's suggestion that he is in love. Certainly, the other characters behave as though Antonio and Bassanio are intimate friends; Lorenzo comments 'My lord Bassanio, since you have found Antonio,/We two will leave you' (1.1.69–70). When Antonio and Bassanio are together, four is evidently a crowd.

But the point I want to emphasize is that neither this scene nor the play as a whole ever conclusively explains why Antonio was originally unhappy. We may assume that the root cause is his complex feelings for Bassanio, or we may follow Graziano in suggesting that Antonio is a cold fish, addicted to seeming wiser than in fact he is. Yet the text never unequivocally states 'Antonio is sad because of reason X'. The play as a whole gives him plenty of reasons for being sad – indeed desperate – yet at the beginning of 1.1 these are implicit rather than explicit. By trying to explain Antonio's melancholy, you have entered into the dynamics of this opening conversation and from there into the central concerns of the play as they open out in this scene. Keep your answer as a record of your first impressions both of the play and of Antonio himself. ❖

This opening enigma warns us that making sense of *The Merchant of Venice* will be a complex process which will involve a range of critical approaches and interpretative strategies. We begin by mapping out the social and historical circumstances which underlie English Renaissance drama before turning our attention to the new literary forms evidenced in plays like *The Merchant*. In this way, we should be able to establish a mediated conversation with the dead.

Social and historical contexts

In the section called 'The discovery of the world and of man' Burckhardt asks 'why did Italy produce no Shakespeare?' (1990, p.204). This is a troubling issue for Burckhardt. How could the Italians, 'the most developed people in Europe' (p.206), fail to produce 'a high development of the drama' (p.205) equal to their achievements in other art forms? His question is indicative of nineteenth-century Romantic views of Italian Renaissance drama and Shakespeare himself. Louise George Clubb observes that the Romantic critical tradition praised 'unclassical' writing at the expense of writing which copied classical examples. Yet the achievement of Italian Renaissance theatre according to Clubb is precisely its 'self-reproducing' recycling of the motifs, characters, plots and situations of classical drama (1989, p.7). Burckhardt and other late Romantic critics looked at Italian drama through Shakespeare-tinted spectacles, attacking it for lacking the originality neither it – nor Shakespeare – ever claimed to have.

Our concern is not directly with the drama of the Italian Renaissance. Burckhardt's question positions Italian theatre against the London stage, and specifically the stage of the pre-eminent Romantic literary icon William Shakespeare; in Burckhardt's words, 'Europe produced but one Shakespeare ... such a mind is the rarest of Heaven's gifts' (p.205). This positioning underlines a paradox: how is it that 'the most developed people in Europe' (the Italians) fail theatrically where a presumably less developed people (the English) succeed? As Clubb's work shows, such a paradox rests on a simplistic understanding of Italian drama. Does it, however, have any relevance to our understanding of the London stage?

Burckhardt's vocabulary now seems rather dated. His discrimination between developed and (implicitly) undeveloped peoples is particularly vulnerable to criticism. Yet despite this, Burckhardt is useful in identifying the problem of how we define Renaissance drama. Is this drama wholly original, or a product of many and varied cultural antecedents? In a sense, this question charts the difference between Romantic readings of literature, which privilege originality, and more recent readings, which seek to locate the literature of the past more firmly in its various contexts. In Clubb's example, the Romantic (or Burckhardtian) reading of Italian Renaissance drama makes the mistake of minimizing its literary context. As a late twentieth-century literary shaman, my aim will be to avoid such an omission. Though we notoriously don't know a lot about Shakespeare's life as a private individual, we do know a great deal about his cultural and literary roots.

Towards Shakespeare's theatre

Exercise

Greenblatt wanted to 'speak with the dead'. I would like you to imagine going further: to travel in time back to the late 1590s to attend one of the first performances of *The Merchant of Venice*. What mental picture do you have of Elizabethan London? Try to write down a few phrases that come to mind before you go on.

Discussion

Imagining London four hundred years ago isn't all that easy. You may have remembered Laurence Olivier's film of *Henry V* (released 1944), with its colourful recreation of a performance of the play at the Globe, or you may have seen images like Wenceslas Hollar's *Long View of London* (Figure 5.1, overleaf). This etching features the best pictorial record we have of the second Globe, rebuilt after the original was burnt down during a performance of Shakespeare's *Henry VIII* in 1613; it has recently been used as vital primary evidence for the modern rebuilding of the Globe (Gurr, 1997, pp.36–47). With these images in mind, you probably have a sense of the beauty of Renaissance London. Hollar's London looks magnificent; as Graham Parry puts it, Hollar 'sees noble prospects everywhere, stately cities lying by great rivers' (1980, pp.14–15). Yet as Parry further notes, Hollar's London depends on careful editing: he removes the 'circumambient squalor of the age' to provide 'not just a direct transcription of the scene, but rather an image of what the cultivated Englishman wished to see' of seventeenth-century London (pp.14–15). ❖

Images like Hollar's, then, can be as misleadingly glossy as Olivier's as guides to the London in which Shakespeare worked. My imagined picture of Elizabethan London is rather smellier, rather more sordidly physical than Hollar's – I would want it to include some of what Parry calls the 'squalor of the age'. Put another way, though Hollar provides a black and white still of how London looked to a court artist in the 1630s, he does not give a full-colour, three-dimensional representation of the scene he witnessed.

But is it possible to get such a view? Yes, if we're prepared to stimulate our imaginations through other sources. Before we consider the theatre which first presented *The Merchant*, I'd like you to take a walk through the streets of London in 1598 in the company of the satirist Everard Guilpin.

Figure 5.1 Detail of Wenceslas Hollar's *Long View of London*, published in 1647 from drawings made in the 1630s, showing the Globe and the bear-baiting house (note that the names were accidentally transposed during the engraving process). Guildhall Library, Dept of Prints, London

Exercise

Read the extract from Guilpin's *Skialetheia*, Satire 5, in *The Penguin Book of Renaissance Verse* (Norbrook, 1993, no. 186). What physical sense does his description focus on? How would you characterize Guilpin's attitude towards London and its inhabitants?

Discussion

Guilpin's London is a pre-eminently noisy environment. His text is an aural assault in which the reader must endure the 'hotch-potch of so many noyses' from squeaking cart-wheels to brawling drunkards. Guilpin ironically shows that the pleasures of 'an idle Citty-walke' are the 'troublesome and tedious ... Chaous of rude sounds' with which London abounds. As I've said, Guilpin was a satirist; you could say that just as it was Hollar's business to make London look as attractive as possible, so it was Guilpin's to make it sound as ugly as possible. There's a lot of truth in this view. As he urges in the final paragraph of this extract, 'The Cittie is the mappe of vanities'. Guilpin takes us round London not to praise it but rather to present it as a tremendous exhibition of human folly – a *fin de siècle* theme park which parades the vices of 'unsufferable inhumanitie' to a cacophonous soundtrack. Moreover, Guilpin makes us uncomfortably aware of the people who live in London in a way Hollar's *Long View* cannot. The university-educated Guilpin disdains these people. They

are the 'unsufferable' and 'rotten-throated' lower orders whose
unholy din abuses the 'Ethicke soule', or moral observer,
commenting on them. But even this apparently realistic description of
London belongs to a literary tradition we can trace back to a classical
original: Guilpin imitates the Roman poet Juvenal, whose Third Satire
provides a similarly unpleasant walking tour of imperial Rome. ❖

Although Guilpin's poem is as bounded by genre and class interests
as Hollar's etching, it does none the less provide a more immediate
sense of late 1590s London: a noisy, amoral city full of vivid human
interactions – carters facing up to each other to see who gives way
first; 'swaggering knaves' arguing over a whore; a Falstaffian 'Ale-
knight' disputing the size of his bar bill. And in the midst of this
colourful scene, a chorus of 'knaves,/Whores, Bedles, bawdes and
Sergeants' pay testimony to their attendance at the popular theatre by
chanting 'Kemps Jigge'. William Kemp was the chief clown with the
Lord Chamberlain's Men, Shakespeare's company, who probably took
the part of Launcelot Gobbo in the first performances of *The
Merchant* (Halio, 1993, p.60). His jigs were bawdy and highly popular
amalgams of dance and song performed at the end of the plays in the
public amphitheatres. Indirectly, Guilpin's tour of London has taken
us nearer to Shakespeare's theatre.

When we think of Shakespeare's theatre, almost inevitably we think of
the Globe and the glorious 1990s reconstruction of it on London's
Bankside. Yet the first Globe wasn't built until 1599, while *The
Merchant* was probably first performed in 1596 or 97 (see Halio,
pp.27–9). So where was the play premiered? *The Merchant*'s debut was
probably at the Theatre, built in Shoreditch in 1576 by James
Burbage, father of Richard, Shakespeare's leading actor (Gurr, 1980,
p.226). We know very little about this theatre in comparison with the
greater information we have on later arenas like the Rose and the
Globe. However, the Theatre was intimately connected to the Globe,
since its dismantled timbers were used as the frame for the building
of the Globe on Bankside in 1599. As Gurr remarks, 'in its basic
layout and audience capacity it must have closely resembled the later
playhouse' (1987, p.13).

So what would the Shoreditch Theatre have looked like? The only
contemporaneous image of the building (see Figure 5.2, overleaf) is
indistinct and relatively uninformative; fortunately, however, there are
descriptions of London theatres from the late 1590s written by two
continental visitors, Johannes De Witt from Holland and Thomas
Platter from Switzerland.

Figure 5.2 Detail of the Theatre and the Curtain, from *The View of the Cittye of London from the North towards the South, c.1597–9*, in the manuscript journal of Abram Booth. Universiteit Utrecht MS 1198 Hist. 147

Read the extracts from De Witt's and Platter's accounts of their visits to London theatres in the Anthology (nos. 54 and 55). What impression do you think these travellers have of the London stage?

Both De Witt and Platter clearly see their visits to London theatres as being of great interest to their countrymen. De Witt, indeed, made a sketch of the Swan theatre (Figure 5.3) which has been a significant piece of evidence for the reconstruction of the Globe's interior (Gurr, 1997, p.28). The key impression, then, which the London theatres made on these European visitors was of something extraordinary – something beyond their local experience. De Witt observes the 'notable beauty' of four London amphitheatres: the Rose, the Swan, the Theatre and the Curtain. Platter similarly gives an elaborate description both of the playing arena and of the various provisions these theatres made for the paying public. ❖

De Witt and Platter must have had experience of theatre-going in Holland and Switzerland, but crucially they had not come across amphitheatres on the scale of the Swan or the Globe; as De Witt notes with obvious wonder, the Swan 'in fact accommodates three thousand people in its seats'. Not many, you might think, compared with the tens of thousands that can be crammed into modern football stadia. But to understand these numbers, we must appreciate that Elizabethan London was on a different scale from that of a modern city. Though its population doubled during the sixteenth century,

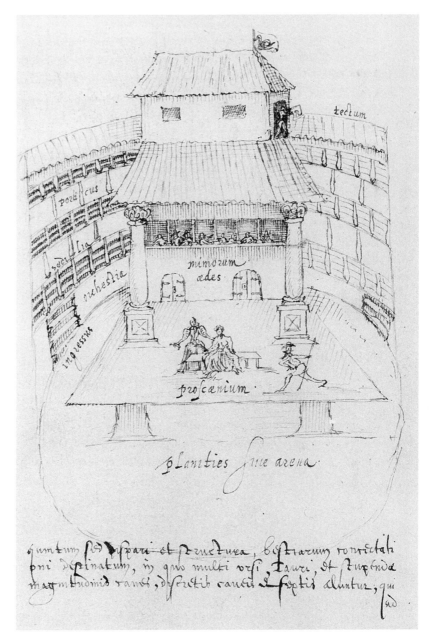

Figure 5.3 The Swan playhouse, a drawing by Arendt van Buchel from Johannes De Witt's sketch made in 1596. Universiteit Utrecht MS 842, fol. 132r

reaching 200,000 by 1600 and making it one of the largest cities in Europe, it was still on a relatively modest scale compared with modern conurbations. In this context, the 'three thousand' paying customers De Witt records in the Swan was an impressively large audience; such a mass assembly would have been rare anywhere in Elizabethan England, since only the largest churches could have accommodated so many people.

The point I want to stress is that in terms of continental European experience, theatres like the Globe and the Theatre itself were highly unusual. There were no Dutch, French or even Italian Globes. This is important because propitious theatrical conditions are vital to the development of sophisticated drama: without viable stages, you don't get complex plays. Burckhardt's explanation of the absence of an Italian Shakespeare makes a related point: 'The stage ... in its perfection is a late product of every civilization' (p.205). In the context of our broad concern in this book with the definition of Renaissance culture, the Elizabethan amphitheatre is an important phenomenon. Are these theatres, which staged the high point of European Renaissance drama, recreations of classical amphitheatres or something rather different?

De Witt's final sentence suggests that the Swan was an imitation of classical theatre design: he sketches it 'since it *appears to imitate* in its shape the form of a Roman structure'. I've highlighted the phrase 'appears to imitate' because it indicates De Witt's uncertainty. He thinks the London theatres must imitate Roman originals – hence his use of the term 'amphitheatres' (*amphiteatra* in his Latin) – but he resists an unequivocal assertion of a relationship between the two. The impression De Witt gives is that he is awed by the scale and beauty of the London amphitheatres, but that he isn't wholly persuaded of their basis in classical design.

De Witt's caution is partly in accord with the views of modern scholars. As you can see from Gurr's description of the amphitheatres in the Reader (no. 15), the external design of the theatres derives from native traditions: animal-baiting arenas (see Figure 5.1) and the coaching inns in which morality plays had been staged. Yet, as John Romayne observes, there was probably a strong contrast between the amphitheatres' plain exteriors and their highly decorated interiors (1997, p.121). The stage in particular would have featured intricate decoration based on classical precedents:

> Amongst the very few descriptive notes on the interior of the theatre which survive, there is enough reference to marbling and columns to suggest that the structure was using and combining referentially classical elements in a way designed to signify 'classical Rome' to the spectator.
>
> (Keenan and Davidson, 1997, p.147)

On the basis of this informed conjecture, the stage of the new Globe is elaborately decorated, featuring, for example, wooden pillars painted to resemble marble and hanging cloths to adorn the discovery space at the back of the stage. The gaudy, almost psychedelic, interior of the new Globe may not embody our idea of classical Rome, but it may have to an Elizabethan audience. Figure 5.4, showing Shylock in a 1998 production of *The Merchant* at the Globe, should give you an idea of the theatre's elaborate interior decor – you can see the painted cloth or arras directly at the rear of the stage area.

So the amphitheatres looked neoclassical to their 1590s audiences, though their design also recalls popular English arenas. But irrespective of their origins, the theatres were impressive to travellers and attractive to large numbers of paying Londoners. At this point we can draw a parallel between the mixed appearance of the Elizabethan theatres and the mixed dramatic modes of the plays presented on these stages. As we shall see with *The Merchant*, while the play has an Italian setting and numerous mythological allusions, it is not an imitation of classical comedy. Rather, like the theatre in which it was first staged, it is an amalgam of modes and motifs. Similarly, *The Witch of Edmonton* (analysed in Book 3 in this series) is a play which amalgamates witch narrative, domestic tragedy and knock-about farce. Such mixing of modes is characteristic of English Renaissance culture.

Figure 5.4 Production of *The Merchant of Venice* at Shakespeare's Globe, 1998, directed by Richard Olivier, Norbert Kentrup as Shylock. Photo: John Trapper

So how did these theatres come into being? And from this, how did they become hosts to the drama of mixed motif in which Shakespeare excelled? To answer these questions we'll need to look at a range of complex factors: religious and demographic change, Elizabethan schooling, and the changing tastes of audiences in the 1590s.

Protestantism and the theatre

The Reformation had an enormous impact on all areas of life in sixteenth-century England. From the 1530s, traditional religious and theological ideas were overturned by a new orthodoxy, Protestantism. By the 1560s and 70s – the period during which Shakespeare was growing up – the polarity between Catholic and Protestant interpretations of Christianity had become ever more acute. Theologians on both sides of the divide underlined the impossibility of remaining neutral or 'indifferent' to religious upheaval. After 1570, when Pope Pius V excommunicated Elizabeth I, English Catholics were put in the invidious position of having to choose between their *religious* duty to conspire against their apostate queen and their *political* loyalty to the crown. If you were a Catholic living in England in the 1580s and 90s you may have felt that you were living through a cold war as you were torn between these competing loyalties. John Donne, who was brought up as a Catholic but subsequently converted to Protestantism, records his spiritual dilemma in 'Satyre 3' (Norbrook, no. 256).

Art – especially visual art and drama – was embroiled in these changes (these are discussed in more detail in Book 3, Chapter 3). The process of reforming the English church, initiated during the latter half of Henry VIII's reign, quickly gathered pace when the Protestant faction at court came to power with the accession of Edward VI (1547–53). Images and other church furnishings were destroyed or sold because they conflicted with the Protestant belief that salvation could not be gained by good works or through the intercession of the saints. After a brief Catholic reaction under Mary Tudor (1553–8), the position of Protestantism as the state religion was confirmed by the policies of Elizabeth I (1558–1603). The Thirty-nine Articles of Religion (1563) were an attempt to define religious orthodoxy. They reflect the English church's growing commitment to Calvinism, which essentially ruled out human free will. But this hardline theology created new divisions between those conservatives – led by Elizabeth – who considered that the outward process of reform had gone far enough and those radical Protestants who considered that a true godly revolution was under way. The latter, who gradually became known as Puritans, demanded both further reformation of the church (removing all vestiges of Catholicism from worship) and the establishment of a culture of godliness based upon moral regeneration and spiritual purity. As part of this reform programme, drama was singled out by Puritan polemicists of the 1580s as a particular object of vilification.

English medieval drama had consisted of two major forms: mystery plays (cycles of plays which dramatized key moments from the Bible, written and performed in local communities) and morality plays (allegorical representations of the soul's conflict with temptation). But although mystery plays were suppressed during the sixteenth century, this was, as Norman Sanders records, a slow and piecemeal process, informed as much by an official desire 'to regulate all popular activities' as by ideological zeal against traditional religion (1980, p.7). Meanwhile, the other traditional form of drama in Britain, the morality play, was used by dramatists like John Bale as a vehicle of Protestant propaganda in the 1530s and 40s. These politicized moralities partly fell into decline with the accession of Elizabeth who, despite her lukewarm Protestantism, was intent on 'not having her religious settlement disturbed by the drama or anything else' (Sanders, 1980, p.21).

The major point I want you to think about here is that the cultural and political processes which informed the Reformation also had a tremendous impact on shaping the kinds of play that were staged in the last two decades of the sixteenth century. Patrick Collinson's distinction between the 'iconoclastic' Reformation culture of the 1540s and the 'iconophobic' Reformation culture of the 1580s suggests that the moralities also declined because religious radicals had re-evaluated the moral role of art (Collinson, 1986). For anti-theatrical controversialists like Philip Stubbes, in his *Anatomie of Abuses* (1583), and the city fathers, who controlled popular activity within London, drama was fundamentally immoral. Because of this disapproval the amphitheatres were located on the fringes of London: Shoreditch and Bankside were areas outside the city walls and hence outside the city fathers' jurisdiction. For Collinson, 1540s iconoclasts rejected traditional Catholic imagery, while 1580s iconophobes had become hostile to artistic representations of all kinds. For Puritan controversialists, representations of God were *less* acceptable than:

> the wanton profanity of secular comedy. So it was that on the eve of its greatest achievements, the English theatre was not available as a medium to explore and present the drama of salvation.
>
> (Collinson, 1986, p.11)

Put like this, we can see that the drama of the London stage, which was both commercial in outlook and secular in content, was made possible by the Puritan rejection of all artistic expression. The moral relativism now especially prized in Shakespearean drama is contingent on the 'iconophobic' abandonment of drama as a didactic tool.

Exercise

Reread Portia's speech on mercy (4.1.181–202), making use of Halio's notes. Do you think there is anything specifically Protestant about Portia's mercy? Make a few brief notes.

Discussion

Though Portia deals with mercy in a way that most sixteenth-century Christians would have endorsed, I think we can detect a Protestant inflection to her speech. Halio notes that 'in the course of justice none of us/Should see salvation' recalls Psalm 143 and the Geneva Bible's fearsome gloss, 'in God's sight all men are sinners'. What Halio doesn't tell you is that underlying this warning is the extraordinarily innovative stress that Protestantism placed on original sin as an ineradicable stain on the human soul. This can best be understood through the ninth Article of Religion, which defines original sin as:

> the fault and corruption of every man, that naturally is ingendered of the offspring of *Adam*; whereby man is very far gone from original righteousness, and is of his own nature inclined to evil ... in every person born into this world, it deserveth God's wrath and damnation.

> (Book of Common Prayer)

In reminding Shylock of the 'course of justice' which necessarily damns all 'of us', Portia implicitly appeals to her Protestant audience's basic theological values, in particular the idea that God's condemnation is only lifted for 'them that believe and are baptized'. This is the Protestant doctrine of justification by faith – that is, the idea that one can only be saved by one's faith in God's mercy as opposed to any good deeds one might do. Read like this, Shylock would be in the classic Protestant double bind: even if he were to show mercy, the good deed would not necessarily bring spiritual good. We should also remember that the fictive scenario of the play is concerned with Catholics and Jewish aliens within Venice. The religious background of *The Merchant* is layered with such rich complications between fact and fiction, between audience and drama. ❖

We should also be aware that Portia's speech on mercy is just one moment in *The Merchant*. It is not the whole of the play's meaning. Though a 1590s audience would have recognized familiar theological concepts within it, the same audience probably would not have seen it as the play's defining moral statement. Halio calls it a 'set speech' (p.197), and it is best understood in this sense: as a performance on the theme of mercy. Portia performs mercy in terms her audience would immediately recognize as orthodox. That orthodoxy is restricted to the Christian Venetians on stage and the Protestant audience: its terminology necessarily excludes Shylock, the Jew, to whom it is ostensibly addressed. Shylock's imperviousness to Portia's mercy could moreover license the anti-Semitism of both the Christian characters *and* the Elizabethan audience.

To recap, the Reformation in Britain was an attenuated process which paradoxically fostered the emergence of commercial drama in London through the ideological shift from iconoclasm to iconophobia. None the less, as Portia's speech demonstrates, the secular drama of Shakespeare's stage is always linguistically alive to biblical allusion and it derives much of its theatrical energy from the sixteenth-century European landscape of theological controversy.

Demographic change

As we've seen, Tudor London was a growing city, doubling its population between 1500 and 1600. This expansion was chiefly due to what Gurr calls 'the growth of a cash nexus in London' – the city's emergence as a major commercial centre (1987, p.50). Such changes in the human geography of London had a decisive impact on its drama. Rapid social change created a large potential audience with complex concerns off which the new drama could feed.

Yet much contemporary literature dealing with social issues was decidedly uncomfortable with such social change. Keith Wrightson observes that the changing shape of social identities in early modern England generated a rhetoric which attempted to discriminate between social groups: he charts the emergence of a language which distinguished the 'better sort' from the 'meaner sort' (1994). For example, Spenser's *Mother Hubberds Tale*, a satiric beast fable, presents an upwardly mobile Fox and Ape as amoral rogues who attempt to revise their social identity through a series of disguises. Yet in *The Ruines of Time* from the same *Complaints* collection (1591) (Oram et al., 1989), Spenser vigorously protests against the attempts of the ruling elite to stifle social promotion:

> O griefe of griefes, o gall of all good heartes,
> To see that vertue should dispised bee
> Of him, that first was raisde for vertuous parts,
> And now broad spreading like an aged tree
> Lets none shoot up, that nigh him planted bee.
>
> (ll.449–53)

This is a satiric portrait of William Cecil, Lord Burghley, Elizabeth's lord high treasurer, whom Spenser believed was hostile to his art and his career. Spenser implies that the elite should 'raise' (or reward) the intelligent (or virtuous) from whatever social background they emerge. Another social commentator, Sir Thomas Smith, had grudgingly made a similar point in *De republica anglorum* (written 1565, published 1583). Yet there's a difference between believing that loyal poets should be promoted and advocating the Fox's individualist ethos: 'Let us our fathers heritage divide,/And chalenge to our selves our portions dew' (ll.136–7). As fictions like *Mother Hubberds Tale* demonstrate, the perception that the social world had become fluid generated anxious debate. Indeed, Greenblatt's *Renaissance Self-fashioning* (1980) has characterized the Renaissance in Britain as a period in which the conception of the individual changes from a static to a mobile model. For Greenblatt, the self becomes something that can be manipulated, or fashioned, at will. Again, Spenser's Fox provides a succinct summary:

> Such will we fashion both our selves to bee,
> Lords of the world, and so will wander free
> Where so us listeth, uncontrol'd of anie.
>
> (ll.167–9)

In other words, sixteenth-century individualists inhabited a highly controlled world. But through their ambiguous self-fashioning, they attempted to redefine themselves as 'Lords of the world', exhibiting a transgressive and socially disquieting sense of their potential freedom of action. Elizabethan London, we can suggest, was a similarly ambiguous social milieu, an expanding commercial centre whose rulers none the less attempted to impose strict controls on social mobility. Such an environment produced a socially varied audience for new plays.

Exercise

Reread Thomas Platter's account of his visit to the London theatres (Anthology, no. 55). What does this tell you about the 1590s audience?

Discussion

Platter identifies three kinds of spectator: those who pay a penny to stand in the yard; those who pay two pennies to 'sit more comfortably' in the galleries, and those who pay three pennies 'to sit in the most comfortable place on a cushion' immediately to the rear of the stage. You can see these elite spectators in De Witt's drawing (Figure 5.3), clearly supporting Platter's remark that these could both 'see everything' and 'also be seen' by others. In Platter's description the amphitheatres embody social stratification. We move up from the lowly groundlings, exposed to all weathers and the discomfort of standing, to the wealthier spectators, simultaneously exhibiting themselves and cushioning their bottoms. ❖

In relation to *The Merchant* we must also consider those people living in London who were not native English. There were numerous European visitors to London and its theatres during Shakespeare's career; Gurr includes an extraordinary anecdote about the Venetian ambassador Foscarini, who visited the Curtain theatre in disguise in 1613 (1987, p.71). Such accounts demonstrate that Elizabethan audiences were not ideologically or culturally monochrome. Yet as tourists rather than residents, Platter and Foscarini are unrepresentative of the vast body of Londoners. The question remains: was there a community of London 'aliens' similar to that in Venice depicted in *The Merchant*?

Exercise

Read pages 1–4 of Halio's introduction. Identify the issue you think is most relevant to an understanding of Shylock and make a note explaining your decision.

Discussion

Halio's account of the treatment of Jews in Renaissance Europe makes sober reading. Jews were seen as a cursed race (because of the widespread belief that they betrayed Christ), who therefore 'could not claim inalienable citizenship in any country'. This is the fact that I would single out because it helps to illuminate how Portia finally undoes Shylock. As an 'alien' Shylock has tried to kill Antonio, a 'citizen' of Venice, and is therefore at the mercy of the duke (4.1.344–59). This detail sharply underlines the alien's anomalous position: he has fewer legal rights than the citizen. Shylock's religious identity puts him at a fundamental disadvantage in sixteenth-century Europe. ❖

You may, however, have chosen a different issue. Halio explains why Jews were popularly seen as usurers and outlines the history of Jews in England after the expulsion of 1290. Here we also learn that Shakespeare could have had first-hand experience of converted Jews living in England. James Shapiro's *Shakespeare and the Jews* summarizes the current state of scholarship on this vexed issue:

> There were Jews living in Shakespeare's England, though probably never more than a couple of hundred at any given time in the whole country, a very small number in a population of roughly four million, and a small number even to the number of aliens residing in London.
>
> (1996, p.76)

Shapiro also argues that sixteenth-century London was a more varied community than we may have assumed, in which aliens comprised a significant minority of London's population. Though the majority of these people were of European origin, 'a small number of Blacks and Jews were crowded within London's walls' (1996, p.181); Anne Laurence estimates that in late sixteenth-century London 'about 5 per cent of the population was from outside England' (1994, p.19). But we should also add that the larger groups of non-English settlers in London were of Scottish, Irish, Welsh, French or Dutch origins: black and Jewish people would have constituted a tiny minority of this immigrant population.

What are we to make of this evidence? For Shapiro, Elizabethan London 'was far from the homogenous world that is all too often nostalgically imagined' (1996, pp.180–1). Thinking back to Laurence Olivier's film of *Henry V*, it's easy to see the cultural depth of this nostalgic construction. As Shakespeare became England's national poet in the eighteenth and nineteenth centuries, so his original audience became an idealized embodiment of white Englishness. Shapiro's study vitally demonstrates that this paradigm never existed. Even during the 1590s the streets (and presumably theatres) of London were not the preserve of a monoglot, monocultural English people of the kind glorified by Olivier's film.

A more culturally varied London has implications for our understanding of its stage. As we have seen, playgoers were socially diverse; now we can see that there was a comparable cultural diversity in sixteenth-century London. Yet, as Gurr's *Playgoing in Shakespeare's London* (1987) shows, we have regrettably few records of the kinds of people who went to the theatres. It would seem unlikely that many of England's tiny Jewish population would have found their way to early performances of *The Merchant* at the Theatre. But this unlikelihood is less immediately important than the emerging complexity of our view of the London stage and its audience. Shakespeare's socially and culturally diverse audience was necessarily interested in plays which reflected its particular concerns. Consequently, *The Merchant* focuses on venture capitalism and legal disputation. It does not, however, journalistically document the financial and legal situation of late 1590s London. Rather, through its Italian setting and its amalgam of different narrative strands, it reflects on experiences which many of its first spectators would have recognized: money lending, court pleading, the desire to make a financially advantageous marriage. We now need to ask what level of education these spectators might have attained.

Elizabethan education

Elizabethan audiences, then, were socially and culturally diverse. They were also living through a period of unprecedented religious polarization. This made them highly attuned to the Bible, yet receptive to the new drama being played at Shoreditch and Bankside. Like any audience, this one demanded that it should be entertained. And *The Merchant* is a sophisticated entertainment.

Sophistication raises the issue of Elizabethan education. How would Shakespeare's audience have responded to his learned and allusive play? Ceri Sullivan has already discussed education and literacy in sixteenth-century England in Chapter 4. She stresses the complex rhetorical skills taught in grammar schools and universities and the gender exclusivity of these institutions. Such an education equipped its male subjects with literary abilities, created by hours of intensive reading and remodelling of classical exemplars. Focusing on Shakespeare's knowledge of Ovid, Jonathan Bate summarizes the kind of curriculum Shakespeare enjoyed (or endured) at Stratford Grammar School:

> The grammar-school curriculum was limited but intense. It depended on learning by rote: Shakespeare and his contemporaries had Latin words and structures ingrained upon their memories in such a way that classical influences would inevitably shape their verbal forms in later life.

(1993, p.19)

As we shall see, *The Merchant* is rich in classical allusions; it is worth noting that Shakespeare's education would have equipped him with a reading knowledge of such important classical authors as Ovid, Plautus and Terence. But for now, let's look at one brief example of what Bate calls 'classical shaping'. When Bassanio first tells Antonio about Portia, immediately after naming her, he adds this qualification: his Portia is 'nothing undervalued/To Cato's daughter, Brutus' Portia' (1.1.165–6). To an audience familiar with Shakespeare's work this looks like an obvious allusion. Because we've seen Brutus's wife Portia movingly portrayed in *Julius Caesar*, we locate Bassanio's Portia – and his sense of her value – through her classical namesake. But we have to be careful: *Julius Caesar* was a later play than *The Merchant*, first performed in 1599. Thomas Platter evidently saw an early performance at the Globe in the same year. In making sense of this allusion, *The Merchant*'s first audience would have been guided not by Shakespeare's play but by its knowledge of his sources – in this case, Plutarch's *Life of Marcus Brutus*. Shakespeare himself would not have read Plutarch in the original Greek. Ceri Sullivan has drawn your attention to the outpouring of classical translations in Elizabethan England. Shakespeare and most of his fellow countrymen would have read Plutarch in Sir Thomas North's 1579 translation.

We can move from this two-line allusion to the play as a whole. I've called *The Merchant* 'learned and allusive'. From one angle, this is undoubtedly true. If you browse through the vast wealth of secondary material this play – like all of Shakespeare's works – has generated, it's hard not to see it as a text bursting with allusions to, and recollections of, other texts. Yet in the late 1590s *The Merchant* existed only as a performed script that you could see acted out at the Theatre. As such, its allusiveness was necessarily conditioned by its primary function: to entertain paying customers. As Ceri Sullivan reminds us in Chapter 4, literacy rates among the labouring classes and women were much smaller than they were with Wrightson's 'better sort' – the more affluent social classes. To return to my earlier question: how would Shakespeare's audience have responded to this learned and allusive play? James Roberts would not have printed it in 1600 if he did not believe there was a market for the text (Halio, pp.84–5). So we can suggest that the various classical allusions the play utilizes formed part of a common culture between the grammar school educated Shakespeare and the majority of his audience: even though literacy rates are unreliable, we should remember that the ability to read was much more widespread than the ability to write. 'Brutus' Portia' could have been comprehensible to someone whose literacy was restricted to reading, or to someone who had heard North's text read out loud. Through a combination of the dissemination of classical translations and the formidable rhetoricity of Elizabethan schooling, sophisticated scripts like *The Merchant* were capable of holding the attention of their diverse London audience.

Renaissance theatre?

We began this section by trying to imagine our way back to an early performance of *The Merchant* at the Theatre in Shoreditch. Since then, we've looked at the appearance of Elizabethan amphitheatres alongside the religious, demographic and educational milieux of that first audience. Along the way, I've tried to convey an impression of London in the 1590s and the way that these overlapping cultural and ideological concerns might have influenced and shaped Shakespeare and his audience. Now let's see what these forces can tell us about Renaissance culture in 1590s England.

This account of the London stage has so far paid little attention to the influence of the court on Shakespearean drama. But as you can see from Halio's introduction (p.59), the first recorded performance of the play was at James I's court in 1605. As elsewhere in Europe, court culture and patronage were a major influence on artistic activity. Shakespeare's company were called the Lord Chamberlain's Men in the 1590s before coming under direct royal patronage as the King's Men in the next decade. Court protection and patronage of the playing companies were vital to the survival of the drama in the face of the city fathers' continued hostility. Yet Shakespearean drama was not exclusively an aristocratic phenomenon, unlike, for example, Ben Jonson's country house poetry. It's worth considering that while court performance was the 'ultimate goal of all the players' as a sign of success, court patronage brought prestige rather than wealth: 'The fee for taking a play to court was £10, comparable to the income they would get from a good day in their common playhouse' (Gurr, 1980, pp.23, 25).

The amphitheatres, moreover, were extraordinary places to stage plays. Though the physical space provided by the court may have been more opulent, we should remember that in the 1590s plays were not primarily designed for such performances. Even the most overwhelming court hall – like the first Banqueting House in Whitehall (1581–2) – would not have had the same adaptability as the amphitheatre stage, with its two playing levels and discovery space at the back of the stage. You can see these features in both De Witt's sketch (Figure 5.3) and the photo from a recent performance at the reconstructed Globe (Figure 5.4).

It is therefore tempting to see the amphitheatre as a distinctive vernacular contribution to European Renaissance culture, designed, as Keenan and Davidson argue, 'to signify "classical Rome" to the spectator' (1997, p.147). Yet the picture is more complicated than this. While stage decoration may have recalled Elizabethan ideas of imperial Rome, the overall design of the amphitheatres remained close to that of the animal-baiting arenas, as Hollar's confused labelling of the second Globe and the bear pit demonstrates (Figure 5.1). Moreover, the similarity of the Globe to the bear-baiting arena makes us alive to the fact that the London stage shared its space with other popular activities like prostitution and the baiting of live animals. You have already experienced Everard Guilpin's satiric negotiation through this milieu. Samuel Rowlands in an epigram of 1600 suggests that playgoing and whoring were cognate activities for young men:

> Speak gentlemen, what shall we do today?
> Or shall we to the Globe to see a play?
> Or visit Shoreditch for a bawdy house?
> (Gurr, 1987, p.214)

Ironically, this picture of playgoing with its associated immorality is similar to that painted by the lord mayor when, in November 1593, he protested to Lord Burghley about the theatres:

> the quality of such as frequent the sayed playes, beeing the ordinary places of meeting for all the vagrant persons & maisterles men that hang about the Citie, theeves, horsestealers, whoremoongers, coozeners, connycatching persones,[1] practizers of treason, & other such lyke ...
>
> (Gurr, 1987, p.210)

---

[1] 'Connycatchers' were professional villains, skilled in a range of deceits from crooked card playing to the cutting of purses. Ben Jonson's *Bartholomew Fair* (first performed 1614) dramatizes a wide range of these activities.

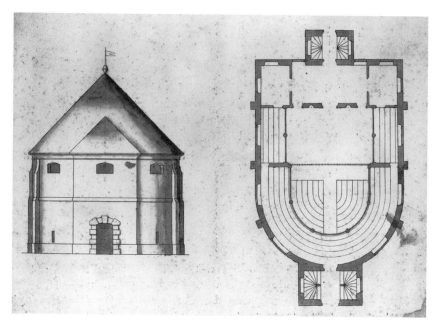

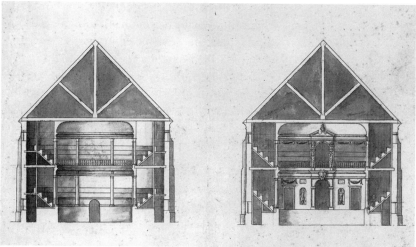

Figure 5.5 Inigo Jones's plans for a roofed theatre, possibly the Cockpit in Drury Lane or the Phoenix. Collection of drawings by Inigo Jones and John Webb, sheets 7B and 7C. Reproduced by permission of the Provost and Fellows of Worcester College, Oxford

So what are we to make of the London stage? Is it chiefly a reflection of European Renaissance culture – a Burckhardtian rediscovery of the classics – or is it rather a separate development embedded in popular dramatic traditions and the more seamy margins of sixteenth-century London?

Such questions are not easy to resolve, especially in the context of the 1590s. After the accession of James I in 1603 the King's Men appear to have aimed to cater more for an aristocratic audience by opening an indoor private theatre at Blackfriars in 1609, at which they could charge higher prices to a smaller audience. *The Witch of Edmonton* was first performed at a rival indoor playhouse, the Cockpit, by Prince Charles's Men in 1621; this theatre was probably constructed according to Inigo Jones's ultra neoclassical plans (see Figure 5.5) (Gurr, 1987, p.22). During the 1590s, however, the major source of revenue for Shakespeare's company was the popular stage of the Theatre.

There is no simple way of making up your mind about these issues. If you go to the new Globe – the best substitute we have for actual time travel – you may be struck (as I was) by the contrast between its plain and familiar exterior and its colourful and unfamiliar interior. In this marvellous reconstruction, it feels as if you are in a building facing in two directions at once. The stage explicitly invokes an idea of the classical past, while the surrounding building is rooted in the indigenous designs of thatched roofs and timber framing. As we shall see in more detail, the plays watched by audiences in the 1590s are similarly lodged between Renaissance literary culture imported from the continent and more native theatrical traditions.

New literary forms

So the London stage came into being through a range of complex and often contradictory factors. Burckhardt's quasi-mystical view that Shakespeare was a singular genius – 'the rarest of Heaven's gifts' (p.205) – begins to look like an inadequate explanation of English Renaissance drama. Of course, Burckhardt wasn't centrally concerned with Shakespeare; this is a passing remark rather than a sustained analysis. None the less, it is indicative of post-Romantic readings of Shakespeare: the all-conquering Bard who seemed to emerge from nowhere to revolutionize literature. From an early twenty-first-century perspective we can see that Shakespeare and his theatre emerged from very specific social and historical contexts. Now we need to look directly at the literary forms Shakespeare inherited and how he adapted and changed them in *The Merchant*.

Origins and ideas of comedy

Comedy is a notoriously slippery category. In this section we shall explore the comic traditions available to Shakespeare in an attempt to decide what kind of comedy *The Merchant* is and how it fits in with Shakespeare's other comedies. Though James Roberts, the printer of the first quarto edition of the play (dated 1600), calls it 'The most excellent Historie of the *Merchant of Venice*' (Halio, pp.84–5), it is not a history play which dramatizes political narrative like *Henry V.*

Roberts uses 'Historie' as synonym for 'tale'. As the rest of the title page shows, he was not categorizing the play's genre so much as describing it as an exciting story to entice readers to buy it. *The Merchant* was accordingly placed among the comedies in the folio of Shakespeare's plays published in 1623. But what is comedy? And what did comedy mean to Shakespeare and his audience?

Exercise

It would now be useful for you to jot down the qualities you associate with Shakespearean comedy. By the end of this section compare your first thoughts with what you've learned. ❖

You may remember an episode of the BBC television programme *Blackadder II*, a pseudo-Elizabethan comedy drama, in which Lord Blackadder quips that his servant Baldrick is the kind of person who would laugh at a Shakespeare comedy. This implies that Shakespeare's comedies were both dated and unfunny to witty Elizabethans if someone as stupid as Baldrick laughed at them. This is a good modern joke. Banking on the television audience's perhaps ambiguous experience of Shakespeare at school, Blackadder reassuringly suggests that Shakespeare was never really funny. *Blackadder II* is a knowing travesty of the Elizabethan period; it looks at the past and its culture through twentieth-century perspectives which insist that expressions like 'Hey nonny nonny', for example (a favourite of Blackadder's other sidekick, Lord Percy), are timelessly ludicrous. Genuine Elizabethan opinion, however, takes a different perspective on Shakespearean comedy. Writing in 1598, Francis Meres helps both to date *The Merchant* (Halio, p.27) and to make a preliminary assessment of Shakespeare as a comic writer:

> As Plautus and Seneca are accounted the best for Comedy and Tragedy among the Latines: so Shakespeare among the English is the most excellent in both kinds for the stage: for comedy, witness his *Gentlemen of Verona*, his *Errors*, his *Loves labors lost*, his *Loves labours wonne*, his *Midsummers night dreame*, & his *Merchant of Venice*.
>
> (Blackmore Evans and Tobin, 1989, p.1970)[2]

Meres's comparison takes us to the heart of scholarly definitions of Renaissance culture. Anticipating Burckhardt's emphasis on the 'revival of antiquity', he gauges Shakespeare's excellence by comparing his work favourably with that of the 'best' classical Latin dramatists, Plautus and Seneca. But how much further does Meres

---

[2] You may be wondering about *Loves Labours Wonne*. Is it a lost play? The Riverside Shakespeare editors comment that 'The play has not survived at least under this name' (Blackmore Evans and Tobin, 1997, p.1970). It's just about possible that it could be an alternative name for *The Taming of the Shrew*, a pre-1598 comedy in which the winning of love is certainly a laborious business!

develop our understanding of Shakespearean comedy? He was not offering a detailed analysis of Shakespeare. Part of his *Palladis Tamia*, this extract is from the section 'A comparative discourse of our English poets with Greeke, Latine and Italian poets', which I would call a thumbnail sketch of 1590s literary culture. In making his sketch, Meres uses the then fashionable vocabulary of classical and continental analogy. In this sense, his analogies have the political goal of asserting that 'our English poets' are as good as 'Greeke, Latine and Italian poets'. In the cultural politics of sixteenth-century Europe, English was a minority language. Patriotic writers like Meres assert the value of writing in English by invoking the standard currency of European culture: the classics. As Bate points out, though literary history has endorsed Meres's association of Shakespeare with Plautus, Seneca and Ovid, it has not followed his claim that William Warner, the writer of a long topographical poem, *Albion's Englande* (1589), was an 'English Homer' (1993, p.2).

Meres is a useful starting point. We will need to look at *The Merchant* in terms of classical comedy. Yet the classical analogy will only take us so far. Unlike *The Comedy of Errors, The Merchant* is not based on a Roman original. As with the amphitheatres, we need to place the play in terms of native as well as classical traditions. Moreover, we need to have a sense of the theoretical understanding of comedy in the Renaissance. Since Shakespeare wasn't an academic dramatist, we need to see how his plays deviate from academic definitions of comedy.

Renaissance comic theory and the influence of classical comedy

Let's begin with sixteenth-century theories of comedy, since they are so strongly based on classical precedent. The humanist understanding of comedy is vigorously presented by Sir Philip Sidney's *An Apology for Poetry*, which you have already encountered in Chapter 4. Sidney's model of comedy ultimately recalls Aristotle's *Poetics*, as well as being informed by the didactic ideas of Horace's *Ars poetica (Art of Poetry)*. In brief, Sidney argues that all literature – including comedy – should have the moral goal of improving the behaviour of its readers and audiences:

> as in geometry the oblique must be known as well as the right, and in arithmetic the odd as well as the even, so in the actions of our life who seeth not the filthiness of evil wanteth a great foil to perceive the beauty of virtue. This doth the Comedy handle so in our private and domestical matters, as with hearing it we get as it were an experience what is to be looked for ... of a flattering Gnatho, of a vainglorious Thraso; and not only what effects are to be expected, but to know who be such by the signifying badge given them by the comedian.

> (Shepherd, 1973, p.117)

321

Sidney's dense prose works by means of analogy. Comedy is like geometry, where you have to know oblique as well as right angles, or like arithmetic, in which you have to know odd as well as even numbers. In the same way, comedy 'handles' the oblique or odd in human behaviour – it represents 'the filthiness of evil' so that the audience can better perceive 'the beauty of virtue'. Sidney's examples are taken from *Eunuchus* (*The Eunuch*) by the Roman writer Terence; this is hardly surprising since, as Marvin T. Herrick notes, Terentian comedy 'laid the main foundations of Renaissance theories of comedy' (1964, p.1). For Sidney, Terence's play equips its readers with a moral yardstick: by representing a flatterer in the character of Gnatho and a boaster in Thraso, Terence shows 'what is to be looked for' from these types of people in everyday life.

Exercise

Let's think about this for a moment. Does this strike you as a sophisticated theory of comedy?

We shouldn't be distracted by the elegance and complexity of Sidney's style. It seems to me that this is an unsophisticated theory of how comedy works. Sidney sees comedy in terms of its moral usefulness – what it can teach its audience. This instruction takes place through comic characters: you see *Eunuchus* and realize that Gnatho is a parasitic flatterer. Armed with this information, you should then be able to recognize and avoid similar people in real life. To take another example, if we map this theory on to *The Merchant*, we could say that the play's lesson is to avoid Jewish usurers like Shylock. But would this offer a satisfying reading or indeed performance of the play? Even allowing for the fact that a 1590s audience had different ideas about Jewishness and usury from our own, this would restrict the rich human interactions the play stages. If Shakespeare wanted to warn his audience about Jewish usurers, why did he bother presenting Shylock in such detail? (Given the very small numbers of Jews in sixteenth-century London, this would constitute a rather impractical warning!) Correspondingly, why did he offset his Jewish villain with a group of Christian characters who embody 'the beauty of virtue' erratically at best? ❖

These are questions we shall return to, but for the moment remember that, though learned, Sidney's theory of comedy is relatively unsubtle. It's worth noting that Sidney's reading doesn't give a full sense of *Eunuchus*: he makes it sound like a dramatic sermon against flatterers and boasters, whereas in fact Terence extends modified dramatic sympathy to both Gnatho and Thraso by the end of the play.

Unlike Francis Meres, Sidney never saw Shakespeare's comedies. *An Apology* was written in the early 1580s (Shepherd, 1973, p.4), and

Sidney was dead by 1586, several years before Shakespeare's earliest plays were written. But it is unlikely that Sidney would have endorsed Shakespeare even had he lived into the 1590s. Discussing the drama he had seen in English, Sidney is disgusted by its ignorance of the classical unities of time and place, which dictated that dramatic action should last no longer than a fictional day and that dramatic location should be restricted to one place. He would not have been impressed by *The Merchant*'s double location or its elongated narrative action. Herrick argues that Sidney's dramatic criticism derives from the Italian critic Lodovico Castelvetro's strict demarcation of tragedy from comedy, based on the Latin models of Seneca and Terence:

> While the dividing line between tragedy and comedy was sharply drawn by most Renaissance critics and commentators, in practice, this line was often blurred, sometimes nearly obliterated when a new type of drama became fashionable.

> (Herrick, 1964, p.87)

This new type of drama was tragi-comedy, a mixed form which amalgamated aspects of each genre. Sidney comments:

> their plays be neither right tragedies, nor right comedies, mingling kings and clowns, not because the matter so carrieth it, but thrust in clowns by heads and shoulders, to play a part in majestical matters, with neither decency nor discretion, so as neither the admiration and commiseration, or the right sportfulness, is by their mongrel tragi-comedy obtained.

> (Shepherd, 1973, p.135)

Here we see Sidney's key requirements: tragedy should produce 'admiration and commiseration' (this paraphrases Aristotle's conception of tragedy), while comedy should produce 'right sportfulness'. Such enjoyment is based on 'delight' rather than just laughter: 'all the end of the comical part be not upon such scornful matters as stirreth laughter only, but, mixed with it, that delightful teaching which is the end of Poesy' (Shepherd, 1973, pp.136–7). True comedy must be elevated above crude slapstick, delighting its audience with moral instruction rather than amoral entertainment. Tragi-comedy is 'mongrel' because it mixes modes and dilutes the distinctive didactic elements Sidney locates separately in tragedy and comedy. Though *The Merchant* is not a tragi-comedy, my guess is that Sidney would have seen it as a 'mongrel' comedy, variously undermined by the indecorous clowning of Launcelot Gobbo, by Portia's disguise and by the laments of Shylock. Where Sidney wants English comedy to follow the model of Terence, Shakespeare characteristically produces drama which exceeds the achievement of such classical models.

So what is the influence of classical comedy on Shakespeare? Unlike his Italian contemporaries, Shakespeare only rarely based his plays on Terentian and Plautine originals. The most sustained imitation of a classical plot is in *The Comedy of Errors*, which Blackmore Evans and Tobin date as Shakespeare's first comedy, written between 1592 and 1594 (1997, p.79). This play reworks Plautus's *Menaechmi* (*The Brothers Menaechmus*) but with added complications. Whereas *Menaechmi* stages the confusions which arise when a twin brother returns to his birthplace and is taken for his twin by his brother's wife, mistress, parasite and father-in-law, the *Comedy* gives the twin brothers twin servants, thus doubling the range and ramifications of the confused identities. As Anne Barton explains, Shakespeare went to Plautus early in his career 'to learn something about the construction of a finely engineered dramatic plot' (Blackmore Evans and Tobin, 1997, p.112).

It has been argued that Shylock derives from Euclio in Plautus's *Aulularia* (*The Pot of Gold*), a paranoiac miser who desperately tries to conceal his money from what he presumes is a similarly cash-fixated outside world. Yet *The Merchant* does not rely on a classical model. As Robert Miola observes in a footnote to his study of Shakespeare's debt to Plautus and Terence, 'Shylock grows beyond the fixed confines of the Plautine original into a character capable of endless refiguration, into one who assumes radically different identities in different productions' (Miola, 1994, p.10, n.21). Shylock exceeds and refigures all the originals – including that of Plautus – from which he derives. Unlike the Antipholus twins of *The Comedy of Errors*, Shylock is not dependent on classical precedent alone.

I stress that Miola makes this observation in a footnote because this indicates how little he finds to say about the direct influence of Plautus and Terence on *The Merchant*. Shylock is just one role in the play, albeit a major one. So are there other kinds of debt to classical comedy evident in *The Merchant*? Barton's comment about *The Comedy of Errors* and *Menaechmi* helps us here: all Shakespeare's comic plots are implicitly 'New Comedic'. That is, they echo the New Comedy initiated by the ancient Greek dramatist Menander. The novelty of Menander's writing lay in its movement away from the satiric 'old' comedy of Aristophanes: in place of Aristophanes' satires on Athenian politics at specific times and places, Menander and his Roman inheritors Plautus and Terence produced depoliticized dramas centring on the conflicts between the old and the young. To take a typical New Comedy plot:

> Glycerium, who is wrongly supposed to be the sister of a courtesan from Andros, is seduced and made pregnant by Pamphilus. He then promises to marry her, but his father, Simo, has already arranged

another marriage for him with the daughter of Chremes. On hearing of Pamphilus's affair Simo pretends that the other wedding will still take place, hoping thereby to discover his son's real feelings. On the advice of his slave Davos Pamphilus raises no objections, but when Glycerium's child is born and Chremes sees it, he breaks off the marriage between Pamphilus and his daughter. Afterwards, he discovers to his surprise that Glycerium is really his daughter, so he marries her to Pamphilus and his other daughter to Charinus.

(Radice, 1976, p.36)

Fathers and sons squabble energetically about whom the sons should marry; wily slaves play one master off against another until the final comic denouement: the courtesan's sister turns out to be the long-lost daughter of a respectable man. This is the plot of Terence's *Andria* (*The Girl from Andros*) as summarized in the second century by Gaius Sulpicius Apollinaris. The play was a staple of the grammar school curriculum in England (Nevo, 1980, p.2); Shakespeare would have known it well. But at first glance, its plot doesn't sound much like that of a Shakespearean comedy. Ruth Nevo clarifies the connection: Donatus, a Latin grammarian of the fourth century CE, based his influential 'formula for comic plots' on Terence's plays; this was 'ceaselessly revised and repeated by the humanist scholars of the Italian Renaissance' (1980, pp.1–2). She quotes Donatus's formula from a 1550 edition of the *Andria*:

Comedy ... ought indeed to be five-parted, the first of which unfolds the argument ... the second completes the same. The third has the increment of turbations and connections ... the fourth seeks a medicine for the turbations ... and is a preparation for the catastrophe, which the fifth demands by right for itself.

(Nevo, 1980, p.2)

Donatus's 'five parts' are the five acts we encounter in modern editions of almost every Shakespeare play. Though it is impossible to say whether Shakespeare included such divisions in his manuscript, those in *The Merchant* are at least as old as the 1623 folio (Halio, p.93). The Donatan scheme gave Shakespeare a basic idea of dramatic form grounded in texts he had been aware of since boyhood. Though Donatus's formula is relatively simplistic, you should be able to see that it fits as a rough outline of the structure of many Shakespearean comedies. *Twelfth Night* (*c.*1601–2), for example, outlines its 'argument' in Acts 1 and 2, introducing Viola disguised as a young man, Orsino's love for Olivia and the Malvolio subplot. Acts 3 and 4 develop this argument (or increase its 'turbations') through Olivia's love for Viola, the gulling of Malvolio and the appearance of

Sebastian, Viola's missing-presumed-drowned twin brother, as a husband for Olivia. Finally, Act 5 stages the 'catastrophe' in which Viola is accused of betrayal by both Orsino and Olivia before Sebastian reappears to reveal Viola's feminine identity alongside the unravelling of the plot against Malvolio. Yet as Nevo reminds us, Shakespeare is never absolutely bound to the Donatan scheme:

> The telos [end] of Shakespeare's early comic plots ... is recovery: the finding of what was missing or lacking at the start ... Shakespeare's protagonists do not know what they want, except in the most superficial sense. They discover as they go along, and so transform the rather arid Donatan scheme into a heuristic device [a means through which characters find out about themselves] of immense potency and flexibility. When his protagonists, like the Romans in their happy ends, get more than they bargained for, it is not simply the bonus ... of a son's light of love turning out to be respectable ... or even the long-lost daughter of the father's best friend, but an illumination of their entire lives.

(Nevo, 1980, p.6)

Nevo emphasizes that the form of Shakespeare's early comedies derives from Terence and Donatus: comic characters are rewarded with bonuses they hadn't anticipated at the outset of the action. So in *The Comedy of Errors*, the merchant Egeon – who in Act 1 was anxious only to save his life – wins the jackpot of recovering his long dispersed family in Act 5. But these Shakespearean bonuses, Nevo suggests, are more than just of a material nature. Whereas in Terence the bonus is that the young and old discover that their outwardly opposed plans are in fact congruent – the desired girl turns out to be the respectable girl – in Shakespeare the bonus carries the audience to a sense of the main protagonists' complex inner life. By the end of *Twelfth Night*, the audience has gained an almost eerie sense of the twinship of the shipwrecked sister and brother, Viola and Sebastian, who meet only in the play's final scene.

Exercise

Now that we've seen the structural influence classical comedy had on Shakespeare, we should be able to move back to *The Merchant*. Flick through the play quickly, noting any acts you think don't fit with Donatus's model.

Discussion

When we map *The Merchant* against Donatus, the major problem is that the 'catastrophe' occurs in Act 4's trial scene. While Act 5 tidies up the ring plot begun at the end of Act 4, it conspicuously lacks the tension Donatus believes it 'demands'. ❖

Though not the focal point of dramatic excitement, Act 5 has become a critically contested area since, as we shall see, its image of aristocratic and conjugal harmony depends on two important exclusions: Shylock from Belmont and Antonio from marriage. So while we need to bear in mind Shakespeare's awareness of New Comedic traditions and their reiteration during the Renaissance, we must also realize that he did not slavishly follow Donatus's model or Terence's precedent. As Nevo suggests, Shakespearean comic plots are more detailed and more emotionally complex than those of either Plautus or Terence.

Native traditions and The Jew of Malta

So what other influences were there on Shakespeare's conception of comedy? In this section we're going to take a quick look at native dramatic traditions: earlier Elizabethan comedy, the morality play and Marlowe's *The Jew of Malta* (*c*.1589–92). This play is an indispensable source for *The Merchant*, exhibiting both the representation of Jews by another major Elizabethan dramatist and the survival of morality play conventions in later drama.

Elizabethan comedy before Shakespeare is extremely varied. There are university plays like *Gammer Gurton's Needle* (1575), a witty imitation of Plautus which transposes his Mediterranean setting to an English village to present a knock-about entertainment concerning the loss of a sewing needle. There are translations of recent Italian comedy, like George Gascoigne's 1566 version of Ariosto's *Gli suppositi* (*Supposes*), which Shakespeare recycled in *The Taming of the Shrew* (*c*.1593–4). There are the popular comedies Sidney mocks for their ignorance of classical decorum and their stretching of credulity: 'After many traverses, she is got with child, delivered of a fair boy, he is lost, groweth a man, falls in love, and is ready to get another child, and all this in two hours' space' (Shepherd, 1973, p.134). Unlikely as this description sounds, there are many plays of this kind. Robert Greene's *Friar Bacon and Friar Bungay* (*c*.1589) and George Peele's *Old Wives Tale* (*c*.1590), for example, are frankly fantastical, featuring casts of magicians, knights errant and damsels in distress. Alvin Kernan observes that such comedy exhibits 'an almost unlimited expression of playfulness and a realisation of freedom from the restraints of the probable' (1975, p.300).

Such drama may seem as distant from Shakespeare as Terence's *Andria*; yet this liberation from 'the restraints of the probable' was important for plays like *A Midsummer Night's Dream* (*c*.1595–6), with its extensive cast of fairies. We know from plays like *As You Like It* (*c*.1599) that Shakespeare was a careful student of the more sophisticated comic fantasies written during the 1580s and 90s by

John Lyly for a court and aristocratic audience. *The Merchant* also depends on its audience's readiness to accept a split location, the folk-tale devices of the casket plot and the flesh bond plot, as well as Portia's disguise. On reflection then, Shakespeare's comedies are embedded in dramatic traditions which count on the audience's readiness to make large-scale suspensions of disbelief. An Elizabethan audience which had enjoyed the magic of plays like *Friar Bacon and Friar Bungay* and *A Midsummer Night's Dream* would have little trouble accepting the fantastic elements in *The Merchant*.

Indeed, Kernan argues that there were two varieties of Elizabethan comedy: 'romantic' comedy and satiric comedy (1975, pp.300–2). Where 'romantic' comedy focuses on amorous adventure, satiric comedy uses clowns – like Diccon in *Gammer Gurton's Needle* – to expose human folly. For Kernan, these two traditions are best represented by the 'romantic' comedies of Shakespeare and the satiric comedies of Ben Jonson (1572–1637). This is orthodox literary history: where Shakespeare's comedies give us the happy endings of multiple marriages, Jonson's expose charlatans and poseurs in all walks of life. But although almost all modern critics of Shakespeare's comedies use a variant of the term 'romantic' comedy, I want to emphasize that this is a vague and potentially misleading description. To begin with, it's very easy to confuse the adjective 'romantic' with eighteenth- and nineteenth-century Romanticism; as we've seen, Burckhardt's ideas about literature are Romantic in origin. When we speak of *The Merchant* as a 'romantic comedy', we are chiefly observing something about its content: this is a play which concerns love and what Robert Ornstein calls the 'adventure of romance', with the vast panoply of fantastic narrative which the term originally denoted (1986, pp.17–18). But even as we make this remark, we notice that it excludes much of what is distinctive about the play: the flesh bond plot and its powerful engagement with the emotions of hatred. If we start to think that the play is about the idealization of romantic love, we minimize its capacity to unsettle and challenge. So while Shakespeare undoubtedly took much from 'romantic' comedy, remember that the term is problematic and be prepared to reshape your sense of *The Merchant*'s genre later in this chapter.

As we've seen, morality plays remained a vital part of dramatic culture in Britain throughout the sixteenth century. Though you may have an idea of moralities as static pieces of traditional drama, they were a flexible mode, undergoing considerable change in use and form: writers like John Bale used the morality genre to convey Protestant ideas during the middle decades of the century. Equally, as David Bevington notes, during the 1570s and 80s elements from the popular 'romantic' comedy we've just looked at were incorporated into hybrid moralities like *Clyomen and Clamydes* (printed 1599), in which allegorical figures share the stage with characters from romance (1962, pp.190–4).

So what is a morality play? Anne Barton gives a succinct definition: 'A Morality is a kind of sermon with illustrations' (1967, p.25). These illustrations typically take the form of allegorical conflicts between figures like Mankind and Everyman, who represent the audience's spiritual condition, and their opponents like Dissymulacyon in Bale's *King Johan*, who represent the Devil and his ministers. The opponent figure became the moralities' most celebrated role: that of the Vice. The importance of these very unclassical plays for the understanding of later Elizabethan drama has been asserted in major studies like Bevington's *From Mankind to Marlowe* (1962). Though the influence of the moralities is clearly visible in Vice-like Richard III and Iago, *The Merchant* exhibits no direct debt to the moralities.

We shall concentrate on *The Jew of Malta*, first because it is a play of the 1590s which is explicitly linked to the moralities, and secondly because of its impact on *The Merchant*. By looking at Marlowe's Barabas we should get closer to Shakespeare's Shylock; moreover, by looking at *The Jew of Malta*'s manipulation of genre, we can compare *The Merchant of Venice*'s analogous strategies.

Exercise

The Anthology includes four extracts from *The Jew*. I'd like you now to read the first three (nos. 56i–iii): the Prologue, 1.1.102–38 and 2.3.176–203. Do you feel Barabas is consistently presented by Marlowe? Think particularly about his two long speeches.

Discussion

Marlowe seems to present Barabas as a thorough-going villain. First he's introduced by Machiavel – a lurid construction of Machiavelli as a bogeyman – as one of his 'climbing followers' who has gained his wealth through Machiavellian 'means'. In the second extract Barabas appears as a wealthy merchant, explaining the benefits trade has brought to European Jews. Finally, he brags of an impressive inventory of misdeeds, from poisoning wells to the indiscriminate slaughter of Christian soldiers. Yet there are contradictions here. The account of Barabas's crimes against humanity – which is addressed to his newly purchased Turkish slave Ithamore to prove his evil credentials – 'does not correspond realistically with what we know of Barabas's life' (Bevington, 1962, p.226). Though later he poisons a nunnery which includes his daughter Abigail, at this stage in the play Barabas has chiefly appeared as a wealthy Jewish merchant persecuted by the Maltese Christian establishment. ❖

How should we account for this discrepancy? Bevington argues that the play is a dialogue between Marlowe's secular values and the restrictive forms of the morality play. In this reading, Barabas is both a Vice figure – 'a universal genius of evil' – and, bewilderingly enough, 'a person of complex human emotions' (Bevington, 1962, pp.226, 222). You will see the complex emotions more clearly in the fourth extract. Greenblatt emphasizes a different aspect of the play by concentrating on Barabas's use of proverbs, like 'who is honoured now but for his wealth' in the second extract. Greenblatt contends that since 'the essence of proverbs is their anonymity', their use serves to 'de-individualize' Barabas (1980, p.208). Barabas's account of his murders makes him 'more vague and unreal, accommodating him to an abstract, anti-Semitic fantasy of a Jew's past' (p.209). In both these readings Barabas's identity is problematic. Bevington sees discrete elements of artistic tradition and innovation in Marlowe's writing, while Greenblatt suggests that Marlowe's point is that Barabas has no identity – he is a patchwork of fantasies enacting the racial anxieties of Elizabethan culture.

I would add that the play's central challenge is its use of macabre humour. In the Prologue Machiavel makes self-consciously outrageous statements like 'I count religion but a childish toy,/And hold there is no sin but ignorance'. As well as establishing Machiavel's standing as an intellectual pariah, these lines are provocative in articulating stylishly what would be unthinkable, or certainly unsayable, outside the theatre. Similarly, after poisoning the nuns, Barabas remarks 'How sweet the bells ring, now the nuns are dead,/That sound at other times like tinkers' pans!' (4.1.2–3). Though these lines report Barabas's gruesome murder of the nuns, they distance us from the awfulness of his actions by comically focusing on his changed perception of bell ringing; indeed Marlowe's Protestant audience may have enjoyed the notion of Catholic nuns being murdered. While it's easy to disapprove of murderers, it's harder to know how to react to one that makes us laugh. In developing the morality play tradition, Marlowe creates a Vice figure who is endlessly ambivalent.

So *The Jew* is a very strange play. Figure 5.6 shows the title page of the first edition, where it is described as 'The Famous Tragedy of the Rich Jew of Malta'. Famous it certainly was, as one of the most frequently performed plays at the Rose theatre in the 1590s (Bawcutt, 1978, pp.1–2). But critics have always been troubled by its designation as a tragedy. Though it ends with Barabas being boiled alive in a cauldron he had prepared for the Turks, the play barely maintains a consistent tragic tone. Since *The Jew* is so important for *The Merchant*, we must look at its generic peculiarities.

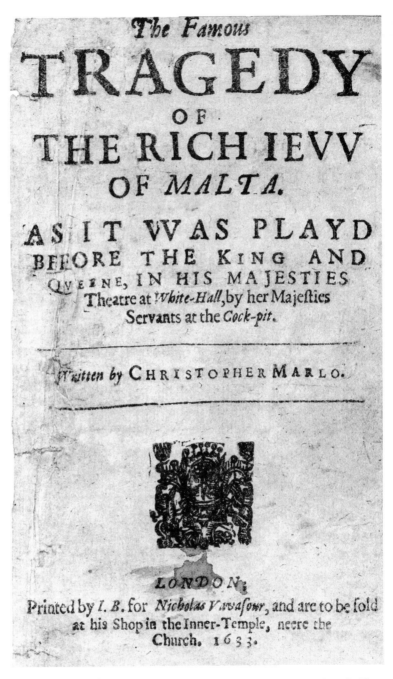

Figure 5.6 Title page of 1633 quarto of Christopher Marlowe's *The Famous Tragedy of the Rich Jew of Malta*. British Library 82.c.22(5). Reproduced by permission of the British Library Board

Exercise

Now read the fourth extract from *The Jew of Malta* in the Anthology (no. 56iv, taken from the start of 1.2, lines 1–225). Like *The Merchant* 4.1, this is a court scene. How do you think the two scenes compare? Do you have more sympathy for Barabas or Shylock?

Discussion

The first observation I would make is that these scenes have radically different locations in their respective plays. In *The Jew* the confrontation between the Jewish outsider and the Christian elite is the second scene, whereas in *The Merchant* it comes towards the end of the play. If we think back to Donatus's formula for comic plots, we can see that this is an important technical issue. Where a scene comes indicates its theatrical importance and how an audience should respond to it. We can put it like this: whereas in *The Jew* the trial scene *propels* the subsequent action (Barabas's terrorist campaign against Christian Malta), in *The Merchant* it *concludes* the preceding action (Shylock's plot against Antonio). In his study of the influence of Marlowe on Shakespeare, James Shapiro argues that this repositioning is Shakespeare's 'decisive revisionary strategy' of Marlowe (1991, p.108). He continues:

> In so doing [Shakespeare] takes what in Marlowe's play provided a barely plausible justification for Barabas's revenge and transforms it into a harrowing and nearly tragic confrontation, reversing the movement of Marlowe's play from potential tragedy to comic farce and steering the play towards the verge of tragedy.
>
> (p.108)

This is an attractive way of viewing the relationship between the two scenes and the two plays. Whereas *The Jew* looks like a tragedy but is actually a farce, *The Merchant* looks like a comedy but gets very close to tragedy. It seems that we should sympathize more with the nearly tragic Shylock than with the amoral Barabas. But we can expand on Shapiro through reading *The Jew* 1.2, especially lines 37–160. This is one of the high points of Marlowe's play: Jew is pitted against Christian as the Maltese elite levy the ten years' tribute money owing to the Turks wholly from the Jewish community. For the governor, Ferneze, the tax is justified on the basis of the Jews' wealth, while for Barabas it reveals the depths of Christian hypocrisy. Like Shylock, Barabas speaks with an impassioned sense of his own righteousness, opposing his Old Testament values to those of the Christians' New Testament. 'The man that dealeth righteously shall live' (1.2.117), he asserts in the manner of the Book of Proverbs, only to be countered by Ferneze's hypocritical moralizing against covetousness (1.2.119–25). As Bevington comments of the next exchange between Barabas and his fellow Jews, 'The dramatist intended his audience to view his "villain", for the moment at least, with genuine sympathy' (1962, p.224).

Yet that moment is brief. As soon as Barabas is left on his own, he reveals that he has been playing the tragic role self-consciously: 'Barabas is born to better chance ... A reaching thought will search his deepest wits/And cast with cunning for the time to come' (1.2.220–4). The scene goes on to show Barabas's scheme for retaining most of his wealth. This is the key difference between Barabas and Shylock in their trial scenes: Barabas is a flexible character, capable of shifting from tragic posturing to Machiavellian scheming in the space of an exit; Shylock is inflexible, sticking to the legal terms of his bond with Antonio. Shylock has no direct soliloquies, whereas this is the central means through which Marlowe reveals Barabas's flexibility directly to the audience. It is in terms of role playing that we can best understand Barabas and see how Shakespeare recasts him in Shylock. Barabas plays a bewildering number of roles which, as Greenblatt argues, ultimately 'de-individualize' him. His repertoire (ranging from merchant, victim, loving father, murderer, penitent, phoney musician to governor) inevitably diminishes the audience's sense of him as a tragic figure. When Barabas shifts rapidly from a tragic to a Machiavellian role, the audience's likely response is knowing laughter at seeing a successful con-man at work. *The Jew* is anti-tragic: by fusing the Vice figure with a Jewish outsider, Marlowe suggests the universality of role playing and hypocrisy. The play's final paradox is that Barabas is undone by trusting the equally duplicitous Ferneze, who turns out to be its most successful exponent of Machiavel's opening lesson.

Shylock lacks Barabas's role-playing faculty. The whole of his identity is at stake in the trial scene, which Shapiro sees as 'a harrowing and nearly tragic confrontation'. Once again we might say that *The Jew* is a comedy that looks like a tragedy while *The Merchant* is a tragedy that looks like a comedy. Such a manoeuvre has been attempted by many recent critics. This comparison should show you that dramatic meaning is at stake in the discussion of genre. If we say that Shylock is a tragic figure, it shapes our subsequent reading and interpretation of the whole play. Shylock becomes the central figure to the exclusion of all others; as you can see from Halio's account of the play's stage history, this interpretation was particularly popular during the Romantic period (pp.65–8). But are we satisfied with this redesignation of *The Merchant*? Are Shylock and the flesh bond plot *unequivocally* more important than Portia and the casket plot? My sense is that both *The Merchant* and *The Jew* excite their audiences by mixing modes and generic signals. Though Barabas and Shylock are potentially tragic figures, both are enmeshed in complex dramatic milieux which refuse to settle either in a wholly tragic mode or in a wholly comic one. Shapiro makes the intriguing point that *The Merchant* is a commercial as well as an artistic response to *The Jew* (1991, p.111). Since *The Jew* was a hit play for the Lord Admiral's Men at the Rose in the mid 1590s, their rivals, the Lord Chamberlain's Men, needed a comparable attraction written by their star dramatist. As Shakespeare's contribution to this commercial struggle, *The Merchant* recodes the older play by transposing its central situation to the conventions of a 'romantic' comedy rather than a revenge tragedy. Artistic innovation on the London stage was often driven by commercial pressure. ❖

Let's summarize what we've learned about the contexts underlying Shakespearean comedy. Native traditions had an important influence on Shakespeare. From the mass of available evidence, I've singled out the 'romantic' comedy of fantastic plots and happy endings and the morality play tradition as it survives in *The Jew of Malta*. We've also explored the influence of neoclassical theory and classical precedent through examining Sidney's *An Apology for Poetry* and Shakespeare's knowledge of Plautus and Terence. At the beginning of this section I asked you to jot down what you understand by the term Shakespearean comedy. We should now be able to formulate some general principles about the contexts of Shakespeare's comic writing.

- Though Shakespeare was aware of the classical theory and practice, he is not a neoclassical writer. His plays do not observe classical unities except in special cases like *The Comedy of Errors* and later *The Tempest*. Secondly, his comedies are not didactic: they do not follow Sidney's theory that comedy should warn its audience against types of people and behaviour. Shakespeare wrote primarily to entertain, and this commercial requirement conditioned what and how he wrote.

- Shakespearean comedy draws on complex native traditions. The loose form and amorous content of his comedies directly recall earlier 'romantic' comedies: framed by marriages between the main protagonists, they focus on issues of love and identity in fantastic locations. But *The Merchant* is not just a play about romance. Its debt to *The Jew* signals Shakespeare's awareness of the morality play tradition which his brilliant contemporary Marlowe had already revolutionized by recasting its Vice figure in the new worlds of his own ambivalent tragedies.

What I hope emerges from this discussion is that *The Merchant* is a play in which classical and indigenous literary modes are mixed to a point where they are almost scrambled. This radical innovation of combining disparate dramatic legacies makes it a play of the Renaissance and aligns it with the hybrid amphitheatre in which it was first performed. It may then be useful to adopt a more modern term to describe the play: it is a problem comedy. This term originated among twentieth-century scholars who sensed that Shakespeare's later comedies like *Measure for Measure* are so troubling that they cannot be labelled comic; in *Measure for Measure* Isabella's virginity is the price demanded by the corrupt judge Angelo for saving her brother's life. A problem play generates such severe interpretative difficulties that it explodes traditional categories like tragedy and comedy. Though you might think that this is a conveniently loose category for plays we can't make our minds up about, Shakespeare's later comedies do become increasingly problematic through the seriousness of the dilemmas they address and the gravity of their treatment. Of course, Elizabethans would not have used this term. One of the questions that you will need to think about as we turn directly to *The Merchant* is how problematic you find it to be. Is it a near tragedy, or do you prefer to see it as a comedy of love?

Studying *The Merchant of Venice*

We now have a contextual map for the first performances of *The Merchant* in the late 1590s. Played on an innovative popular stage, it emerges from a complex literary and dramatic culture indebted variously to continental humanism, classical precedent and native traditions. With these vital contexts in mind, we return to the play itself. I shall be adopting two interrelated approaches. First, we'll explore the play's presentation of its Italianate settings. Since this book is concerned with the interrogation of Renaissance culture, Shakespeare's Italy is of particular interest: how did Shakespeare represent Italy? What values did it embody for his audience? Secondly, we'll consider the dynamic which structures the play around the *inclusion* of some characters and the *exclusion* of others. Examining *The Merchant*'s others and lovers will underline the play's creation of dramatic roles and the ways in which they embody Renaissance ideas of the self.

Shakespeare's Italy

The traditional sense of the difference between Venice and Belmont goes something like this: 'Venice is a world of money, and Belmont is a world of love' (Leggatt, 1974, p.122). It looks like an attractive dichotomy, juxtaposing the mercantile world of Venice with the fairy-tale world of Belmont.

Exercise

Read 1.1 and 1.2, paying special attention to what these scenes tell us about Venice and Belmont. Do you agree with Leggatt?

Discussion

On a first reading Leggatt's distinction looks persuasive. The Venetian characters talk about Antonio's merchandise and Bassanio's 'disabled ... estate'; in Belmont conversation focuses on Portia's unsuitable suitors. Yet the danger of this reading is that it overlooks the similarities between Venice and Belmont. As we saw at the beginning of this chapter, 1.1 is concerned with love almost as much as money: love is present as a possible explanation of Antonio's melancholy, in the relationship between Antonio and Bassanio, and in Bassanio's description of Portia. This description in turn presents Portia in financial terms: she is 'richly left'; her hair is 'a golden fleece'. These images then prepare us to read Belmont not just as a world of love but as a world of inheritance. Portia's inheritance dominates 1.2. It establishes her as an aristocratic lady of leisure while restricting her erotic autonomy: she cannot choose a husband for herself but must be guided 'by the will of a dead father'. Love and money now look intimately connected in Venice and Belmont. I am not suggesting that Bassanio's 'rich' description of Portia undermines the love plot; the point is rather that we cannot inoculate Belmont from the mercantile values of Venice. ❖

Before we leave this comparison we should notice that Portia's conversation is more satiric than romantic. Shakespeare recycles a scene he first wrote for *The Two Gentlemen of Verona* (*c*.1594) in which Julia and Lucetta flirtatiously discuss Julia's suitors. In *The Merchant* the scene becomes a set-piece exhibition of Portia's wit and a first indication of the linguistic and intellectual resources she has at her disposal: 'he doth nothing but talk of his horse, and he makes it a great appropriation to his own good parts that he can shoe himself. I am much afeared my lady his mother played false with a smith' (1.2.39–43). While such mockery is genuinely comic, it is also indicative of a toughness in Portia: the ability to judge – harshly if necessary – which she will reveal more dramatically in the trial scene. She is no light-headed romantic heroine.

So it begins to look as though the distinction between Venice and Belmont is far from absolute. In both places love and wealth are the protagonists' key preoccupations. Let's now take a closer look at these places and the different values they embody.

Venice

Burckhardt analyses Renaissance Venice in 'The state as a work of art' (pp.58–65). He presents it as an example of the commercial rather than the artistic civilization of the Renaissance: 'In Venice ... the supreme objects were the enjoyment of life and power, the increase of inherited advantages, the creation of more lucrative forms of industry, the opening of new channels of commerce' (p.63). In the light of our previous discussion, 'the increase of inherited advantages' reminds us powerfully of both Bassanio's depletion of his inheritance and Portia's as yet untapped resources.

Exercise

Now read Halio's section 'The "myth" of Venice' (pp.24–7). How far does Halio's Venice modify Burckhardt's?

Discussion

Though Halio writes chiefly about Elizabethan ideas of Venice, his account is basically in accord with Burckhardt's. He stresses Venice's allure to Elizabethans as a wealthy and ancient republic which enjoyed a distinctive legal system and the reputation for being a pleasure-loving city. Burckhardt similarly emphasizes the power of Venetian 'Public institutions' (p.59) and the enormous wealth of fifteenth-century Venice. Elizabethan Venice was then an idealized location, exemplifying excellence in both trade and law. Where Halio diverges from Burckhardt is in his account of the Venetian treatment of Jews. Unlike England's small numbers of Jews, who were unable to practise their religion openly (Halio, pp.3–4), Venetian Jews were tolerated though ghettoized. ❖

We catch a fascinating glimpse of the ghetto in the travels of the English writer Thomas Coryat, whose attempts to convert Venetian Jews to Christianity in 1608 led to him being chased by a hostile crowd (Shapiro, 1996, p.115). Figure 5.7 shows the graphic depiction of this story in which Coryat is pursued by a Jew intent on circumcising him – in the words of Lawrence Whitaker's

Figure 5.7 Detail 'G' from title page of Thomas Coryat, *Coryat's Crudities*, 1611. British Library c.32.e.9. Reproduced by permission of the British Library Board

commendatory poem to Coryat's book, '[be]ware Tom, I advise thee,/And fly from the Jews, lest they circumcise thee' (Shapiro, 1996, p.115). Renaissance Venice was an amalgam of the commercial and the exotic. This is very much the city's profile in *The Merchant*.

Exercise

Reread 1.3. What does this scene tell you about Venice? You might like to make a list of its most important attributes.

Discussion

Money is unavoidable in this scene – its first words are 'Three thousand ducats'. Indeed, much of the conversation Shakespeare stages is what we might call shop-talk. Bassanio and Antonio negotiate a loan with Shylock – a professional money lender – and part of the scene's brilliance is its exact recording of the tensions inherent in such negotiations. Shylock mulls over the proposition aloud while Bassanio nervously prompts him – 'May you stead me? Will you pleasure me? Shall I know your answer?' (1.3.7–8). Yet we soon find out that money is not regarded equally by all the characters – or rather, the making of money is not regarded equally. The opening dialogue is alive with these tensions – note the different values Shylock and Bassanio assign to the word 'good' (1.3.12–17) – before exploding in the argument about usury. Shylock has already explained his reservations about Antonio. As a venture capitalist, he has 'squandered' his wealth 'abroad' in his far-flung argosies, an illustration that such entrepreneurial activity is fraught with risk (1.3.20–4). Antonio correspondingly disdains both Shylock's 'usances' and his biblical justification of the principle of lending money for interest. He reinterprets Shylock's telling of the story of Jacob and Laban as an example of the value of 'thrift': in Antonio's terms, this was 'a venture ... Jacob served for' (1.3.84–90). Venice is a financial centre which is itself divided in practice and ideology. The Christian elite are either venture capitalists like Antonio or prodigal aristocrats like Bassanio, who suddenly require the help of a Jewish usurer they habitually despise.

The friction between Jew and Christian is the other major focus of this scene. Shylock hates Antonio 'for he is a Christian' (1.3.38–49). In this great speech, frequently cut in modern performances that present Shylock as a wholly tragic figure (Halio, p.74), Shylock reveals a hatred driven both by Antonio's opposition to usury and by his Christianity. Antonio returns this hatred with – ironically enough – interest. Shylock's emotive account of the mistreatment he has received from Antonio produces an open reassertion of that antipathy: 'I am like to call thee so again,/To spit on thee again, to spurn thee, too' (1.3.126–7). Shakespeare's Venice is a place where hatreds based on social identity and religious affiliation are openly acknowledged. After this frank exchange of hatred it seems unlikely that Shylock and Antonio will be able to strike a deal. Yet they do so through the mechanism of Shylock's 'merry bond' (1.3.170), which alerts us to the emphasis placed in this scene on Venetian law. As a money lender Shylock operates through legally binding contracts, through which he can extract further financial penalties if the borrower fails to repay him at the stipulated time. His bond with Antonio is then from the outset profoundly paradoxical: he presents it as a friendly joke, whereas in fact the flesh bond will give him a legal claim on Antonio's 'fair flesh' (1.3.147). ❖

Venice emerges from this pivotal scene as a place of overlapping and conflicting interests. Money, whether in the form of Antonio's ventures or Shylock's loans, dominates the social world. Beyond Shylock's house in Act 2, what we chiefly see of Venice is a gossipy market place: the Rialto. The other major Venetian milieu is the court of law in Act 4, where legal claims are put to definitive judgement. Law is critical to *The Merchant* because Venice is a commercial centre, a place in which members of different cultures trade and intermingle. Shakespeare's Venice – a dramatic idea based on a real place – stages the dialogue between the antagonistic value systems of Christian and Jew.

Belmont

Whereas Shakespeare's Venice is a fictionalized version of a real place, Belmont is a wholly fictional place. Belmont derives from the play's major source, Giovanni Fiorentino's *Il pecorone*, which Halio summarizes on pages 14–16 of his introduction. As you can see, Shakespeare made important changes to this fictional location. In Fiorentino's story, Belmonte is dominated by the Lady's provocative law: 'whoever arrives here must sleep with her, and if he can enjoy her, he must take her for wife and be lord of the seaport and all the surrounding country. But if he cannot enjoy her, he loses everything he has' (Brown, 1964, p.142).

Exercise

Reread 1.1.161–76 and 2.1. What chiefly differentiates Shakespeare's Belmont from Fiorentino's Belmonte?

Discussion

The clearest difference is that Portia does not put her suitors to the sex test. Fiorentino presents Belmonte as a place of glamour and barely stifled sexual excitement. Bassanio stresses Portia's moral virtues as well as her wealth: 'she is fair, and fairer than that word,/ Of wondrous virtues' (1.1.162–3). Similarly, Portia lacks the autonomy of the Lady of Belmonte; as she explains to Morocco, she is barred 'the right of voluntary choosing' by her father's casket test (2.1.16). Shakespeare has sanitized Fiorentino's story by making his

Belmont a place where female sexuality is still governed by male authority. Indeed, Bassanio's assertion of Portia's virtue is borne out by her own remark: 'If I live to be as old as Sibylla, I will die as chaste as Diana unless I be obtained by the manner of my father's will' (1.2.103–5). ❖

You will notice that Portia doesn't directly explain *why* she will obey her father's will; I would suggest that the remark emphatically distinguishes Portia from figures like the Lady of Belmonte: as she is obedient to her father's will, so she will implicitly be obedient to her future husband. It begins to look as though Leggatt is right. Belmont is a 'world of love' inhabited by the ideal Elizabethan romantic heroine: wealthy, beautiful and chaste.

Exercise

Reread the casket scenes: 2.7, 2.9 and 3.2. Can you now think of a better definition than a 'world of love' for the Belmont of these scenes? Think particularly about the repetition of the casket device.

Discussion

Part of our difficulty here is that just as money is so much a part of Venice, so love is a major part of Belmont. The ecstatic exchange between Portia and Bassanio (3.2.139–85) centres on their intense, almost unspeakable emotions: 'Myself and what is mine to you and yours/Is now converted'; 'Only my blood speaks to you in my veins'. But when we read these scenes in sequence, we do find more to say about Belmont. My definition would be that Belmont is a world of formality and ritual. It is a self-contained court, or at least an aristocratic country house with many of the trappings of a court. Note how Portia invests Bassanio as her husband: as she was 'the Lord/Of this fair mansion, master o'er my servants,/Queen o'er myself', Bassanio now takes on these roles and prerogatives (3.2.166–9). Belmont is represented through courtly formality. In these scenes, we witness a repeated action with three minor variations. Three different suitors choose three different caskets; and as in most fairy tales, the third suitor makes the right decision. ❖

Such repetitions partly identify Belmont as a fairy-tale environment where beautiful princesses are won by questing heroes. Yet as you can see elsewhere in this book, such ritualized behaviour was a fundamental characteristic of Renaissance courts; in Chapter 3 Anabel Thomas describes the elaborate festivities which accompanied Count Galeazzo Maria Sforza's 1459 visit to Florence. In that chapter the point is made that 'prestigious rivalry' underlines such displays of court culture. Similarly, we are made aware from Act 1 onwards that in going to Belmont, Bassanio is competing for Portia:

... the four winds blow in from every coast
Renowned suitors, and her sunny locks
Hang on her temples like a golden fleece,
Which makes her seat of Belmont Colchis' strand,
And many Jasons come in quest of her.
O my Antonio, had I but the means
To hold a rival place with one of them,
I have a mind presages me such thrift
That I should questionless be fortunate.

(1.1.168–76)

As we would expect from a speech uttered in Venice, this makes it clear that Bassanio can only 'rival' the other suitors if he has the financial 'means' to keep up with the opposition, which in turn underlines the importance of wealth in Belmont. Note the stage directions in the three casket scenes which indicate that each suitor is attended by a 'train' of followers; to play the courtly game, you have to cut the appropriate figure.

You may have noticed that both in this speech and in 3.2 Shakespeare makes repeated mythological allusions, chiefly to the story of Jason and the Argonauts. We could say that Belmont is a world of myth. This is another important context for reading Belmont. Unlike Fiorentino, Shakespeare presents his Belmont through a filter of allusions to Ovid's *Metamorphoses*. Why does he do this? Partly because such allusiveness is a function of what Bate calls 'the Renaissance habit of thinking in terms of parallels between present experience and mythological precedent' (1993, p.151). As the golden fleece was to Jason, so Portia is to Bassanio. He verbalizes his sense of her value through this mythic vocabulary, in the process transmuting Belmont into Colchis, where Ovid located the original golden fleece. Myth is a form of shorthand, a poetic short-cut which links the present to a shared pattern of meaning.

Such analogies can set up troubling resonances. Though Bassanio and Graziano view themselves as Argonauts, Portia interprets Bassanio as Hercules rescuing Hesione from a sea monster (3.2.53–62). You may wonder if these discrepancies matter. They do in as much as the chosen myths open up wider patterns of meaning of which the speaker may not be wholly aware, or in control. One short example would be that Morocco's misremembering of the story of Hercules and Lichas is indicative of a discrepancy between his heroic rhetoric and his comic inadequacy as Portia's suitor (2.1.32–8; see Halio's note, p.129). Hercules was one of the greatest Greek heroes, whereas

Jason was more of an opportunist; Bate goes so far as to suggest that Ovid's Jason is a parody of his Hercules (1993, p.153). In construing Bassanio as Hercules, Portia connects Hercules' liberation of Hesione to the role she believes Bassanio will fulfil for her. 'Live thou, I live' – if Bassanio heroically makes the right choice, his survival of the test guarantees Portia's own survival. This application of the myth briefly opens the possibility that Bassanio's success will endow Portia with the autonomy denied to her by her father's will. This pattern of meaning is very different from the one invoked by Bassanio and Graziano: 'We are the Jasons, we have won the fleece' (3.2.239). As Bate argues, this identifies Portia and Nerissa as fleece-like treasure which will enrich the Venetian travellers: 'The success of Bassanio and his friend as Argonauts is nothing more than a means of compensation for the loss of Antonio's argosies' (1993, p.152). We might add that the love story of Jason and Medea (whose witchcraft enables him to win the fleece) is a profoundly unsettling precedent: Jason ultimately jilts Medea, who murders their children in revenge.

What then do these mythical allusions add to our sense of Belmont? First, myth conveys an idea of Belmont as a fairy-tale world – somewhere in which Shakespeare's characters can become like the celebrated figures of classical myth and literature. As in Bassanio's speech to Antonio, the Jason myth communicates both a concrete idea of Portia's value and a shimmering sense of the romance of Belmont. Though we may be sceptical of Jason's heroism, we should not underestimate the power of myth to construct a 'golden' image of Belmont as an aristocratic counterpoint to mercantile Venice. Secondly, myth heightens a sense of Belmont as a formal, courtly milieu. In construing Bassanio as Hercules, Portia prepares him for the roles she wants him to assume: Herculean liberator and 'new-crowned monarch'. This allusion works alongside the casket device and the music Portia requests to give the scene a sense of courtly solemnity. Like the Medici court analysed by Anabel Thomas in Chapter 3, Belmont displays an appetite for antiquity, here shown in words rather than bronze reliefs. Finally, mythical allusion complicates Belmont by making it susceptible to the darker resonances explicit in the Ovidian myths. The best example of this is the so-called love duet between Lorenzo and Jessica which begins Act 5.

Exercise

Reread 5.1.1–24, paying attention to Halio's notes. What tone do you think the actors should adopt for this dialogue?

Discussion

I've seen the dialogue performed in several different ways. Sometimes the actors are flirtatious, exchanging the myths as a part of their love play; sometimes they seem unsettled by the words they say to each other and by each other's company. There are two kinds of problem in Shakespeare's text. First, the lyric tone encourages us to trust the languorous sexuality of night-time in Belmont. When Lorenzo says 'In such a night as this,/When the sweet wind did gently kiss the trees/And they did make no noise', he eroticizes the wind and the trees by making them 'kiss': the natural world seems to mirror Lorenzo and Jessica as lovers. Because the speech is mellifluous, we may assume that the emotional reality between the lovers is correspondingly amorous. But the second problem is that the stories the lovers swap are all tragic:

> to the mythologically literate members of Shakespeare's audience, these allusions would have been shot through with irony ... Cressida is probably lying with Diomede as Troilus mounts the walls; Pyramus and Thisbe will soon be dead; Aeneas will not return to Carthage.
>
> (Bate, 1993, p.155)

This enormously complicates how the lines should be performed. Though not everyone in an Elizabethan or modern audience would recognize these allusions, my guess is that the best performance will be one that tries to bring out some of the irony Bate identifies. ❖

A lot is at stake in Act 5; the way in which you read these lines will have a decisive effect on the way you interpret Belmont. If you take it that the tone is predominantly flirtatious, and that in any case only a few members of the audience would have been 'mythologically literate', you will probably be content to see Belmont chiefly as a world of love. But if you're not wholly convinced by Lorenzo and Jessica's love, and remember that these were very well-known classical stories – after all, Shakespeare had already dramatized the story of Pyramus and Thisbe in *A Midsummer Night's Dream* (*c.*1595–6), while Marlowe's *Dido, Queen of Carthage* (*c.*1586) had retold Aeneas's desertion of Dido – you will probably want a different definition of Belmont.

But what? As I reminded you earlier, Belmont is a fiction. We all have ideas of Venice which are independent of *The Merchant*, whereas Belmont exists only in the play. Because we know about it in reality, we can easily think that Venice is more than just a 'world of money'; Belmont however remains a fictitious environment, a no-place like Sir Thomas More's *Utopia*. But we need to go further than distinguishing between factual and fictional locations. Belmont is construed and presented to the audience through Venice: we first hear about it in Venice through Bassanio, for whom it embodies a chance for both love and financial redemption. Belmont then looks like a place of Venetian wish fulfilment, yet it also mirrors Venetian values and aspirations. As an aristocratic court, it is an exclusive milieu in which wealth is an inherited fact rather than something competed for in the market place. What Bassanio competes for is Portia herself. The casket test implicitly identifies her as a commodity – as she says to Bassanio before he chooses: 'I am locked in one of them./If you do love me, you will find me out' (3.2.40–1). Finding 'Fair Portia's counterfeit' in the lead casket entitles Bassanio to Portia and provides a counter metaphor to the financial one: Bassanio *gives* himself emotionally to Portia as he *receives* her as his prize (3.2.140); he has hazarded himself in order to win infinite emotional and financial rewards. You will have to make up your own mind about how satisfactory you find this fusing of quest motifs with financial metaphors. The point I want to stress is that love in Belmont remains unsettled and unsettling. Immediately after Bassanio chooses the right casket, we learn the bad news about Antonio which clouds and complicates the romantic idyll. Similarly, Lorenzo's and Jessica's evocation of Ovidian lovers emphasizes the proximity of tragedy to Belmont.

We began this section with Leggatt's distinction between Venice and Belmont. How far have we modified our sense of Shakespeare's Italy? Leggatt makes Venice and Belmont into distinct worlds with contrasting, antagonistic value systems. In a play with two different locations, this effect is almost inevitable – *As You Like It* contrasts Duke Frederick's corrupt court with the innocent world of the Forest of Arden. But with *The Merchant* I suggest we avoid such dichotomies. To understand the play we need to juxtapose Venice and Belmont, but in the process of making that juxtaposition we often find that the contrasts are far from absolute. As a court Belmont is a locus of inherited wealth, while Venice is a market in which such wealth can be lost, as Bassanio's plight testifies. But to argue that money or love characterizes one place and not the other is to simplify the rich overlapping resonances between the two places and plots. That said, the central distinction I would make between Venice and Belmont is in terms of the openness of each milieu. As we've seen, Venice is a cosmopolitan environment with a thriving Jewish community, whereas Belmont is an exclusive aristocratic court. We must now turn to this tension between exclusion and inclusion.

Others and lovers

I've mentioned the exclusion of Shylock from Belmont and Antonio from marriage. I'd like you now to reread the rest of Act 5, trying to pinpoint where these exclusions take place.

Shylock is not named in Act 5. He is alluded to explicitly as 'the wealthy Jew' (5.1.15–17) and implicitly as 'The man that hath no music in himself' (5.1.83–8). The first allusion sites Shylock outside of Belmont by recapping Lorenzo's and Jessica's elopement: they have 'run from Venice/As far as Belmont' with Shylock's wealth. The second passage recalls 2.5, where Shylock exhibited his dislike of music:

> ... when you hear the drum
> And the vile squealing of the wry-necked fife ...
> ... stop my house's ears – I mean my casements:
> Let not the sound of shallow fopp'ry enter
> My sober house.
>
> (2.5.29–36)

C.L. Barber argues that this speech identifies Shylock as an anti-festive figure: someone who like Malvolio in *Twelfth Night* ludicrously and self-importantly disdains normative social activities like drinking and partying (1959, p.165). Lorenzo goes further. For him, the music-hater 'Is fit for treasons, stratagems and spoils ... Let no such man be trusted' (5.1.85–8). As 4.1 demonstrates, Shylock's 'stratagems' almost succeed in killing Antonio. Lorenzo's speech clarifies the need for Belmont to exclude Shylock. Not only is he an anti-festive figure, he is a character who cannot be absorbed into this apparently benign world of harmony and love. Again, though, we need to be alive to the discrepancies which circulate throughout this play. Though it is tempting to view Lorenzo as the play's spokesman, we must remember his relationship to Shylock. He has strong incentives for wanting to exclude from Belmont the father-in-law whose ducats he has stolen.

Antonio's exclusion is less direct than Shylock's and more debatable. Portia welcomes him to Belmont (5.1.139–41), yet almost as soon as this has happened the characters become embroiled in the unravelling of the ring plot. At the moment when marital harmony has broken down Antonio dolefully observes, 'I am th'unhappy subject of these quarrels' (5.1.238). Though the 'quarrels' are eventually resolved, the ring plot draws attention to Antonio's comparative isolation in Belmont. The other Christian characters have paired off (3.5.35–6 implies that even Launcelot Gobbo has a sexual partner) while Antonio stands alone. The play's final exit continues to give directors an interesting conundrum: how to get the solitary Antonio off stage. Do you leave him by himself as the newly married couples retire to their bedrooms, or do you have him exiting arm in arm with Bassanio and Portia? If you leave Antonio alone, you respect the fact that Shakespeare, unlike Fiorentino, has not equipped his merchant with a wife (see Halio, p.15) and imply that he remains melancholy, excluded from his dearest friend's new relationship. If you make Antonio leave with Bassanio and Portia, you signal his inclusion in the harmonious resolution of the ring plot, but will then have to cope with the sexual innuendo which crackles in the play's final lines: two of the couples are after all exiting to their first night in bed together. ❖

'Romantic' comedy is implicitly a genre of inclusion. Through the final marriages, different and often conflicting characters are assimilated into a social and dramatic institution which is larger than their differences. Hymen, the classical god of marriage, appears at the end of *As You Like It* (5.4.125–44) and clarifies this principle: 'I bar confusion,/'Tis I must make conclusion/Of these strange events ... 'Tis Hymen peoples every town,/High wedlock then be honored'. Marriage resolves differences and populates the community. But *As You Like It* is a much lighter, more genuinely 'romantic' comedy than *The Merchant*. In this section of the chapter we will examine the others and lovers who inhabit Belmont and Venice through three overlapping case studies. In studying the roles of Shylock, Antonio and Portia we should be able to answer some key questions about *The Merchant* as a whole: why are Shylock and to a lesser extent Antonio excluded from the finale? Is the play finally so unsettling that we have to revise its comic status?

The Jewish other

In the twentieth century Shylock has become an increasingly problematic role. In an era which has witnessed the genocide of European Jews by Nazi Germany, Shakespeare's depiction of Shylock as a bloodthirsty miser has seemed racist in the extreme. As a theatre script *The Merchant* has become burdened with the concerns of recent times, as you can see in Halio's discussion of the play's stage history (pp.73–83). But we need to understand Elizabethan attitudes towards Jews. As Halio's section on 'Shakespeare and Semitism' underlines, the dominant cultural paradigms (or models) of Jewishness derived from folk tales, anecdotes and prejudice because first-hand experience of practising Jews was so limited (pp.1–13); Chaucer's *Prioress's Tale* (*c.*1393–1400) embodies this tradition in presenting Jews as murderers of Christian children. A good example of Elizabethan representation of Jews is Thomas Nashe's picaresque travel narrative *The Unfortunate Traveller* (1594), in which the hero Jack Wilton falls into the hands of Jewish villains in Rome. Nashe's Jews, Zadoch and Zachery, are no more than two-dimensional stereotypes, avaricious psychopaths intent on killing the beleaguered English hero; Figure 5.7, the engraving of Coryate being pursued by a Venetian Jew, embodies a related idea of the Jewish other as a bogeyman.

Such evidence seems to construct a model of reading which interprets *The Merchant* in the same way that we approach texts like *The Unfortunate Traveller* and *The Jew of Malta*. The logic goes like this: just as Nashe and Marlowe represent Jews as archetypal villains, so Shakespeare follows suit in his own drama about Jews. Precisely because Shakespeare *was* a product of his culture (as this chapter has been suggesting) he replicates the exclusionary thinking which characterized that culture. Let's see if this argument works in practice.

Exercise

Reread 3.1, then read the extracts from C.L. Barber and Ruth Nevo in the Reader (nos. 16 and 17). Which interpretation of Shylock's role strikes you as being the most convincing?

Discussion

I chose Barber and Nevo not because they are the most up-to-date critics, but because they have each been highly influential, and because in this case their analyses are diametrically opposed. Barber, reading Shylock as an anti-festive miser, argues that he is a comic demonstration of the human 'degraded into mechanism' (1959, p.180). This is why he refers to Jonson and Molière: in his reading, Shylock has surrendered his humanity to his obsession with cash and so becomes a dramatic cousin of figures like Volpone and Harpagon, who are both comic misers. Any reading which humanizes Shylock is for Barber a falsification of what he sees as Shylock's mechanistic conceptualization of the human body and his reduction of the emotional to the material. Barber's Shylock is there to be laughed at: 'the process of *making fun of* a person often works by exhibiting pretension to humanity to show that they are inhuman, mechanical, not validly appropriate for sympathy' (1959, p.181). So when Shylock bemoans the loss of Leah's ring, the appropriate response is derision because it shows that he understands only possessions, not emotions.

This is a powerful reading which warns us against sentimentalizing Shylock. Barber's study cumulatively suggests that Shylock is a figure like Malvolio who exists as a lightning conductor for comic abuse. Yet Barber's reading is partly undermined by a piece of critical sleight of hand. He quotes the phrase 'O my daughter! O my ducats!' as though it were a part of Shylock's direct speech. Yet as Nevo observes, this phrase is actually embedded in Salarino's and Solanio's 'burlesquing of Shylock's outcry' in 2.8 (1980, p.132). This is a vital detail, since, as Nevo argues, there is a crucial difference between the Christian's abusive *reporting* of Shylock's laments and the actual *staging* of these laments in 3.1. Nevo characterizes these speeches as a biblical 'Jeremiad', suggesting that in 3.1 we experience a genuine sense of Shylock's anguish as a deserted father. For Nevo, the appropriate analogy for Shylock at this point is Lear, not Molière's Harpagon: a tragic father to be empathized with rather than a ludicrous father to be laughed at. This is why Nevo emphasizes her belief that Shylock only decides to claim the flesh bond *during* 3.1: Shylock's homicidal desire for revenge is actuated by the Christians' taunts. Rather than revealing Shylock as a machine, 3.1 makes him a quasi-tragic figure, invested with true Shakespearean gravitas.

I imagine that this is not an exercise you find at all easy – I don't find it easy myself. Making up your mind about a figure as problematic and intriguing as Shylock should never be a simple task. If we read 3.1 from the perspective of Elizabethan ideas of Jewishness and usury, we will probably think that Barber makes the more compelling case. Like Nashe's villains, like Marlowe's Barabas, Shylock is a bogeyman whom we are invited to despise. Because we imagine Elizabethan England as an unsentimental and tough environment, we could take Barber's view that Shylock is 'a clear-cut butt' (1959, p.183). Yet we can make a case that would allow Shylock a measure of pathos, even on the stage of the Theatre in the late 1590s. To begin with, we cannot be certain how Elizabethans responded to dramatic aliens: Othello, 'the Moor of Venice', is unequivocally a tragic hero. Though there is some evidence that *The Jew of Malta* was interpreted by some as a licence for attacks on aliens resident in London (Shapiro, 1996, pp.184–6), the play as we know it is more of an incitement to misanthropy than racial hatred.[3] The fact remains that Barabas is the play's central character, the hero-villain who generates the action; my suspicion would be that Elizabethan audiences, like their modern counterparts, would have enjoyed his antics theatrically even as they disapproved of them morally. We should also note that Elizabethans were not as unsentimental as Barber implies. One of the most popular plays of the 1580s and 90s was Thomas Kyd's *The Spanish Tragedy*, which centres on the efforts of Hieronimo to avenge the murder of his son Horatio. It is a highly emotive play, featuring many long laments by Hieronimo. Given that Spain and England were at war in the late 1580s, it is suggestive that Elizabethan theatre-goers were prepared to empathize with the woes of this Spanish hero, though we should remember that *The Spanish Tragedy* is explicitly tragic.

---

[3] As you can see from Figure 5.6, *The Jew* was first printed in 1633, 40 years after Marlowe's death. Various scholars have speculated that the text published at this time represents an edited version of Marlowe's original, which would mean that the play presented at the Rose in the 1590s could have been substantially different from the play we now know. See Bevington's and Rasmussen's commentary in their edition of *Doctor Faustus and Other Plays* (1995, pp.xxviii–xxix).

But the strongest argument in favour of Nevo's reading would be the primary evidence she adduces: the text of *The Merchant*. In particular, I find Barber's reading of 3.1 hard to accept because the text is so far removed from plays like Jonson's *Volpone* or Plautus's *Aulularia*, in which the main protagonists' focus on money becomes an obsession which distorts all other perceptions. In the dialogue with Tubal which Barber quotes at length, the words arguably do not expose Shylock as a machine but as a suffering and flawed individual. Investing emotional value in material objects, as Shylock does with Leah's ring, is after all a universal human activity. With Barber's reading in mind, M.M. Mahood comments:

> Much of Shylock's language is as comically repetitive as the 'sans dot' ['without dowry' – Harpagon's battle-cry] of Molière's miser; yet the declaration 'I would my daughter were dead at my foot, and the jewels in her ear: would she were hearsed at my foot, and the ducats in her coffin' ... echoes with a kind of psalmodic passion the very different repetitiousness of Hebrew poetry. The same voice of lamentation, obscuring the solipsistic nature of what is said, is heard in 'no sighs o'my breathing, no tears but o'my shedding'.
>
> (1987, p.33)

Mahood reminds us of the poetic resonance of the Bible in sixteenth-century England.[4] The biblical timbre of Shylock's laments gives them a resonance which Elizabethan spectators would have recognized immediately and possibly responded to. A character who says 'I would my daughter were dead at my foot, and the jewels in her ear' is unlikely to produce derisive laughter. Indeed, throughout this scene, Shylock's words are memorable because they are actuated by the pain of his situation. Though Shylock is undoubtedly solipsistic (or self-absorbed) his language is here elevated above the ludicrous. Moreover, the violence of Shylock's imagery signals the seriousness of the threat he embodies – unlike Harpagon or Euclio, he has by this stage of the play become a dangerous man. ❖

But where does this leave us? Does Shakespeare simply replicate the exclusionary attitudes characteristic of his culture, or does his play do something different? Shakespeare's attitudes as a private individual are irrecoverable – all we can comment on are the effects produced by his text. *The Merchant* is vastly different in tone from a work like *The Unfortunate Traveller*, though it is not a plea for racial tolerance.

[4] The major English translation was the Geneva Bible (1560), made by Marian exiles, but Mahood notes that Shakespeare shows more familiarity with the Bishops' Bible (1568) at this stage in his career. The King James Bible (1611) was shaped and informed by these earlier translations, but was too late to be used substantially by Shakespeare.

Note, for example, the treatment of Morocco. His first speech identifies him as a Moor – he tells Portia 'Mislike me not for my complexion' (2.1.1). After his unsuccessful suit, Portia comments in an aside, 'A gentle riddance. Draw the curtains, go./Let all of his complexion choose me so' (2.7.78–9). As the couplet closer of the first casket scene, these brisk lines are calculated to raise a laugh, especially through Portia's recycling of Morocco's word 'complexion'. Modern audiences rarely laugh at such casual racism, but this is no reason to assume that Elizabethans would not have enjoyed the line. Shylock is a different kind of other. He lacks Morocco's exaggerated self-importance and is handled in much greater detail. Quite simply, Shakespeare gives us the opportunity to care much more about Shylock than he does about Morocco; his is a role we can identify with and invest in. This is how I would deal with the readings of Barber and Nevo: both are possible interpretations activated by Shakespeare's script. Difficult though this is, the best reading is one which steers a course between the extremes of seeing Shylock either as a fall guy or as a tragic hero. Shylock's role emerges from a network of historic and folkloric models with a strong exclusionary bias into something which transcends these cultural stereotypes. He is a psychologically credible other.

The Christian outsider

As I noted earlier, Antonio's exclusion is more debatable than Shylock's. An influential view has juxtaposed the exclusion of Shylock as a bitter, vindictive materialist with the inclusion of Antonio in Belmont and the household of Bassanio and Portia. According to this reading, *The Merchant* distinguishes between opposing approaches to the use of wealth: the miserly, closed approach of Shylock as against the venturing, open approach of Antonio and Bassanio. Joseph Pequigney summarizes the emotional grammar he discerns in *The Merchant*:

> The graspers and hoarders lose; the givers gamble and win ...

> Antonio is the referent of the title because, besides being the protagonist to Shylock's antagonist, he gives and hazards the most. All his wealth is risked in foreign trade and then seemingly lost ... he lets go of Bassanio, on account of whom he loves the world ... he ventures the pound of flesh and is ready to lay down his life for his friend ...

> The moral law peculiar to this comedy coincides with the law common to all Shakespearean comedies, according to both of which felicity and, in cases of suffering, equitable to [sic] superabundant compensation await the virtuous ... and this Antonio is no exception.

(1995, pp.190–1)

For Pequigney, Antonio's final inclusion depends upon his financial and emotional hazarding. As a giver to Shylock's hoarder, he ultimately deserves the 'superabundant compensation' which awaits all virtuous comic characters. This model of comic bonuses is similar to Nevo's theory of Shakespearean comedy as a mode of self-discovery which we have already encountered, but note the shift in emphasis. For Pequigney, venture capitalism and emotional openness are cognate activities. If you hazard your wealth abroad, you will be emotionally open; if you hoard it at home, you will be emotionally closed.

Pequigney's Antonio is heroic: a noble self-sacrificer, constantly putting the interests of his beloved friend ahead of his own. Pequigney suggests a comparison between Antonio and Christ by juxtaposing Antonio's long speech to Bassanio at 4.1.261–78 with Christ's remark, just before the Crucifixion: 'Greater love hath no man than this, that a man lay down his life for his friends' (John 15.13). Read in this way, Antonio assumes the stature of an incomparable hero. But is this our experience of the character – and the drama – Shakespeare actually wrote?

Exercise

I'd like you now to reread 4.1, paying particular attention to Antonio's role. Do you agree with Pequigney's reading?

Discussion

For me, Pequigney's account is far too idealized. Though he is right in thinking that the play turns on moments of hazarding, as 3.2 demonstrates, his sense of Antonio's selflessness is questionable. Antonio presents himself as a human sacrifice in the lines 'I am the tainted wether of the flock,/Meetest for death' (4.1.113–14), but a sacrifice for what or to whom? Halio's note points out the echo of the story of Abraham and Isaac, in which God provides Abraham with a ram – the 'tainted wether' – to substitute for Isaac. Does Antonio then believe he is an offering to God – a Christian martyr to be butchered by the heathen Shylock – or does he reveal some unspecified psychological neurosis (see Halio, p.49, n.1)? Mahood warns against making the play a theological allegory:

> To view the play in this light it is necessary to believe that Shakespeare's use of a phrase or reference always reflects his reading of Scripture and that its biblical source was immediately evident to the audience; that an Elizabethan audience would have considered theological matters a proper concern for comedy; and that it was ready ... to attribute a distinct moral meaning to the play it had witnessed. None of these assumptions can be made with confidence.
>
> (1987, p.187)

Such allegorical readings view the trial scene as a demonstration of the superiority of the new law to the old: Christian mercy eclipses Hebrew legalism. This interpretation depends on accepting the assumptions Mahood questions and on believing Antonio's self-presentation as a sacrificial victim. ❖

Is there another way to view his role in this scene? Theatrically, these lines serve both to build the mounting tension and to present Antonio as a character who wants to die. But why should he? His farewell speech to Bassanio helps us here:

> Commend me to your honourable wife.
> Tell her the process of Antonio's end.
> Say how I loved you, speak me fair in death.
> And when the tale is told, bid her be judge
> Whether Bassanio had not once a love.
>
> (4.1.270–4)

Antonio almost sounds like the dying Hamlet, asking Horatio to 'draw thy breath in pain/To tell my story' (*Hamlet* 5.2.344–9). But Hamlet wants his story told to clear his 'wounded name' to the outside world, whereas Antonio's death wish is specifically directed to Bassanio's 'fair wife' to communicate to her the intensity of the bond between the two friends. Why? Not presumably as a wedding present, but rather as a posthumous challenge: '*You* think you love Bassanio, well *I* died for him!' At issue here is Bassanio's affections, not his body: who loves him most and whom he loves most. Given this stimulus, it is no surprise that Bassanio replies that Antonio's life is more precious to him than his own, Portia's 'and all the world' (4.1.279–82). From this evidence, I would suggest that the 'heroic' Antonio is no more convincing than the 'tragic' Shylock. Both roles are more complex and dramatically enigmatic than such characterizations allow for. As *the* Merchant of Venice, Antonio is the play's major subject: the subject of his friends' speculation in 1.1, the subject of Shylock's homicidal grudge in 4.1 and finally 'th'unhappy subject of these quarrels' in 5.1. But as a 'protagonist' (remember Pequigney's use of this word) Antonio is curiously passive. Unlike Barabas, he is never shown energetically pursing his 'ventures'; rather he is always the subject of other characters' actions, whether in the form of Bassanio's demand for cash or Shylock's demand for his flesh. Dramatic heroes – even Hamlet – are usually more active and more engaging of the audience's attention than Antonio. Shakespeare's venture capitalist seems to be a rewrite of Marlowe's in a minor key.

In recent years the homoeroticism of Shakespeare's work has been explored by scholars like Pequigney: since sodomy was illegal in sixteenth-century England, such interpretation depends on revealing what may have been latent in familiar texts. In this case, Pequigney emphasizes the non-sexual character of the relationship between Bassanio and Antonio. In his reading of the ring plot, Antonio is incorporated into the Portia–Bassanio marriage by standing as guarantor of Bassanio's fidelity (Pequigney, 1995, p.191). It seems to me that Pequigney is right in thinking that Bassanio and Antonio are not presented as homosexual lovers – Bassanio discusses his marriage project directly with Antonio who then finances it. Yet there is a definite competition within the play's final scenes for Bassanio's affections – a desire especially on Antonio's part for emotional pre-eminence. This desire is short-circuited by Portia's interventions: in the trial scene she saves Antonio's life; through the ring plot she gives him a role in Belmont; finally, through the discovered letter, she provides him with material returns on his original ventures. Portia then appears as a mediator of conflict and a fulcrum between Belmont and Venice and their competing values.

'A second Daniel'

All readings and performances of *The Merchant* must grapple with the role played by Portia. It is Shylock who identifies the cross-dressed Portia as a type of Daniel (4.1.220), who, as Halio notes, judges righteously in the apocryphal story of Susanna and the Elders. But as the trial turns against Shylock, Graziano appropriates the analogy for his sarcastic onslaught on Shylock: 'I thank thee, Jew, for teaching me that word' (4.1.337). Hebrew scripture is used to reinforce Christian justice in its victory over a latter-day Jew. Graziano's irony – and the irony of the scene as a whole – is in revising Shylock's conception of justice.

Exercise

Have another look at the trial scene. Are you convinced by Portia's solution to the flesh bond (4.1.302–9)?

Discussion

Numerous critics have pointed out the flaws in Portia's solution to the flesh bond; as Halio notes, 'The right to take the pound of flesh would assume the right to take the blood necessarily spilled in the process, unless the bond specifically stated that blood should be omitted' (p.203). Portia puts forward a case which is dramatically rather than legally convincing. ❖

What then is the dramatic function of the trial scene? I would say that it tests what kind of play *The Merchant* will finally be: the comedy of love intimated in 3.2, or the revenge tragedy anticipated in 3.1. So the actual scene is neither comic nor tragic: both modes are potentially present as the scene skilfully holds the outcome in the balance. In her role as Balthasar, Portia ensures the comic outcome for the Christian characters at least. By undermining Shylock's bond, she liberates Antonio; through the ring plot which closes this scene, she enables Antonio to find an emotional place within Belmont which is not directly in competition with her relationship with Bassanio, while rerouting the play back to the comic tone of the earlier Belmont scenes.

So far so good, but our real problems are not so much with Portia saving Antonio as with the Christians' stipulation that the humiliated Shylock should convert to Christianity (4.1.376–96). As I indicated earlier, our responses to Shylock are shaped by our own cultural norms: we find this conversion under duress hard to accept. Elizabethan audiences would have reacted differently. Even so, Shapiro's study reveals that contemporaneous attitudes to the conversion of Jews were not as uniform as we might expect. Elizabethans may simply have read Antonio's action as a demonstration of Christian mercy. Radical Protestants may have seen Shylock's conversion as symbolic of a wider process in which their own distinct values were endorsed by the conversion of the Jews (Shapiro, 1996, pp.140–6). Equally, some may have been sceptical about the genuineness of Jewish conversions, like the seventeenth-century writer Thomas Calvert for whom it was dubious whether 'any Jew will heartily convert and turn to Christ' (Shapiro, 1996, p.165).

Shakespeare does not provide Shylock with a detailed response to his conversion beyond the three words 'I am content' (4.1.389); this proved so frustrating to Olivier that he gave his Shylock an off-stage howl of anguish to make up the perceived shortfall (Mahood, 1987, p.50). While Barber would see this as a sentimentalization of Shylock, we can suggest that the tension between Christian mercy and Shylock's elliptical response is an essential part of the writing. In saving Antonio, Portia destroys the Shylock the play has so far presented: you may take it that his conversion foreshadows the creation of a 'better' Christian Shylock, but Shakespeare gives us no hint that this will occur. It may be that, in answer to Halio's question, you conclude that Shylock is not worth saving (p.11); it may be that Shylock was jeered off stage by 1590s audiences with Graziano leading the chorus of disdain, but Shakespeare's text remains enigmatic. When Shylock says he is 'not well' (4.1.392), it is hard to resist the feeling that we have witnessed the erosion of a distinctive identity. In this context, Nevo's idea that the play contains 'two Shylocks' is useful: one is a 'burlesque ogre' – the miser the Christians are keen to exclude – the other is a 'human being possessing a gloomy and savage dignity' who so often unsettles audiences and readers (1980, p.136).

I think the other thing we can say about Portia as Daniel is that while she saves Antonio – and therefore saves the audience from witnessing a scene of excruciating violence like the blinding of Gloucester in *King Lear* – she also licenses another goading attack on Shylock which arguably does not show the Christian Venetians as consistently merciful or virtuous. While Shylock enjoys Christian mercy through the duke's pardon (4.1.364–5), the scene's dramatic tone transfers the anticipated violence of Antonio's death to the realized violence of the verbal assault the Christians – led by Graziano – make on Shylock. Remember that Shylock leaves the stage to Graziano's quip that if he had been Shylock's judge, he would have had him hanged (4.1.394–6).

Portia's legal performance enables the Christian characters to return to Belmont and the relationships to which they have attached supreme importance. For the space of an act, she takes on a role which goes beyond the conventional behaviour of a noblewoman. Like Helena in *All's Well that Ends Well* (*c.*1602–3), Portia is a resourceful heroine whose actions are not confined by her gender. But again, we have to be careful: Shakespearean comedies end with marriages after which his distinctive heroines become wives and presumably mothers: the autonomy which continues to delight us in characters like Portia, Rosalind and Helena is something of a holiday intermission between the 'real life' of being either a daughter or a wife. Moreover, as Rosalind explicitly signals in the Epilogue to *As You Like It*, part of the feminine autonomy Shakespeare plays with in the comedies is contingent on the gender ambiguities generated by having female parts played by boy actors. You can see the dizzying ironies between the real and the unreal this would have presented to an Elizabethan audience in Portia's remark to Nerissa about their cross-dressing: 'When we are both accoutered like young men/I'll prove the prettier fellow of the two' (3.4.63–4).

Renaissance drama?

One of the most striking aspects of the Renaissance in Britain is how late it occurs. Shakespeare was born in 1564 – the year Michelangelo died, aged 89. The diffusion of Renaissance culture to Britain was a slow process; in the case of drama, we have seen that the social and economic conditions for a new secular drama were in place only by the later decades of the sixteenth century. Shakespearean drama draws on a wide range of traditions: unlike artists such as Michelangelo, Shakespeare's work was not chiefly stimulated by the imitation of classical precedents. In this chapter we've looked in detail at the native and classical traditions available to Shakespeare and their impact on *The Merchant*. We should now be able to ask what we mean when we call this play a Renaissance drama.

In Burckhardt's terms, *The Merchant* lacks a central concern with the revival of classical culture which he argues characterized the Italian Renaissance; the play's Italy is an amalgam of contemporary reportage and fairy tale. Yet Burckhardt still sees Shakespeare as a singular creative talent – a Renaissance artist of the highest rank. The play also features several densely enigmatic roles which have proved endlessly reinterpretable since the 1590s. You may feel that roles like Shylock and Portia embody Burckhardt's idea that there is a discovery during the Renaissance of a modern conception of the self. As our discussion of Shylock demonstrates, part of the difficulty we experience in making sense of his role is that Shakespeare confers a complex personality on him which we cannot ignore.

Does this mean then that Shakespeare's characters are examples of Burckhardt's modern individuals? My answer would be yes and no. Since part of the novelty of Shakespearean drama is the sense of vivid interior life he bestows on his characters, he does contribute to our ideas of the self. Ambivalent though Marlowe's Barabas is, he lacks the psychological nuances of Shylock and, as Greenblatt argues, is 'de-individualized'; he is a stereotype drawn from folklore, prejudice and fashionable ideology. By contrast, *The Merchant* gives a disquietingly intimate sense of involvement in the pursuits of its characters. My favourite example of this is during 2.6: as Graziano and Salarino gossip about Lorenzo and Jessica, Graziano comments 'All things that are,/Are with more spirit chasèd than enjoyed' (2.6.13–14). At a stroke, Shakespeare initiates the doubts about Lorenzo's and Jessica's relationship which accumulate through the play: Graziano makes us feel like the jaded roué he implies Lorenzo will become.

Yet we need to remember that our ideas of the self have partly been constructed by generations of reading Shakespeare in particular ways. In other words, though Shylock is a more complex role than Barabas, he was drawn from the same traditions and prejudices as Marlowe's character. Similarly, although it is tempting to read Portia as an independent woman of the Renaissance, Shakespeare carefully locates her within patriarchal institutions. Compared with her fictive original, the Lady of Belmonte, Portia is a much more restricted character. Moreover, Portia was originally performed by a 'bragging Jack' boy actor (3.4.77); rather than an independent creation, Portia remains on a material level a role staged at a specific place and time.

So is *The Merchant* a Renaissance drama? Ultimately, this depends on what we mean by 'Renaissance'. If we use the term to date specific cultural artefacts, then we can say unequivocally that *The Merchant* is a product of English Renaissance culture. But I think we can say more. In this study of the play I have emphasized the complex social and literary traditions on which Shakespeare draws. English Renaissance culture is characterized by these kinds of assimilation or synthesis, as we have seen in our study of the amphitheatres. In formal terms, *The Merchant* amalgamates a vast range of sources into a coherent and deliberately problematic drama. Like Spenser's *The Faerie Queene*, it is a dazzling formal achievement, exemplifying the artistic skill and intellectual resources of 1590s literary culture. In calling *The Merchant* a Renaissance drama, we both link the play to these vital contexts and accommodate its strangenesses to the very different cultural climate of the present day.

Bibliography

All quotations from and line references to *The Merchant of Venice* are from Halio's edition, The Oxford Shakespeare; all quotations from and references to Shakespeare's other plays are from Blackmore Evans's and Tobin's The Riverside Shakespeare.

BARBER, C.L. (1959) *Shakespeare's Festive Comedy: A Study of Dramatic Form and its Relation to Social Custom*, Princeton, NJ, Princeton University Press.

BARTON (RIGHTER), A. (1967) *Shakespeare and the Idea of the Play*, Harmondsworth, Penguin.

BATE, J. (1993) *Shakespeare and Ovid*, Oxford, Clarendon.

BAWCUTT, N.W. (ed.) (1978) C. Marlowe: *The Jew of Malta*, The Revels Plays, Manchester, Manchester University Press.

BEVINGTON, D. (1962) *From Mankind to Marlowe*, Cambridge, Mass., Harvard University Press.

BEVINGTON, D. (ed.) (1997) C. Marlowe: *The Jew of Malta*, Revels Student Editions, Manchester, Manchester University Press.

BEVINGTON, D. and RASMUSSEN, E. (eds) (1995) C. Marlowe: *Doctor Faustus and Other Plays*, Oxford, Oxford University Press.

BLACKMORE EVANS, G. and TOBIN, J.J.M. (eds) (1997, 2nd edn) W. Shakespeare: The Riverside Shakespeare, Boston, Mass., and New York, Houghton Mifflin.

Book of Common Prayer (1968) London, Eyre & Spottiswoode.

BROWN, J.R. (ed.) (1964) W. Shakespeare: *The Merchant of Venice*, The Arden Shakespeare, London, Methuen.

BURCKHARDT, J. (1990) *The Civilization of the Renaissance in Italy*, trans. S.G.C. Middlemore, Harmondsworth, Penguin; first published 1858.

CLUBB, L.G. (1989) *Italian Drama in Shakespeare's Time*, New Haven, Conn., Yale University Press.

COLLINSON, P. (1986) 'From iconoclasm to iconophobia: the cultural impact of the second English Reformation', The Stenton Lecture 1985, University of Reading.

GREENBLATT, S. (1980) *Renaissance Self-fashioning: From More to Shakespeare*, Chicago, University of Chicago Press.

GREENBLATT, S. (1988) *Shakespearean Negotiations*, Oxford, Clarendon.

GURR, A. (1980, 2nd edn) *The Shakespearean Stage: 1574–1642*, Cambridge, Cambridge University Press.

GURR, A. (1987) *Playgoing in Shakespeare's London*, Cambridge, Cambridge University Press.

GURR, A. (1997) 'Shakespeare's Globe: a history of reconstructions and some reasons for trying' in J.R. Mulryne and M. Shewring (eds) *Shakespeare's Globe Rebuilt*, Cambridge, Cambridge University Press.

HALIO, J.L. (ed.) (1993) W. Shakespeare: *The Merchant of Venice*, The Oxford Shakespeare, Oxford, Oxford University Press.

HERRICK, M.T. (1964) *Comic Theory in the Sixteenth Century*, Urbana, Illinois University Press.

KEENAN, S. and DAVIDSON, P. (1997) 'The iconography of the Bankside Globe' in J.R. Mulryne and M. Shewring (eds) *Shakespeare's Globe Rebuilt*, Cambridge, Cambridge University Press.

KERNAN, A. (1975) 'The plays and the playwrights' in C. Leech and T.W. Craik (eds) *The Revels History of Drama in English: 1576–1613*, vol. 3, London, Methuen.

LAURENCE, A. (1994) *Women in England 1500–1760: A Social History*, London, Weidenfeld & Nicolson.

LEGGATT, A. (1974) *Shakespeare's Comedy of Love*, London, Methuen.

MAHOOD, M.M. (ed.) (1987) W. Shakespeare: *The Merchant of Venice*, The New Cambridge Shakespeare, Cambridge, Cambridge University Press.

MIOLA, R. (1994) *Shakespeare and Classical Comedy: The Influence of Plautus and Terence*, Oxford, Clarendon.

NEVO, R. (1980) *Comic Transformations in Shakespeare*, London, Methuen.

NORBROOK, D. (1993) *The Penguin Book of Renaissance Verse: 1509–1659*, ed. H.R. Woudhuysen, Harmondsworth, Penguin.

ORAM, W.A., BJORVAND, E., BOND, R., CAIN, T.H., DUNLOP, A. and SCHELL, R. (eds) (1989) E. Spenser: *The Yale Edition of the Shorter Poems of Edmund Spenser*, New Haven, Conn. and London, Yale University Press.

ORNSTEIN, R. (1986) *Shakespeare's Comedies: From Roman Farce to Romantic Mystery* Newark/London and Toronto, University of Delaware Press/Associated University Presses.

PARRY, G. (1980) *Hollar's England: A Mid-Seventeenth-Century View*, Salisbury, Michael Russell.

PEQUIGNEY, J. (1995) 'The two Antonios and same-sex love in *Twelfth Night* and *The Merchant of Venice*' in D.E. Barker and I. Kamps (eds) *Shakespeare and Gender: A History*, London, Verso.

RADICE, B. (trans.) (1976) Terence: *The Comedies*, Harmondsworth, Penguin.

ROMAYNE, J. (1997) '"Totus mundus agit histrionem": the interior decoration scheme of the Bankside Globe' in J.R. Mulryne and M. Shewring (eds) *Shakespeare's Globe Rebuilt*, Cambridge, Cambridge University Press.

SANDERS, N. (1980) 'The social and historical context' in T.W. Craik (ed.) *The Revels History of Drama in English: 1500–1576*, vol. 2, London, Methuen.

SHAPIRO, J. (1991) *Rival Playwrights: Marlowe, Jonson, Shakespeare*, New York, Columbia University Press.

SHAPIRO, J. (1996) *Shakespeare and the Jews*, New York, Columbia University Press.

SHEPHERD, G. (ed.) (1973) *P. Sidney: An Apology for Poetry*, Manchester, Manchester University Press.

WRIGHTSON, K. (1994) '"Sorts of people" in Tudor and Stuart England' in J. Barry and C. Brooks (eds) *The Middling Sort of People: Culture, Society and Politics in England, 1550–1800*, Basingstoke, Macmillan.

Anthology and Reader sources

Johannes de Witt, Remarkes on the London theatres: *Shakespeare's Globe Rebuilt*, ed. J.R. Mulryne and M. Shewring, Cambridge, Cambridge University Press, 1997, Appendix C, p.189 (Anthology, no. 54).

Thomas Platter, Visits to London theatres: *Shakespeare's Globe Rebuilt*, ed. J.R. Mulryne and M. Shewring, Cambridge, Cambridge University Press, 1997, Appendix C, p.189 (Anthology, no. 55).

Andrew Gurr, Physical conditions of the London stage: *Playgoing in Shakespeare's London*, Cambridge, Cambridge University Press, 1987, Chapter 2, pp.14–22 (Reader, no. 15).

Christopher Marlowe, from *The Jew of Malta*: ed. D. Bevington, Revels Student Editions, Manchester, Manchester University Press, 1997, pp.17–19, 24–6, 28–36, 57–8 (Anthology, nos. 56i–iv).

C.L. Barber, The merchants and the Jew of Venice: wealth's communion and an intruder: *Shakespeare's Festive Comedy: A Study of Dramatic Form and its Relation to Social Custom*, Princeton, NJ, Princeton University Press, 1959, Chapter 7, pp.163–9 (Reader, no. 16).

Ruth Nevo, Jessica's monkey; or The Goodwins: *Comic Transformations in Shakespeare*, London, Methuen, 1980, Chapter 7, pp.128–40 (Reader, no. 17).

Glossary

all'antica ancient or classical; usually used with reference to the art and architecture of the Greeks and Romans

architectural orders see **orders**

belvedere raised construction or summer-house from which the surrounding scenery might be viewed

blazon part-by-part description specifically of a beloved's body

cantus firmus an existing melody that becomes the basis of a new composition through the addition of other parts

capital head or crowning feature of a column or pillar

cappella 'chapel', meaning either the building itself or the body of singers who performed in it

cardinal (or 'natural') **virtue(s)** in scholastic philosophy, justice, prudence, temperance and fortitude (courage), characteristic of good governance

chant in the context of this course, synonymous with 'Gregorian chant' and 'Plainsong' – the monophonic music (i.e. single-line melodies) used in the celebration of Catholic liturgy

coffered recessed panels, usually square or polygonal, decorating a vault or a ceiling

colophon end-piece in a manuscript or book, often ornamental, providing the writer's or printer's name and other details such as date of completion; also the device used by a publisher on the title-page of a book

conceit far-fetched comparison, made for the wit it exhibits or the surprise it arouses in the audience

condottiere (plural *condottieri*) mercenary captains or generals, usually drawn from the minor Italian nobility

copia abundant resources of language

Corinthian order third order of Greek architecture; an Athenian invention of the fifth century BCE, later developed by the Romans, who provided the prototype for the Renaissance form. Corinthian columns are fluted and more slender than either **Doric** or **Ionic**, and the **capital**, while varying in design, is often ornamented with elaborate acanthus leaf foliage

cornice horizontal moulded projection crowning a building; uppermost part of an **entablature**

decorum observation of standards of behaviour and action appropriate to one's social position; like *magnificentia*, with which it was commonly associated, it too derived from Aristotelian ethics

deliberative rhetoric branch of rhetoric which attempts to sway the audience's will through appeals to the praiseworthy or possible

diet meeting of the estates of the realm

dispositio selection and ordering of arguments

Doric order first, i.e. earliest, of the three orders of Greek architecture. The columns, which are sturdy, tapering and fluted, have simple **capitals** consisting of an echinus (a round, convex moulding) surmounted by a square abacus (flat slab). In the course of its later development the order became subdivided into Greek Doric and Roman Doric, the columns of the latter acquiring a base

ekphrasis from Greek, a particularly clear or lucid description

elocutio clothing topics in words

emblematic art in which the meaning is encoded in a series of symbols or allegories

entablature upper part of an order, consisting of architrave, frieze and **cornice**

fantasie Italian plural of the word for the imaginative faculty. However, in this sense it refers to the bizarre, fanciful or exotic representations invented for a masque, pageant or other formal entertainment. Often such representations carried an allegorical or mythological reference

Gothic art form of the Middle Ages characterized by an absence of classical features. Examples include: in architecture the use of the pointed arch, and in writing the use of Germanic as opposed to Roman or italic script

gradatio scheme which mounts by degrees to a climax, through parallel constructions in words or matter

historiated decorated with artistic historical, legendary or emblematic designs

humanism not coined until the late eighteenth or early nineteenth century, the term is loosely employed by historians to denote the revival of interest during the Renaissance in the values of a liberal arts education which stressed human as opposed to transcendental values

hyperbole a **trope** of exaggeration

impresa (plural *imprese*) a personal emblem or device, often with an associated motto, which was employed as a self-advertisement. Unlike heraldic symbols and devices, the *impresa* was chosen, not inherited; nor did it provide a necessary indication of rank. Creating new, recondite *imprese* was a widespread intellectual game for those with a

Renaissance humanist education in classical literature

incipit (Latin 'here begins') the first few words and/or notes with which a work of literature or music commences

inductivist the inductive method, which characterizes most modern science, is based on the premise that theoretical understanding of cause and effect in nature is founded on the systematic acquisition of verifiable facts (usually through repeatable experiments)

International Gothic (sometimes known as the international style) late form of Gothic art of a naturalistic kind that first found expression at the courts of France and Burgundy at the end of the fourteenth century, and which later spread to Italy, Germany and Bohemia. The new realism was confined to details, particularly to details of landscape, of animals and of costume. Objects were characterized by harmonious, flowing lines and delicate colours verging on prettiness – totally unlike the austere, humanistically inspired realism of the great Florentine masters, Masaccio and Donatello. A celebrated example of the International Gothic is the Wilton Diptych in the National Gallery, London

inventio in classical and medieval rhetoric, inventio or 'invention' was the first of the five 'parts' of oratory, and referred to the process of finding and elaborating material relevant to the rhetorician's argument

invenzione creation of elaborate schemes or allegories for paintings; during the Renaissance these were frequently devised by humanists employed at court

Ionic order second order of Greek architecture, which originated in Asia Minor in the mid sixth century BCE. The **capital** of an Ionic column is characterized by two laurel volutes (spiral scrolls)

istoria narrative or event depicted in a work of art

lauda (plural *laude*) non-liturgical religious song, of greatest importance first in the thirteenth and then again during the fifteenth to sixteenth centuries, with texts usually in Italian, less often in Latin

loci communes (Latin for 'commonplaces'; same as Greek *koinoi topoi*) the term is a vague one because of its rather indiscriminate use. A commonplace was a general argument, observation or description that a speaker could memorize for use on any number of possible occasions. Thus an American senator who knows he will be asked to speak extempore on 4 July might commit to memory reflections on the courage of the Founding Fathers or tags from the Declaration of Independence. Other traditional *loci* include: the inevitability of death; the active versus the contemplative life; a short, celebrated life versus a long, obscure one. Collections of such rhetorical commonplaces were often produced with the aim not only of listing the things that people generally considered persuasive but also of categorizing the methods that had persuasive effects. Proverbs ('*sententiae*') such as 'time flies' were also drawn upon as a source of pithy wisdom. As a possible starting-point for discussion, Aristotle included the 'commonplace' in his definition of 'invention', i.e. the process of discovering the relevant material for a discourse

locus amoenus 'the pleasant place', demonstrated in Virgil's *Eclogues*

lost wax one of the standard methods of producing bronze cast sculpture in the fifteenth and sixteenth centuries. It is sometimes also known by its French name of *cire perdue*. The procedure was as follows: a full-size clay model was made first. Then, depending on the size of the sculpture, either a plaster mould covered the whole model, or else moulds were taken of the individual parts. Wax covered the inner surfaces of the moulds and the resulting shells were then separated from the plaster moulds. A core of clay, horse dung and hair, sometimes supported by a metal armature, was roughly shaped according to the piece to be cast, slightly smaller in every dimension, but otherwise corresponding to the plaster moulds. The wax shells were reassembled over the core. They were covered with ash and water to ensure fire resistance and then clay was packed over them. Vents were inserted at the top and bottom through the outer layer. A uniform heat melted away the wax shells. The same amount of liquid bronze was then poured into the intervening space. The outer layer and the core were removed, and the surface smoothed with files and burnishers. Sometimes the surface was also deliberately patinated. The core and the moulds could be re-used for other versions of the same subject

lyric personal, short verse; the lyric voice is the subjective tone noticeable, for instance, in **Romantic poetry**

magnificentia pursuit of grandiose and magnificent display by rulers derived from the revival of the Aristotelian theory of that name

mannerism late phase in the development of the Italian Renaissance characterized by extreme artificiality and elegance

masque spectacular court entertainment which mixed music, dance, poetry, and intricate and expensive staging

metaphysical term now generally applied to a group of seventeenth-century poets, chiefly Donne, Carew, Herbert, Crashaw, Henry Vaughan, Marvell, Cleveland and Cowley. They reacted against the conventions of Elizabethan love poetry and wrote a more witty, ironic and, at the same time, more passionately intense and more psychologically probing poetry. Instead of writing melodious lines on the lady's beauty, or even on her indifference, the metaphysicals penned colloquial and often metrically irregular lines filled with arresting and original metaphors and similes. Such far-fetched and ingenious images were known as '**conceits**'. Originally merely a 'concept' or 'idea', the conceit came to mean a striking parallel drawn between two highly dissimilar things

motet sacred vocal composition in Latin which may – or may not – have a liturgical function

negotium everyday duties or work that has to be performed

order classical architecture employed a prescriptive system of components. An order in this system comprised a column with base (usually), shaft, **capital** and **entablature**, decorated and proportioned according to one of the accepted modes – **Doric**, **Ionic**, **Corinthian**, Tuscan or Composite. Each order had a specific repertoire of ornament which characterized the entablature and the capital of the column. The three basic orders in antiquity, in descending order from the most elaborate to the least, were the Corinthian, the Ionic and the Doric. The names reflect their origin in early Greek architecture. Renaissance architecture employed two further orders, the Composite and the Tuscan, the former combining motifs from the Corinthian and Ionic orders, the latter being even plainer than the Doric. The main descriptive accounts of the orders were provided by Vitruvius in his *On Architecture* (first century CE) and by Alberti in his *Art of Building* of 1452 (first published in 1485)

otium leisure

panegyric high praise

pendentive spherical triangular space formed by the intersection of a dome with two arches radiating from supporting columns

pilaster decorative feature which has the appearance of a flattened column projecting slightly from the wall

polyphony music that simultaneously combines several lines, as distinct from **monophony**, which consists of a single melody

predella platform on which an altarpiece is set, often decorated with sculpture or painting relating to the main subject of the altarpiece

register social context from which a word is drawn

renovatio in Latin, 'renewal'; shorthand for the revival of classical antiquity in the Renaissance

representational art which seeks to portray reality as it appears

retardataire from French, to hold back or to be old-fashioned

retrograde backwards, i.e. beginning with the last note and ending with the first

Romantic poetry late eighteenth-century verse which, in response to the earlier neoclassical aesthetic, featured a return to the lyric voice and poetic sublimity, especially in describing the links between humanity and nature

rustication masonry marked with sunken joints to give the illusion of a roughened surface

scheme (Greek *schema*, Latin *figura* from which the word 'figurative' derives) in the special rhetorical sense, 'scheme' means a rational change in meaning or language from the ordinary or simple form; in other words, any form of expression which deviates from the norm, e.g. hyperbole, or metaphor. 'He ran quickly down the street' is literal; 'he hared down the street' is figurative

seigneurs land-owning nobility

sententiae see **loci communes**

Signoria Italian form of address equivalent to 'Lordship/Ladyship', which can also mean 'rule' or 'dominion'. The term is also applied to the Palazzo della Signoria (the palace of the ruling council), the seat of government of the republican city of Florence. The assembly, consisting of seven 'priors' elected from the leaders of the city's major trade guilds, was known as the *Signori* (gentlemen). Built between 1299 and 1310, the Signoria today serves as the chief residence of the city's mayor and as an important museum

solmization designation of pitches by means of conventional syllables rather than letter names. The system was first recorded in the eleventh century, and from it developed our modern tonic sol-fa. The syllables most commonly used in western cultures are *doh* (or *ut*), *re, mi, fa, soh* (or *sol*), and *la*

sonnet fourteen-line poem which often split in two, between an eight- and a six-line unit (Italian form) or three quatrains and a couplet (English form)

specula principum handbooks of advice for rulers

sphinxes considered in the ancient world to be 'repositories of arcane wisdom' (Hall, 1974)

sprezzatura careless grace or studied nonchalance cultivated by courtiers

studiolo private apartment reserved for contemplation, study and recreation

syncope ellision of words

synecdoche a **trope** which employs a part for a whole

theological virtue(s) faith, hope and love/charity (agape), three pre-eminent graces of the Christian life identified by the apostle Paul in 1 Corinthians 13.13, came to be named the three 'theological' virtues in contrast to the four Platonic or 'natural' virtues of wisdom, courage, temperance and justice (*Republic* Book 4). To describe a virtue as 'theological' is to say that its distinctive quality is rooted in the character of God and that it may be bestowed on humanity by God alone. 'Natural' virtues, on the other hand, may be acquired through self-discipline and training

tiburio often translated as the 'lantern' or the 'spire' of an Italian church. It refers to the architectural structure over the main crossing of the church between the transepts and the chancel

topos (plural *topoi*) see **loci communes**

triglyph in a Doric frieze, the rectangular area between the metopes (square spaces, often decorated with relief sculpture), ornamented with three vertical grooves

triptych painting consisting of three hinged panels, often created for altarpieces

trope turning of meaning given to a word, such as metaphor performs

Vitruvian canon ancient ideals in architecture based on the writings of the Roman Vitruvius (fl. first century BCE/CE). The use of the Vitruvian orders of columns (**Doric**, **Ionic**, **Corinthian**) reflected concerns about social as well as aesthetic priorities

Acknowledgements

Grateful acknowledgement is made to the following sources for permission to reproduce material in this book:

Palisca, C.V. (ed.) (1988) 'Score of "Motet: Tu solus, qui facis mirabilia" by Josquin des Prez', *Norton Anthology of Western Music*, 2nd edn, vol. 1, Associated Music Publishers.

Figure 3.1: Hollingsworth, M. (1996) *Patronage in Sixteenth Century Italy*, John Murray (Publishers) Ltd.

Figure 4.7: Lubkin, G. (1994) *Renaissance Court: Milan under Galeazzo Maria Sforza*, University of California Press. Copyright © 1994 The Regents of the University of California.

Figure 4.8: Duncan-Jones, K. (1991) *Sir Philip Sidney, Courtier Poet*, Penguin Books Ltd.

Every effort has been made to trace all the copyright owners, but if any have been inadvertently overlooked, the publishers will be pleased to make the necessary arrangements at the first opportunity.

Index